D0906082

STUDIES IN THE SOCIOLOGY OF SEX

STUDIES IN THE
SOCIOLOGY OF SEX

Edited by

JAMES M. HENSLIN
Southern Illinois University, Edwardsville

APPLETON-CENTURY-CROFTS
Educational Division
MEREDITH CORPORATION   New York

ACKNOWLEDGMENT

For the contributors to this volume I have nothing but the highest praise and admiration—both for their courage to do this type of research (in the face of opposition, which although of diminished proportions, is still with us) and for their excellent cooperation, patience, and understanding as their manuscripts were altered to accommodate my "editorial suggestions."

J.M.H.

CONTENTS

SEX BY FORCE

OCCUPATIONS AND SEX:
WHERE THE OCCUPATION INVOLVES SEX

OCCUPATIONS AND SEX:
WHERE THE OCCUPATION IS SEX

HOMOSEXUALITY

AN OVERVIEW OF SEX RESEARCH

The Sociological Point of View

JAMES M. HENSLIN

What does sociology have to do with sex? Perhaps some people might question the relevance of sociology in the study of sexual behavior, and they might be viewing sex (no voyeuristic pun intended) as a very personal matter to which sociology is inapplicable. Sociologists would agree that sexual behaviors (including sexual practices, sexual involvements, sexual desires, attitudes, and motivations, etc.) are indeed characteristics of individuals and that, because these behaviors frequently are very intimate in nature, that they are in many ways extremely personal matters. As a result, the sociologist who is studying sexual behavior ordinarily looks at individuals as the objects of his study. But, when he does so, because he is a sociologist, he looks beyond the individual in order to understand behavior. Although individuals are engaging in whatever behavior is being described and analyzed, the individual is a member of social groups. The sociological perspective is that human behavior is not understandable apart from social group membership, and that this membership is so strong and pervasive that it also affects ideas and behaviors in this so very personal and intimate realm of behavior.

The sociological point of view, then, is that while it is individuals who engage in any given sexual behavior, it is their group membership that shapes, directs, and influences the forms

1

or patterns that their sexual behaviors take. People often have difficulty seeing the validity of applying this sociological orientation to their own culture, where customary sexual behaviors seem so "natural." Because the visibility of the group influences are minimized due to close proximity to the subject, these sexual patterns appear to members of the culture in which they take place to be primarily, if not exclusively, expressions of desires from *within* the individual. These group influences become more apparent if we take a cross-cultural perspective. In doing this, we see that particular sexual practices or behaviors vary markedly from one bounded grouping of people to another (such as from one tribe to another). This perspective makes the group base influencing the directions such behaviors take more visible to us. The cultural anthropologist would attempt to abstract from each tribe or grouping of people the cultural factors that determine or direct these behaviors. He would emphasize certain aspects of their culture, especially their beliefs about status, leadership, the sacred, the profane, the world of the spirits, conception, warfare, or manhood, and, in so doing, he would note their pervasive influence upon the sexual behaviors which typify that particular grouping of people.

Sociologists and social psychologists also look for and emphasize the influence of group membership upon the behavior they are studying. In this volume, for example, such group influences upon behavior are examined by Goethals in his cross-cultural examination of factors affecting permissivity in premarital sex and by Davis in her study of the development of deviant motivation in the prostitute. When it comes to motivations for sexual behavior, one might think that they are individualistic and separate from a group base or origin. Davis does view motivations as being personal, that is, she agrees that it is a person who possesses the particular motive for behavior, but she does not see motives as individualistic in the sense that they are separated from a group base. On the contrary, she traces motivations for prostituting oneself to a socialization process whereby interaction in particular groups is the key to understanding these motivations. Even such an individualistic and personal matter as sexual orgasm is not without a social base, as is documented by Shope.

Although sexual behaviors have a biological base, it is membership in groups which shapes or gives direction to the expression of this sexual drive. Since different groups have differing sets of expectations, as well as differing patterns of reinforcements, values, and beliefs, this sometimes leads to markedly differing sexual behaviors from group to group, even though the groups are within the same society. Symond's article on mate-swapping is an example of sexual behaviors at variance with the dominant ethos of the broader society, yet there is also a group base for these variant behaviors, and they are normative or rule-governed within the group in which they take place.

Not only does membership in a given culture, in a particular social class, or in a certain age and sex grouping shape sexual behavior, but so does membership in occupations. Expectations and patterned practices of sexual behaviors can differ from occupation to occupation. Such patterns are analyzed by Henslin in his study of sexual access to females in the male-dominated occupation of cabdriving. Cummins analyzes informal mechanisms of sexual social control by the police, while Henslin and Biggs deal with expectations of denial of sexuality in vaginal examinations. Social bases of recruitment into stripteasing, as well as the use of visual sex for financial gain, are analyzed by Skipper and McCaghy.

Markedly differing sexual practices of other social groupings that are described and analyzed in this volume include Humphreys' study of impersonal sex in public restrooms and Kirkham's study of patterns of homosexual behavior in prison. In these studies the influence of the particular group upon its members' sexual practices is especially evident. The sociological perspective directs us not to view homosexual behavior as due to a person's peculiar proclivities but as the logical outcome of *social* forces. Homosexual behavior in a situation of blocked access to females, as in Kirkham's study, is an excellent example of this sociological understanding.

Gordon, in his content analysis of American sex manuals,

documents major changes in American sexual orientation and practices from the nineteenth to the twentieth century. His study, with that of Chappell, Geis, Schafer, and Siegel on rape and Goethals' on premarital sex, represents an analysis of a broad social base in influencing sexual behaviors. The study of forcible rape demonstrates a highly relevant group base to this sexual activity which we ordinarily conceive as being solely individualistic. It also seriously calls into question the view that rapists are psychopathic, leading us to examine the *social* forces which determine even such things as rape rates and, if we might call it that, "styles of rape."

In addition to the papers already mentioned, Manning and Henslin each study various aspects of abortion—from the maintenance of respectable appearances and the process of making the decision to abort and of neutralizing the violation of internalized norms to how the abortion system functions on the college campus. Finally, Sagarin closes this volume by providing us with an overview of sociological sex research.

Although there is so very much that we still do not know about the sexual behavior of man, it is refreshingly instructive, in order to see how far we have come in sex research, to look back a few years to see where we once were. This perspective can be gained quickly by examining the early writings of a sociologist whose name is still held in respect today, W. I. Thomas. (His reputation is not based on what I shall cite, I hasten to add.) In *Sex and Society,* published in 1907, Thomas says that there seems to be "a connection between an abundance of nutrition and females, and between scarcity and males, in relatively higher animal forms and in man" (pp. 4–5). He concludes, "More boys are born in the country than in cities, because city diet is richer, especially in meat" (p. 5). He also says, "More children are born from warm-weather than from cold-weather conceptions, but relatively more boys are born from cold-weather conceptions" (p. 6). He adds, however, "These facts are not conclusive, but they all point in the same direction, and are probably sufficient to establish a connection between food conditions and the determination of sex" (p. 9).

Besides orienting the reader to the sociology of sexual behavior, this volume is designed to provide the reader with an overall view of what sociologists are currently researching in sex. However, in three ways it is unrepresentative of the sociology of sex. First, the papers in this volume, with the exception of Goethals', are all analyses of various aspects of sex in American society. These presentations are culturally limited because American sociologists, for a variety of reasons, appear to be fascinated with American society and culture: consequently, in our own ethnocentrism we seldom look beyond the confines of our own culture. And, given our current practices of professional training in sociology (there being, for example, no requirement for the doctoral candidate to do cross-cultural research), this state of affairs is likely to continue for some time.

Second, the final choice of topics has been limited because it was not possible to locate, for each area of sex, sociologists whose research was at the point where they could report their findings. Consequently, certain topics on which research is being done, such as nudism, pornography, voyeurism, transvestism, extramarital sex, seduction, sadomasochism, and sexual behavior under the influence of drugs, are not included. Therefore, no claim is made that topics covered in this volume are the only subjects currently being analyzed by sociologists.

Third, the selections in this volume are unrepresentative of sociological sex research because in one respect I have purposely chosen to make them so. Sociologists sometimes are accused of forgetting about people (e.g., George C. Homans, "Bringing Men Back In," *American Sociological Review 29:* 809–818, 1964), that is, the people sociologists study frequently become reduced to mere numbers in statistical tables or to an analysis of levels of significant differences. Agreeing that this is frequently the case and that it is undesirable, I have consciously kept this problem in mind and have purposely chosen papers which, hopefully, do not forget people. People, with their particular motivations, needs, desires, beliefs, aspirations, aberrations, and sometimes even humor, should come through clearly in these selected research studies. At the same time, however, relationships between the individual and his group, whether that group be the family or the peer group on the college campus, in prison, or in an occupation, or whatever, are emphasized. But this, of course, is the sociological approach in research.

It is hoped that this volume will stimulate further research by sociologists into sexual behavior, that area of human life which is both so complex and fascinating, yet so crucial for a thorough understanding of man.

CROSS-CULTURAL OVERVIEW OF PREMARITAL SEX

Factors Affecting Permissive and Nonpermissive Rules Regarding Premarital Sex

GEORGE W. GOETHALS

INTRODUCTION

While the severity of control may vary, all societies to some de-gree structure the sexual activity of the unmarried. As Whiting and Child pointed out in their cross-cultural study of socializa-tion (30), the degree of variation is, indeed, extremely wide, ranging from societies who encourage and find amusement in the sex play and attempted intercourse of children to those soci-eties who punish sexual deviation from the norm of chastity with extreme severity. The social scientist cannot permit himself the luxury of assuming that the variation exists for merely quixotic reasons. Whenever wide variations in any behavior are found, he must address himself to the question of why these exist. This re-sponsibility to understand variation is particularly intriguing

The research mentioned in this paper was supported by funds from the William F. Milton Fund, Harvard University. It must be made clear that this particular report, while it makes references to preliminary findings of that research, does not in any way constitute a final form of the empirical study that will be published subsequently by this author and Professor John W. M. Whiting.

For purposes of clarity, theoretical and ethnographic materials are listed in separate bibliographies.

I would like to acknowledge the assistance given to me in this project by Mary Murphy.

when it comes to sexual behavior because of the central question which must be answered over and beyond the phenomenon of variation: Why has man typically placed such extremely strong prohibitions upon an activity which has such powerful gratification? This question is not easy to answer either from the point of view of theoretical considerations or from the view of empirical research. However, by examining a number of different theoretical positions, it may be possible to come to some kind of synthesis, and by reviewing what little empirical research exists, we may be able to come to some conclusions about the present state of research strategy and methodology. This paper proposes to undertake the following tasks: first, to review the theoretical materials which are presently at the investigator's disposal; second, to evaluate the existing empirical research which bears upon comparative studies; and, third, in the light of the first two questions, suggest a point of view for future research that is both theoretical and methodological.

FOUR THEORETICAL POSITIONS

The Psychoanalytic Position

The psychoanalytic position concerning sexual behavior and its meanings to the individual is, of course, the major concern of Freud's work. However, the precise theoretical contribution of this particular school to any study of sexual behavior cannot be understood thoroughly without some review of the crosscurrents that existed in Freud's own thinking about the expression of sex, particularly sex outside of the marital context. In what is probably his final and clearest summary of his whole theory of personality, Freud makes a significant statement: "From the beginning it had been our contention that men fell ill due to a conflict between their impulses and the inhibitions set up against them" (13: 83). Freud's whole theory of neuroses as well as his somewhat pessimistic point of view on man's fate hinged upon his conviction that man was always in deep conflict between the demands of primitive instincts (and the word *instinct* is important) and those inhibitions learned and the controls internalized as the process of socialization in the family proceeded. Thus, there is a fascinating paradox in the work of Freud: on the one hand, he sees the expression of sex as important to the healthy personality; and on the other hand, as we shall see below, he views the inhibition of sexual instinct as imperative to a functioning society.

Freud's concern with sexual instinct and its inhibition came not only from the clinical data that he collected from his patients, but also from the general intellectual tenor of his time. The influence of Darwin's thinking on Freud's general outlook has been mentioned by many writers, and it is not my intent here to review the work of Rieff (26) and others who have so brilliantly discussed this dimension of Freud's intellectual stance. What is important, to repeat, is that Freud saw man in an evolutionary context, viewing his instincts and their present state of inhibition as part of a long and lengthy process which postulated man as a species in evolution and not, as other points of view might have proposed, the ultimate in God's handiwork.

In a number of papers, Freud (7, 9, 10, 11) discusses at great length the way in which social coherency was related to man's eventual capacity to control the sexual instinct and, by controlling it, to create a family context wherein children could be kept from the undisciplined expression of this most powerful of human capacities. Freud was convinced that parents socialize their children, indeed that they must do so, in order to avoid living with the consequences of undisciplined libido (9). It is interesting that Freud is consistent in this position, both in his first lectures and in his last discussions of human personality (11, 13).

> In its own interests, accordingly, society would postpone the child's full development until it has attained a certain stage of intellectual maturity, since educability practically ceases with the full onset of the sexual instinct. Without this the instinct would break all bounds and the laboriously erected structure of civilization would be swept away. Nor is the task of restraining it ever any easy one; success in this direction is often poor and, sometimes, only too great. At bottom society's motive is economic; since it has not means enough to support life for its members without work on their part,

it must see to it that the number of these members is restricted and their energies directed away from sexual activities on to their work —the eternal primordial struggle for existence, therefore, persisting to the present day. (9: 273)

In what many consider to be his final reprise to his whole point of view on mankind, *Civilization and its Discontents* (11), Freud presents the position that civilization itself cannot survive or progress without strict inhibition of the sexual instinct. Thus, the psychoanalytical position, as expressed by Freud and thinkers subsequent to him, sees the inhibition of sex—and its sometimes disastrous consequences—as part of the price evolutionary man must pay for the creation of his social structure and his civilization.

> The liberty of the individual is not a benefit of culture. It was greatest before any culture, though indeed it had little value at that time, because the individual was hardly in a position to defend it. Liberty has undergone restrictions through the evolution of civilization, and justice demands that these restrictions shall apply to all. The desire for freedom that makes itself felt in a human community may be a revolt against some existing injustice and so may prove favourable to a further development of civilization and remain compatible with it. But it may also have its origin in the primitive roots of the personality, still unfettered by civilizing influences and so become a source of antagonism to culture. Thus the cry for freedom is directed either against particular forms or demands of culture or else against culture itself. (11: 60–61)

The Cult of Chastity

If the Freudian position proposes that sexual inhibition is important for maintaining civilization itself, a brilliant review by Havelock Ellis (4) suggests another possible interpretation on the value placed upon nonmarital sex. It is interesting that although Ellis is using European sources for the most part, some of his ideas seem to apply to other sections of the world. This theoretical position is very different from the psychoanalytic one but has its own explanatory power and equally complex rationalization.

Ellis observes that from the earliest times of recorded history various civilizations, for unexplained reasons, have placed a tremendous value upon physical virginity. The best known example of this is, of course, the vestal virgins of ancient Rome. But the general currency of this particular example has caused us to overlook the fact that the cult of virginity has been much more widespread than this example demonstrates. For example, in ancient Sumeria and other countries in the Middle East, the most honored positions in law and government were required to be fulfilled by women who were physically intact. The idea emerges that the person who is physically "uncorrupted" will be more competent and more fair by the fact of her own virtue, in judging the virtues of others (25: 40–75). It is interesting that this same theme is very much a part of the whole Arthurian cycle.

The cult of abstinence is found, however, not only in Medieval Europe, but among the Plains Indians who felt that no man before going on a raid or going hunting should indulge in sexual intercourse. Thus, chastity and abstinence in many societies and at different historical times have been seen as salubrious conditions related to man's competence and facility in other areas of living.

One of the most interesting threads in the development and history of sexual rules is one which may help explain one of the complexities of our present-day thinking about sexual behavior—the evolution from the notion of the virgin warrior to the idea of courtly love, which in its turn led later to the conclusion that romantic love is a necessary prerequisite for sexual activity. Thus, this point of view—the positive insistence on and reference to chastity not only as part of better physical functioning but also as a prerequisite to the relationship between men and women—is a thread that, although utterly different from that proposed by Freud, is important to understanding our contemporary sexual attitudes and behaviors. Despite our more liberal traditions, we still view virginity, particularly female virginity, as a talisman and as an assurance of sexual happiness. While this idea may be naïve, it is nonetheless a deeply held belief in Western society.

The Anthropological Position

The anthropological position is pragmatic. It has none of Freud's pessimism about the expression of sexual behavior, nor does it have the romantic and idealistic notions contained in Havelock Ellis's review. Although Freud does allude to some of these ideas in *Totem and Taboo,* he does not develop them in the direction or with the precision of the social anthropologist. In a very early article by C. S. Ford (5) and in an extremely sophisticated cross-cultural study by G. D. Murdock (23), the anthropological point of view is expressed and may be summarized as follows: Culture, to use Ford's phrase, "consists of the tried and true solutions of the problems of living" (5: 135). One problem faced by every society regardless of its level of civilization is that of inheritance and descent. Thus, the anthropologist sees the various rules pertaining to premarital sex as man's attempt to give coherency to the transfer and inheritance of property. Unless the kinship lines can be kept unambiguous and paternity assured, social chaos would exist. It is interesting to contrast this anthropological position with that of Freud since both seem to come to the same conclusion, that is, the control of sex is necessary for social institutions to function. However, it should be pointed out that the anthropological position is related almost entirely to questions of *social structure* whereas the psychoanalytic position is related almost entirely to the problem of *control of instincts.*

The Parental Authority-Rivalry Hypothesis

Finally, another interesting hypothesis which derives at least in part from psychoanalytic theory proposes that the control of sexual behavior exists to preserve for older men access to younger women and in addition may represent, at least symbolically, the last act on the part of parents to impose their will and authority on their children. Freud speaks (10, 11) of the primal father and the rivalry which exists between him and his sons. In an empirical study published some years ago, Whiting, Kluckhohn, and

Anthony (28) propose that initiation rites, which Freud would define as symbolic castration, are perpetuated by the parental generation to keep the sexual behavior of the adolescent under control. In his classic monograph *Facing Mount Kenya,* Jomo Kenyatta (18) reveals how the Kikuyu structure the sexual behavior of the adolescent so that parental authority is maintained and sexual behavior properly patterned. As mentioned before, this particular theoretical position concerning parental authority derives from a variety of sources and is separate and distinct from the other theoretical positions reviewed previously.

Summary of Theoretical Positions

As can be seen, the sources of testable hypotheses for the study of premarital sexual behavior are numerous and varied. They range from Freud's concern with the evolution of man to the rather functional notions of the social anthropologist, and as if this were not enough, there are the brilliant, though somewhat romantic, speculations of Havelock Ellis. The fascinating conclusion, however, for one who has worked for some years in this area, is that each of these hypotheses seems to gain empirical support in different sections of the world. One conclusion that will be tentatively offered is that no *one* theoretical position can be used to generate sophisticated hypotheses for research in this area.

DISCUSSION OF TRENDS FROM
EMPIRICAL RESEARCH

For a number of years John W. M. Whiting and I have been engaged in a number of pilot studies on premarital sexual behavior, using the Human Relations Area Files and the Cross-Cultural Method. This particular method has been employed as described by Whiting in a previously published work in which he also discusses the methodological difficulties regarding matters of scaling and measurement (30). While the material that follows is in no way to be interpreted as a report of that "in progress" research, certain trends have emerged which can be discussed at this particular stage in light of the theoretical hypotheses reviewed earlier. I would like to emphasize that what is reported here in no way prejudices the complete findings of the empirical study. Yet, preliminary findings are often intriguing not only in themselves but also as a point of departure for related research. To repeat: what follows is a discussion of a preliminary nature of trends that seem to be emerging from these pilot studies and which seem to be congruent with parallel research findings published in 1964 by Murdock (24).

Before reviewing these empirical leads, one general conclusion can be drawn from the various theoretical positions which have been reviewed. People seem to control the sexual behavior of the unmarried for two primary reasons: they may control it because they place a very high value of an ideological nature upon physical chastity, or on the other hand, they may control the sexual behavior of the unmarried for completely pragmatic reasons which revolve around the problems created by unwanted pregnancy. In an overall test of these alternatives, the preliminary data show that the worldover, concerns about pregnancy are far more potent than ideals concerning chastity when it comes to the control of premarital sex generally. Yet, interestingly enough, those societies which have the strongest and most powerful sanctions against premarital sexual behavior are those which have these same sanctions based upon ideological as opposed to pragmatic reasons. Further, it is interesting to observe that these societies for the most part are found around the Mediterranean and in the Middle East, such as among the Albanians (S1), Sicilians (S11), Serbs (S12), Spaniards (S14), and Tunisians (S5 & S9).

Female-based and Male-based Families. One of the findings that has emerged clearly has been the fact that there is a profound difference in the control of sexual behavior depending on whether males or females are in a position of power and authority. In essence, as males gain more and more authority both within the society at large and specifically within the family as an isolated unit, the sanctions *against* sexual behavior become more and more severe. Severity of sanctions, thus, seem to have what might be called a patrilineal and patrilocal bias, as is indicated by the Serbs (S12) and Annamese (Vietnam) (S8). Conversely, in those societies which are matrilineal and matrilocal in their orientation, such as the Hopi (S7) and the Trobrianders (S10), sanctions upon premarital sex, if they exist, are extremely mild. One explanation of this, but by no means the only one, is that when the young woman stays at home with her mother as a consequence of the marriage pattern in her culture, her personal safety and security is not affected by a pregnancy whether she is married or not. It must be remembered that this is only one explanation, and, as will be suggested later, there are alternatives.

The Social Complexities. Social complexity does indeed have an effect on the patterning of sexual behavior. Stated generally, small societies tend to be quite permissive while large societies tend to be restrictive. Murdock (24), testing ideas derived from social evolutionary theory, proposes that societies which have become complex must control the sexual behavior of their members so that the work of a complex society with its involved division of labor may be accomplished. This does not mean that a complex division of labor requires a greater control of sexual behavior; it does mean, however, consistent with the ideas of Freud, that civilized, complex societies must sublimate their energies into the complex work that must be done to keep a complex set of institutions functioning.

The Social Complexity—Social Class Trend. In the pilot studies an attempt was made to replicate Murdock's findings, and these were indeed substantiated. However, a corollary to this test was the conclusion that it was not the degree of complexity that made a difference in the control of sexual behavior, but rather the *kind.* For example, it was discovered that in societies which were highly developed and complex but whose social organization was essentially of a caste nature (i.e., they had slaves and captives to carry out the day-to-day work) in which the status of the various members of the society was ascribed rather than achieved, such as the Azande (S3) and the Lepche (S6), sexual attitudes tended to be generally permissive. Conversely, when the complexity of the society existed because of the presence of achievable status and social position, such as the Nupe (S13), Shilluk (S2), and the Wolof (S4), thus being analogous to social class in modern industrial society, sanctions upon sex became more severe.

Summary

In general, thus, it can be stated with some confidence that complexity of social structure does make a difference in determining how premarital sex is patterned and controlled. Small societies, particularly those which invest women with power and authority, ordinarily tend to be permissive while the converse is true when males are in positions of power. While these findings are of interest in and of themselves, the theoretical "second thoughts" that they generate are possibly more important than these preliminary findings. It is to these that attention is now directed.

DISCUSSION AND IMPLICATION OF THE FINDINGS

These findings, although tentative, raise questions of a substantive nature as well as lead to issues in research, methodology, and theory. Possibly the most crucial issue relevant here is the theoretical reconsideration which these data, in the light of other relatively recent contributions, throw upon this whole complex area.

This requires digression into two quite different areas: the work of Alfred Kinsey and his associates and some reconsiderations of orthodox psychoanalytic theory. Kinsey (19, 20) made two very important general conclusions about human sexual behavior. These are summarized in his second volume, *The Sexual Behavior of the Human Female* (20: 567–687). The first of these conclusions is that the patterning of male and female sexual activity is quite different when seen from the point of view of its chronology. The male is seen as being intensely active during his teens and twenties, whereas the female, at least in the model case, is found as slowly reaching her peak of activity in her twenties and early thirties. After the twenties, the male's sexual behavior seems to go into a slow but steady decline, while the female continues, for the rest of her life, at whatever level of activity she had reached in her twenties and thirties. Possibly the most important aspect of this comparison between males and females is that the sexually active woman is far more active sexually throughout her life in any dimension than is the sexually active male. A further important finding is that while females typically have a different nexus of arousal than males and typically are aroused by direct physical stimulation, those females who do respond to what Kinsey calls "psychologic" stimulation respond with intensity far greater than any male. Kinsey's work, whatever its demerits—and a great deal has been written about his methodology and conclusions—demolishes once and for all the image of the sexually acquiescent female. His findings also demolish the stereotype of the Victorian female, disinterested and disgusted with anything to do with sex, active only at the insistence of her animalistic husband.

By reading Ernest Jones' magnificent biography of Freud (17), or better yet, Freud's letters to his fiancee (6), one becomes impressed not only by Darwin's influence on Freud, which has been alluded to before, but also by the tremendously intense impact upon Freud's mind of the Victorian times in which he lived. While it is very clear that Freud broke taboos in the sense of talking about sex, it is equally clear that he found it convenient to adopt the Victorian stereotype concerning the female. In his two key essays (12, 14) Freud makes it very clear that feminine sexuality tends to be, as he terms it, "actively passive." And further, he also makes it clear that the sexual life of a woman is focused not around her physical gratification but rather around the love that she can lavish on her children. To be somewhat harsh about it, Freud sees women as second-class psychic citizens with a second-class sexual life. This particular tradition of viewing the feminine psyche has continued to be part of our thinking about the human female, whether one refers to the point of view of Helene Deutsch (3), Freud's gifted pupil, or to the work of such literary figures as Simone de Beauvoir (2).

Possibly the most direct assault upon the idea of the woman as sexually passive (psychoanalytically defined) and the male as a superior being in a functioning society has been undertaken by Bruno Bettelheim in his monograph *Symbolic Wounds* (1). In a fascinating summary of anthropological and psychoanalytic theory, Bettelheim reviews not only what from his point of view are the functional meanings of initiation rites, but, in addition, he subjects to heavy criticism what he calls the *androcentric bias* of those who have written about questions of gender and sexuality. He points out that "genital envy," particularly "penis envy," so much a part of psychoanalytic thinking concerning the female, has caused us to be blind to the fact that the male's envy of the female's capacity to have children may be a far more critical and psychological problem for males than penis envy is for women. Bettelheim summarized his position succinctly:

> But in regard to what counts most, nature *permits* each person only one sex. Hence a desire for the bodily characteristics and functions of the other leads to a psychological impasse to become like the other sex (which is desired) implies giving up one's own sex (which is feared). This impasse has been little recognized as a conditioning factor in so-called castration anxiety. That the anxiety reaches more deeply than parental influence can account for was recognized by Freud. So he looked to racial memory traces for its cause and concluded that we are born with a fear of losing our sex organs. I believe, instead, that our desire for the characteristics of the other sex is a necessary consequence of the sex differences. Fulfillment of that desire would imply losing our own genitals— hence the inexorable nature of castration anxiety in both sexes. (1: 147)

Bettelheim thus sees the relationship between the sexes as being one in which pride and envy are a complex admixture, with women being as active sexually and as concerned about their genital capacity as any male. Bettelheim, thus, *from a theoretical point of view,* does to the study of women what Kinsey had done in an empirical fashion. These two contributions taken together cause us to scrutinize and carefully refine the point of departure for our whole exploration into the realm of sexual activity, particularly pre-marital sexual behavior. Therefore, in the light of our findings and these new theoretical and empirical perspectives, another look at our data and another level of interpretation is required.

If women are as sexually active biologically as are males and if their level of activity can surpass that of any male, then it would stand to reason that when they are in positions of authority they will indulge themselves as much as possible. The data involving matrilocal and matrilineal societies do, indeed, support this conclusion. When women are in control, sexual behavior tends to be extremely permissive and extremely active.[1]

This point of male anxiety concerning the sexuality of women is, of course, pivotal for any research in this area and must be recognized as such. Our data suggest that when men come into position of control, they begin systematically to circumscribe the sexual behavior of the unmarried female, and it is proposed in this paper that the threat to the male of the sexually active woman is a reality and a reality that has been far too long neglected in research on sexual behavior. It will be noted that both in our study and in Murdock's, social complexity is always related to male authority and a male-based family, and, coincident with this is heavy-handed sexual control.

Finally, one may raise the question as to why those societies which have social classes are even stricter in their regulation of sex than those which are simply large. The explanation offered here is that males are not only worried about the problem of their sexual adequacy, and thus project some of their own anxieties into their daughter's lives, but, in addition, in a relatively open society where achievement creates the male position, it would be disastrous to the father's ego for his daughter to become impregnated by someone who is not socially acceptable. Thus, many patternings of sexual control may have to do not only with males' deep fear of their sexuality and its adequacy but also with the problem of hypogamy.

This article must not be concluded without reference to the

---

[1] Parenthetically, it might be noted that one of the most interesting quirks of behavioral science history is the fact that Ralph Linton's ethnography of the Marquesan society, reviewed by Abraham Kardner in his book, *The Individual and His Society,* revealed not only the intense sexual activity of women when they were in control of a society but, even more important, the intense male anxiety that was generated in societies where women had sexual liberty. Abraham Kardner, *The Individual and His Society* (New York: Columbia University Press, 1939).

brilliant paper by Mary Jane Sherfey (27), which on a far more sophisticated level abolishes once and for all the whole psychoanalytic interpretation of "female sexuality":

> In these primates and in women, an inordinate cyclic sexual capacity has thus evolved leading to the paradoxical state of sexual insatiation in the presence of the utmost sexual satiation. The value of this state for evolution is clear: with the breeding premium going to the primate females with the greatest pelvic edema, the most effective clitoral eroticism and the most aggressive sexual behavior, the satiation-in-insatiation state may have been an important factor in the adaptive radiation of the primates leading to man—and a major barrier to the evolution of modern man.

> The rise of modern civilization, while resulting from many causes, was contingent on the suppression of the inordinate cyclic sexual drive of women because (a) the hypersexual drive and the prolonged pregnancies was an important force in the escape from lactation asexuality. Women's uncurtailed continuous hypersexuality would drastically interfere with maternal responsibilities; and (b) with the rise of the settled agriculture economies, man's territorialism became expressed in property rights and kinship laws. Large families of known parentage were mandatory and could not evolve until the inordinate sexual demands of women were curbed. (27: 127–128)

CONCLUSIONS

In the light of the previous discussion, I will make a few general concluding remarks in the hope that they will help those in the several behavioral sciences with any research of a comparative nature that they choose to undertake pertaining to sexual behavior.

First, it is extremely clear that social and cultural variations in any form of sexual behavior, particularly premarital sexual behavior, are open to the same wide degree of variability that Kinsey found in individual human beings. Even with a carefully selected world, in research spanning a six-year period, linguistic sample pilot studies have been able to generate only the most crude, although highly suggestive, findings. The degree to which sexual behavior is affected by such matters as climate, intricacies of family organization, or sexual training in childhood needs to be considered carefully in any study undertaken.

Second, it is clear that many of the assumptions behind research on sexual behavior must be revised in light of new knowledge concerning the female's orientation toward sexual behavior. While it is indeed true that Murdock has demonstrated empirically the validity of some of Freud's ideas concerning social organization, it is also clear that this is but a small step in a very complicated area. Sherfey's brilliant review of psychoanalytic material and her sophisticated handling of materials from primatology must be applied to any program of research on sexual behavior. While psychoanalytic theory in general, as well as specific hypotheses drawn from anthropology, can generate interesting and even significant findings, they in no way illuminate as much as we would like in this complex area of human behavior.

Finally, it is very clear that much more work is required upon identifiable, different, intact, social, and ethnic groups. Unless such work is done, particularly by sociologists, variations between groups will never be seen clearly in terms of their own legitimate parameters.

REFERENCES

(1) Bettelheim, Bruno. *Symbolic Wounds, Puberty Rites, and the Envious Circle.* Chicago: Free Press, 1954.

(2) de Beauvoir, Simone (1952). *The Second Sex.* Translated and edited by H. M. Parshley. New York: Alfred A. Knopf, 1953.

(3) Deutsch, Heléne. *The Psychology of Women.* Vol. 1. New York: Grune & Stratton, 1945.

(4) Ellis, Havelock (1905). "The Function of Chastity." Chap. 5. "Sex in Relation to Society." Part 3. In *Studies in the Psychology of Sex,* Vol. 2. New York: Random House, 1935, pp. 143–177.

(5) Ford, Clellan S. "Society, Culture and the Human Organism." *Journal of General Psychology 20:* 135–179, 1939.

(6) Freud, Ernst L., ed. *Letters of Sigmund Freud.* Translated by T. and J. Stern. New York: Basic Books, 1960.

(7) Freud, Sigmund (1912). *Totem and Taboo: resemblances between*

the psychic lives of savages and neurotics. New York: Moffat,
Yard & Co., 1918.

(8) Freud, Sigmund (1918). Contributions to the Psychology of Love.
The Taboo of Virginity. Vol. 4. Collected Papers. London:
Hogarth Press, 1950, pp. 217–235.

(9) Freud, Sigmund (1920). "The Sexual Life of Man." Lecture 20.
In A General Introduction to Psychoanalysis. New York: Liveright Publ. Corp., 1935.

(10) Freud, Sigmund (1922). Group Psychology and the Analysis of the
Ego. Translated by J. Strachey. London, Vienna: The International Psychoanalytic Press, 1922.

(11) Freud, Sigmund (1930). Civilization and Its Discontents. Translated by Joan Riviere. London: Hogarth Press, 1957.

(12) Freud, Sigmund (1931). Female Sexuality. Vol. 5. Collected
Papers. London: Hogarth Press, 1950, pp. 252–272.

(13) Freud, Sigmund (1933). "The Anatomy of the Mental Personality." Lecture 31. In New Introductory Lectures on Psychoanalysis. New York: W. W. Norton and Company, 1933, pp.
82–112.

(14) Freud, Sigmund (1933). "The Psychology of Women." Lecture
33. In New Introductory Lectures on Psychoanalysis. New
York: W. W. Norton and Company, 1933, pp. 153–185.

(15) Goethals, George W. "The Sexual Revolution: Cross-Cultural
Perspectives." In A Report of the Twentieth Annual Conference, National Association of College and University Chap-
lains and Directors of Religious Life. Boston: Boston University Press, April, 1967.

(16) Jacobsen, Thorkild. How Did Gilgamesh Oppress Uruk, Acta-
Orientale 8: 62–74, 1929.

(17) Jones, Ernest. The Young Freud. Vol. 1. Sigmund Freud. London: Hogarth Press, 1953.

(18) Kenyatta, Jomo. Facing Mt. Kenya. New York: Random House,
Vintage Paperback, 1962.

(19) Kinsey, Alfred C.; Pomeroy, Wardell B.; and Martin, Clyde E.
Sexual Behavior in the Human Male. Philadelphia: W. B.
Saunders Co., 1948.

(20) Kinsey, Alfred C.; Pomeroy, Wardell B.; and Martin, Clyde E.
Sexual Behavior in the Human Female. Philadelphia: W. B.
Saunders Co., 1953.

(21) Malinowski, Bronislaw. Sex and Repression in Savage Society.
New York: Harcourt, Brace & Co., 1927.

(22) Malinowski, Bronislaw. "The sexual life of savages in north-

western Melanesia: an ethnographic account of courtship, marriage and family life among the natives of the Trobriand Islands, British New Guinea." New York: *Eugenics 28:* 603, 1929.

(23) Murdock, George P. *Social Structure.* New York: Macmillan Co., 1949.

(24) Murdock, George P. "Cultural Correlates of the Regulation of Premarital Sex Behavior." In *Process and Pattern in Culture,* essays in honor of Julian H. Steward, edited by Robert A. Manners. Chicago: Aldine Publishing Co., 1964, pp. 399–410.

(25) Pritchard, James B., ed. *Ancient Near Eastern Texts Relating to the Old Testament.* 2nd ed. Princeton, N.J.: Princeton University Press, 1955.

(26) Rieff, Phillip. *Freud: The Mind of the Moralist.* New York: Doubleday & Co., Anchor, 1961.

(27) Sherfey, Mary Jane. "The Evolution and Nature of Female Sexuality in Relation to Psychoanalytic Theory." *Journal of the American Psychoanalytic Association 14:* 28–128, 1966.

(28) Whiting, John W. M.; Kluckhohn, Richard; and Anthony, Albert. "The Function of Male Initiation Ceremonies at Puberty." In *Readings in Social Psychology,* edited by Eleanor E. Maccoby, Theodore M. Newcomb, and Eugene L. Hartley. New York: Henry Holt & Co., 1958, pp. 359–370.

(29) Whiting, John W. M. "Methods and Problems in Cross-Cultural Research." In *The Handbook of Social Psychology,* edited by Gardner Lindzey and Elliot Aronson, Vol. 2. Reading, Mass.: Addison-Wesley, 1954; 1968, pp. 693–728.

(30) Whiting, John W. M., and Child, Irvin L. *Child Training and Personality: A Cross-Cultural Study.* New Haven, Conn.: Yale University Press, 1953.

(31) Whiting, John W. M., Goethals, George W., *et al.* "Factors Affecting Pre-Marital Sexual Permissiveness." Several unpublished papers. Department of Social Relations, Harvard University, Cambridge, Massachusetts, 1962–69.

SUPPLEMENTAL REFERENCES

S 1. Durham, M. Edith. *Some Tribal Origins, Laws, and Customs of the Balkans*. London: George Allen & Unwin Ltd., 1928.

S 2. Evans-Pritchard, Edward Evan. *The Divine Kingship of the Shilluk of the Nilotic Sudan*. Cambridge, England: University Press, 1948.

S 3. Evans-Pritchard, Edward Evan. *Witchcraft, Oracles and Magic Among the Azande*. Oxford: The Clarendon Press, 1937.

S 4. Gamble, David P. *The Wolof of Senegambia: Together with Notes on the Lebu and the Serer*. London: International African Institute, 1957.

S 5. Goethals, George W., and Rolde, Edward Jackson. "Tunisian Village: A Study of Social Change in a Tunisian Village." 1966: Cambridge, Mass. Unpublished monograph, School of Public Health and the Department of Social Relations, Harvard University.

S 6. Gorer, Geoffrey. *Himalayan Village; An Account of the Lepches of Sikkim*. London: M. Joseph, 1938.

S 7. Kroeber, Alfred L. *Zuni, Kin and Clan*. Anthropological Papers of the American Museum of Natural History. Vol. 18. Part 2. New York, 1917, pp. 135–152.

S 8. Langrand, Gustave. *Vie Sociale et Religieuse en Annam: monographie d'un village de la cote Sud-Annam* [*Social and Religious Life in Annam: The Study of a Village on the Coast of Southern Annam*]. Lille: Editions Univers, 1945.

S 9. LaMacchia, Linda; Steere, Carole; Ware, Janet; and Ware, Lewis. "Rural Life of Tunisia: Summer Observations 1967." Internal Report 1. Cambridge, Mass.: Harvard University, 1967.

S10. Malinowski, Bronislaw. *Argonauts of the Western Pacific: An Account of Native Enterprise and Adventure in the Archipelagoes of Melanesia New Guinea*. London: George Routledge & Sons Ltd., 1922.

S11. Maxwell, Gavin. *The Ten Pains of Death*. New York: Dutton Publishers, 1960.

S12. Mijatovic, Chedo. *Servia of the Servians*. New York: Charles Scribner's Sons, 1914.

S13. Nadel, Siegfried Frederick. *Nupe Religion*. London: Routledge & Paul, 1954.

S14. Pitts-Rivers, J. A. *The People of the Sierra*. Chicago: University of Chicago Press, Phoenix Books, 1952.

SEXUAL ORGASM

Sexual Responsiveness in Single Girls

DAVID F. SHOPE

As greater sexual freedom has developed in America, so has scientific interest and research into sexual behavior. Such scientific endeavors have led to theorizing and research in the area of female sexual responsiveness. This paper is an attempt to refine further our knowledge in this realm, and it is laid on the foundation established by earlier researchers, such as Gilbert Hamilton (1929), Lewis Terman (1938), Alfred Kinsey (1948, 1953), and Masters and Johnson (1966), who established some of the major landmarks in sexual research. Clifford Adams (1946, 1953) has set much of the tone for my current thinking in this area. In fact, the research reported in this paper is a natural outgrowth of these earlier studies, and is a preliminary report of the findings to date. Since the study of female sexual responsiveness is in its infancy, it is entirely possible that many of our concepts will change as we gain more knowledge. When considering the results of this investigation, its exploratory nature must be kept in mind.

The Problem

Female sexual responsiveness is on a continuum that ranges all the way from practically no response to orgasm, which is usually thought of as the peak of sexual-tension release. For the majority of women (and for their men), orgasm is the expected end result of coitus. Yet, not all women achieve orgasm. What factors differentiate women who achieve an orgasm from intercourse and those who never find this release? In order to answer this question, a comparison was made between women who usually or always reach climax from intercourse and those who never do. A study was made of single girls of college age and background who had never been married but who had engaged in coitus for at least a three-month period prior to the research.

Some Previous Explanations

Several explanations have been given to account for some females having greater sexual responsiveness than others. Two such explanations are based on greater physiological potential and differential overt sexual experience. For example, Hamilton (1929: 195) postulated that orgasm adequacy was related to menarche, and Kirkendall (1961: 939) cites other scientists who felt that the sex drive is basically biological. The folklore of sex drive equates it to other physiological drives such as hunger and thirst, but it is obvious that many persons can and do live without sex. The idea that prior sexual experience will be helpful in producing sexual adjustment appears in several writers' works, and it is implied that this adjustment includes orgastic ability. Kinsey (1948: 386–391) discusses the role of premarital sexual experience and states that insofar as possible this experience should be orgastic. Christensen (1958: 185) feels that premarital experience without orgasm could teach one "not to respond."

No differences were found in the physiological measures pursued in this investigation. These include degree of lubrication, age at menarche, number of days menstrual period lasts, and amount of cramps experienced during the period. A related item was the time of month that the subject felt most easily aroused. There were no significant differences between the groups, and 40 percent of the women in each group could report no time.

Experience has also been a prime explanation for the differences between the responsive and nonresponsive, but this is not the explanation for the differences in our groups. Both groups were equally experienced as measured by the age they began petting, age they began intercourse, number of men with whom they petted, number of coital partners, or number of times they had engaged in coitus. Additionally, both groups had equal numbers of oral-genital experiences, and approximately the same number of subjects in each group had engaged in self-stimulation. This does not negate the role of experience in learning, however, because there is the matter of intensity and quality of experience. Experience and attitude are complexly related, and it is not possible in a nonlongitudinal study such as this to tell which comes first. Although this is a matter for future research, one cannot help but be impressed with the number of young people who have a first experience in spite of negative attitudes only to have these attitudes themselves softened. Thus, actual experience may either confirm or deny the attitudes that one has been taught. Few of my subjects expressed more than minor regret over losing their virginity, and the majority were glad that they had, in spite of the fact that they at one time held virginity at marriage as a major goal.

Terman (1938: 381) suggested that female orgastic ability may be an inherited trait which is either evolving in or out of the human race. He cites the fact that there is little evidence that female animals are capable of orgastic responsiveness, and the specific personality traits he measured showed no relation to orgastic ability. This study confirms his thesis as regards to general personality as he measured it (I used about the same traits) but can offer no evidence on the genetic theory beyond demonstrating that specific sexual attitudes do affect orgastic achievement.

The Subjects

The subjects in this study ranged in age from eighteen to twenty-three years and had attended college for at least two years. All were unmarried and were engaging in sexual intercourse. Of these females, eighty were reaching climax from their coital activities while sixty-five were not, even though they had engaged in coitus no less than fifteen times. No subjects with known mental pathology were included. Subjects were selected from among volunteers who came to the school marriage clinic for counseling on such problems as contraception, value orientations, and other routine matters. Other subjects were chosen from among the general college population who had heard about the project or from the author's marriage classes. It is not known how representative this sample is, but in two instances 100 percent of the marriage classes volunteered.

The Procedures

Information was gathered by asking each subject to complete the Adams' Marital Happiness Prediction Inventory (MHP) and from her participation in two or more in-depth, semistructured interviews. The MHP measures personality dimensions which have been found to be predictive of both marital happiness and sexual adjustment. It has a validity of $r = .60$ and a reliability of $r = .90$ when used with a college population. Some of the interviews were cross-validated by having another interviewer complete the second session with certain subjects. Both interviews (first and second) yielded approximately the same data.

In each case the girls were asked only to give what they believed to be their best estimate of how they usually felt during the activities discussed and were reminded that there could be no right or wrong answers.

For some of the data reported, there were less than eighty orgastic subjects and less than sixty-five nonorgastic subjects due to a change in some of the questions after the first 40 girls in each group had been interviewed. When this has been the case, the discrepancy has been reported.

Reported Reasons for Engaging in Coitus

Coital orgasm is considered by most of these subjects to be the height of sexual interaction. A glance at Table 1 makes it clear that the relationship between a woman's reason for beginning intercourse and her ability to achieve orgasm is slight. It should

TABLE 1. REASON FOR FIRST ENGAGING IN COITUS

Reason	Number of Orgastic Subjects Reporting Each Reason	Number of Non-orgastic Subjects Reporting Each Reason
Curiosity	19	14
Love for male	15	12
Just seemed a natural outcome of the relationship	11	5
Date asked for it	6	7
Needed self-fulfillment	4	0

This table is based on an orgastic group of N = 55 and a nonorgastic group of N = 38.

be pointed out that these are the reasons given for first engaging in coitus and not the reasons why some of the subjects continue. Reiss (1967: 19) has pointed out that modern college students often set a standard that permissiveness with affection is acceptable, but this was not the case with the majority of subjects in this study. *Curiosity* vied with *love* as the chief reason for beginning intercourse, which may be an indication that females are becoming more interested in sexual participation as natural or that they are rejecting the double standard more; that is, women are becoming more realistic and depending less upon traditional ideological reasons for participating in coitus. Many subjects felt that their coital activity was a natural outgrowth of their sexual relationships with men and should be expected. If this *just seemed natural* category is combined with the *needed fulfillment* category, there is evidence that women who see sex as a natural part of themselves are more likely to reach orgasm. All four orgastic girls in this last category explained their need for fulfillment as stemming from sexual arousal and not as a psychological need. It is interesting that no nonorgastic women felt this need either as physically or psychologically based. Since the data is incomplete and the N is small, more evidence will be needed in this area before any justifiable conclusions can be reached.

Nonsexual Variables

Let us now examine some of the "nonsexual" factors which were studied. The data relating to these variables can be found in Table 2. There has been much speculation concerning the role of religion, family background, dating and general personality characteristics in regard to the manner and degree to which they affect female sexual responsiveness. To gain some insight into these variables, each subject was questioned about her relationship with her parents, age she began dating, number of partners she considered as steady dates, and her own self-rating concerning her degree of religious devoutness. Neither religious devoutness, age at first date nor the number of men considered as steady dates proved to differentiate the groups.

Parental conflict was divided into conflict with her mother and conflict with her father. Although there was no significant difference in the groups considering the amount of conflict they had with their mothers, there was a trend for the orgastic girls to have less conflict. This trend, if continued, might indicate that the daughter who most highly identifies with her mother is the most capable of orgasm, or it might simply mean that orgastic girls communicate less with their mothers concerning antagonistic subjects and are less dependent on them for making behavioral decisions; that is, she may feel more free to "be herself" without dependence on others. This latter interpretation is supported by other data in this study.

Significantly fewer of the orgastic girls had conflict with their fathers. This possibly indicates that girls who have not learned to reach orgasm have not identified with the male most likely to influence their attitudes toward men—their fathers. Adams (1953: 58), Frankl (1952: 128–130), and others have noted that women who have more conflict with their mates are less orgastic. It would seem that a father who teaches his daughter to feel positively toward men by his own behavior with his wife and family would be giving her a basic attitude toward males which would enhance her orgastic potential. Greater identification with both parents, if this is what less conflict represents, may produce a generalized

TABLE 2. NONSEXUAL ITEMS INVESTIGATED

Item	Category Description	Orgastic Subjects		Nonorgastic Subjects		Level of Significance
		No.	%†	No.	%†	
Religious devout-	None/little	19	(24)	20	(30)	
ness	Some	26	(33)	22	(34)	NS*
	Much/very much	35	(43)	23	(36)	
	Total	80	(100)	65	(100)	
Conflict with	None/little	23	(58)	8	(32)	
mother	Some	7	(17)	8	(32)	NS
	Much/very much	10	(25)	9	(36)	
	Total	40	(100)	25	(100)	
Conflict with	None/little	29	(72)	11	(44)	
father	Some	8	(20)	7	(28)	.05
	Much/very much	3	(08)	7	(28)	
	Total	40	(100)	25	(100)	
Predicted marital	Lowest quartile	26	(33)	16	(24)	
happiness	Middle quartiles	39	(49)	44	(68)	NS
	Upper quartile	15	(18)	5	(08)	(.06)
	Total	80	(100)	65	(100)	
Predicted sexual	Lowest quartile	34	(43)	34	(53)	
adjustment	Middle quartiles	36	(44)	25	(38)	NS
	Upper quartile	10	(13)	6	(09)	
	Total	80	(100)	65	(100)	
Average number of men dated as steadies		3.7		3.5		NS
Mean age in years at first date		15.1		15.02		NS
Personality stability	Lowest quartile	36	(45)	21	(33)	
related to sexual	Middle quartiles	37	(47)	26	(39)	.01
adjustment	Upper quartile	7	(08)	18	(28)	
	Total	80	(100)	65	(100)	
Training of daugh-	Yes	15	(38)	18	(72)	
ters more restric-	No	25	(62)	7	(28)	.01
tively than sons	Total	40	(100)	25	(100)	

* Not Statistically Significant at the .01 or .05 levels.
† Rounded off to nearest whole number.

acceptance of loving relationships which enhances sexual responsiveness.

The general personality characteristics measured by the MHP include sociability, tendency to become annoyed, agreeableness, capacity to be realistic in one's outlook, social prejudice, freedom from repression, flexibility, the subject's standards and ideals, and her general family background and family attitudes. When compared for these personality characteristics, the groups did not differ significantly although there was a very definite trend for more of the orgastic girls to be most agreeable than the nonorgastic ones. Twenty-eight of the orgastic girls were in the upper half of the agreeableness scale while only nine of the nonorgastic girls were in this category. To be agreeable as measured by this instrument is about the same as being more submissive and fits the social definition of the female role more precisely. This latter measurement also fits closely with Maslow's notion that the more dominant women are less sexually satisfied unless subdued (1963: 100). Consequently, this seems to be another facet of the woman's general attitude toward both her mate and others, and this attitude produces a psychological set either to "give up" to the other person or to aim for control of that person.

In a statistical sense one personality characteristic measured by the MHP, Personality Stability, did prove significant in differentiating the groups by indicating that orgastic women tend to be less stable, or, in other words, more emotional. This trend has continued in our newer data and therefore might be a reality factor; however, since it is only one of twenty-four [1] personality characteristics measured by the MHP, this is likely a chance statistic.

Since the MHP yields an overall score predictive of both marital happiness and sexual adjustment, the groups were compared to disclose whether or not coital orgasm before marriage was predictive of either marital happiness or sexual adjustment. The chi-square for these items reveal no predictable difference, but there is a very definite trend for more of the orgastic girls to have higher predictions for marital happiness. Since 1963 when

---

[1] The twelve personality items measured by the MHP are normed for both marital happiness and sexual adjustment separately.

the first data were collected to the present, this relationship between orgasm has grown closer to significance, going from a probability of .10 to the present .06. This is sheer speculation, but I cannot help but wonder whether this reflects the newer, more free sexual attitudes; that is, currently it is more feminine to be more accepting of sexuality than it was only a few years ago. Nevertheless, the data do not bear out the contention that premarital orgasm is useful for predicting marital happiness or marital sexual adjustment.

Elsewhere Shope and Broderick (1967) have published evidence that virgins have both a greater chance of marital happiness and of sexual adjustment regardless of whether the nonvirgin is experiencing orgasm or not.

Subjects were not asked directly about their own beliefs concerning the "double standard" of sexual behavior, but 40 of the orgastic and 25 of the nonorgastic girls were asked whether or not they intended to rear their daughters more restrictively than their sons. This data yielded highly significant differences in the group with 62 percent of the orgastic women indicating that they did not intend to rear their daughters more restrictively, while only 28 percent of the nonorgastic women answered this way. Both sexes, most orgastic girls believed, would be reared to regard sexual morality as important but would be expected to develop their own ideas of what is and is not proper. I suggest that this offers further evidence that orgastic girls tend to want to control others less.

Although broad, general personality traits seem only slightly correlated with female coital-orgastic responsiveness, the more specific sexual attitudes of these women indicated pronounced differences between the groups. In our society, I believe, sexual relationships are considered special by most people; for example, sexual interaction is not considered by most to be of the same intensity as sharing a meal. The fact that specific sexual attitudes differentiate orgastic from nonorgastic women has led me to hypothesize that females do not manifest their personality traits in the sexual situation as they would in other situations. I have called this the female's "special sexual personality." Thus, a woman might react to a man in a superior manner in nonsexual interaction, but once she perceives the relationship as containing some element of sex, she is likely to react differently. Few orgastic women will want to outperform their mates. What is needed here is data on general personality characteristics which are operative in the actual sexual encounter between men and women. Additionally, there are specific sexual attitudes toward her mate, her self-concepts, and her sexual behavior. Thus, a woman might be dominant with men other than her sexual partner or husband, but she might try to role-play a more submissive part when interacting with her significant male or males.

Attitudes Toward Mate

An examination of Table 3 indicates that there are definite differences between the groups in their relationships with and attitudes toward their mates. The orgastic women reported more satisfaction with both their general adjustment and their sexual adjustment to their mates. The mixture of general and sexual satisfaction is a complex one in which each contributes something to the other. In some cases general satisfaction did not take place until the girl felt herself sexually fulfilled with her mate. This sexual fulfillment did not depend on orgasm since some girls who reported this trend became satisfied that their men were good sexual partners before reaching orgasm with them (it might be correct to say *for them*). For the majority, of course, intercourse took place after they felt a good general adjustment to the man. This reported adjustment, it should be pointed out, depended upon the subject's perception of the situation with her mate and could not always be verified objectively; consequently, it is the woman's perception of her mate as satisfactory that is conducive to her coital orgastic capacity with him.

At first it was a surprise to find that more of the orgastic girls pretended to have an orgasm when in fact they had not. Further interviews with these women revealed that the pretense was primarily to please their partners, and that they had a qualitively higher desire to please sexually than the nonorgastic females.

Significantly more of the nonorgastic women felt that they

TABLE 3. ATTITUDES TOWARD MATES POSITIVELY RELATED TO ORGASM

Item	Category Description *	Orgastic Subjects		Nonorgastic Subjects		Level of Significance
		No.	%†	No.	%†	
General adjust-	Most	62	(78)	26	(40)	
ment to mate	Middle	13	(16)	29	(45)	
	Poor	5	(06)	10	(15)	0.1
	Total	80	(100)	65	(100)	
Sexual adjustment	Most	60	(75)	26	(39)	
to mate	Middle	17	(21)	26	(39)	
	Poor	3	(04)	13	(21)	0.1
	Total	80	(100)	65	(100)	
Pretense of climax	Usually	5	(12)	4	(10)	
when one is not	Occasionally	8	(20)	2	(05)	
achieved	Rarely	9	(23)	2	(05)	0.1
	Never	18	(45)	32	(80)	
	Total	40	(100)	40	(100)	
"Giving in to mate"	Never	28	(70)	10	(40)	
in regards to	Sometimes	11	(27)	5	(20)	
coitus	Often	0	(00)	4	(16)	0.1
	Usually	1	(03)	6	(24)	
	Total	40	(100)	25	(100)	
Sex drive compared	About same	47	(75)	14	(29)	
to mate's	Stronger	11	(17)	16	(33)	0.1
	Much stronger	3	(05)	14	(29)	
	Much weaker	2	(03)	04	(09)	
	Total	63	(100)	48	(100)	
Desire for coitus	As often	28	(70)	17	(43)	
compared to	More often	10	(25)	21	(52)	.05
mate's	Less often	2	(05)	2	(05)	
	Total	40	(100)	40	(100)	
Willingness to dis-	Freely	76	(95)	47	(72)	
cuss sex with	Sometimes	3	(04)	11	(17)	
mate	Rarely/Never	1	(01)	7	(11)	0.1
	Total	80	(100)	80	(100)	

* The *most* category was originally titled *perfect to almost perfect adjustment;* the *middle* category, *there could be some improvement;* and the *poor* category *poorly or not at all adjusted.*

† Rounded off to nearest whole number.

were forced to "give in" to their mates in regard to intercourse. This feeling of being pushed into sexual intercourse was one of the most profound factors separating the groups. There is a qualitative difference between being required to please one's mate and pleasing him out of personal choice. I believe this factor needs considerably more research effort than it has received thus far. A woman can be happy because she willingly pleases her man in non-tabooed areas but find her happiness dampened by being "forced" to submit in more or less prohibited areas. The word *forced* does not mean physical force, but the psycho-socio-moral implications that without giving in she might lose her mate, might not be fulfilling her duties as a wife, be less than normal, or a myriad of other implications. Any woman might engage in sexual behavior with her mate for a variety of reasons other than her personal desire and yet feel that this behavior is improper and, given a real choice, would not indulge in it.

Research with married women has shown that those couples who regard their sexual drives as about equal have the better sexual adjustment (Adams 1953: 60; Wallin and Clark 1958: 247–254). The orgastic girls in this study were significantly more likely to see both their sex drives and their desire for coitus as about equal to their mate's; whereas, the nonorgastic subjects were most likely to feel that their mate's sex drives were much stronger than theirs. Many of the latter group felt that their mates emphasized sexual relationships "too much." That this is primarily a matter of attitude is attested to by the fact that both groups had approximately the same amount of experience over the same amount of time. I shall return to the matter of experience later. There is, I believe, little justification to the view that men have a greater biological need for sexual expression than do women. Several writers share this belief (Kinsey 1953: 688–689; Chesser 1956: 24-25; McCary 1967: 203–205). In all probability, sexual drives are primarily conditioned by the culture in which one lives, and ours has overemphasized male sexuality, a condition which many females will no longer accept. The feeling of sexual equality is conducive to sexual responsiveness and raises further questions concerning the desirability of rearing our daughters to believe that men generally have stronger sex drives than women.

Still another bit of evidence which leads me to conclude that orgastic women have more intense relationships with their mates is the fact that the great majority reported that they were able to discuss sex with their mates and do so as freely as the male. They could talk on his terms and in his language, and many subjects reported that they initiated such sex discussions. Many more of the orgastic women volunteered that they enjoyed discussions of sexual intimacy.

Self-attitudes

Orgastic girls in this sample see themselves as sexual beings more often than do nonorgastic girls. Some of the above data suggest this interpretation, but Table 4 offers further evidence on this point. Orgastic women considered themselves more free of sexual inhibitions than nonorgastic ones, although many of the latter also felt themselves to be free of such inhibitions. This feeling of being personally inhibited sexually is also evidenced by the greater degree to which outside noises tended to disturb the nonorgastic girls.

More orgastic women reported that they had initiated petting some of the time. They either did things directly related to having the male pet them, or they had begun the petting process by touching him sexually. In the first instance some of the girls had removed their blouses, for example, before the men had touched them in a directly sexual way. Petting was defined as, at least, having one's covered breasts fondled with the clear and conscious knowledge that the purpose was to promote sexual arousal. Since very few subjects in either group were willing to pet on their first three or four dates, it is evident that they felt they must "know the man" before they were willing to pet with him; consequently, the greater willingness of the orgastic women to initiate petting cannot be laid to differences in promiscuous attitudes. Most college females, at least of the author's acquaintance, follow the standard that before becoming sexually involved they must know and like the man.

Acknowledged guilt was not an important factor for either group; in fact, the overwhelming majority of subjects in both

TABLE 4. ATTITUDES TOWARD SELF POSITIVELY RELATED TO ORGASM

Item	Category Description	Orgastic Subjects No.	%	Nonorgastic Subjects No.	%	Level of Significance
Amount of sexual	None/little	59	(74)	25	(38)	
inhibition	Some	19	(24)	24	(36)	.01
	Much/very much	2	(02)	16	(26)	
	Total	80	(100)	65	(100)	
Amount disturbed	None/little	51	(64)	23	(35)	
by outside noises	Some	21	(26)	22	(33)	.01
	Much/very much	8	(10)	20	(32)	
	Total	80	(100)	65	(100)	
Satisfaction with	Entirely adequate	13	(16)	7	(11)	
sex education	Reasonably adequate	30	(38)	19	(29)	.05
	Rather inadequate	19	(24)	11	(17)	
	Very inadequate/none	18	(22)	28	(43)	
	Total	80	(100)	65	(100)	
Ever initiated	Yes	32	(80)	19	(76)	NS*
petting	No	8	(20)	6	(24)	
	Total	40	(100)	25	(100)	
Amount of pleasure	None/little	0	(00)	1	(05)	
from initiating	Some	5	(15)	7	(37)	
petting †	Much	4	(12)	5	(26)	.05
	Very much	23	(74)	6	(32)	
	Total	32	(100)	19	(100)	
Desire to become	None/little	4	(10)	10	(40)	
more sexually	Some	8	(20)	3	(12)	.05
responsive	Much	15	(38)	5	(20)	
	Very much	13	(32)	7	(28)	
	Total	40	(100)	25	(100)	

* Not significant at the .05 or .01 levels.
† Based only on those who initiated petting.

groups denied more than a medium amount of guilt which definitely (and usually quickly) melted into little or no awareness.

The orgastic women in this study indicated that they were much more satisfied with the amount of sex education they had received. Most of this sex education came from either their peers or their dates, but the source of sex education, parents, teachers, peers, or dates, did not significantly differentiate the groups. Apparently, the "faulty sex education" which is written about so much and which is ascribed to learning sex from one's peers did not affect the capacity of these subjects to reach an orgasm. Likely, only certain self-referent ideas would produce the kind of inhibition that deters responsiveness, and men do not ordinarily communicate ideas to their dates if they find these will inhibit her. Perhaps, we need to find out more about this kind of "sex education." It should be pointed out that orgastic girls might have felt that their sex education was satisfactory because they were reaching orgasm; if so, this is the well-known psychological *halo effect*. By the same token girls who were not reaching a climax from coitus might have felt their sex education was less satisfactory because of this.

Each subject in this study was asked to rate her desire to become more sexually responsive than her current capacity. Using a four-point scale which ranged from none to very much, it was found that more of the coitally orgastic females wanted to become even more sexually responsive. Two-thirds of the orgastic women felt that they wanted to be from *much* to *very much* more responsive. Only half the nonorgastic subjects felt this way. The rest apparently had little interest in becoming more sexually arousable. This interest in becoming more sexually arousable is another reason I have ascribed the term "seeing themselves as sexual beings" to the orgastic women. This is another case where the evidence is based on only forty orgastic and twenty-five nonorgastic girls. An interesting sidelight is the reflection of the four orgastic women who did not want to become more sexually responsive. All four stated they felt this way because they did not see how they could possibly become more responsive. Among the seven nonorgastic females who did not want to become more responsive, two gave as their reason: "It is not right."

For some diffuse reason the others did not want to achieve greater sexuality. The information in Table 4 indicates that twenty-eight of the orgastic women and twelve of the nonorgastic ones wanted to become much to very much more sexually arousable. How many would actively do something about achieving this greater sexuality is not known, but each subject has agreed to a follow-up interview after one to two years. Perhaps then the answer will be known.

Thus, the orgastic woman is clearly more satisfied with herself as a "sexual being" as evidenced by her freedom from inhibition, the fact that she is less easily disturbed during coitus, her greater willingness to initiate petting, her larger satisfaction with her sex education, and her stronger desire to become more sexually responsive. Up to this point we have seen that female sexual responsiveness is related to attitudes toward her mate, attitudes toward herself as a sexual person, and some so-called nonsexual variables. I, of course, have pointed out that these factors do not operate in a vacuum but are interrelated, although we cannot at this time specify the degree or complexity of the correlations.

Table 5 provides us with data concerning the outcomes of actual sexual expression. Remember all of these women were engaging in coitus as well as all other forms of sexual expression mentioned in this paper so we are clearly dealing with actual, not potential, behavior. That the orgastic females become more aroused from intercourse and enjoy it more is to be expected. Some nonorgastic subjects claim to enjoy coitus more than some of the orgastic ones so that it cannot be said that orgasm is necessary to the enjoyment of coitus, but it certainly helps.

The bulk of the women who were orgastic wanted more intercourse soon after the first coital act had been completed. The orgastic experience itself is so highly satisfying that the climactic female is ready to begin intercourse almost immediately and is certainly interested in maintaining some sexual contact with her mate. A typical remark by an orgastic subject might be, "Well, yes, I want to lie close to him when we are done and enjoy his affection, but I don't want him to quit either." (*Quit* meaning, she does not want her mate to stop sexually stimulating her). Also, nonorgastic women usually liked their men's attention after

TABLE 5. RESULTS OF SEXUAL EXPRESSION POSITIVELY RELATED TO ORGASM

Item	Category Description	Orgastic Subjects No.	%	Nonorgastic Subjects No.	%	Level of Significance
Arousal from coitus	None/little	0	(00)	1	(04)	
	Some	1	(03)	3	(12)	.02
	Much	8	(20)	12	(47)	
	Very much	31	(77)	9	(37)	
	Total	40	(100)	25	(100)	
Enjoyment of coitus	None/little	0	(00)	6	(09)	
	Some	1	(01)	4	(06)	.01
	Much	8	(10)	14	(21)	
	Very much	71	(89)	41	(64)	
	Total	80	(100)	65	(100)	
Desire for more coitus almost immediately	Never	3	(08)	4	(16)	
	Sometimes	10	(25)	11	(44)	.05
	Often/ usually *	27	(67)	10	(40)	
	Total	40	(100)	25	(100)	
Enjoyment of oral stimulation of breasts	None/little	5	(06)	10	(15)	
	Some	13	(16)	21	(32)	.02
	Much	34	(43)	18	(28)	
	Very much	28	(35)	16	(25)	
	Total	80	(100)	65	(100)	
Enjoyment of petting	None/little	1	(01)	10	(15)	
	Some	14	(18)	23	(36)	.01
	Much	25	(31)	22	(34)	
	Very much	40	(50)	10	(15)	
	Total	80	(100)	65	(100)	
Arousal from petting	None/little	0	(00)	6	(09)	
	Some	13	(16)	22	(34)	
	Much	24	(30)	21	(32)	.01
	Very much	43	(54)	16	(25)	
	Total	80	(100)	65	(100)	
Relaxation follow- ing nighttime coitus	Complete	37	(93)	30	(75)	
	Increased energy	2	(05)	2	(05)	.05
	Nervous tension	1	(02)	8	(20)	
	Total	40	(100)	40	(100)	

* Originally these were two separate categories.

intercourse, but the more purely affectional nature of the relationship was emphasized.

The orgastic subjects also became more aroused and received more enjoyment from their petting activities. It is not clear whether their greater satisfaction with petting is the result of achieving climax in intercourse or whether it contributes to coital climax. What is more understandable is that these attitudes toward sexual expression have a global effect on the individual, and it is more probable that each contributes something to the other which builds a woman's sexual image of herself. Additionally, orgastic women enjoyed oral stimulation of their breasts to a significantly greater degree than nonorgastic ones. They also became more sexually aroused from this activity.

Once coitus is completed, more orgastic women tend to feel relaxed. As Masters and Johnson (1966: 6, 27, 294) have pointed out, a woman responds with her entire body to sexual stimuli, and if orgasm is not reached, muscle tension may remain for hours. Thus, a physiological basis has been established for the role of orgasm in producing relaxation, and when psychological relief is added to this, it is apparent that orgasm, however produced, can be useful in producing individual peace of mind. Much more research is needed on the function of orgasm in producing relief from muscular and everyday psychological tensions. To what extent is the failure to relax following coitus responsible for a wide variety of family difficulties? What factors other than orgasm account for this relaxed feeling? That orgasm contributes to marital happiness cannot be doubted in most cases; at least, this is the finding of Adams (1953: 65) and Gebhard (1966: 95), and our own data, although just short of statistical significance, support the conclusion that premarital, coital orgasm increases the likelihood of marital happiness. To the extent, then, that orgasm helps produce relaxation, it would be expected to enhance happiness if the assumption that relaxed people find it easier to be happy is valid.

Based on forty orgastic and twenty-five nonorgastic women the following data have proven significant. Orgastic females were more interested in sexual experimentation, became more aroused when fantasizing about sex during rest (nonsexually active) periods, and use the kind of thinking and movements they feel will enhance their sexual responsiveness. These data are set forth in Table 6.

Several conclusions seem warranted from the data in Table 6. Orgastic girls are more interested in thinking and acting in a sexually tension producing way during coitus, and when not actively engaged in coitus, they can fantasize themselves into a higher degree of sexual responsiveness than nonorgastic girls as a group. They are more willing to control themselves toward increased sexual arousability or overt sexual expression, and they can abandon themselves to sexuality when in situations where abandonment is called for. Some orgastic girls could not keep from becoming aroused during coitus, but for the majority, they sought to give up inhibiting controls.

Conclusions

Certain tentative conclusions concerning the capacity of a female to reach a coital orgasm seem warranted from this exploratory study. These have been subjectively divided into categories in regard to items which are not directly sexual in nature (nonsexual items), factors related to a woman's attitudes toward men, concepts expressing her own sexuality (sexual self-attitudes), and, as each woman reported experiencing them, her overt sexual responses.

The orgastic woman is relatively free from conflicts with her parents and especially her father. She wants to rear her own daughters so that they, too, will enjoy sex to the fullest extent. She, the orgastic girl, is more likely to be emotionally unstable than is her sister who never reaches orgasm from coitus, but clinical data suggest that she uses this emotionality to enhance her sexual responsiveness. Orgastic girls who score high on emotional stability are apt to be more free to let their emotions go in the sexual situation. She likes men in general and has a good adjustment to her mate in most areas of their lives including the sexual.

Orgastic women see themselves as having about the same sex drives as their men, and they can communicate their sexual feeling, verbally and nonverbally, more easily than nonorgastic fe-

TABLE 6. FACTORS AFFECTING AROUSAL

Item	Category Description	Orgastic Subjects No.	%	Nonorgastic Subjects No.	%	Level of Significance
Enjoyment of sex-	None/little	0	(00)	3	(12)	
ual experimenta-	Some	5	(13)	5	(20)	.05
tion	Much	13	(33)	11	(44)	
	Very much	22	(54)	6	(24)	
	Total	40	(100)	25	(100)	
Arousal from	None/little	6	(15)	8	(32)	
phantasizing	Some	15	(38)	10	(40)	.05
about sex	Much	8	(20)	6	(24)	
	Very much	11	(27)	1	(04)	
	Total	40	(100)	25	(100)	
Control over	1 *	26	(64)	4	(16)	
thinking during	2	11	(28)	2	(08)	
coitus	3	2	(05)	3	(12)	.01
	4	1	(03)	11	(44)	
	5	0	(00)	5	(20)	
	Total	40	(100)	25	(100)	
Control over	1 *	26	(64)	3	(12)	
movements dur-	2	10	(25)	5	(20)	
ing coitus	3	3	(08)	5	(20)	.01
	4	1	(03)	8	(32)	
	5	0	(00)	4	(16)	
	Total	40	(100)	25	(100)	

* 1 = Begin coitus by controlling to enhance responsiveness, gradually lose control.

2 = Begin coitus by controlling to enhance responsiveness, partially maintain throughout.

3 = Begin coitus by controlling so as "not to get carried away," gradually lose control.

4 = Begin coitus by controlling so as "not to get carried away," partially maintain.

5 = Begin coitus by controlling so as "not to get carried away," fully maintain throughout the act.

males. They simply do not believe that they are sexually inhibited and act as though they were not when in the appropriate situation. They themselves define, for the most part, the appropriateness of the situation. An orgastic woman has pleasure out of giving herself to her mate and in seeing him become aroused, but she also feels good about her own capacity to be stimulated and can gradually allow herself to focus almost exclusively on the physical feelings she is receiving from the latter stages of coitus. She chooses to become involved and is seldom forced by psychological pressures into coitus.

Since the reinforcement from a sexual climax is so intense and is so far away in time from the punishing agents of society, it would seem that once reached, this acme of sexuality would become built into every subject. The fact that it is not indicates that the internal-mediating factors of each girl have varying degrees of effectiveness with her. These factors then become the punishing agents which prohibit a girl from reaching climax, and instead of being far away in time, they are with her at the very moment the act of intercourse is taking place, administering a more powerful negative reinforcement than the positive reinforcement she is receiving from coitus. Indeed, coitus, under these circumstances, can become a negative reinforcer to general sexual responsiveness. Some of these negative reinforcers have been shown to be covert hostility toward men (maybe overt hostility also), a belief that her own sex drive is not strong enough, an air of indifference to the desirability of reaching orgasm, deliberate attempts to keep her sexual feelings down, and a refusal to condition herself or get into situations where she would be naturally conditioned to increased sexual responsiveness. If these feelings and attitudes can be modified, I believe, the nonorgastic girl can become increasingly responsive and eventually attain coital orgasm in most instances. So long as she carries her own negative reinforcers with her, she has less chance of becoming responsive.

Comments from two of the subjects sum up much of the difference between the groups. The nonorgastic girl stated, "I read where at age thirty many women reach their peak of sex-

ual responsiveness, so I'll just wait for my orgasm until then."
From the orgastic girl, "I just enjoy everything about sex. There
isn't anything I wouldn't try to make it even better."

REFERENCES

Adams, Clifford R. "The Prediction of Adjustment in Marriage."
    Educational and Psychological Measurement 6 (Summer): 185–193,
    1946.
Adams, Clifford R. "An Informal Preliminary Report on Some Factors
    Relating to Sexual Responsiveness of Certain College Wives." Re-
    port to the American Association of Marriage Counselors at Penn-
    sylvania State University, 1953. Mimeographed.
Chesser, Eustace. *The Sexual, Marital, and Family Relationship of
    the English Woman*. London: Hutchinson's Medical Publications,
    1956.
Christensen, Harold T. *Marriage Analysis*. New York: Ronald Press,
    1958.
Frankl, Victor. "The Pleasure Principle and Sexual Neurosis." *Inter-
    national Journal of Sexology 5:* 128–130, 1952.
Gebhard, Paul. "Factors in Marital Orgasm." *Journal of Social Issues
    22* (April): 88–95, 1966.
Hamilton, Gilbert. *A Research in Marriage*. New York: Charles and
    Albert Boni, 1929.
Kinsey, Alfred, *et al. Sexual Behavior in the Human Male*. Phila-
    delphia: W. B. Saunders Co., 1948.
Kinsey, Alfred, *et al. Sexual Behavior in the Human Female*. Phila-
    delphia: W. B. Saunders Co., 1953.
Kirkendall, Lester. "Sex Drive." In *The Encyclopedia of Sexual Be-
    havior,* edited by Albert Ellis and Albert Abarbanel. New York:
    Hawthorn Books, 1961, Ch. 2, pp. 939–948.
McCary, James L. *Human Sexuality*. New York: Van Nostrand,
    1967.
Maslow, A. H. "Self-Esteem (Dominance Feeling) and Sexuality in
    Women." In *Sexual Behavior and Personality Characteristics,*
    edited by Manfried F. DeMartino. New York: Grove Press, 1963,
    Ch. 4, pp. 71–112.
Masters, William, and Johnson, Virginia. *Human Sexual Response*.
    Boston: Little, Brown & Co., 1966.

Reiss, Ira L. *The Social Context of Premarital Sexual Permissiveness.* New York: Holt, Rinehart and Winston, 1967.

Shope, David F., and Broderick, Carlfred B. "Level of Sexual Experience and Predicted Adjustment in Marriage." *Journal of Marriage and the Family 29* (August): 424–427, 1967.

Shope, David F. "The Orgastic Responsiveness of Selected College Females." *Journal of Sex Research 4* (August): 206–219, 1968.

Terman, Lewis. *Psychological Factors in Marital Happiness.* New York: McGraw-Hill, 1938.

Wallin, Paul, and Clark, Alexander. "Cultural Norms and Husbands' and Wives' Reports of Their Marital Partner's Preferred Frequency of Coitus Relative to Their Own." *Sociometry 21* (September): 247–254, 1958.

Zehv, William. "Which Woman Enjoys Sex Most." *Sexology Magazine 35* (April): 622–624, 1969.

From an Unfortunate Necessity to a Cult of Mutual Orgasm: Sex in American Marital Education Literature 1830–1940

MICHAEL GORDON

INTRODUCTION

The history of the sex manual is not a long one. Prior to the twentieth century, the topic of sex was, if not a taboo at least one to which few authors were audacious enough to devote a book. Consequently, in this paper we shall attempt to delineate changes in the approach to sex in domestic education literature, from an unfortunate procreative necessity to the *ne plus ultra* of married life. In order to do this, I must first define the term "sex manual."

The sex manual is actually a variety of a more inclusive form of domestic education literature: the marriage manual. The latter is best defined as a book written to serve as a guide to the highways and byways of married life. Not all marriage manuals, however, are identical. While some deal with mate choice, the economics of home management, relations with in-laws, and so

The author would like to thank Esther Barsky, Charles Bernstein, Robert Kernish, and Roslyn Strokoff for their assistance in this project. The research was supported by a Temple University Faculty Grant and a University of Connecticut Research Foundation Grant. An abbreviated version of this paper was presented at the 1970 meetings of the American Sociological Association under the title, "From Procreation to Recreation: Changes in Sexual Ideology, 1830–1940."

forth, others omit these topics or place less emphasis on them. There is, then, considerable variety in what is found in the pages of works that can be properly spoken of as marriage manuals.

Since the turn of the century, and especially since the 1920s, many manuals have one or more chapters devoted to the topics of sex and contraception. Such books are not actually sex manuals. It is our contention that this term is best reserved for those volumes which are entirely or almost entirely devoted in a pedagogical manner to various aspects of sexual behavior. In the course of this paper we will have occasion to refer to both these types of books, since we find few sex manuals published before the 1920s.

THE BOOKS

The books discussed in this paper were selected as part of a larger study of the general topic of American nineteenth- and twentieth-century domestic education literature.[1] Nineteenth-century manuals were chosen somewhat differently from those of the twentieth century. The *American Catalog of Books* was consulted as the primary source of nineteenth-century manuals because it is generally agreed to be the most reliable and comprehensive source for the period. An attempt was made to locate all books listed in it under the headings of "Marriage" and "Sex." These were supplemented by others taken from various bibliographic sources. All in all, sixty-one nineteenth-century books were used in this study. The twentieth-century manuals were chosen by means of a random sample of titles taken from the *Cumulative Book Index* for each decade from 1900 to 1939 under the same headings. These were supplemented by others which did not appear in the group because of sampling procedures but which

[1] The author is currently engaged in a study of American domestic education literature from the nineteenth century to the present. This study deals with a variety of aspects of domestic life, for example, mate choice, marital adjustment, etc. See Michael Gordon, "The Ideal Husband as Depicted in the 19th Century Marriage Manual," *Family Coordinator 18* (July 1969): 226–231; and Michael Gordon and M. Charles Bernstein, "Mate Choice and Domestic Life in the 19th Century Marriage Manual," *Journal of Marriage and Family 32* (November 1970): 665–674.

were extremely important from the perspective of the history of the sex manual, for example, Stone and Stone, *A Marriage Manual*.[2] In most cases we will not discuss the statistical frequency with which particular recommendations appeared in print or attempt any sort of statistical analysis; our main concern here is presenting a history of ideas, or more simply, "ideal" patterns of sex behavior over a hundred-year period.

THE NINETEENTH CENTURY

As we have already indicated, the nineteenth century did not see much in the way of books devoted exclusively to sex behavior, but we do find manuals concerned with what was then referred to as "sexual physiology." Works of this kind generally discuss the genital organs, the dangers of masturbation, the nature of conception, gestation and parturition, various postparturitive factors, and occasionally birth control, abortion, and sexual relations.[3] These works come as close to sex manuals as anything published in the century. To a great extent, their contents typify the general attitude toward sex that prevails at the time. That is to say, sex is viewed, and this is true even of those who take a relatively liberal perspective, as means to an end rather than an end in itself; nonprocreative sex is never *fully* accepted throughout most of the nineteenth century.

The "Dangers" of Sexual Excess

One of the prime aspects of this topic covered both in the books on sexual physiology as well as the more general marriage man-

[2] Hannah M. Stone and Abraham Stone, *A Marriage Manual* (New York: Simon and Schuster, 1935).

[3] The dangers of masturbation, a particular preoccupation of nineteenth-century authors, are frequently and vividly set forth: "Tobacco and alcohol are not so potent to rob man of the high prerogatives of manhood, as this humiliating, self-abusing vice" (Augustus K. Gardner, *Conjugal Sins Against the Laws of Life and Health* . . . [New York: G. J. Moulton, 1874; first published in 1870 as *The Conjugal Relations*], p. 69). For an interesting perspective on this problem, see Robert H. MacDonald, "The Frightful Consequences of Onanism: Notes on the History of a Delusion," *Journal of the History of Ideas 28* (1967): 423–431.

uals, is the excessive expenditure of sexual energy. Discussions of the dangers of intemperate sexual behavior are common, and there is a continuing concern with the frequency with which sexual intercourse should take place as well as the proper time for it, for example, the morning or the evening. The debilitating effects of sexual indulgence are supposedly experienced by both sexes: "The sexual act is an exhausting one. It takes hold of the whole body, and demands the best energies of the system. It requires so much of nerve-force that it ought always to be followed by a period of rest." [4]

The male is seen as the one who bears the brunt of the dangers of sexual excess. This would appear to be related to notions about the "spending" of semen, which is thought of—if not spoken of—as "vital fluid." "The spermatic secretors are composed of the most precious properties which the blood is comprised. Thus it is that the vital resources of the individual are severely taxed when any undue strain on them takes place." [5] If men are not restrained in their sexual indulgence, the results are seen as grave indeed. "The ordinary results of an abuse of the conjugal privilege are, in the man, very much the same as those brought on by self-abuse. Locally there is an overexcitation, irritability, and possibly inflammation. The digestion becomes impaired, dyspepsia sets in, the strength is diminished, the heart has spells of palpitation. . . ." [6]

In order to avoid these unquestionably serious results, mod-

[4] Henry G. Hanchett, *Sexual Health* (New York: Chas. T. Hurlburt, 1887), pp. 25–26.

[5] E. B. Duffey, *The Relation of the Sexes* (New York: Wood and Holbrook, 1876), p. 30. It is interesting to note that this idea has a long history in both Western and Oriental thought. R. B. Onians in his *The Origins of European Thought about the Body, the Mind* . . . (Cambridge: Cambridge University Press, 1951), pp. 109–110, claims that in early Greece "it was natural and logical to think that the 'life' or Ψυχη issuing from a man must come from the 'life' or Ψυχη in him, from his head, therefore, and, helping that location, to see in his seed, which carries the new life and which must have seemed the very stuff of life, a portion of the cerebro-spinal substance in which was the life of the parent."

[6] George Napheys, *The Physical Life of Woman* (Philadelphia: David Mc-Kay, 1890; first published in 1869), p. 179.

eration in sexual indulgence was recommended, although this term has different meanings for different authors. Some suggest continence, except when children are desired; others feel once a lunar month is adequate; and still others argue for no more than once a week, although qualifications based on the man's occupation are generally given. A fairly typical position is the following:

> The frequency with which sexual intercourse can be indulged without serious damage to one or both of the parties depends, of course, on a variety of circumstances—constitutional stamina, temperament, occupation, habits of exercise, etc. Few should exceed the limit of once a week; while many cannot safely indulge oftener than once a month. But as temperance is always the safe rule of conduct, if there must be any deviation from the strictest law of physiology, let the error be on that side.[7]

Sex was clearly not something to be entered into with a light heart and an anxiety-free mind.

Relative Sensuality

Attitudes toward the relative sensuality, or in the words of the times, "amativeness," of the sexes are not as "Victorian" as one might expect. While most authors are of the belief that masculine needs are both greater and stronger than those of their feminine counterparts, women are not always presented as desireless creatures. "In fact, it seems to be true through life that distinctively sexual desires are, on the average, less imperious in the female than in the male." [8] Perhaps as strong a view as can be found on the weakness of female sensuality is the following: "There can be no doubt that sexual feeling in the female, is, in a majority of the cases, in abeyance, and that it requires positive and considerable excitement to be roused at all; and, even if roused (which in many instances it never can be), is very mod-

---

[7] R. T. Trall, M.D., *Sexual Physiology and Hygiene* (New York: Fowler and Wells, 1897; first published in 1866), p. 295.

[8] Hanchett, *op. cit.*, pp. 37–38.

erate, compared with that of the male." [9] The point here is that while this author is rather conservative in his view of female sensuality, he never denies the possibility of its existence, which is something we might expect, given prevailing stereotypes of the nineteenth-century notions of female sexuality. Actually, at least two authors argue that females are in fact more sensual than males.[10] For the most part, however, women are presented as creatures who *may* enjoy sexual relations but do not find abstinence unbearable.

Winds of Change

We have already noted that sex in the nineteenth century was not generally seen as something which was to be enjoyed apart from its procreative function. However, in the latter half of the century, and particularly in the last two decades, we see signs of the beginning of an acceptance of sex as something which can be beneficial to the marriage apart from its role in producing offspring.

> Whatever may be the object of sexual intercourse, whether intended as a love embrace merely, or as a generative act, it is very clear that *it should be as pleasurable as possible to both parties.* . . . There must be mental harmony and congeniality between the parties. Each must be able to respond to the whole nature of the other—bodily, morally and intellectually, to the extent that there shall be no sense of discord, no feeling of repugnance, but on the other hand, an utter abnegation of selfhood [ital. mine].[11]

Other authors go even further in their acceptance of marital sex. "The sexual relationship is among the most important uses of

[9] Albert H. Hayes, *Physiology of Woman* (Boston: Peabody Medical Institute, 1869), p. 226. The reader should not conclude that female orgasm was unrecognized at this time. "In the female an Orgasm is not always experienced, and may even know not what it is, though they may be capable of considerable excitement. When it does occur, it is exhibited in the same way as in the other sex, though often much more intensely . . ." (Frederick Hollick, *The Marriage Guide* [New York: T. W. Strong, 1860], p. 358).

[10] One author attributes this to what he sees as the fact that the act is less debilitating for the female. Michael Ryan, *The Philosophy of Marriage* (Philadelphia: Lindsay and Blakiston, 1873), pp. 122–124.

[11] Trall, *op. cit.,* pp. 291–292.

married life; it vivifies the affection for each other, as nothing else in the world can, and is a powerful reminder of their mutual obligation to each other and to the community in which they live." [12] As we shall show, this point of view will become predominant in the twentieth century, but at the end of the nineteenth century it exists only in an incipient form.

Birth Control

To some extent, the general attitude toward sex in the nineteenth century is reflected in the discussions of birth control. Continence is the most frequently mentioned method. For some authors this means intercourse perhaps once or twice a month, but for the majority who use this term, it is the complete abstinence from sexual relations except when children are desired.

> By the use of the term continence is meant: "The voluntary and entire absence from sexual indulgence in any form, and the having complete control over the passions by one who knows their power, and who, but for his pure life and steady will, not only could, but would indulge them." [13]

Nevertheless, continence is seen more as an ideal pattern than one which is readily realizable. Thus, we find both the rhythm method and intercourse without emission, or "Karezza," as it was known, being recommended quite often.

Despite the impact Knowlton's *Fruits of Philosophy* was supposed to have had both in this country and in Britain, douching, the method recommended by Knowlton, was not popular with the writers of nineteenth-century domestic education literature. Several of them do mention it, but generally in the context of a review of undesirable (or ineffective) birth control practices.[14] Included here would also be the condom, disliked both as an

[12] Henry Guernsey, *Plain Talks on Avoided Subjects* (Philadelphia: F. A. Davis, 1882), p. 103.

[13] John Cowan, *The Science of a New Life* (New York: J. S. Ogilvie, 1869), p. 115.

[14] It has been claimed that "the first edition was apparently read to pieces since nowhere in present-day libraries is a copy to be found" (Sidney Ditzion, *Marriage, Morals and Sex in America* [New York: Bookman Associates, 1953], p. 320).

irritant and because of its negative effect on sensation, and Car-
lile's sponge.[15]

1900 TO 1919

In many ways the period from 1900 to 1919 is a transitional one.
While nineteenth-century attitudes are by no means completely
abandoned, there is definitely a more positive orientation to the
role of sex in marriage.

Echoes of the previous century are heard in the recurring
references to the dangers of masturbation and the generally ambivalent attitude toward birth control; however, discussions of
these matters are, for the most part, more sophisticated than those
encountered in the nineteenth century. Some do, for example,
categorically condemn masturbation as a dangerous evil; others
merely claim its danger is to be found in the guilt it produces
or in the possibility of its becoming habitual. In point of fact,
one author even condones masturbation for spinsters and widows,
although his attitude toward male masturbation is somewhat less
liberal.[16]

Of greater significance is the growing acceptance of nonprocreative marital sex, something we saw take root in the late nineteenth century. Admittedly, this acceptance is hemmed about
with certain proscriptions, but, as we shall see, it is a far cry from
the attitudes prevailing throughout most of the nineteenth century. A physician writing at the time had the following to say on
sex in marriage: "The Great Power which controls us does not
intend that misery in sex relations and mating shall be our lot.
No other state but that of happy and joyous sex relations can
keep the world moving and progressing." [17]

---

[15] Worthy of comment is the fact that withdrawal as a means of contraception is frowned upon by a number of authors because of its supposedly
negative effects on both sexes. A variety of nervous diseases in the male are
seen as the result of this practice, and the female is also believed to be deprived of the important and "soothing" effects of emission.

[16] See, William Lee Howard, *Sex Problems in Worry and Work* (New
York: E. J. Clode, 1915), p. 31.

[17] William Lee Howard, *Facts for the Married* (New York: E. J. Clode,
1912), p. xii.

Other authors are even more direct in their praise of marital sex:

> Those who believe that sex relations are for racial purposes only, are welcome to their belief, and are welcome to live up to it. (How few of them do, though, honestly and consistently?) We must reiterate our opinion that the sex instinct has other high purposes besides that of perpetuating the race, and sex relations may and should be indulged in as often as they are conducive to man's and woman's physical, mental and spiritual health.[18]

This acceptance extends beyond merely acknowledging the propriety of sex in the context of marriage. It also includes discussions of sexual satisfaction, in the form of simultaneous orgasm—something which was lacking in the nineteenth-century literature and which indicates the degree to which attitudes have shifted.

Relative Sensuality

The concern with synchronized orgasm is part and parcel of the new conception of female sexuality that emerged at this time and cannot be understood without an appreciation of it. In the nineteenth century, female sexual needs and desire were felt, for the most part, as we have already indicated, to be less than those of the male. By the early twentieth century, however, there is emerging a belief in the existence of female sexual desire, as well as its right to be satisfied. Nevertheless, the nature of female sexuality is seen as unique: women are felt to be more passive creatures whose sexual needs have to be awakened and called forth by their husbands. "Men's sexual appetites are, on the average, far keener and more insistent than those of a normal woman. Women's desire for sexual gratification often needs clamant awakening." [19] This proviso notwithstanding, there seems to be agreement on the fact that once "awakened" women's sexual needs are strong. "It is a great mistake, then, to assume that sexuality is a quality that belongs to man in larger measure than to wom-

[18] William J. Robinson, *Woman Her Sex and Love Life* (New York: Eugenics Publishing Company, 1929; first published in 1917), pp. 286–287.
[19] Patrick Geddes and Arthur J. Thompson, *Sex* (New York: Henry Holt and Company, 1914), p. 189.

an." [20] Without this recognition of woman as a sexual creature in her own right, this concern with simultaneous orgasm obviously could not have arisen.

Sexual Satisfaction in Marriage

The stress placed on mutual orgasm is not as great as that which we find later in the century, but it is present in a number of books published at that time. Writing in 1904, Talmey argued: "The hygienic rule in regard to duration is, therefore, briefly this: The man must adjust himself to the condition of the woman so that they reach the culmination at the same time." [21] Not all of the authors who deal with orgasm in the woman maintain it has to be simultaneous with that of the male; the major consideration is that she achieve climax. One writer devotes an entire chapter to the disabilities and neurotic symptoms women may suffer when their sexual needs are not satisfied.

Associated with this accent on female orgasm is a companion interest in sexual technique. What we have here are *the beginnings* of a phenomenon which Lewis and Brisset have called the "sex as work ethic." [22] This "ethic" is clearly revealed in the following excerpt from a manual published in 1919. "Its [sex's] perfect accomplishment is an art to be cultivated, and one in which expertness can only be obtained by wise observation, careful study of the factors involved, and a loving adaptation of the bodies, minds, and souls of both parties to the act. It is no mere animal function." [23]

[20] Grace R. Adkins, *The Sex Life of Girls and Young Women* (Cincinnati: The Standard Publishing Company, 1919), p. 42.

[21] Bernard S. Talmey, *Woman* (New York: Practitioner's Publishing Company, 1912; first published in 1904), p. 178. The first mention of mutual orgasm in a marriage manual we have come across is in George W. Savory's *Marriage: Its Science and Ethics* (Chicago: Stockham Publishing Company, 1900), p. 323. Savory also feels mutual orgasm is associated with the creation of healthy children: ". . . For then only [when mutual orgasm is present] can come that full delight in the ultimation of love by which superior children can be begotten" (p. 323).

[22] Lionel Lewis and Dennis Brissett, "Sex As Work: A Study of Avocational Counseling," *Social Problems 15* (Summer, 1967): 8–18.

[23] H. W. Long, *Sane Sex Life and Sane Sex Living* (New York: Eugenics Publishing Company, 1922; first published in 1919), p. 88.

The same author goes on to offer one of the first detailed descriptions of technique in sexual intercourse. Similar, although not as lengthy, discussions are to be found in other books of the period. This, then, is an extension of rationalism to the sexual sphere.

Birth Control

The topic of birth control is particularly interesting during this period, for, in many ways, the heritage of the nineteenth century is much more in evidence than it was with regard to general sexual attitudes. This is seen in the frequency with which abstinence and continence are recommended as birth control techniques.[24] However, where change is seen is in the general attitude toward birth control. Many more writers are now in favor of it, but they do not discuss birth control technique, and it is a fairly safe assumption—in some cases statements to this effect are made—that their reluctance stems from fear of prosecution under the still prevailing Comstock Laws.[25] Yet, despite the fact that more authors than previously are in favor of birth control, their attitude continues to be ambivalent. On the one hand many are committed, or at least appear to be, to the importance of pleasurable sexual relations, while on the other hand many are still laboring under the sex-for-procreation ethic. Consequently, we find those who advance abolishing prudery in sexual relations arguing a few pages later that birth control techniques should be used only in cases of serious illness, extreme poverty, and so on. Unques-

[24] These are followed by the rhythm method and Karezza in order of frequency, so that the techniques discussed do not reflect much change.

[25] Writing in 1918, Marie C. Stopes had the following to say on this matter: "It is important to observe that Holland, the country which takes *most* care that children shall be well and voluntarily conceived, has increased its survival-rate and has thereby not diminished but increased its population, and has the lowest infant mortality in Europe. While in America, where the outrageous 'Comstock Laws' confuse wise scientific prevention with illegal abortion and label them both as 'obscene,' thus preventing people from obtaining decent hygienic knowledge, horrible and criminal abortion is more frequent than in any other country" (Marie C. Stopes, *Married Love or Love in Marriage* [New York: The Critic and Guide Company, 1918], p. 143).

tionably, this is a period of important transition in thinking on the legitimacy of contraception.

1920 TO 1939

The decade following World War I saw dramatic changes take place in the manners and mores of American society. It was during this time that the "Genteel Tradition" breathed its last gasps, leaving in its wake an opportunity for exploration and experimentation in all areas of life. Sexual behavior was among the areas that felt the impact of this new liberation. Many of the supposedly current changes in sexual behavior, bemoaned by the preservers of morality, actually took place in the 1920s. This liberalization of sexual behavior is, to some extent, seen in the marriage manuals of the time.

Nonmarital Sex

The shifts in attitudes toward sex outside of marriage are rather interestingly revealed in the marriage manuals. The issue is generally framed in terms of a comparison between marital and nonmarital sex. The latter is less frequently endorsed than it is discussed in such a way as to highlight the benefits of conventional morality. That is to say, while we see an unequivocal development of concern with this topic, and to a certain extent a recognition of it, the authors who manifest it are seldom willing to discard completely conventional morality in favor of an alternative ethic. Actually, for some, this behavior—and we are talking for the most part about nonadulterous premarital sex—must be viewed in terms of the involved individuals' commitment to prevailing morality.

> I do not think the union of true lovers apart from marriage is impure. I believe that such lovers make a very serious mistake—a mistake that may turn out to have been cruel. I believe that society is utterly right in condemning such unions. . . . But impure is not the word to apply to them. They are clean and beautiful compared to the bodily intimacies of those who marry without love.

And yet I do not think that even emotionally they can ever be perfect. Sexual intimacy is not the perfect and sacramental thing which it is meant to be unless both parties come to it with free and untroubled minds, feeling that what they do is a right and happy thing. But in the union of unmarried persons there generally lurks some half-hidden sense of shame. Some part of the being of one or the other really endorses society's standards, and even love cannot dispel the shadows thus created.[26]

Note that the point of concern to this author is the guilt created by the commitment to society's standards: he does not argue that the act itself is inherently evil or immoral. Another author nearly echoes the same sentiment: "Free love will only be a success in the case of extremely normal individuals for whom the sexual relationship means solely physical gratification." [27] Writers such as these have clearly come to grips with the existence of behavior which questions prevailing ideas of appropriate sexual conduct. They apparently cannot argue logically that sex in the context of a love relationship is more immoral than sex in a loveless marriage, but they are unable to abandon completely conventional ideas.[28]

More revolutionary ideas are found during this time in discussions of "adultery." For example, "When circumstances, either temporary or permanent, bring it about that the maintenance of sex monopoly imposes a real sacrifice upon one or the other partner, husband and wife might well be free to agree whether the sacrifice imposed does not outweigh the advantage to be derived from monopoly." [29] Judge Ben Lindsey, author of the influential

[26] A. Herbert Gray, *Men, Women, and God* (New York: Association Press, n.d.; first published in 1922), p. 63.

[27] Andre Tridon, *Psychoanalysis and Love* (New York: Brentano's, 1922), p. 97.

[28] Perhaps the most unqualified affirmation of premarital sex, at least for men, is found in a book published in 1923. "Speaking generally, therefore, we may say that of all the ways for dealing with the vigorous sexual impulse of young men during the preconjugal period, an intimacy, regular intercourse with a beloved and loving sexual partner, is the happiest and most moral" (Abraham Buschke and Friedrich Jacobsohn, *Sex Habits* [New York: Emerson Books, 1923], p. 119).

[29] Robert C. and Frances W. Binkley, *What Is Right with Marriage* (New York: Appleton, 1929), p. 216.

The Companionate Marriage, had the following to say on this matter:

> I suggest . . . that the proper view for society to take of . . . [extra-marital sex] is to recognize that some persons have an inclination toward varied sex experiences, and that some haven't; and that it is no function of society to discriminate against those who have such inclinations provided they duly respect and consider the genuine rights of other people. Within that limit, their conduct is as much a personal matter, to be personally determined, as the choice of one's politics or religion.[30]

Points of view such as these, *while clearly in the minority,* are significant to the extent that they provide some indication of the reorientation of attitude toward sexual behavior that was beginning to take place at the time.

Relative Sensuality

If we look at attitudes toward female sexuality in these decades, we find that no drastic shifts have taken place. In fact, there is considerable consistency with what was found in the first twenty years of the century: female sexual needs are different from rather than less than those of the male, and, to some extent, the difference lies in their having to be awakened or called forth by the male. Statements to this effect are now encountered with remarkable frequency. Of the books that deal with the question of sex differences in sensuality, almost all contain some variation on this theme:

> No doubt women differ greatly, but in every woman who truly loves *there lies dormant* the capacity to become vibrantly alive in response to her lover, and to meet him as a willing and active participant in the sacrament of marriage [ital. mine].[31]

> Woman's sex life is more complicated, that is, more diffused and more elaborate, than that of the man, and on account of this her

[30] Judge Ben B. Lindsey and Wainwright Evans, *The Companionate Marriage* (New York: Boni and Liveright, 1927), p. 82.
[31] Gray, *op. cit.,* p. 145.

desire for primary sex experience, that is, coitus, may not be felt so quickly or so consciously as man's.[32]

The sex impulse in a woman is much more general, more inspired, more spiritualized, and much more intimately interwoven with her personality and her character than the purely genital impulse in man.[33]

This point of view is well represented throughout this period, although it is not very frequently presented in Freudian terms, something we might expect given his influence during this period.

Also of interest are the attempts made to explain these differences in male and female sexuality. For many of the persons writing at the time, the sources of these differences are to be found less in biology than in culture:

Man's sex life is comparatively steady, woman's more periodic, man's more narrow and direct, woman's more diffused. Part of the basis for this psychological difference may lie in the fact that women have been less honestly informed than men.[34]

If we ask ourselves how these differences in the sentiments of men and women have come into existence, we shall find that in the first place we must ascribe them to differences in the education of the two sexes.[35]

The point should be made that many other authors see this difference as an essential part of feminine nature without exploring its sources.

During these two decades, then, this picture of the uniqueness and what some may see as inferiority of female sexuality, however explained, prevails. Women are increasingly granted their right to full participation in *marital* sexual relations. Furthermore, as we shall show, it is now felt to be the husband's re-

[32] Ernest R. Groves, *Marriage* (New York: Henry Holt and Company, 1934; first published in 1933), p. 235.

[33] Fritz Kahn, *Our Sex Life* (New York: Alfred A. Knopf, 1943; first published in 1937), p. 60.

[34] Elizabeth and Forrester Macdonald, *Homemaking* (Boston: Marshall Jones Company, 1927), p. 49.

[35] Bernhard Bauer, *Woman and Love* (New York: Boni and Liveright, 1949; first published in 1927), p. 35.

sponsibility to see to it that she exercises this right and to make sure that she experiences sexual satisfaction.

Sexual Satisfaction in Marriage

What sets the tone for these two decades is the near-unanimous agreement on the pivotal place of sex in marriage. The following quotation characterizes the generally current attitude: "The act of sex is appropriately the central fact in the psychological situation of marriage, for in the act a complete system of domestic behavior, both active and passive, can be anticipated." [36] With this emphasis on the crucial role played by sex in marriage there is, as one might expect, a parallel concern with the importance of achieving a satisfactory sexual adjustment. This is seen in the number of authors committed to the "sex as work" ethic. Moreover, there is, as has been indicated, an increased emphasis on the woman's right to sexual satisfaction (read: her right to experience orgasm). All three of these themes are found in the marriage literature of this period. The 1930s, as we shall see, are, however, to be distinguished from the 1920s in terms of the stress on discussions of sexual technique.

Development of an adequate, if not sublime, sexual adjustment in marriage is presented in terms of a goal toward which the couple should work and strive. It is not uncommon for us to encounter the sexual relationship's being described in terms of "artistry":

> Marriage, in its physical aspect, is an art in itself, the cultivation of which is within the reach of all married people whatever their station in life, or quality of intellect. Those who have cherished and refined this art are the people who made a life long success of marriage. Such people are not only supremely happy, but they benefit greatly in mind and body, for it is an established fact that the physiological conditions of a normal sex life have the greatest beneficial effect on the whole system. [37]

[36] Binkley and Binkley, *op. cit.*, p. 125.
[37] Isabel E. Hutton, *The Sex Technique in Marriage* (New York: Emerson Books, 1936; first published in 1932), p. 86.

By the use of the terms "art" and "artistry" we have an indication of the conception of sexual adjustment. This is now not seen as something which grows out of two physically and psychologically healthy persons expressing and finding satisfaction for their sexual needs. Rather, it is something which must be *cultivated* and *developed* through conscious effort and involvement.

> *If there be a conscious program* [to achieve sexual adjustment], *and this is the inevitable result whenever people attempt to deal rationally with any undertaking,* it must be built upon one or the other opposite conceptions of the art of love. In the one case there is a straining after an objective performance which is assumed to be indispensable in happy married life. On the other hand, there is a realization that their path to happiness the two must find together by adventuring and exploring within their own sex character. What they are to achieve must be as individual, as natural an outcome of their comradeship as is their association in its other aspects. [Emphasis added.] [38]

This accentuation of the conscious and conscientious pursuit of sexual satisfaction is characteristic of manuals published in both decades, but is more often encountered in those of the 1930s.

Sex adjustment is, during these years, defined in terms of the achievement of simultaneous orgasm, and we see crystallize what we have chosen to call "the cult of mutual orgasm." A majority of those writing in these two decades express concern that the couple achieve simultaneous orgasm: "Thus, while it is imperative that the woman should release her own deep impulses and give them full and unashamed expression, it is essential that the husband, with a deep effort of the subconscious will, attune his climax simultaneously with that of his beloved." [39]

Not all those writing at the time argue that the orgasms of the pair must be in unison. One author is strongly opposed:

[38] Groves, *op. cit.,* p. 240.

[39] Margaret Sanger, *Happiness in Marriage* (New York: Blue Ribbon Books, 1926), p. 139. When we use the term "cult of mutual orgasm" we do not mean to suggest that concern with mutual orgasm first arose at this time. The reader knows that this is obviously not the case. What we are suggesting is that for the first time there existed a preoccupation with this phenomenon of sufficient magnitude to describe it as a cult.

This book unqualifiedly recommends succession as infinitely superior to simultaneity. Only by the arrangement of the love episode in such a way that in every love episode the husband's erotic acme follows, even after the lapse of several minutes, the wife's, can the spiritually deleterious results of mentally autoerotic simultaneity be avoided. Only thus can the most inexpressible joy be experienced by both husband and wife. Only thus can they be said to be erotically, perfectly mated.[40]

It should be emphasized that the above view is not typical; most of the authors who deal with orgasm maintain that it should be experienced simultaneously. The 1920s and particularly the 1930s do see this feeling reaching a point which may appropriately be described as a preoccupation or cult.

A crucial aspect of this concern with synchronized orgasm is the new, and in some cases detailed, discussions of sexual technique.[41] There are two areas treated in such discussions, although both are not hit upon by all authors: foreplay and positions in intercourse. It should be obvious that the emphasis on foreplay is related to the prevailing conception of female sexuality.

Many men, during their courting days, are great lovers, but after marriage they take too much for granted, and as man's erotic nature is usually more quickly and easily aroused than woman's, they neglect the preliminary loving so necessary to women, to prepare them for the full pleasure and gratification of their sex life.[42]

. . . Preliminary petting or courting is absolutely essential to successful and gratifying intercourse.[43]

The preliminary lovemaking referred to in these quotations involves, as one might expect, the stimulation and titillation of "erogenous zones." Actually, it is of interest to explore this whole

[40] Wilfrid Lay, *A Plea for Monogamy* (New York: Boni and Liveright, 1923), p. 155.

[41] "Patience on the part of both, and an attempt to improve their technique, would save many couples from the divorce courts or loveless bitter lives" (Esther B. Tietz and Charles K. Weichert, *The Art and Science of Marriage* [New York: Whittlesey House, 1938], p. 43).

[42] Don Cabot McCowan, *Love and Life* (Chicago: Pascal Covici, 1928), p. 168.

[43] Thurman B. Rice, *The Age of Romance* (Chicago: American Medical Association, 1933), p. 35.

idea of foreplay and the context in which it arose.[44] Perhaps there is no better way to do this than to look at the topic in terms of a book that was among the first, and clearly among the most influential, to broach these topics: Van de Velde's *Ideal Marriage*.[45]

Van de Velde and his Heritage

Van de Velde's book is a sex manual par excellence; it is unquestionably the most detailed and rationalized treatment of sexual behavior to see the light of print. To read its elaborate table of contents is to explore every crevice of the anatomy of sexual behavior from "varieties of erotic kiss" to "household remedies for frigidity and passivity." Of course, in the present section our interest is limited to sex technique, but one has to emphasize how this area is merely one part of the Dutch doctor's discussion of the manifold aspects of the complex subject which he calls "ideal marriage."

His section on "love play" includes among other topics: "the love bite," "significance of erogenous zones," "hints on technique," and "the genital kiss," to name only a few of the many areas covered, and stimulated.[46] It is difficult in a brief space to convey how intricate the sexual process is presented as being, how demanding of the couple if ideal marriage (read: bliss) is to be achieved, and how diligently the zones and techniques must be studied. It suffices to say that with the publication of this book, marital sex migrates from the realm of something which merely has to be worked at or is merely an art to something which becomes virtually an academic discipline. To this extent *Ideal Marriage* cannot be said to be typical of these decades, though its

[44] One might look at this concern with sexual technique as a form of ritual magic. That is to say, as the sexual rights of women gained acceptance, sexual intercourse probably became a more anxiety-laden area for men, and, hence, it is not surprising that we see this new concern with technique.

[45] Th. H. Van de Velde, *Ideal Marriage* (New York: Covici-Fried, 1930). The quotations that follow are taken from the first British edition (William Heinemann, 1930). This book is currently in its forty-fifth printing and has sold more than one-half million copies.

[46] Van de Velde is the first author to discuss oral-genital sex. See his part 3, chapter 8.

publication date is at the midpoint of the two; rather, it represents, if Weber will forgive us, a *real* ideal type, that is, not a hypothetical construct with no empirical reality, but the ideal type come to life.

Despite the exaggerated character of this book, it is a watershed of sorts, for we find in the 1930s a spate of publications (Stone and Stone, Hutton, etc.) which are similarly committed to foreplay and technique. Moreover, these books deal with positions in sexual intercourse, a topic which tends to set off the books of the thirties from those of the twenties.[47] Again, this is a concern which is voiced at length first in Van de Velde, and it is also voiced by him in the most unequivocal way. He lists the reasons he feels it important to discuss positions in intercourse: "(a) The increase of sexual pleasure; (b) The prevention of hygienic dangers or injuries; (c) The control (promotion or prevention) of conception." [48] This ordering is not without significance, since most other authors who discuss this topic tend to focus on (b). For example, "In our western civilization we have somehow developed the feeling that there is only one right posture in the sexual act and that it is not quite decent to discuss any variations. However, one can see on reflection that there are *good hygienic grounds* for experimentation with a number of different postures. (Emphasis added.)" [49]

The closest we come to a hedonistic rationale for varying positions, apart from Van de Velde, is the following: "This (position) is not particularly practical or convenient, *but in some instances it is found to be a stimulating variation. (Emphasis added.)*" [50] Nonetheless, it (the quotation, that is) indicates that sex is not only fun, but it can be better fun if the couple tries to use their imaginations in regard to varying sexual positions.

Perhaps the only other significant point to emerge in the 1930s is that of masculine sexual stimulation. The reader will re-

[47] Apart from general statements concerning precoital preparation and stimulation, discussions of sexual technique are, for the most part, absent from books published in the 1920s.

[48] Van de Velde, *op. cit.*, p. 317.

[49] Millard S. Everett, *The Hygiene of Marriage* (New York: The Vanguard Press, 1932), p. 125.

[50] Stone and Stone, *op. cit.*, p. 176.

call that the issue up until this time has been the assertion of the importance of recognizing and satisfying woman's sexual need. It is telling that at the height of this argument there also develops an interest in male sexuality. In a book published in this country, a female British physician had the following to say on the subject: "The woman must be ready to help the man if his reactions are slow and if he is tired or not able to achieve erection easily. She must master the subject of love play and learn what helps sexual response in him." [51] This point, which again is found first in Van de Velde, is of utmost importance for understanding the perspective on marital sexuality as play, which is emerging. We have not introduced this theme before, and it may sound paradoxical in view of our emphasis on the "sex-as-work" theme, but it should be kept in mind that we are dealing with changing approaches to sex from its nineteenth-century position as a procreative necessity to its mid-twentieth-century view as a form of recreation—recreation, admittedly, at which one must work hard.[52] Sex is now recreation which both sexes are impelled to take part in and mutually desire. Therefore, the new woman should be prepared to assert her own sexuality in the face of the occasional lapse of her husband's interest or energy. This should not be seen as suggesting any redefinition of the male's role; he is still seen as the sexually aggressive partner.

Birth Control

Associated with the rise of the idea of "work at sex because it's fun" are, as one might expect, shifts in attitudes toward birth control, or at least changes in the way in which it is discussed. This, however, really does not take place until the 1930s. At least half of those writing in the 1920s appear to approve of birth control, although there are many who equivocate. The fact that those who are favorably disposed do not discuss technique may

[51] Hutton, *op. cit.,* p. 92.

[52] On this point see, Nelson N. Foote, "Sex As Play," in *Mass Leisure,* ed. Eric Larabee and Rolf Neyersohn (Glencoe, Ill.: The Free Press, 1948), pp. 335–340. Also see, Jetse Sprey, "On the Institutionalization of Sex," *Journal of Marriage and the Family 31* (August 1969): 432–440.

be due to the previously mentioned legislation which prevented the dissemination of birth control information. For example, a manual republished in 1922 includes the following paragraph: "The pages running from 699 to 708 have been eliminated from this edition on the ground of legal considerations. It is against the law of the U.S.A. to print, publish, or circulate any literature that deals with 'prevention'." [53]

Judge Ben Lindsey in his well-known *The Companionate Marriage* offers this in the way of birth control information to a woman whose letter asking for birth control information he includes: "My answer to Mrs. Ellis and to every other woman who wants to know what has already been accomplished in the way of scientific contraception is to write to the Birth Control League, at 104 Fifth Avenue, New York City." [54] As we have already indicated, not everyone writing in the 1920s was as favorably, though discreetly, committed to birth control as the reformist jurist. In *The Doctor Looks at Marriage and Medicine,* Joseph Collins argues: "No one can practise any form of contraception, save relative continence, habitually, without being injured spiritually, and few without being injured bodily." [55] Others also are committed to the view that birth control is only suitable for the sick, the mentally ill, and the indigent—healthy people with no financial problems have no right to contraception.

The 1930s witnessed some important changes in the legal realm which opened up the path for the dissemination of birth control information. The Comstock Laws of 1873 which had long lost their "propriety" also lost their "validity," resulting in the appearance of contraceptive information in the marriage manual. In view of this new development, one might think that the literature of the time would contain a deluge of such material. Interestingly enough, this is not the case. The books of this period are fairly well split between those which equivocate or are disposed to birth control under special circumstances (for exam-

[53] Iwan Bloch, *The Sexual Life of Our Time* (New York: Allied Book Company, 1922; first published in 1908), p. 698.

[54] Lindsey and Evans, *op. cit.,* p. 237.

[55] Joseph Collins, *The Doctor Looks at Marriage and Medicine* (Garden City, N.Y.: Doubleday, Doran and Company, 1929), p. 43.

ple, poor health) and those which are completely in favor of it. As one might expect, those in favor of birth control at this time are those more apt to discuss sexual technique and those who seem to be committed to the play function of sex. This is not to say that those who are opposed to the unqualified use of birth control also are opposed to or fail to see the value of sex for marriage; rather, it is a matter of many of them being put in the difficult position of having to wrestle with seemingly contradictory values, although as we have seen in previous periods this is no novelty.

From the perspective of social change, it is of value to look at the birth control techniques being recommended by the heralds of the new sexuality. One of the ironies of this period is that Van de Velde is the negative case: the author committed to the complete rationalization of sexual pleasure who at the same time hedges on birth control.

> This basis implies that physical sexual relationships, through sound knowledge and appropriate technique, are directed and developed so as to give permanent and complete satisfaction to *both* partners, to intensify their mutual love, and contribute to a life of lasting happiness together. This basis, therefore, does not *necessarily* include the practical methods of contraception. *For such methods as are known and practised to-day* often contravene the demands of Ideal Marriage, by diminishing stimulation, disturbing and dislocating normal reactions, offending taste, and effectually ruining spontaneous *abandon* to the act of communion.[56]

One wonders how Van de Velde would have viewed the pill. In any case, others writing at the time begin to advocate the use of the diaphragm as the least disruptive and most efficient birth control device, and this appears to be, in the marriage manual literature, the birth control innovation of the 1930s. The Stones have this to say with regard to this technique.

> The ideal contraceptive still remains to be developed. It should be not only harmless and entirely reliable, but also simple, practical, universally applicable and esthetically satisfactory to both husband and wife. None of the methods in use today meets all the necessary

[56] Van de Velde, *op. cit.*, p. 317.

requirements. Generally speaking, I would say that the vaginal diaphragm in conjunction with a contraceptive jelly is probably the most adequate and satisfactory method available at present.[57]

It should be pointed out that the Stones as well as at least one other author discuss the intrauterine device which was first being experimented with at this time. So then, what we see in the period of the 1920s and 1930s is not so much a dramatic shift in attitude toward birth control, although this shift is present in more than an emergent form, but rather the creation of an atmosphere which permits the dissemination of birth control information.

CONCLUSION

We have traced changes in the approach to sex in domestic education literature from a pariah topic to a virtual preoccupation. This has been manifested in the changes in conceptions of female sexuality, as well as the changes in the role of sex in marriage, definitions of sexual adjustment, and birth control advice. At this point it is necessary to raise the question of just what all this means. We have not claimed that the marriage manuals we have been dealing with reflect actual shifts in behavorial patterns or even changes in the values of their audience. The manuals, in the most conservative sense, it could be claimed, contain nothing more than the opinions and attitudes of their authors, whose expertise is often self-proclaimed. The question of the actual impact adult education literature has upon its readers is a complex one, and the available evidence suggests that it is ambiguous at best, although there have not been any studies which focused specifically upon domestic education books, other than child training manuals.[58]

Why then bother to study marriage manuals? There are several reasons for doing this. To begin with, we will not be able to unravel the relationship between such literature and actual

[57] Stone and Stone, *op. cit.,* p. 123.
[58] For a discussion of this topic see Michael Gordon, *"Infant Care* Revisited," *Journal of Marriage and the Family 30* (November 1968): 578–583.

behavior until further research is carried out, and studies such as this one may provide some of the necessary comparative material. Secondly, having a picture of shifts in expert opinion on sex allows us to assess what effect, if any, larger social and cultural currents have upon them. For example, to what extent was the acceptance of female sexuality linked to the increasing number of women in the work force? Finally, as social history, the attitudes contained in the marriage manuals are in and of themselves of interest apart from any functional relationship they may have with any other phenomena.

Epilogue

After completing this paper the reader may have a sense of being left dangling in air. Where can the sex manual go after the cult of mutual orgasm? Unfortunately, at present, we are unable to answer this question. Our analysis of the period from 1940 to 1969 is not yet in a form which permits even broad generalizations.[59] All we can say is that those of us who are on the "right" mailing lists know that, if nothing else, the adage "one picture [or better, one color photograph] is worth a thousand words" is one to which many publishers of today's sex manuals are committed.

[59] As this book goes to press, the author has completed some further analysis of these data. See, Michael Gordon and Penelope J. Shankweiler, "Different Equals Less: Female Sexuality in Recent Marriage Manuals," *Journal of Marriage and the Family,* forthcoming.

SEX AMONG SWINGERS

Sexual Mate-Swapping:
Violation of Norms and
Reconciliation of Guilt

CAROLYN SYMONDS

INTRODUCTION

In order to get ideas for further research, I conducted a preliminary study of mate-swapping—or swinging as it is better known
by those who engage in it—in Southern California. This paper is
an analysis of some of the information gathered in that study.
In it I touch on some aspects of collective behavior and also focus on how people enter into an area of sexual behavior which
society, in general, considers to be deviant, their modes of entry
into swinging, how they began violating previously internalized
norms and how they reconcile violating them.

Definition

Swingers' definitions of swinging vary considerably. Therefore, I
am proposing the following functional definition which follows
closely the actions of swingers and the behavior they require of
people they label as swingers. Swinging requires one of two things,
or perhaps both: *Willingness to swap sexual partners with a couple with whom they are not acquainted and/or to go to a swinging party and be willing for both parties to have sexual intercourse with strangers.*

This does not mean that swingers have to be married; both unmarried couples and singles may swing or attend parties. It also does not mean that long-time or closer relationships do not evolve over a period of time or that a process of selectivity cannot be involved, but rather that selectivity initially is based on physical attraction and immediately obvious aspects of the personality rather than on beliefs, commitments, or intellectual attributes. There are probably many couples who swap sexual partners or who share a bed with their friends who would never think of going to a party or having intercourse with strangers. This type of couple or individual is not considered in this study.

Swingers observed at parties and social functions as a part of this study are generally of middle socioeconomic status. They are predominantly Caucasians with a few Negro men and an occasional Oriental. There are some European accents heard among the Caucasians. The swingers generally appear in couples (although not necessarily married), and the few singles that are seen are usually male. Swingers range in age from early twenties through early forties, judging by appearance, with the largest number falling between twenty-five and thirty-five years. Informants agree that this is the general trend of swinging in Southern California. However, there were reports of parties consisting of singles only and also of parties where the youngest people appeared to be in their late forties. From reports and observations of other areas and states within the United States, it appears that although the definition remains the same, the types of people, general rules, and taboos differ. Perhaps there are regional differences, but at this time the reasons for the differences are unknown.

Swingers in Southern California fall into one of two categories: there may be others but this distinction was sufficient for this study. In the first category are persons who use swinging as a form of recreation and who make room for it in their lives by giving up some other form of recreation such as card playing or bowling. It might fill needs for socializing, exercise, or perhaps sexual variety or conquest. These nonideological swingers are labeled *recreational swingers*. The second group are basically philosophical utopians who dream of forming a community and living all aspects of their lives in that environment. They want to share not only sex with their fellow communitarians but also provision for food and shelter, childrearing, education, and other areas of living. Swingers who have this ideological base are referred to as *utopian swingers*. The type of swinger cannot be determined by the method or manner of introduction into swinging behavior; therefore, the basic swinging philosophy is not of major concern in this paper.

METHODS

This study was initially conceived when I became aware that a large number of my personal friends and acquaintances were swingers. This presented me with some ethical problems which were not insurmountable and provided opportunities to learn about personal feelings, rationale, activities, and behavior. To gather the data for this study, I supplemented general observational techniques with interviews. I spoke with friends who had experiences with mate-swapping, conducted ten depth interviews with swingers, visited a night club catering to swingers and interviewed its managers, attended meetings of a national group of swingers, attended swinging parties, witnessed unplanned sexual encounters, and joined a small discussion group of female swingers.

The sample for depth interviews was arbitrarily selected by asking some of the people I met at swinging parties or other functions, and a few I already knew socially, if they would consent to be interviewed. With such a small number of depth interviews, all of the minority groups (Europeans, Negroes, singles, ex-swingers, utopians) represented appear to be overly represented. The sample is as follows:

1 European	9 U.S.-born
1 Negro	9 Caucasian
3 Singles	7 Marrieds
1 Ex-swinger	9 Current swingers
4 Utopian swingers	6 Recreational swingers
6 Women	4 Men

The ratio of six women to four men represents a reversal of the sex ratio in swinging. In one case a husband and his wife were interviewed (separately) and in four cases only the wife was interviewed because it was difficult to make convenient appointments with the men.

My biggest problem was getting invitations to swinging parties. I attended four planned parties and, in addition, received details of numerous parties and sexual events from respondents and informants.

I also benefited from contact with social science students who were also swingers. They were able to contribute insight into the processes of swinging because they were involved in it, had developed an awareness of the sociological and psychological implications, and thus could bring into the open things that non-swingers might not think of considering.

METHODS OF INTRODUCTION
INTO SWINGING

Paperback Books

Because of the great public interest in the subject of sexual behavior, many books are published, some dealing directly or indirectly with mate-swapping. A number of books, written mainly by psychologists or psychiatrists, discuss swinging as neurotic or deviant behavior. Roger Blake [1], Albert Ellis [2], and Frank Caprio [3] are representative authors of this type of publication. They are concerned with sexual behavior in general and at some point, for whatever reason, refer specifically to sexual mate-swapping

Another type of book gives the impression of actually being written by swingers. One example is William and Jerrye Breed-

---

[1] Roger Blake, *Casebook: Female Behavior* (Ohio: Century Books, 1966).
[2] Albert Ellis, "Wife Swapping," in *Suppressed* (Chicago: New Classics House, 1965), ch. 5.
[3] Frank S. Caprio, "Miscellaneous Variations in Sexual Behavior," in *Variations in Sexual Behavior* (New York: Grove Press, 1955), pt. 4.

love's *Swap Clubs* [4] and another is *Sex Rebels* [5] which was written by a couple who managed a swap club magazine and is a discussion of their experiences with this venture. In addition, there are innumerable books on the market which claim to present information on the mate-swapping scene. These popular paperbacks include titles such as *Male and Female Sexual Deviations, A Study of Wife Swapping, Marriage Roulette, The Promiscuous Breed, Metropolitan Swap Set!, The Swinging Bisexuals, Swinging Marriages, Games of the Mate Swappers,* and *A Study of Group Sex in Wife Swapping.*

A third type of book is concerned with the sexual revolution in general with specific reference to mate-swapping. The best known is Lawrence Lipton's, *The Erotic Revolution.* [6] Swingers are sometimes said to specifically symbolize this revolution.

Personal Aids

The paperback books may introduce people to the idea of mate-swapping and may give some notion of the mechanics of it; however personal ads are more useful for making direct contact with other people.

Occasionally a personal ad will be seen in a daily newspaper indicating that a "broad-minded couple wants to meet other couples for mutual enjoyment." Such an ad in a large popular newspaper, however, is apt to lead to police harassment.

Many swingers, or prospective swingers, use the underground press to make contact with others. There is an Underground Press Syndicate which includes *The Los Angeles Free Press, San Francisco Oracle, East Village Other, Fifth Estate, Graffiti, Modern Utopian,* as well as other publications. Some of these publications are difficult to locate; others are sold freely on newsstands.

[4] William and Jerrye Breedlove, *Swap Clubs* (Los Angeles: Sherbourne Press, 1964), p. 44.

[5] Matt and Kathleen Galant, *Sex Rebels* (San Diego: Publisher's Export Co., 1966).

[6] Lawrence Lipton, *The Erotic Revolution* (New York: Pocket Books, 1966).

Many of the publications carry personal ads, lists of sexual libertarian organizations, or advertisements for publications.

There is an even smaller self-selecting market for a number of publications (sometimes advertised in the Underground Press), or clubs centered around publications which exist for the purpose of running ads and making swingers (and other sexual behavior deviants) aware of each other. These involve titles such as *Select, The Group, Response, The Swinging Set, The Personal Approach,* and *Kindred Spirits.* They print ads, pictures, and advertisements. They sometimes contain articles centered around a sexual theme. They offer a mail forwarding service so that initially ads are not answered directly, but names, addresses, and phone numbers become known only after the correspondents decide to make them known. This type of publication is not seen on display in a general newsstand, and frequently advertises that it is delivered by mail in a plain wrapper.

Function of the Mass Media

Mass media (here considered to be newspapers, magazines, and books available to general or selected readership and although the Underground Press consider themselves in opposition to the mass media, in this paper they are considered as a part of it) introductions to swinging behavior contribute to the growth of the swinging movement by (1) giving evidence that there are many people who engage in this behavior, (2) presenting a source of contact if desired by others, and (3) presenting a broad range of available sexual behavior so that a newcomer or prospective swinger can use this as a norm to guide his behavior. In effect, the information disseminated by mass media gives swingers and prospective swingers a sense of belonging and security. It educates concerning expectations and behavior of other swingers. The mass media introduction to swinging is of particular interest to those people who feel vague dissatisfaction in their marriage, are consciously aware of marital problems, or who have come to a point in their marriage where they feel a desire to expand or to experiment.

RECRUITMENT

Most of the respondents had been introduced to the idea of swinging before they were given, or desired, the opportunity to actually engage in swinging behavior themselves. The initial exposure was either through mass media or friends and acquaintances they knew were swingers. One couple, however, was introduced to the idea while visiting with another couple. In the course of their conversation, the subject of swinging parties was brought up, followed by an invitation to a party later in the week, which they attended. Until that time they had never heard about swinging.

Some of the single men were eager to get involved in swinging situations because they thought it would eliminate much of the meaningless socializing and courtship-like rituals required to get a girl to go to bed. This was accomplished by inserting or answering ads in swinging publications or in some manner getting invitations to parties.

One couple had come to the United States as adults and began swinging when a man who worked with the husband approached him and asked about the parties he heard about in Europe that involved mate-swapping. He asked the husband if he could arrange to have one of those parties. The husband indicated that he had never had one before, but he supposed that he could, and invited the man and his partner over to his house one evening. Neither he nor his wife had had extramarital relations up to that time, and he did not tell her that the couple was invited for the purpose of mate-swapping. The two couples sat around for awhile, and then the husband took the female guest out of the room. His wife related:

> It was kind of rough. You know, you walk into your own bedroom and there is your husband with someone else in bed. So anyway I was sort of put down and I kept talking to this guy and he was very attracted to me and I felt that if I ever had sex with anyone it would have to be someone special. But he and I just talked so my husband swung and I didn't. This man was very handsome,

very bright, and very nice. All things that I like in a man. So the next time I saw him we swung and that was my first extramarital experience. He was colored. Each time he would come over he would bring a different girl so I was having more of an affair but my husband was swinging. We both liked the arrangement very much. I liked having the same guy and he liked different girls.

A male single swinger was introduced to swinging by a physical seduction. He was taken to a house for what he thought would be a social evening, by a man he knew to be a swinger. He was shown scrapbooks of polaroid pictures of people in sexual situations. The host and hostess were the only people in the pictures who were recognizable. The hostess was extremely attractive and sat by him looking at the pictures with him. As he related:

> I found this somewhat disconcerting, and then my friend started making advances toward her. Pretty soon his clothes were off, and hers were off and so were mine and her husband had his polaroid camera going. He was a voyeur. That's how I got started swinging.

One couple began swinging within six months after they were married. A number of their friends were swingers and although they intended to wait for a year or so to begin, he just could not wait. He did not want to be tied to a monogamous relationship, and he wanted to see if swinging was "really going to work." He thought that once one was sexually free one would not have any hang-ups. He now realizes that this is a fallacy, but in the meantime insisted in indulging in behavior that put a good deal of pressure on his wife and stress on the marriage.

Another couple talked of it and discussed it with their friends for several months before they decided to try it. When they did decide to experiment with swinging they propositioned another couple who were as novice as they. Within a short time both couples expanded their contacts and also became involved in party situations.

A female single invited to a party had the impression that it was some kind of a sex party. She described the difference between her expectations and what she found as follows:

> There were about fifteen people there, more men than women. Now I don't care for an uneven number, but at the time I didn't

have any idea what was going on. It was very flattering to have
three or four men making love to me at the same time. That had
never happened to me before and it was very nice, not at all like
I expected. I expected it to be a glorified fraternity orgy, a lot
of drinking, a big brawly loud thing.

There was very little drinking. Very quiet. Very dignified. It
was a nice, quiet, intelligent group of people. Entirely in the
nude. I just wasn't prepared for it. Nice soft music and soft lights
and soft pleasant people. I went once a week for awhile, then I'd
quit for awhile when I found something that I thought was better.
But I still like swinging.

Another respondent and her husband began answering ads
in the swingers' and underground press. They had very few couples with whom they had had continuing contact, but as a result
of these contacts they began associating in circles where there
were other people with similar thinking. They initially began
answering the ads because they wanted to expand their marriage,
the wife explained:

My husband and I had gotten to the point where we loved each
other so much that we didn't want the other to go without anything desired or even thought about.

We didn't know where to turn to express this new-found feeling, especially as it applied in the sexual area. At first we talked
only to each other. Then we attempted to seduce friends, but the
people we knew were not in the same period of development so
this proved unsuccessful.

ETHNOGRAPHY

On the first anniversary of their opening, a nightclub catering
specifically to swingers held a celebration. Upon entering it looked
like any bar, anywhere: dark, bar with about twenty stools, small
tables, three-piece combo, a dance floor with booths on either side,
a buffet lunch at the far end of the dance floor. People were
greeted casually and told to sit where they liked. The waitress who
took orders was friendly. As it got late, more people arrived. A
woman requested a number from the pianist and simultaneously
patted him in a friendly manner. There was a sign over the food

which read: "Thanks for a groovy year, lovers" and signed by the managers.

It was difficult to tell the help from the customers; all were dressed in casual street clothes. Most of the people were attractive couples under forty, a few stags. The waitresses embraced the customers that they knew as they arrived. A man mentioned that the place was full of hard core swingers.

People began to dance—not particularly modern dances but the jitterbug and other older types. The dancing was suggestive and the men had a tendency to explore the women's bodies as they danced. The waitresses danced with customers. The crowd was racially mixed. Both men and women were obvious in scrutinizing the opposite sex. A man joined my husband and me, and with two consorts I was given more attention than when I had just one.

A waitress stopped to talk. She was concerned because her kid brother had a job there as a dishwasher but he did not know what kind of a place it was. Her problem was that she did not know whether to tell him, or let him find out for himself. The management makes a practice of never telling the help in advance that the place caters to swingers. New help are impressed with how well-mannered and friendly the customers are, and how they seldom have drunks. By the time they discover that the customers are mainly swingers, the help is already biased toward them.

Friday and Saturday nights are "pick-up" nights and have a different flavor. Where the anniversary party was rather lackadaisical and seemed to be an end in itself, weekends are a means to an end with the desired end being a satisfactory connection with another couple or perhaps with a party.

On a routine Friday night the place is apt to be full. There is a combo and dancing. Most of the women wear mini-skirts, and both men and women appear to be under forty and fairly attractive. The place is crowded, and couples are steered by waitresses or the managers and asked to share booths with other couples; frequently there are at least two more people in a booth than it was made to hold. Nobody seems to mind the crowded facilities, and there is an assumption that anybody who is there is also a swinger. The old-timers recognize and are purposefully friendly to the newcomers. Nonetheless the assumption seems to be that they know what they're doing.

As the evening wore on and approached closing time, some of those who had not yet made connections became somewhat frantic. Couples moved from booth to booth, talking, pointing to other people, and then moving on. People were leaving, two or three couples at a time; the crowd was beginning to thin out.*

While behavior at nightclubs assumes an overall middle-class flavor, the behavior observed at private gatherings is apt to be more specifically oriented. The differences between the utopian and recreational swingers becomes more apparent in private settings. Small weekend gatherings of utopian swingers are apt to include hiking, swimming, music, good food, radical discussion, as well as sexual activity.

A pair of recreational swingers were accidentally invited to a weekend party at the home of utopian swingers. They thought the people as well as the activities at the party were rather strange. As they related:

> The people were weird, and the host was outlandish in his behavior. He went overboard in trying to be a good host and making it with every woman regardless of her appearance. The hostess was strange and glassy eyed; I'm sure she was using some kind of hard dope.

In contrast, the utopians reported on the same incident, and the hostess told of the arrival of the very straight couple:

> It was a terrible mistake. When they arrived they stood out like sore thumbs and were obviously misfits. We had been smoking grass, but quit as soon as they arrived. I was very annoyed at my husband for inviting people who didn't fit in.
>
> Another couple arrived. He'd invited them without even meeting them. Fortunately the two couples fit right in with each other, and they left before too long. One of the women had never been to a swinging party before.

Utopians refer to recreational swingers as square people, and the hostess said that she just could not talk with square people around and did not say anything all the time they were there. She said, "They are just not à part of my family, and I wish that he hadn't invited them."

> I was invited to a recreational swinging party, which was attended by about thirteen people. Initially, the people sat around with their

* From the author's fieldnotes—Ed.

mates, engaging in small talk. As soon as everyone had arrived, the hostess undressed; everyone else did so gradually, some doing so in the bedroom and others in the living room. Some of the women undressed because there was a man giving back rubs on the living room floor, and he insisted that they take off their clothes. It was strictly a back rub, never developing into anything more erotic.

People wandered in and out of the living room. There was food and hard liquor and mix for people to prepare their own drinks. One of the bedroom doors was closed, indicating that there was something special and private going on. Nobody entered that room unless specifically invited. The other bedroom had a large bed and people joined and left rather casually. There was group conversation, but people were mostly separated into couples with little physical group interaction.

This party lasted far into the night. Some couples left to go to another party in another town but returned later during the weekend and continued partying. The hostess complained later that it took hours to launder all of the dirty towels and sheets from the party. However, she considered it to be a success.*

Control of Behavior

Directions for appropriate behavior can be considered as being on a continuum, with very flexible rules of etiquette at the one end, and taboos at the other. Taboos involve the forbidden, unclean, or dangerous; have a mystical sanction that keeps people from committing certain acts; and are strongly expressive of social values. Most of the information about the "etiquette-taboo continuum" was obtained by attending private events, listening to what people said about behavior of the people around them, and asking direct questions of the respondents concerning their perception of what takes place. This subject requires more study, and the material discussed here should be considered as posing questions or hypotheses for further research.

The swingers in this study are on the whole responsible middle-class people who conform in public to the norms of middle-class behavior. They are not heavy drinkers and, therefore, are not prone to become obnoxious because of intoxication. Swingers usually have been observed to pass over or try to tol-

* From the author's fieldnotes—Ed.

erate uncomfortable situations when they happen, and then to try to manipulate events so they are not repeated. Recreational swingers finding themselves in uncomfortable situations will generally leave as gracefully as they can (note the example given above of the recreational swingers at the utopian party).

The utopian swingers attempt to control behavior by selective recruitment. They were at one time part of a national organization and advertised in the underground press. They later changed the name of their organization to keep out unwanted recreational swingers whom they felt did not fit into their philosophy. This covert selection of utopian companions is apparently preferable to any overt screening mechanism.

Contact of swingers between swinging sessions is a form of behavior that falls under group control, perhaps being placed at the etiquette end of the behavorial norm continuum. Guidelines that are appropriate for one group of people are not necessarily appropriate for another. For one group of recreational swingers, it is important that there be no telephone contact with the opposite sex between functions; whereas, another group always has telephone contact, although they have no sexual contact between functions. The utopian swingers, on the other hand, expect to have both sexual and nonsexual contact with people they swing with if they find themselves attracted to them. The only known instance of limits being set by utopians on themselves or mates is when an individual begins spending too much time outside the marriage. Contact between swinging occasions is an area in which etiquette is of greatest importance to the recreational swingers and of less concern to the utopian swingers.

Propositions to initiate a sexual encounter at parties vary from a simple "Will you go with me?" to involved exercises in role-playing. Very few people really like to be rejected, and this is as true for the swingers as for anyone. The more chance there is for rejection, the less direct the proposition will be. One method occasionally employed is for a person, rather than making a verbal overture, to take the other person by the hand and lead her (the propositionee usually being female) to the bed. This is a difficult type of proposition to refuse and if the propositionee allows herself to be led, it implies approval and acceptance. On the other hand, if she objects, the initiator can insist that he was merely taking her to the kitchen for a drink or for something to eat. Propositions at swinging functions, as in the society at large, are usually initiated by the male. There is occasional discussion about this among the swingers, and plans to rectify the situation are frequently resisted as highly by the males as by the females. Males are apt to feel that there is as great a risk in the chance of not being propositioned at all as there is in the chance of being refused. Females frequently find it difficult to overcome their socialization by making direct overtures.

Females have said that they take the initiative at parties, but when questioned about how they do it, it frequently turns out that they make themselves obviously available by word and gesture, leaving the overt proposition or initiative to the male. However, many women are very skilled in attracting the man in whom they are interested, and even though they cannot verbalize exactly what they do, overt techniques are undoubtedly involved: manners of undressing, or not undressing; sway of the hips when crossing a room; posture and manner of standing, tilt of head so that a woman looks at the man through half-closed eyelids; obviously scrutinizing a man; offering a cigarette or drink in a suggestive voice that gives the impression of offering a body. The techniques both of enticement and proposition do not appear to vary a great deal from those found in the society at large. The main difference is that in the swinging environment they are expected and desired, and frequently accepted.

Group pressure has never been observed or reported to be put on any individual to swing with any other specific individual. However, an individual himself may exert personal pressure on another person to swing, perhaps by the type and repetition of propositions. It is generally expected that a person attending a swinging party is a swinger, and likewise there is an expectation that he or she will at some time swing.

There is a stated rule about the necessity of washing between each sexual contact. Even though this rule is verbalized by people in various swinging circles, it admittedly was not followed closely. This is partly due to the difficulty of determining when one sex contact is completed and another started in flexible and rotating group situations.

The washing rule is established more as an ideal than an enforceable guideline, and it is postulated to have a certain amount of symbology attached. Many swingers, especially utopian swingers, admit that the feeling of the need for frequent washing is lessened in proportion to the closeness of the group. There is less washing done with a group of people who know and like each other well. The greater the feeling of unfamiliarity, the more washing is accomplished.

Complete nudity is the usual behavior at parties, but cues are sought from the hosts as to when to disrobe. Hosts who do not disrobe are sanctioned both because they violate the norm of nudity and also because they withhold the necessary behavioral cues for comfortable disrobing of guests. Sanctions for hosts involve complaints (gossip) in their absence, and boycotting of their future parties. Sanctions for individual guests who don't disrobe vary with the reasons and with the occasion. A newcomer to swinging who did not disrobe would probably have difficulty getting invitations to future parties. An old-time swinger was known not to disrobe because of recent surgery. Although she attended a party when she could not participate, she was known to be a swinger, and it was therefore acceptable behavior.

Alcohol may be consumed at sexual functions but seldom in great quantity because of its tendency to numb sensitivity and inhibit mental functioning. The usual sanction for excessive use by guests is not being invited back.

Marijuana is preferred by the utopian swingers for its relaxing and uninhibiting effects. However, if nonutopians are present at a party or social gathering, the utopians refrain from obvious use of marijuana. Their main concern is the illegality of marijuana.

Passing on venereal disease can certainly be considered taboo among swinging circles. Occasionally gonorrhea breaks out. The swingers in this study have a great sense of social responsibility so that the word is spread rapidly and everyone exposed obtains an immediate checkup. Sanctions against people who might not get their checkup after exposure include harassment from other swingers and eventual ostracism. Occasionally rubber prophylactics are used, but some consider them more offensive than abstinence.

"Swinging pills," large doses of antibiotics taken to prevent venereal diseases, once were frequently used by the swingers of this study. Use of "swinging pills" now is considered an undesirable practice because one rapidly develops an immunity to any one type of antibiotic and because they sometimes mask symptoms while the disease continues unchecked and unknown.

Male swingers are concerned about erections. Concern about getting an erection when it is not appropriate depends upon the individual's background. A man from a nudist background is embarrassed if he gets an erection "too soon": "When I'm in a swinging association, in a group, I'm still kind of half embarrassed if I have an erection. I don't want to be too obvious and I'll slip out of there any way that I can get out of it. A lot of men are kind of proud of it, but I'm not." Sanctions for "premature" erections are usually applied internally by the individual himself.

A second, more serious, concern is the fear of *not* getting an erection in the sexual situation. Nonerection under these circumstances is usually considered a sign of failure by the men, who are apt to be more upset about it than the women. Some women take it as a personal insult if a man does not respond to her and maintain his response with an erection; however, the mature experienced woman is aware that erections are not perpetual and that there are many variables involved. A man who occasionally fails to obtain erection is accepted as normal within the swinging situation, although any one experience is painful for the man. However, the man who consistently fails to achieve erection is considered to have a problem, and he begins to be a topic of conversation and to be pressured into seeking professional assistance. In one case it was decided that the man had some unexpressed homosexual needs and a party was planned with two males especially invited to help the man fulfill his homosexual needs.

On the whole there is little bisexuality among males, and in some circles it is taboo. However, bisexuality among females is considered normal in most swinging circles, and pressure is exerted upon individual females to let themselves become involved, at least passively, with other women. Many of the females enjoy bisexual activity, some of them learning to enjoy it to be sociable or to please their mates. The men enjoy watching. Men have been observed, after hours of sexual activity, to eat chocolate and watch female interaction and thereby become sufficiently revived to rejoin the sexual activity.

Freely giving names and addresses of swingers to other swingers has been observed to be taboo. Usually both couples are consulted before a name or a phone number is given out. Even when an occasional swinger heard about and desired to contact me, there would be a long explanation and introduction and names of people mentioned who were mutual acquaintances. Apparently this norm is so ingrained that it was enforced even when applied to me, and I wanted contact with a variety of persons.

Sanctions against deviance from norms appear to be mild, usually involving avoidance or gossip. Gossip as a means of behavioral control is effective only within a subgroup. Although swingers will seldom speak directly to others about the things they don't like, they want the information to get to them. The respondents occasionally attempted to use me in this manner. I have been requested to: (1) Tell a woman that she did not smell good (although there was some question about whether the cause was internal, which could be controlled by diet, or external, to be controlled by bathing); (2) Tell a man that he was not an adequate sex partner and teach him how to be; and (3) Direct to the "right" circle people who had inadvertently begun swinging in the wrong ones.

Problems Encountered in Swinging

In describing some of the etiquette, rules, and sanctions in the section above, some of the problems that swingers encountered were discussed involving specific swinging situations. Here, more general problems will be reviewed pertaining to the marriage relationship, the family, and difficulties that arise because of the swinging behavior.

Many couples enter the swinging situation with some specific understanding between them as to what is permissible behavior, the type of relationships they will have, and so forth. The utopian swingers are less afraid of emotional involvement than the recreational swingers and any negative effect that it might have on their marriage. This would fall in line with their ultimate desire for community and an expanded living relationship. There was one utopian couple where the man enjoyed a variety of women, once saying that he would like to swing with 365 girls a year; but the woman preferred affairs with one or two different men. She was willing to swing at parties, but if one of her lovers was not there she did not find it particularly enjoyable. At a later date her husband did get involved in an affair, and she was very patient in guiding him, from her experience, in handling his emotional involvement so that it would not be disruptive to their marriage. For the first time, under the impact of the difficulties he was having, he realized how very competent his wife had been during the past several years in maintaining her emotional involvements so that they did not interfere with their marriage relationship.

Another couple, a pair of dedicated communitarians, began swinging at the beginning of their marriage because the husband was intent on avoiding monogamy. He thought that once he was sexually free he would not have any other type of hang-up. Both the husband and the wife became involved in a number of affair-type relationships. It is difficult to determine the effect it had on their marriage because they started when they were first married. However, he has since decided that it takes more than sexual freedom to make a person generally free.

Whereas utopian swingers are usually in agreement with their mates as to what is desirable, and the problem remains one of each couple finding a workable compromise for themselves, the recreational swingers have a further difficulty in that when they enter the swinging situation they are not always in agreement as to desirable limits and restrictions for behavior and involvement. One couple began with rather rigid requirements of each other: no sexual contacts with people of the opposite sex between formal swinging sessions. In this case the man had a strong tendency toward extramarital emotional involvement, and both he and his wife were aware of this and were afraid that it might be upsetting to their marriage. As time passed and they became more secure in the general swinging situation, he felt they really did not know whether he could handle an emotional involvement unless they experimented. She much preferred to have freedom for individual relationships but was still hesitant because of doubts about his ability to remain "cool." Finally they made a verbal agreement that they could have individual affairs aside from the swinging situations. She had a number of opportunities which she declined because at that point there wasn't anyone in whom he was interested. She was afraid that he would feel rejected if she became involved in an affair and he did not.

Another recreational couple had a similar problem with the freedom they felt they could individually handle and that their marriage could tolerate. With recreational swingers the agreements are usually determined to satisfy the person with the least amount of tolerance, and any change is based upon the ability of that individual to change. With recreational swingers the emphasis is upon maintaining (or in some cases, saving) the monogamous marriage relationship.

Although the long-range plans and goals of the utopians are such that they have potential for a greater impact on the society, their numbers appear to be considerably smaller. Only one family of utopian swingers who had children was closely observed, but a number of the recreational swingers had children of varying ages. The utopian swingers do not attempt to maintain a conventional front for their children. Although they are not explicit about their activities, the children frequently know more than the parents and friends realize. There was a joke among the adult swingers that when the son reached the age of sixteen, one of the adult women would initiate him sexually. The parents were not aware that the son knew of this until at the age of thirteen he discovered that he was growing pubic hair and joyfully announced to them that perhaps he could be initiated at the age of fourteen instead of waiting until he was sixteen.

Recreational swingers were much more concerned about their children discovering their activities. Informants stated that they could not hold parties because of the children. Those swingers who had children in their teens sometimes found them unapproachable in their attempts to liberalize their children's sexual attitudes. Because of the way their children were raised, the parents found it necessary to maintain a façade of straight-laced behavior, even as they became sexually liberal. Many admitted that this was a problem which they did not know how to handle, and that they did not even know how they would like things to be. Some of them were not sure that they wanted their children to be brought up in a sexually free environment. Some couples had raised their children in a comparatively sexually free environment, but they were afraid that although the children had a great deal of sexual freedom, they did not realize how overtly sexual the parents were. One couple was waiting with mixed emotion for the day that they would attend a party that one or both of their children were also attending. It did happen, but without some of the problems that they had feared. The children were sophisticated enough to realize that their parents, too, had active sex lives.

The general topic of childrearing was of concern to both utopian and recreational parents. If they were too permissive and open, they experienced the fear that the children would talk about it in inappropriate surroundings. On the other hand, if they were secretive, there was the chance of discovery plus their own feelings of hypocrisy to contend with. While becoming more open and honest with their mates, some of them were simultaneously more guarded with their children.

Another problem area, not as encompassing as relationships between parents and children, concerns the definition of situations. If one half of the couple begins to define a social setting as a swinging setting, their individual behavior will begin to change within that setting. This can be a matter of concern to the other half of the couple who does not perceive the situation as a swinging setting but suddenly observes that the spouse is acting in an apparently inappropriate manner. A few swingers have been observed to be so much on the alert for indications of sexual behavior and responses that they perceive sexual behavior that nobody else is aware of. This type of situation has not been reported to be serious enough to break up a marriage or cause a couple to drop out of swinging, but it has been reported to be the basis of severe arguments.

Benefits of Swinging

In spite of some of the problems that swinging brings into a couple's life, especially if they have children, there appear to be benefits as swinging continues to grow in popularity (or at least becomes more open to public awareness). In Southern California where swingers tend to be undemocratically selective, to be known as a swinger almost automatically means that a person falls within a certain range of age and physical attractiveness. There can be a certain amount of personal satisfaction in being acceptable in this ingroup.

Some people find satisfaction in being socially popular, in being invited to parties, and in being invited over by other couples (which is perhaps the equivalent of being invited out on dates). There is social satisfaction in hosting successful parties and in having two or three couples over for a social-sexual evening. Some couples claim to have made friends through swinging, with people who hold values similar to their own.

Most of all, people find enjoyment in the situation that encourages sexual experimentation. For the first time, some of them begin to view their bodies as a source of pleasure. Some women have stated that as they have become more sensually aware of their bodies as sources of pleasure, their need for orgasm has decreased. And, as the need for orgasm decreases, the actual number of orgasms that they experience increases.

THEORETICAL

Swingers are aware that their behavior is deviant, and that it is not generally acceptable to the society in which they live. Gouldner and Gouldner [7] suggest various ways that people handle pressures caused by their deviant behavior. The first method is to

---

[7] Alvin W. Gouldner and Helen P. Gouldner, "The Forms and Sources of Deviance," in *Modern Society*, ed. Robert K. Merton (New York: Harcourt, Brace & World, Inc., 1963), pt. 4, ch. 14.

drop their deviant behavior. There are probably a number of people who do not begin swinging because of societal pressures, but dropping out as a result of pressures felt by being deviant is not broadly known, and probably dropouts are credited to more specific things such as problems with children rather than to general pressures caused by deviancy.

A second method of responding to outside social pressure is to pretend compliance with the norm and to be secretive about the deviant behavior, in this case swinging. This reflects the behavior of all swingers contacted in this study. Only a few are verbal about their swinging activities, and then they are careful around whom they talk. They feel sure that people where they work or in their nonswinging environment would be shocked if they knew that they were swingers. This is particularly true of the recreational swingers. The utopian swingers have a tendency to surround themselves, at least in their nonworking life, with people who possess the same philosophy. Even those who promote swinging and attempt to spread its philosophy are careful with whom they talk, and they bring up the subject only if the listener is seen as extremely broad-minded and liberal, or as someone they desire to proposition.

The third method of handling deviancy is to band together with others of their kind so that there is mutual reinforcement. This method is partially used by swingers. When swingers congregate in their nightclub they let down their guard. They talk rather freely and frankly, they look at each other frankly, propositions are made openly, and the manner of dress and dancing is frequently suggestive. However, a person entering this setting accidentally would not necessarily know that this was a congregation of swingers. The impression gained is that of a warm, friendly nightclub, hardly anybody obnoxiously intoxicated, the music good and the dancing relaxed. In this case, even though the swingers are banding together, there is nothing that outwardly identifies them as deviants because the actual sexual behavior is still confined to private settings. It is in the private settings, at parties and small groups, that the deviant behavior becomes apparent. And, there they have each other for external and subsequently internal reinforcement.

Moving away from methods of handling deviant behavior after it has once occurred, the question may be asked how people take the first step that leads them to break norms which they have themselves internalized. How do they compromise values that are thought to be traditionally held by this society? In pursuing this question, three points will be considered.

1.   The Southern California swingers in this study are middle-class intellectual people with interest in concepts and symbols and with strongly verbal orientations.

2.   People in this society are exposed to a variety of conflicting values, norms, and behaviors throughout their lives.

3.   The swingers in this study are capable of and willing to make decisions within their experience and knowledge concerning how to handle their own problems, conflicts, and desires.

These points will now be considered in greater detail:

1.   Although no formal index of social position was employed in this study to classify the social status of the subjects, the determination that these swingers are generally in the middle socioeconomic class is based on observation of their behavior in public places and the occupation and general life-style of respondents and informants.

We have noted previously that the swingers maintained behavior appropriate to middle-class behavior when they were in public places. We shall now look briefly at their occupations and general life-styles.

Most of these swingers were employed in occupations or professions that deal primarily with concepts or manipulation of symbols. For example, the swingers in this study are known to include one or more of the following occupations: physician, lawyer, social worker, college professor, teacher, engineer, computer analyst, artisan (electrician, plumber), writer, businessman (insurance manager), model, actress, high-level clerical, bookkeeper, student, and housewife. Moreover, these swingers, including the artisans, were eager to talk about their experiences, problems, and theoretical and practical solutions to the problems they perceive.

Their life-style, as reflected in the location of their homes and choice of home furnishings, appeared to be solidly middle class. Their homes were in respectable neighborhoods and comfortably furnished. The artisans appeared to differ from middleclass behavior in that they were not upwardly mobile and were not pushing for promotions or for better jobs. They expressed satisfaction, pleasure, and pride in their work and were not pushing their children to succeed or to go to college.

2. People in this society are exposed to a variety of conflicting values, norms, and behaviors throughout their lives.

As illustration, a study published in 1951 [8] noted changes in the focus of publications for the United States Department of Labor Children's Bureau's *Infant Care* bulletin from 1914 through 1945. These bulletins reveal a change from a moral, puritan ethic that cautions the mother against indulging the child or allowing him sensual pleasure to a "fun-morality" where thumb-sucking and masturbation are seen as parts of the experience of growing up and exploring the world or as a result of boredom. Even if the message in these bulletins was not faithfully followed, it nonetheless illustrates an intellectual change in the approach to sexuality and sensuality in childrearing.

Further evidence of societal conflict concerning sexual behavior and attitudes is gained from a study made by Albert Ellis in 1950 and updated in the 1960s.[9] Ellis' research shows conflicting attitudes concerning premarital sex relations in the 1950s and '60s. Anti-adulterous attitudes were more prevalent in the '50s than in the '60s. In the 1960s the liberal attitudes were stronger and more straightforward. The attitudes toward sexual promiscuity were "confused, muddled, and unhealthy," with a little more liberalism found in 1960.

[8] Martha Wolfstein, "The Emergence of Fun Morality," *Journal of Social Issues* 7 (1951): 15–25.

[9] Albert Ellis, *The Folklore of Sex* (New York: Grove Press, 1961). This study involved examining fiction and nonfiction books listed in certain newspapers on January 1, 1950; reviewing New York newspapers on that day and sampling newspapers from across the United States; viewing all motion picture and stage productions playing on Broadway; and reviewing available radio and television shows on NBC and CBS and samplings of shows broadcast over other broadcasting systems; review of all types of popular magazines on the newsstands; all "Hit Parade" songs and popular songs printed in magazines. A small sample of scientific journals were also reviewed for comparison. A very similar study was repeated in early 1960.

In 1950 the views of sexual intercourse were somewhat contradictory, but in 1960 they were less conflicting and more universally accepted as a good thing. In the area of sexuality for women, Ellis found that numerous publications make the assumption that what is right for boys is wrong for girls. However, on the whole the attitudes toward female sexuality were mainly liberal and permissive. He also found that the demand for frigidity and purity was disappearing and that a view of the female as "oversexed" was becoming predominant. He feels that this view is as unrealistic as the previous view of women as sexless.

Before the industrial revolution women were obligated to accept their role as helpmate to men and husbands. Before jobs became available to them, women had no independent means of support.[10] Besides the value placed on virginity and fidelity, virtue was very practical for birth-control purposes. With separate incomes, females are no longer financially dependent upon men, particularly their husbands. With almost foolproof birth control techniques, women have a degree of sexual freedom they have never before experienced. Educational opportunities are also increasing for women.

The college experience can be one full of conflict, with the expectation that the girl both excel academically and also appeal to males so that she will not become an old maid. This sometimes requires that she conceal some of her interests and "play dumb" on dates.[11]

Religion is generally viewed as socializing people into strict sexual morality, and as a traditional source of guilt and conflict concerning disapproved activities. Well-known research, popu-

[10] For a discussion of the change from traditional to nuclear family, see Ralph Turner, "The Family," in *Sociology*, ed. Broom and Selznick (New York: Harper & Row, 1968).

[11] See "Cultural Contradictions and Sex Roles," *American Journal of Sociology 52* (Nov. 1946): 184–89. See also Bruno Bettelheim, "The Problems of Generations," *Daedalus 91* (1962). This mentions the conflict faced by the adolescent girl who expects, from early age, that her main fulfillment in life will be concerned with marriage and children. However, her education parallels that of boys whose realization comes through work and achievement in society. "To make matters worse, the years in college or even graduate school have further prepared the female elite to seek self-realization in work while society at large continues to stress that they must find it in motherhood."

larly known as the "Kinsey Report," states: "Degrees of religious devotion did correlate with the incidences of the various types of sexual activity, and devoutly religious backgrounds had prevented some of the females and males from ever engaging in certain types of sexual activity." [12] In line with this finding of Kinsey, I also found that the degree of previous religious devotion affected the comfort and guilt feelings of the respondents. Those who experienced the greatest discomfort were those who had been religiously devout in a religion concerned with morality in sexual behavior, while those who were less devout or who were exposed to a broad range of religious beliefs experienced the least discomfort.

Felt internal conflict or guilt between religious teachings and swinging activities can lead an individual to review and revise past religious beliefs. This was the case with a female respondent who had been brought up as a strict Roman Catholic. She admits that sometimes she still has the feeling that "good girls don't do that kind of thing." But the physical and emotional enjoyment she gets out of swinging and the closeness with a few couples who have become warm friends compensate for the indirect guilt feelings, and she rationalizes them into a minority position.

A swinger may maintain an identity with his religion but consider himself a "backslider." A male respondent said, "Swinging is not compatible with my religion which preaches fidelity, and the Ten Commandments which teach that thou shalt not covet thy neighbor's wife, and thou shalt not lust . . ." He does not accept these teachings and does not think that his behavior will "mess him up" with God.

3.   The middle-class intellectual people of this study who have been exposed to conflicting values and norms throughout their lives are capable and willing to make decisions within their experience and knowledge about how to handle their problems, conflicts, and desires. Rational thought is an important part of their experience. Some swingers want to save a marriage; some want to expand and get fuller enjoyment out of a marriage; some

    [12] A. C. Kinsey, W. B. Pomeroy, C. E. Martin, and P. H. Gebhard, *Sexual Behavior in the Human Female* (Philadelphia: W. B. Saunders Co., 1953), p. 687.

swingers want to have fun. They have all given thought to "how things should be," which is a necessary step in accepting that kind of behavior for themselves. There are probably many mechanisms at work, but after a person is willing to accept certain behavior, it is easier for him to consider engaging in that behavior if he desires.[13]

Besides the trend toward a single sexual standard, the woman's role in the marriage relationship is apt to become that of being her husband's best friend.[14] This is certainly true in the swinging relationships. Although the husband and wife may not be best friends, there is enough communication between them that they consider themselves friends. The trend toward more communication between husband and wife has partly to do with the increasing amount of education of females, especially in the middle class, and increasing of parallel areas of interest and information. When the overlapping interests of couples is narrow, neither is a satisfactory audience for the other.[15]

Some of the respondents had an awareness from childhood of conflicting values in the society with which compromises and decisions must be made. For example, one woman noticed that the preacher was driving a Cadillac while she used bubble gum money for the collection. This probably helped her to later disregard her mother's moralizing concerning sexual behavior when mother's behavior did not reflect mother's moralizing verbaliza-

[13] Edward C. Tolman, "Value Standards, Pattern Variables, Social Roles, Personality," *Toward a General Theory of Action,* ed. T. Parsons and E. Shils (New York: Harper Torchbook, 1962), pt. 3. In this chapter Tolman argues that value standards are ways of believing, even though a person "knows" what is good this does not mean he will necessarily want it. Not only must he hold a particular value *standard,* but the value must also be activated by a need aroused. Types of needs are also discussed. This is not seen to contradict the argument just presented. With swingers, the need or desire sometimes follows the rationale. In either case the rationale is usually adequate to allow the individual swingers to be reasonably comfortable with new behavior.

[14] Morton M. Hunt, *Her Infinite Variety* (New York: Harper & Row, 1962). Also see Ernest Burgess and Harvey Locke, *The Family: From Institution to Companionship,* 2nd ed. (New York: American Book Co., 1953).

[15] Mirra Komarovsky, *Blue-Collar Marriage* (New York: Random House, 1964). In this class the less educated couples hold more traditional notions about the "right" of men to silence (p. 132).

tions. Experience with this type of intellectual handling of conflict and guilt made it easy for her to accept the swinging experience. She decided that it was what she wanted to do and she did it.

Another respondent claims that she never felt guilt about sex. She adopted an attitude when she was young that sex was good for her, and this helped her through her early premarital sexual experiences and later her extramarital experience. She was raised in a small town where townspeople went out of town to engage in deviant behavior. This gave her a good background for comfortable acceptance of the swinging experience.

Some of the single people involved in swinging were rejecting the meaningless routine required as preparation to have sex with someone. They tired of the phony compliments and catering before it was appropriate to make a sexual approach. As pointed out by Ellis in his research, sex attitudes as expressed in the public media are so conflicting that a wide range of acceptable (or unacceptable) attitudes and behaviors are available to choose from. In many cases public media contradictions verify personal experience for singles and marrieds alike who in turn learn to depend on their own judgment for decisions involving their behavior.

SUMMARY AND CONCLUSIONS

In studying mate swapping (swinging) in Southern California I have explored the process by which people enter into deviant behavior and how they reconcile their deviant behavior after it occurs. In doing this I have concluded that these swingers are middle-class with an intellectual and verbal orientation, that they have been exposed to conflicting values and behaviors throughout their lives, and that they are capable of making decisions concerning their behavior based on their experience and knowledge (which also involves their experience with conflicting values). They have defined swinging behavior in positive terms, as the appropriate behavior to meet whatever needs they have. By continuing to swing they have determined that the consequences of swinging are good.[16]

For any other social class these three points might not be appropriate. For some other class a fun-and-games emphasis might be more legitimate with less importance attached to an intellectual approach. However, in this circle, almost every swinger with whom the subject was discussed had a well thought out and easily verbalized position concerning attitudes toward swinging.

I have done further probing in other geographical areas of the United States, and it appears that behavior in Southern California is regional behavior. Different behavior seems prevalent in other locations. If this is so, then there are perhaps different mechanisms at work in other areas to help the individual swinger to easily internalize new values to adequately cope with his behavior.

Even if the new values are not immediately internalized, but initially rationalized, this seems to be an important step for later internalization. It is necessary for the swinger to maintain a low enough guilt level that it does not interfere with daily living. Until the internalization takes place, swinging is intellectually defined as appropriate and the consequences of it defined as good.

---

[16] James M. Henslin, "Guilt and Guilt Neutralization: Response and Adjustment to Suicide," in *Deviance and Respectability: The Social Construction of Moral Meanings*, ed. Jack D. Douglas (New York: Basic Books, 1970), pp. 192–228. In this paper thirteen techniques of guilt neutralization following a suicide are identified. These include such techniques as defining others or impersonal factors as causal agents; defining suicide as inevitable; and defining suicide in positive terms, and, in effect, viewing the suicide as "good." This last method of neutralizing guilt after suicide can be applied appropriately to the swingers in their attempts to neutralize their guilt for breaking norms and accepting behavior in themselves that is deviant to the society. They define their behavior in positive terms.

ABORTION

Criminal Abortion:
Making the Decision and
Neutralizing the Act

JAMES M. HENSLIN

INTRODUCTION

Abortion,[1] the termination of an intrauterine pregnancy before the fetus has reached viability, is a pervasive fact of American society. In addition to *therapeutic* (legally induced) abortion, which until 1969 to 1970 occurred only about 8 to 10,000 times per year in the United States (Tietze 1968), there are also about 400,000 *spontaneous* abortions (miscarriages) which account for the termination of approximately 10 percent of all pregnancies (Nesbitt 1959: 97). More significantly though, approximately 1,000,000 American women undergo *criminal* abortions each year, that is, they have abortions that are illegally induced. Estimates for criminal abortions per year in the United States range from a minimum of 200,000 to a maximum of 2,000,000, with one million being the commonly accepted figure (Bates and Zawadzki 1964: 3).

Considering the estimated number of annual abortions in the United States from all three types, therapeutic, spontaneous, and criminal, therapeutic abortion has been playing an insig-

---

[1] It is interesting to note how ancient abortion is. Our earliest record of an abortifacient goes back almost 5,000 years, to somewhere between 2737 and 2696 B.C. in China. (Himes 1936: 14).

nificant role. Until very recently, in fact, the number of legal abortions had been decreasing because of a growing consensus among physicians that chronic medical conditions seldom require the therapeutic termination of pregnancy. In New York City, for example, therapeutic abortions displayed a consistent downward trend for the twenty-year period 1943 through 1962, declining 65 percent, from 5.1 to 1.8 per 1,000 live births. The frequency of therapeutic abortions declined "by each county within the city, by each maternal age and parity group, by each ethnic group, by each type of hospital service, and by each indication for intervention" (Gold *et al.* 1965: 971). At present, however, this trend in therapeutic abortion is undergoing a sharp reversal with the changing laws of 1969–1970 in such places as Hawaii, Maryland, New York, and Washington, D.C.

While therapeutic abortions were decreasing, criminal abortions appear to have increased correspondingly. In New York City, for example, deaths due to criminal abortion comprised one in four puerperal deaths among whites and one of every two among nonwhites (Gold *et al.* 1965: 965). The pervasiveness of illegally induced abortions and their negative consequences is further demonstrated by the fact that in 1961 over 3,500 patients were treated for infection following abortion in a single medical facility, Los Angeles County Hospital (Kistner 1965), while in just a five-year period over 20,000 women were treated for complications of abortion in the Cook County Hospital (Lash, Webster, and Barton 1968).

That Americans have negative attitudes toward abortion is commonly accepted as fact, but the assertion of statements about widespread attitudes without documentation is a risky business. In this situation we, fortunately, do not have to rely on common experience and assertion since proscriptive attitudes toward abortion by Americans have been documented. The National Opinion Research Center, interviewing a representative sample of 1,484 adult Americans in December 1965, found that while the majority of respondents favored abortion in cases of endangered health of the pregnant woman, rape, and the possibility of a defective child, only 21 percent approved of abortion for economic reasons, because the pregnant woman was unmarried, or because a married woman wanted no more children. Moreover, in spite of doctrinal differences concerning abortion, religion does not make a significant difference in determining attitudes toward abortion (Rossi 1966). It will be most interesting to see the changes American attitudes toward abortion undergo as the legal abortion experience becomes more common.

Although we are currently changing our abortion practices in some areas of the country, therapeutic abortion still comprises but a small proportion of American abortions, and until recently it accounted for perhaps only one percent of our induced abortions (10,000 of 1,000,000). Although abortion is a frequently occurring event in our society, because only a handful of our states have changed their abortion laws, legal abortion is inaccessible to the vast majority of American women, and its most common type is proscribed and covert. Who are the clients for criminal abortion? Most of them are married women who already have children (Bates 1964: 4; Gebhard 1958: 9). Induced abortion among married women is the most prevalent at younger ages when wives feel that they are not ready for children. It is estimated that younger wives deliberately abort over one fourth of their conceptions. The abortion rate then appears to decline as they feel that they can responsibly take care of children, only to increase with later years in life when the couples feel that their families are sufficiently large (Gebhard et al. 1958: 119).

Illegal abortion is a deviant activity which, for the most part, involves persons who are conforming members of society. Because of situational factors of a temporary nature, they enter into a transitory deviance. How do they come to the decision to violate normative proscriptions? Additionally, how do they protect their self-concept from definitions of deviance while they knowingly deviate from a widely held norm? In this paper we shall deal with both these subjects: we shall examine the process of deciding to abort, then focus on mechanisms used to protect the self, mechanisms that minimize unfavorable psychological consequences of abortion.[2] We shall analyze particularly the process

2 Protective mechanisms appear to be quite successful since only about 9 percent of abortionees experience psychological difficulties following illegally induced abortion (Gebhard et al., 1958: 208–210). Compare, however, the

of neutralization which enables abortionees, in spite of their
deviant activity, to retain their identity as conforming, normal
members of society.

Methodology and Sample

Twenty-two white female respondents who had undergone abortions were interviewed. Their ages at the time of the abortion
ranged from 16 to 33 (mean: 21.5); sixteen of them were single,
five married, and one divorced. At the time of the interview, no
respondent had less than a high school education nor more than
a master's degree (mean education attainment: 13.9 years). Gaining access to women who have had an abortion is, at best, difficult. Working through campus contacts, I interviewed women
who had experienced abortion, while other students interviewed
for me their friends who had had abortions. In each case an
open-ended interview was used, with the interviews being taped
in fifteen cases and notes taken during the interview with the
other seven respondents. Protocols of these interviews are the
basis of this paper. Race, age, marital, and education characteristics of this sample reflect the origin of contacts from the university community.

THE PRE-ABORTION PHASE

The Dilemma

During this phase the abortionee-to-be finds herself with an unwanted pregnancy. In most cases in this sample (sixteen of twenty-

---

study in Sweden in which it was found that 26 percent experienced self-
reproach following *legal* abortions—14 percent mildly so, 11 percent seriously
so, and 1 percent to the point that their working capacities were impaired
(Ekblad 1955: 233–234). It is probable that the methodology of the Kinsey-
Gebhard study minimized psychological consequences of abortion due to the
gap in time between the experience and the reporting of that experience. It
is also possible that Ekblad's sampling maximized such consequences since
there was a psychiatric base for the abortions in his sample. Compare also
the 20 percent who reported having nightmares following their abortion experience, as reported by Lee (1969: 105–106).

two), she is a *single* girl, who finding herself pregnant, is faced with the dilemma of marrying someone whom she is not yet ready to marry, marrying someone she feels perhaps she should not marry, not getting married and giving birth to a child out of wedlock with all of its associated stigma, or having an abortion with its attendant problems.

Sometimes she at first does not realize how complicating her pregnancy will become, thinking that she will tell her boyfriend and they will be married. It can then come as a rude shock to her that he wants nothing more to do with her. For example:

> He was nasty about it. I guess we both were before it was all over. He even threatened to accuse me of promiscuity if I tried to force him to marry me—said I could never prove anything. After that I just gave up.

And:

> He'd already left and gotten himself another chick. He wasn't getting anything from her, so he was hanky-pankying around me. When I called and told him I was pretty sure I was pregnant, he said, "Forget it! I've already found someone else, and I'm going to marry her."

In other cases, this message is delivered more subtly but nonetheless just as effectively:

> He said, "Well, (name), we'll get married. But things will really be bad, you know. You know things will really be rough." He all but said, "If you want to, I will. But I don't really want to." So what could I say?

In other cases, even though marriage is a viable option, the dilemma still exists. For example:

> The man was perfectly willing to go through with marriage. But I didn't particularly want to. And I didn't—I felt like I didn't— want to get pushed into a marriage and have a seven month baby and all that business. And people would talk and all this.

The *married* woman with an unwanted pregnancy finds herself in a similar dilemma: the birth of the child would bring about what she defines as undue strain on her marriage, this strain usually having a financial base but also including such things as a desire for personal freedom, independence, or travel, her evaluation of her husband and/or herself as being too immature or irresponsible for a child at this point, having enough children already, or feeling that the marriage currently is "too shaky" to support a child. The following two examples illustrate the financial base of the felt dilemma for married women:

> We already had three children. We could support them comfortably, but another child would put a crimp in our budget. Besides, I work so that my family and I can live more comfortably. I would have had to quit work, and there would have been some things we would go without that we otherwise could have had.

And:

> We were both students, and neither of us had a job. We were living in the front half of his parent's house. They didn't like me anyway, and he wanted to finish his education. And he didn't want to have to stop and get a job and support a child. And I rather agreed with him. I didn't want to have a child while we were living with his in-laws, with his parents, in a rather poor section of town. That would just sort of stop us there. We couldn't get any farther because we'd have to take care of the child.

The *divorced* woman, upon becoming pregnant, finds herself in a dilemma similar to that of the pregnant single girl. Additionally, if she already has children from her first marriage, she can find things even more complicating, as:

> If my ex-husband found out, he could really make trouble for me. He could take me into court and take the children away from me by proving I'm an unfit mother. That's how I felt when I walked out of the doctor's office—I could just see myself sitting in court, obviously pregnant, not married, trying to prove to a judge, who's most likely married, that I'm a fit mother. You know that I just had an affair, that it was the only time and that it wouldn't happen again—who's going to believe you? The whole thing sounded ridiculous and unreal.

The Decision

Finding herself in this dilemma, the woman makes what is usually a very difficult decision, that abortion is her way out of the dilemma. In making this decision, she receives the help of significant others (all cases). Shortly after finding out that she is pregnant, she tells those she feels she can trust, usually a close girlfriend, her parents, or the imputed impregnator (boyfriend or husband).[3] Through the influence of these people, she makes her decision to abort.

Sometimes the significant other tells the woman in a subtle way that she should have an abortion, as:

> My mother said that I was old enough to make up my own mind, and—so—she didn't say anything, but she said, "You know what you can do." She didn't tell me that she thought I should do anything, you know, different from what I said, but . . .

At other times this desire is communicated in a less subtle manner, as:

> [My boyfriend] told me to have the abortion, so I just said, "Fine. I'll have the abortion." I didn't even argue with him. I thought, "What's the use? I'll just do what he wants me to." I was just sick of the whole mess.

In some cases this decision is made after a serious discussion. For example, a girl with her father:

> We discussed the alternatives. And I mentioned the word abortion. And, uh, and then my father, after he had talked to the, the father of the child—and I had said I didn't want to have him put the screws on, I thought he'd been pressured enough, that I didn't want to marry anybody who was going to act like that—he said, "Well, then I guess we'll just have to do the other thing." And several things ran through my mind because I knew there were a

---

[3] Compare the finding by Ball (1967: 294) that patients in the abortion clinic he studied only rarely go to the clinic without a "supportive other." Compare also Lee's (1969: 53–57) report of the persons consulted in the decision to abort.

couple of other alternatives, and I said, "Which other thing?" He said, "You know, the, uh, . . ." I don't remember now what he said, but he kept trying to avoid the term.

Or in the case of the married woman in the sample, the decision is made after a rational discussion with her husband:

We wanted a family from the first, but with both of us in school—John with two more years to go, we couldn't do it. Before we were married, his parents promised that they would help us make our bills, with the stipulation that we would hold off on a family until John was graduated from ——— school. So we could have never gotten married without having this help.

I went home that afternoon and fixed John's supper [after having her pregnancy confirmed]. I guess I was thinking that would help things along. After we ate, I took him into the living room and told him. He was very surprised and very happy. But soon we sat down and started thinking more realistically. We discussed our alternatives, and decided on an operation. John had to finish school. He had a goal, and worked very hard toward it since high school. He now has a 4.5 average. That is a lot of hard work. We could not see throwing it away—not to work in a factory. I guess it's the hard way to get an education, but no way is easy.

There are cases, however, where the abortionee is not involved in the decision, such as the sixteen-year-old girl in our sample:

I hadn't thought of abortion. I didn't know there was such a thing. . . . My parents—my mother told me what to do and took me to the place.

Neutralization Techniques in Making the Decision

Neutralization techniques have been analyzed as processes by which social controls are rendered inoperative in juvenile delinquents (Matza and Sykes 1957) and as processes by which individuals protect their self-concept following the suicide of a significant other, suicides in which some feel that they might have had causal complicity (Henslin 1970; Henslin forthcoming). In the former, neutralization techniques are those justifications or rationalizations that neutralize, turn back, or deflect *in ad-*

vance "disapproval flowing from internalized norms and the social environment" (Matza and Sykes 1957: 666–67). They precede the deviant act, helping to make the act possible. In the latter, neutralization techniques build a protective shield around the self *after an act,* either eliminating or helping to reduce guilt in significant others following a suicide, by placing responsibility for the suicide beyond the self, thus allowing easier acceptance of the death (Henslin 1970).

It is during this pre-abortion phase that neutralization techniques begin to come into play, helping the girl to make her decision final, to go through with the abortion, and setting the stage for adjustment to her act. In making the decision to abort, the technique of *conceptualizing the abortion as the lesser evil* appears to be the overriding factor that enables the woman to come to this decision. Abortion is defined as being a lesser evil than are such things as a lower standard of living, the termination of educational plans, going through with a bad marriage, or the stigma attached to unwed motherhood.

For whatever the reasons, these women define their whole social existence as becoming humiliatingly changed if they were to go through with the pregnancy, with abortion being defined as the lesser evil.[4] For example:

> If I had it, there would be several months before it was born that I couldn't work. Then, even when I was able to go back to work, what school would hire an unmarried teacher with a baby? . . . I decided it was the only thing I could do.

Another neutralization technique that is helpful in making the decision to abort is to define the act as *altruistic* regarding the child with whom she is pregnant.[5] For example:

> I knew if we got married that would be—you know. And if I kept the baby, it wouldn't be fair to the baby. And if I gave it up for adoption, it just seemed to me really that it would be better for the baby if I . . .

[4] Very similarly, Matza and Sykes (1957) report that one of the major neutralization techniques used by juvenile delinquents is their "appeal to higher loyalties," where other norms held to be more pressing are accorded precedence.

[5] Similarly, altruism is a technique used by persons to overcome guilt following suicide (Henslin 1970).

And:

> I believe it's better not to have children at all if you think you'll
> resent their presence. Children are sensitive to things like that. . . .
> I sincerely believe that my mother felt that my sister and I were a
> hindrance. For a long time this hurt me. . . . I wouldn't wish that
> on any child.

Abortion, after the woman goes through a tumultuous evalu-
ative process, is finally viewed as "the only way out," "the only
possible solution," or "the only thing I could do,"—not as an act
desirable in itself, but as an act that is less repulsive in its consequences than those that would develop if the pregnancy were
allowed to go full term. Such views, where abortion is considered
to be the lesser evil of possible alternative courses of action, become the major neutralizer by which internalized proscriptions
against abortion are overcome, the decision is finalized, and the
girl can go through with the act.

Locating the Abortionist

Once the decision has been made that abortion is the solution
to her dilemma, the girl is now faced with the problem of finding an abortionist.[6] Most commonly the solution to this problem
is provided for her by the significant other with whom she confided her pregnancy. Ordinarily this person either already knows
of an abortionist, knows someone who has had an abortion, or
by "asking around" finds out how to contact an abortionist. Frequently there are several significant others involved in this communications network, such as a girlfriend who knows a girlfriend
who . . . , or a father who contacts a doctor who, in turn, contacts
a surgeon, etc. The following table gives a breakdown in order
of frequency of those persons in this sample most responsible
for locating the abortionist:

[6] It should be noted that opting for abortion not only removes a dilemma,
but is in itself a dilemma-producing decision. For example: "I was afraid because I was so far along. . . ." and "I have always heard of this back alley
stuff, but never, never thought it would happen to me. I never even thought
I could lower myself to be in a situation, but there I was." and "I'd heard all
these scary stories about abortionists with the dirt under their nails and all
this sort of stuff. . . . And I was scared."
See the following selection in this volume.

Who Located The Abortionist

Relationship to the Girl	Frequency
Doctor	6
Parents	5
Girlfriend	4
Boyfriend	3
Other relative	
(Sister and sister-in-law)	2
Self-induced abortion	2
	N = 22

It is interesting that in this sample the most frequent contact with the abortionist is a physician, whether he be the family doctor, a gynecologist, or an osteopath. When doctors pass on such information, they are frequently reluctant go-betweens in the communication network of criminal abortion. Several respondents made such requests of their doctors, but were refused. In some instances, however, the doctor himself makes the suggestion for abortion. For example:

> He [the gynecologist] gave me this woman's phone number. Well, first he asked me what I was going to do. I didn't want to tell him about the abortion, even though this is what [my boyfriend] wanted. So I told him I felt sure that the guy would not want me to have it, and then he said, "Would you like to have the number of an abortionist?" And I said, "Yes. Well, I probably should take it along because this is probably what I'll do." And I was reasonably sure at the time that this is what I would do. He was very open about it. He was all for abortion, and he said most of the doctors today are. And he said usually they wait for the patient to say something to them first, but he said something to me first, and he felt it should be legalized, of course. And he said this woman is very good, and there was nothing to worry about. And I said, "Being alone as I was, would that make a difference?" And he said he didn't think so, but that she would have to decide this when I talked to her. And he gave me some pills, and he sent me a prescription later, after he found out I did it, for pain and infection. He also furnished a doctor's statement for work cause I was out a week. He was a very, very nice man.

In another case, to help one of my respondents, a chiropodist contacted four doctors whom he knew had been performing abortions. He found that three of them were no longer performing abortions, however, and he would not recommend the fourth "because he was a butcher." The chiropodist finally recommended a midwife in St. Louis who has been performing abortions for twenty-five years.

These latter two examples of doctors who took the initiative in contacting an abortionist are not typical, however, and based on evidence from these interviews, it would seem that doctors' reluctance to serve as go-betweens in the abortion communication network is more easily broken down where there are "established" abortion centers that have operated fairly openly over a long period of time, abortion centers that have facilities for keeping girls overnight and, if need be, for several days, and centers that appear to have a good record of patient care. It should be noted that this conclusion is highly tentative.

There are, of course, disreputable doctors who communicate such information for a kick-back from the abortionist. That this was possibly the situation with one of my subjects is indicated by the respondent whose doctor took her telephone number, gave it to an abortionist, and then: "The abortionist called me every day. I never called her. . . . He had her call me. He probably got a cut in it."

The most unusual way of locating an abortionist that came up in this sample was the mother who "looked in the Yellow Pages under midwife." It seems that the Bell Telephone System is correct—"you *can* find anything you want in the Yellow Pages."

THE ABORTION PHASE

In this paper I will not analyze the abortion phase, although it is fascinating. We have, for understandably obvious reasons, a gap in our literature on this subject. The best analysis in the sociological literature of abortionists at work is that by Ball (1967). His analysis, however, does not deal with the abortion itself but, rather, deals with features of the setting and interaction that surround the abortion. Nor does his analysis by any means exhaust the types of abortion clinics, mills, centers, or just plain places where abortions take place. One would presume that they differ widely, each having its own characteristics, types of clientele and practitioners, and, ultimately, its effects on the abortionee's adjustment to her act.

Some idea of the variety connected with this phase is gained by pointing out that in just this small sample alone abortions were obtained in both the St. Louis and Chicago metropolitan areas, were performed by both whites and blacks, with the abortionists ranging from surgeons in sterile surroundings through midwives in "semi-sterility" to a housewife placing her "patient" on her living room coffee table and using an ice pick on her. The price range was also tremendous in this sample, varying from nothing in the case of a physician who performed an abortion as a favor to a friend, and twenty-five dollars in the case of a medical school drop-out who charges "only expenses" for the abortions that he performs, doing them primarily as favors for friends, to one thousand dollars in the case of a woman who went to a Chicago abortion mill. It is interesting to note that there is no direct correlation whatsoever between the fee charged by the abortionist and the quality of the abortion. Rather, an inverse correlation appears to exist on the extreme ends of the fee range, with the best care being received from the physician who performed the abortion free and the abortionist with medical training who charged just twenty-five dollars for "his expenses," while the woman who paid the one thousand dollar fee received the poorest treatment of all, having her intestines punctured, almost losing her life from hemorrhaging, and being hospitalized for a full month following the abortion! (It is also interesting to note that, in spite of the serious medical ramifications of this woman's abortion, she refused to give the police the name of her abortionist, even when directly questioned by them.)

THE POST-ABORTION PHASE

How do women who have knowingly engaged in an act defined by society as deviant, one which they, themselves, also ordinarily define as deviant, and one moreover for which they are liable to punishment by law, avoid incorporating the pejorative label of "deviant" into their self-concept? For this answer there are many aspects of abortion that we could examine. For example, we could look at abortion settings that are designed to minimize or deny deviance, such as the use of middle-class props and medical terminology within a pseudo-medical framework (Ball 1967).[7] We could also profitably utilize the concept sociologists call "situational deviance," where an individual who is ordinarily a conforming member of society finds himself in a situation in which he engages in a deviant act, but he does so only on a temporary basis, moving quickly back into his conforming, nondeviant style of life. Also, we could emphasize the covert or "secrecy" aspect of abortion, which, since, few people know of the act, makes it difficult for the label "deviant" to be successfully applied to the individual. It also might be profitable to look at the reasons why abortion does not lead to a "subculture of abortionees," seeing what difference this makes for the application of the deviant label. Finally, we might want to pay attention to the fact that with abortion there is ordinarily an absence of degradation ceremonies (Garfinkel 1956).

Although these are probably highly relevant and significant concepts and variables, we are going to examine a different type of data: responses that the respondents themselves have made that demonstrate ways in which they define their act such that it neutralizes deviance and guilt. In spite of having violated both societal proscriptions against abortion and, in many cases, their own internalized norms, most of these girls are quite successful in neutralizing feelings of deviance or feelings that they have done something for which they should feel guilt. Unfortunately our data do not permit us to analyze the process through which individuals go from the time they consider abortion to some given period following the abortion. Accordingly, we are limited to studying post-facto self-reports of the abortion experience, ab-

---

[7] For contrast, we could also examine abortion that takes place within situations of "cultural-denial-of-deviance," where, as in Japan, abortion is accepted as a technique of population control, is legal, is inexpensive, pre-abortion counseling is provided, and the abortion occurs within a medical setting.

stracting and analyzing the techniques these respondents used to cope with their transitional experience with deviance. It is to these techniques that we shall now turn.

The first major neutralizing technique used by these respondents is that of conceptualizing abortion as the *lesser evil*. The initial conceptualizing process through which the girl made her decision to have her abortion also helps her adjust to the fact of abortion. In making her decision, she concluded that abortion was the lesser of the evils surrounding her, and, in making the choice she did, she defined herself as opting for the less evil choice. As such, as long as she maintains the definition that the other choices open to her were more evil than abortion, she can define herself as having done what she was socialized to do—to choose the least evil of any action open to her. It may be that the act she chose was "wrong" according to society's and her own definition, but, at the same time, the other choices were even "more evil."

Specifically, these respondents felt that abortion was preferable to having the child and ruining the lives of significant others, such as one's husband or parent, or ruining one's own life; that abortion was better than having the child and shifting the responsibility for raising the child onto others; that it was better than ruining the child-to-be with resentment that he or she had been born; and better than losing the children one already has.

A related neutralization technique used by these respondents is not only to define abortion as being, although a negative thing, a "less evil," but also to view it as a *"positive good."* It seems that this would be easiest to do where the individual is surrounded by others who support such a view and encourage the act. The process of arriving at such a conceptualization is indicated by the following respondent who appears to have been encircled by protective, supportive, significant others who both pointed and paved the way to abortion as the correct solution to her dilemma. Note her repetitive use of the phrase "best thing" when she refers to abortion:

> (My mom) thought it'd be the best thing, and I figured it would be, too. . . . After my mom told me, I started to talk to my girl-

friend, and she decided it would probably be the best thing for me, too. . . . I told him (boyfriend) I'd probably get one, you know. He said he'd help pay, you know. He thought that would be the best thing. . . . I went to the doctor when I found out I was pregnant, a doctor here in town. And she also mentioned about abortion, too. . . . I always told myself that, you know, I'd probably get one if I didn't get married, cause to me that would be the best thing for me. . . . I think it's (abortion) a good idea. I think they should legalize it.

Another neutralization technique is for the respondent to define herself as having little or *no choice* in the matter. Where choice is minimal or nonexistent, the act is viewed as not being willful, and this means a lowered perceived responsibility for the act or even no responsibility at all. Phrases that recur by persons using this technique are: "We could see no other way to turn," and, "It seemed the only way out of the problem." If such a definition of the self's responsibility can be successfully held, a protective shield can be erected that overcomes internal and external recriminations for the act.

In utilizing this "no choice neutralization technique," others are defined as having made the choice, with the self being defined as only a very reluctant or even an unknowing participant in the act. Our sixteen-year-old respondent, for example, defines herself as having not been involved in the decision whatsoever: "I never thought whether it was right or wrong. They (parents) told me what to do, and I did." And, another respondent states (emphasis added):

He (boyfriend) insisted that I do this. *I* was against it. . . . I knew that *I* didn't want to . . . but when you have someone saying, "Well, this is what *I want you* to do," and *he didn't want* to get married, and *he wouldn't let* me just have the child like *I wanted* to do—so *I* really didn't have a whole lot of choices, you know what I mean.

She defines others as exerting their will upon her, as forcing her to do something she did not want to do. Even though she finally "decides" to have the abortion, she defines herself as not wanting the abortion: "They changed my mind . . . but I still didn't want to when I did. When I made up my mind to, I didn't want to."

Another neutralization technique is to seek an *interactional validation* of the act and of the self-concept. They seek out significant others, especially parents, boyfriends, and girlfriends, who will maintain the definition that abortion was good or that it was preferable in the circumstances or that they had no choice, etc. For example:

> I discussed this with this person I told, and she felt, "Why ruin another person's life? Why be unhappy and ruin your own life when you're so young? Granted I did make a mistake by getting pregnant —so why should three other people be penalized by making this mistake?" This is the way she felt, and that's why she did help me.

Possibly *atonement* is an additional neutralizing technique, a means of overcoming guilt. For example, one could conceptualize that subsequently becoming pregnant and giving birth to a child is a "re-doing" of the earlier "pregnancy-abortion-event," that a new pregnancy and a resultant birth is a "wiping away" of the negative act of abortion. This neutralizing conceptualization seems to be indicated by the following respondent who said:

> The mistake is past, if it was a mistake. At any rate, we can do nothing about it now. Now we have to look to the future. In another year John and I will hopefully have the start of our own family. Thoughts of being a mother have entered my mind frequently since the abortion. I really look forward to that day!

Unfortunately, there are no cases in this sample of persons who have borne children since the abortion and who have expressed that this helped them. In fact, one could hypothesize that future children would even increase feelings of guilt and deviance by reminding the woman of what she did not have, perhaps of what she had "done away with." We shall, however, have to leave the resolution of this question to further research.

Other specific techniques that these respondents demonstrated, although doing so only minimally, include *thought avoidance,* that is, trying not to think about the act, and increased *church attendance.*

The final technique of neutralizing guilt that we will discuss is *denial of a victim*.[8] I assume that a woman who expects to terminate her pregnancy with the live birth of a child conceives of herself during her pregnancy as nurturing a live human being in her womb. At least it is common for pregnant women to refer to their enlarged midriffs as "Junior." For example, when movement in the uterus is noticed, some women frequently say, "Junior is kicking."[9]

For a woman who expects to terminate her pregnancy with abortion, however, to conceptualize her pregnancy as "a child" or even that of a developing individual or human being would probably be to increase guilt or the possibility of guilt both prior to and following her abortion. If, however, she is able to conceptualize her pregnancy in nonhuman terms, she is able to reduce or to even eliminate guilt. It is common for these respondents to refer to that which was inside their uterus as an "it" instead of as a child. For example:

> I didn't even know I had passed it! When I came out of the bathroom, (the nurse) checked the stool. She came into the bedroom and told me I was finished. It couldn't have been very big. I didn't even notice it had passed!

One respondent even defined this "it" as being about the same as "other junk": "I could hardly tell the difference in it and the tube and the other junk. It was just a small blob."

When the abortionee defines the "it" which she "passed" as "not-a-child" but as, rather, only a small inanimate "blob," she is maintaining that there is no victim to her act. Consequently, she need feel little or no guilt concerning her act. Who should feel guilty about "passing a blob"? Who is a deviant for such an inconsequential act?

Some women, by the use of such neutralizing techniques as outlined above, are so successful in preventing feelings of guilt that they not only express no feeling that they have been involved in deviance or that they have done something for which they should feel guilt, but they additionally express happiness and gratitude about the act of abortion. For example:

[8] This is one of the major techniques analyzed by Matza and Sykes (1957).
[9] I am grateful to Miss Kathleen Sivok for this point. I also wish to thank Janey Fauke, Jacqueline Huch, and Cheryl Richey for interviews they conducted.

After I did have the abortion, I had a kind of new beginning again. . . . I was always grateful because I'd always felt he'd (my father) given me a new lease on life. There were times when I couldn't believe my good fortune. And everyday that—at least for the next nine months—practically everyday I would think, "Well, you know, I wouldn't be here doing what I am, enjoying myself or whatever I happen to be doing and being free of that sordid situation or that unpleasant situation if it weren't for my father."

And another respondent, one who had induced her own abortion, although not as glowing in her terms, expresses gratitude that her act was successful:

I was grateful. The only reason I would have felt regret I think is if I had been forced into a marriage, I mean, if it [the abortion] hadn't worked. I hadn't planned on it not working. I was gonna try something else, you know. . . . But, yeah, I wanted that abortion.

Failure of Guilt-Deviance Neutralization

By emphasizing neutralization in this paper, I do not want to give the impression that all the respondents were successful in protecting their self-concept from moral recriminations concerning their act. This is just not the case, and such a conclusion would be extremely misleading. Some women failed to neutralize societal norms regarding abortion, and, not being able to overcome their own acceptance and internalization of these norms, they are unsuccessful in neutralizing or mitigating the guilt that followed their act of norm or conscience violation. As a result, a tremendous guilt burden plagues them, one that begins with a "guilt quandary" when they first think of abortion and one that can then continue for years afterwards. For example, one respondent who was unable to neutralize the effect of her act on her self conceptualizes abortion as killing. She expressed some of the questions, doubts, self-searching, and self-recriminations that have haunted her for the three years since her abortion when she said:

I was scared, and I wondered if I was doing the right thing. And there's always doubt in your mind because, of course, there's always that feeling that you are killing a life-to-be. And although I have

> certain feelings about whether it would be better for the child to
> live in a bad environment and mentally hurt him, I don't know
> whether it would be better to kill him before he took his first
> breath. I had mixed emotions. . . . I wondered, and I didn't know
> if I had done the right thing. Of course, this will drag on a per-
> son's mind whether I did the right thing. . . . I wish it could be
> completely blotted out of my mind. I just don't know if I did the
> right thing.

And another respondent seems to not even have had the "comfort of doubt" that the above respondent exhibits that of at least
not knowing whether she was right or wrong. She states that although "everyone says that that (fetus) isn't life," she still defines
conception as being under the control of God and abortion the
same as capital punishment—the taking of human life:

> I don't think that anyone has the right to take life. Now granted
> everyone says that that isn't life. God, he controls all of this. And
> I feel the way I do about capital punishment—and it's completely
> different. But I just don't think any human being has the right, to
> say, to take a life. And I just can't see it. I mean God did this for a
> reason, and who are we to take a life of a human being, deprive
> them of the privilege of living?

Since guilt is not an automatic response to some objective situation but is, rather, a learned response to a perceived event (Henslin 1970), it is easy to see how holding definitions of abortion as
"killing a life-to-be," "killing someone before he takes his first
breath," "taking the life of a human being," or "depriving someone of the privilege of living" result in feelings of guilt or self-
reproach.

DISCUSSION

Although this research sheds some light on the decision-making
and neutralization processes in abortion, it is highly exploratory
in nature, is not definitive, and, in many ways, raises more questions than it answers. Questions that this paper leads to, but for
which it provides no answers, relate primarily to differential responses to the act of abortion.

For example, why are some women highly successful in handling a "rhetoric of legitimization" (Ball 1967: 296), in manipulating a set of symbols that neutralizes definitions of deviance and guilt, while others are not? Why do some women seem little bothered, while others are plagued with guilt for years over the same act? On what basis are certain neutralization techniques chosen over against others? What are major guiltogenic factors? How does differential exposure to guiltogenic factors affect the definitions held by the actor? For example, how does differential internalization of normative proscriptions against abortion determine later reactions to abortion? How about differential exposure to "accusing others"? We can ask the same question concerning differential exposure to guilt-reducing or neutralizing interactional factors, for example, supportive others. These are some questions which, hopefully, other researchers will try to answer.[10]

Although we can presently say little concerning the bases of success in utilizing these various neutralization techniques, our data does indicate that the person who is most successful is the one who conceptualizes abortion as a neutral or a positive act, and the person who is the least successful is the one who conceptualizes abortion as murder. The following quote by a respondent who is making a purposeful effort to avoid thinking of abortion as murder, gives some insight into such neutralizing conceptualization: "Since then (the abortion), I haven't thought about it much. I never really have considered the baby. I know

[10] As abortion becomes more acceptable in the United States, corresponding changes in neutralizing techniques should also take place. Just as the problems faced by women undergoing abortions will change as abortion is redefined from deviance to a medical matter (removing the illegal and "back alley" stigmatizing aspects of their behavior), so should aspects of their conceptualization of their act. One would presume that the act, being no longer legally deviant, although perhaps still being defined interpersonally as deviant for a long time to come, will yield greater support to conceptualizations of the act that protect the self concept, shielding it from labels of deviance. It is even possible that we are currently not too far from the day when abortion will be readily available in these United States, as evidenced at least by a bill introduced to the United States Senate, April 23, 1970, by Senator Robert W. Packwood, an Oregon Republican, that would permit a woman to have an abortion anywhere in this country if a licensed doctor performed it (*St. Louis Post-Dispatch*, April 26, 1970).

some people refer to abortion as murder, but I never have thought of it this way." But the basic question of why some persons can successfully maintain this neutralizing definition of the situation while others cannot remains unanswered.

A promising possibility in handling some of these questions is to utilize the theory of cognitive dissonance (Festinger 1957), although we have not applied it as such in this paper. We would expect, for example, that knowingly violating an internalized norm will set up internal dissonance between an actor's self concept and the knowledge of his act. This tension should, in turn, be followed by mechanisms that function to reduce the tension. Hopefully, the above exploratory analysis of neutralization techniques in abortion is a first step in determining such factors. In this light, we can reconceptualize the data into types of techniques by which the actor (1) manipulates cognitive elements by reconceptualization, for example, the "less evil" and "no choice" techniques, (2) seeks out others who will through interaction validate her self-concept, and/or, (3) chooses certain neutralizing acts, for example, atonement, avoidance, and church attendance. Hopefully such ideas can be rigorously applied by sociologists engaging in future research in this area about which we presently know so little.

REFERENCES

Ball, Donald M. "An Abortion Clinic Ethnography." *Social Problems 14* (Winter): 293–301, 1967.

Bates, Jerome E., and Zawadzki, Edward S. *Criminal Abortion: A Study in Medical Sociology.* Springfield, Ill.: Charles C Thomas, Publisher, 1964.

Ekblad, Martin. "Induced Abortion on Psychiatric Grounds: A Follow Up Study of 479 Women." *Acta Psychiatrica Et Neurologica Scandinavia,* suppl., Vol. 99, 1955 (Donald Burton, translator).

Festinger, Leon. *A Theory of Cognitive Dissonance.* New York: Harper & Row, Publishers, Inc., 1957.

Garfinkel, Harold. "Conditions of Successful Degradation Ceremonies." *American Journal of Sociology 61:* 420–424, 1956.

Gebhard, Paul H.; Pomeroy, Wardell B.; Martin, Clyde E.; and Christenson, Cornelia V. *Pregnancy, Birth, and Abortion.* New York: Paul B. Hoeber, Inc., 1958.

Gold, Edwin M.; Erhardt, Carl L.; Jacobziner, Harold; and Nelson, Frieda G. "Therapeutic Abortion in New York City: A 20-year Review." *American Journal of Public Health 55:* 964–972, 1965.

Henslin, James M. "The Construction of Social Meanings Following a Suicide." In *Existential Sociology,* edited by Jack D. Douglas. New York: Rand-McNally Company, forthcoming.

Henslin, James M. "Guilt and Guilt Neutralization: Response and Adjustment to Suicide." In *Deviance and Respectability: The Social Construction of Moral Meanings,* edited by Jack D. Douglas. New York: Basic Books, 1970, pp. 192–228.

Henslin, James M. "Strategies of Adjustment: An Ethnomethodological Approach to the Study of Guilt and Suicide." In *Survivors of Suicide,* edited by Albert C. Cain. Springfield, Ill.: Charles C Thomas, Publishers, forthcoming.

Himes, Norman E. *Medical History of Conception.* Baltimore, Maryland: Williams and Wilkins, 1936. (As quoted in Bates and Zawadzki 1964: 14).

Kistner, Robert W. "Medical Indications for Contraception: Changing Viewpoints." *Obstetrics and Gynecology 25:* 285–288, 1965.

Lash, Abraham; Webster, Augusta; and Barton, John J. "A Survey of over 20,000 Abortions at the Cook County Hospital (1961–1965)." *Transactions of the American Association of Obstetricians and Gynecologists 79:* 110–113, 1968.

Lee, Nancy Howell. *The Search for an Abortionist.* Chicago: The University of Chicago Press, 1969.

Matza, David, and Sykes, Gresham M. "Techniques of Neutralization: A Theory of Delinquency." *American Sociological Review 22* (December): 664–670, 1957.

Nesbitt, Robert E. L., Jr. "The Outcome of Pregnancy Complicated by Threatened Abortion." In *Spontaneous Abortion,* edited by David N. Danforth. New York: Paul B. Hoeber, Inc., 1959, pp. 97–109.

Rossi, Alice S. "Abortion Laws and Their Victims." *Trans-Action* (September–October 1966), pp. 7–12.

Schur, Edwin M. *Crimes Without Victims.* Englewood Cliffs: N. J.: Prentice-Hall, 1965.

Tietze, Christopher. "Therapeutic Abortions in the United States." *American Journal of Obstetrics and Gynecology 101:* 784–787, 1968.

Fixing What You Feared:
Notes on the Campus
Abortion Search

PETER K. MANNING

This paper describes and analyzes the vicissitudes of the search for an abortion by unwed coeds on a Midwestern college campus. It is an attempt to demonstrate how active social control in the form of medical agencies and agents creates a limited range of action alternatives for an abortion-seeking population.[1] The salient features or stages of the search for an abortion are constructed as the person confronts, defines, and manages the social situations entailed in coping with problems. Its primary concern is to identify those features which when present culminate in an abortion, and when absent, lead to other, alternative outcomes.[2]

I would like to thank Donald W. Ball, Nancy Howell Lee, and Nanette J. Davis for helpful comments.

[1] A more complete study of the social control of abortion is now being executed by Nanette J. Davis, "Contextual Features of Abortion Markets: Social and Economic Exchange of a Risk Commodity," Dissertation in progress, Michigan State University, Department of Sociology. Her concern is with the patterning of a high, inelastic demand for abortion services by the exchanges among social control agents such as hospital boards, local branches of organized medicine, individual physicians and clergymen. A set of alternatives of differential cost are established by the bargaining and negotiation over the rules carried on by these power groups.

[2] I have also described the methodology of this study as an example of analytic induction in *Introduction to Social Science Methods*, ed. Robert B. Smith (New York: The Free Press, forthcoming). Arguments which simply rely on such structural descriptions, commit, among other things, the ecolog-

Depending on one's methodological purity, this study is generalizable only to these coeds and their experiences, the abortion-seeking population of one Midwestern university, all Midwestern universities, or the search as it takes place on all campuses where abortion is illegal. The focus of this study is limited in that it does not cover a number of important issues, and it describes only a portion of the possible experiences.[3] Most pregnancies are not aborted, most abortions are performed for married women, most abortions are sought and obtained in large, urban areas and an increasing number are being performed in states where the operation is legal.[4]

A natural history approach organized the research; that is, abortion or searching for an abortion was not assumed to have a universal meaning, but a meaning that shifted as events unfolded. Within each of the identified states, the persons involved encountered charactertistics, problems and defined them in fairly consistent fashion. Thus, although an outside observer might identify a set of objective and constraining social and biological conditions and associated contingencies, they may or may not be

---

ical fallacy, leading to the claim, based on statistical generalizations, that a certain type of female is permissive, while others are not. Vincent makes clear in his *Unmarried Mothers* (New York: Free Press of Glencoe, 1969, paper ed.) that unwed mothers do not differ significantly at the attitudinal and demographic level from other girls in a control sample. It is the situational and aleatory processes which explain the differences.

[3] Such issues as the need for legal reform, the political implications of abortion, changing public attitudes toward abortion, the suffering and mental anguish caused women by "sexist" laws, and the consequences of abortion policy for world population are beyond the scope of this paper. See, for coverage of these issues, Nancy Howell Lee, *The Search for an Abortionist* (Chicago: University of Chicago Press, 1969) and literature cited therein; L. Lader, *Abortion* (Indianapolis: Bobbs-Merrill, 1966); Edwin Schur, *Crimes Without Victims* (Englewood Cliffs: Prentice-Hall, 1965); Alan F. Guttmacher, ed., *The Case for Legalized Abortion Now* (Berkeley: Diablo Press, 1967); Harold Rosen, ed., *Abortion in America* (Boston: Beacon Press, 1967); Jerome Bates and E. Zawadzki, *Criminal Abortion* (Springfield, Ill.: Charles C Thomas, 1964); George Devereaux, *A Study of Abortion in Primitive Societies* (New York: Julian Press, 1955) and Paul Gebhard *et al., Pregnancy, Birth and Abortion* (New York: Harper & Brothers, 1958) and the massive compendium, Robert Hall, *Abortion in a Changing World,* two vols. (New York: Columbia University Press, 1970).

[4] See Lee, *op. cit.,* ch. 1.

taken into account by the actors themselves. Admittedly, there are a set of "objective" social facts such as the raising of money, obtaining transportation, and contacting an abortionist, but they are not universally or uniformly perceived and defined. As Becker writes ". . . each stage requires explanation, and what may operate as a cause at one step may be of negligible importance at another step." [5] In short, the research investigates the social processes by which an abstract term, "abortion" is given concrete meaning as a result of the definitions people confer on it at given periods of time, and the action implications which flow from those concrete or situated definitions.

SOME ECOLOGICAL AND DEMOGRAPHIC MATTERS

A college campus, ecologically and demographically, is characterized by large numbers of young males and females regularly interacting within a bounded setting and many subsettings. More specifically, the ecology allows a degree of privacy, for example, regular visitation hours in dorms, ease of access to the opposite sex, and regularized settings and occasions for dating. These generalizations simply get the scene, action, actors and settings together.

In this context, sexual relationships of great diversity are an everyday affair. Since it is an everyday affair, sexual intercourse does not require an explanation as deviance; like eating lunch, it happens routinely.

Therefore, we may assume that many premarital pregnancies are the result of what Lemert calls "primary deviation," polygenetic in origin, diverse in meaning and significance, widely distributed in a given population and of little consequence to the self and role of those engaged in it.[6] Reasons advanced by a group of young unmarried mothers for their out-of-wedlock preg-

---

[5] Howard S. Becker, *Outsiders: Studies in the Sociology of Deviance* (New York: Free Press, 1963), p. 23.

[6] Edwin M. Lemert, *Social Pathology* (New York: McGraw-Hill, 1951), pp. 75–76 *passim*.

nancies are probably representative of college students finding themselves pregnant.[7] These include such diverse accounts as the "failure" of consciously utilized birth control devices by either sex, risk-taking or thrill-seeking in a gamble with pregnancy, forgotten birth control pills, "trying it" to see, passions of the moment, attempts by females to "trap a husband," or to play on male vulnerability, male aggression or exploitation, the result of regular cohabitation or intercourse among couples in love, mutual indifference, and so forth.

These ecological, demographic and social arrangements allow for the regular production of a rate of pregnant females. At the campus where the research is being conducted, a Midwestern State University of over 40,000 students, 18 percent of the student body is married, and 41 percent of the students are females. Knowledgeable people estimate that from two to three girls a day recognize the need for advice or counsel for their pregnancies. Approximately 1,000 girls a year seek aid. They are the known tip of an "iceberg," and they, in turn, may represent less than half the actual numbers of unwanted pregnancies on the campus.[8] The most important consequences of these actions are patterned by formal agencies of control.

SOCIAL CONTROL: AT LARGE AND ON THE CAMPUS

Social control is the process by which human transactions, exchanges of demanded goods and services and human affection, are shaped and patterned by the arbitrary boundaries established by socially dominant political-economic groups. The legal designation by dominant groups of certain human exchanges as immoral or illegal results in the differential treatment via stigmatization and criminalization of some human wanderings. Edwin

[7] Vincent, *op. cit.*, ch. 2, "Unwed Mothers' Attitudes."

[8] A local crisis intervention clinic opened near the campus in the summer of 1969. In the first two months of operation on a twenty-four-hour basis, they received eighty-seven contacts on the general topic of "problem pregnancy." A group of campus ministers are cooperating with the clinic to provide abortion-relevant information.

Schur, in an excellent review of relevant literature in the area of abortion, drug addiction and homosexuality, concludes:

> . . . usually the professed aim of legislation against deviance is to eliminate the offending behavior . . . In all three problem areas, the effect of the policies employed has been to regulate, and not to eliminate . . . *the repressive policies discussed in this book represent societal decisions as to how the various demanded goods and services are to be allocated.* Embodied in these decisions is an insistence that social approval shall not attach to the transactions in question; but also implied is the recognition that the particular goods and services shall in one way or another be made available. The woman is to be relieved of her unwanted pregnancy, even if reputable hospitals are not to cooperate. The drug addict is to obtain his drugs, but not from legitimate medical sources . . . Yet for one reason or another it has been "arranged" that these social problems shall remain insoluble.[9]

Legal controls upon the allocation of goods and services insures that a level of ever-present demand will not be satisfied through legitimate sources.[10] The process of labeling which occurs illustrates that the central consideration in the study of deviance and control is the *reaction* of an audience to the social identities, including behavior, of the defined deviant person or group.[11]

[9] Schur, *op. cit.*, p. 176.

[10] Some functionalistic arguments portray social control as a means of maintaining group boundaries, reinforcing social solidarity and reasserting the morality of the dominant groups over deviant morality. The process of rule-making by these dominant groups creates or generates deviance; deviance can be said to be a function of the rules created to control it. A sociological example of this argument is Kai T. Erikson, *Wayward Puritans* (New York: John Wiley and Sons, 1966); similar points are made using an economic metaphor by Herbert Packer, *The Limits of the Criminal Sanction* (Stanford: Stanford University Press, 1968). The most important implications of this argument are that deviance is not controlled in any absolute sense, but that it is patterned by social control. When named deviations are brought under control, they nevertheless survive. It is likely that new institutionalized or refined sorts of evasions will emerge over time. For a general treatment of this process, see Robin Williams, "Patterned Evasion of Norms," pp. 372–396 in *American Society* (New York: Alfred A. Knopf, 1960) and Joseph R. Gusfield, "Moral Passage: The Symbolic Process in Public Designations of Deviance," *Social Problems 15* (Fall, 1968): 175–188.

[11] For examples of this perspective, see Lemert, *op. cit.*, Becker, *op. cit.*, and John Lofland, *Deviance and Identity* (Englewood Cliffs: Prentice-Hall, 1969).

Within narrowly defined "political" territories, such as college campuses, campus police, health centers, and counseling centers, habitually modify and transform broader legal rules to suit the exigencies of current situations. They transform cultural premises and rules, legal and otherwise, into *strategies* of enforcement and *tactics* in attempts to *successfully* carry out their mandates.[12] The tactics of control agents are seen in interpersonal encounters in which specific meanings of vague moral rules are negotiated, defined, transformed and practically interpreted. In many cases, these encounters loom largest in the nature and creation of deviant roles and selves.

For example, at the university where the research was conducted, the policy of the campus health center, in part because no obstetrician-gynecologist is in residence, is to provide no prenatal care.[13] Therefore, a demand for help exists which is not met by the formal control agencies. Consequently, as in the social structure at large, one expects to discover an *infrastructure* growing up around these persistent human problems in order to illegally supply the demanded services. A parallel and sub-rosa demimonde will exist, a distorted reflection of the legitimate structure, refracted by the impact of the control system itself. This is true whether the demand be for homosexual contacts, "relevant" education through Free Universities, marijuana, abortion, information on student activities (some universities have hired informants in student dorms, in radical groups, and in student activities), or textbooks.

The availability of services in *both* structures is apparently known to students as a part of their everyday/anyday lives, what Schutz calls the "common-sense reality of everyday life." [14] In a

[12] I have dealt with the strategy and tactics of the police as an attempt to manage the appearance of effective accomplishment of their mandate in "The Police: Mandate, Strategy and Appearances," in *Crime and Justice in American Society*, ed. Jack D. Douglas (Indianapolis: Bobbs-Merrill, 1971).

[13] Furthermore, students define the health and counseling centers as the allies of administration (which in fact they are); cf. Szasz's trenchant remarks on the role conflict of the campus psychiatrist, "The Psychiatrist as Double Agent," *Trans-Action 4* (October 1967): 16–24.

[14] Alfred Schutz, "Common-sense and Scientific Interpretation of Human Action," *The Collected Papers*, vol. I, ed. M. Natanson (The Hague: Martinus Nijhoff, 1964), pp. 3–47.

recent class survey, for example, 57 percent of the students surveyed said they could obtain an abortion for someone, or knew someone who could arrange it; 87 percent responded that they either "might be able," or knew "exactly who" to contact in order to obtain marijuana within a single day; 43 percent made the same claim about obtaining the "services" of a prostitute.[15] This testifies to the social distribution of knowledge, that is, the fact that although a high percentage of people are aware of the existence of various "deviant worlds," this awareness is differentially distributed in the social organization.

It is apparent also that the extent of overlap among these various social worlds, which exist insofar as interaction and shared meaning occurs, is an empirical question. The nature of deviancy and related knowledge is, of course, secretive and private; although many individuals may have such information, they do not know others also have it, nor do they routinely seek it. This is an example of "pluralistic ignorance." [16] The primary necessary condition for an abortion search by an unwed coed on a college campus is being pregnant. As a potentially discrediting and stigmatizing consequence of sexual relations, unwed pregnancy is a secret which is largely *unshareable* except with perhaps closest same-sex peers.

In the situation of the differential distribution of information comprising an *open network,*—that is, where people in contact with each other do not know all the others known by the people they know [17]—previous research suggests that information will take a "two-step flow" pattern from the information sources to "opinion leaders," in this case to knowledgeable persons within

15 Class Survey (N-35), MSU Fall Term, 1969.

16 The concept of pluralistic ignorance was first used by Floyd H. Allport, *Social Psychology* (Boston: Houghton Mifflin Co., 1924).

17 The term network has been redefined in several ways since its initial definition by Elizabeth Bott, ". . . a set of social relationships for which there is no common boundary," (*Family and Social Network* [London: Tavistock, 1967], p. 59. We follow a definition provided by Stebbins, ". . . ego's sustained orientation toward a particular alter which is perceived by ego to be reciprocated by alter." Networks should be seen as shared predispositions to act. See Robert Stebbins, "Social Network as a Subjective Construct: A New Application for an Old Idea," *Canadian Review of Sociology and Anthropology 6* (1969): 1–14, quote at p. 3.

the abortion infrastructure, and thence to the seekers or search-ers. It is my alternative contention that the network itself is *created* by the search, *located* by the searching, *defined* via the transactions carried on between the knowledgeable informants (referees), the abortionists and self-defined candidates, and begins to function as a result of the actor's involvement in it.[18]

This conceptualization of the nature of the "system" coin-cides with the notion of the differential social distribution of knowledge, the phenomenology of the actor, and the repressive action of the legitimate "helping agencies." The secretive nature of the information involved insures that the flow will by-pass the official control agents (dormitory assistants, housemothers, coun-selors, physicians and the health center) who are theoretically defined as linked into larger systems of help and nurturance.

WHAT IS FEARED: THE PREGNANCY

A majority of American females believe that intercourse and pregnancy ought to be reserved for marriage.[19] Most girls learn at a very early age to fear premarital conception. If pregnancy becomes a reality, however, several *logical* options are available, although the girl may not be aware of them, consider them, or take them into account at any point. The logical options shown in Figure 1 are behavioral alternatives for an initial set of preg-nant girls.

The most significant choice is between marriage, either to the biological father or another man, and nonmarriage. The de-

[18] Lee's work (*op. cit.*) distinguishes three levels of information relevant to the search for an abortionist. They are the *formal level* of mass media in-formation, factual articles on the existence of abortion as an alternative, etc. The second level is that of *gossip*, particular experiences of persons who com-municate to each other about these experiences. The third level of informa-tion comes about *as the search begins:* the search creates the information and makes it available to the searcher.

[19] This generalization collapses very important age, race and educational differences. For our population, it is a *very slight* majority: 55 percent of a sample of female college students believe in abstinence. I. L. Reiss, *The Social Contest of Premarital Sexual Permissiveness* (New York: Holt, Rinehart and Winston, 1967), Tables 2.6, 2.7.

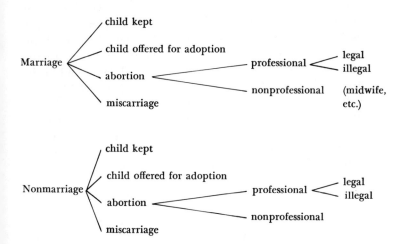

Figure 1. Logical Options for the Pregnant Coed

cision to marry follows pregnancy in 20 to 30 percent of all marriages, a fact suggested earlier by Kinsey's estimate that 50 percent of women are no longer virgins at the time of their marriage.[20] Among the married, most children are kept, some are aborted or lost through infant mortality, and very few are given up for adoption. Although it is estimated that the vast majority of abortions (200,000 to 1.2 million a year) are performed by physicians, until recently, only a small percentage of them were performed legally.[21] Among the unmarried, the order reverses, with most pregnancies unsanctioned by *ex post facto* weddings, being aborted, a large proportion of children born being given up for adoption, with a very small number being kept by mothers.[22] A decreasing number of abortions are apparently being performed in hospitals, a situation which changes in the laws in Colorado, Hawaii, Maryland, Washington, D. C., and North

[20] See Ronald Freedman and L. Coombs, "Childspacing and Family Economic Position," *American Sociological Review 31* (October 1966): 631–648. and Gebhard *et al., op. cit.*

[21] Lader, *op. cit.,* p. 22.

[22] Gebhard *et al., op. cit.,* cited in Lader, *op. cit.,* p. 59.

Carolina and New York may alter in time.[23] The inescapable conclusion is that abortion is both a flourishing and growing enterprise in response to a fairly inelastic demand in American society. Given the social costs of the stigma of public knowledge of an illegitimate child, the narrow range of acceptable legal reasons, the vast range of human situations and involvements which produce intercourse, and the isolation of most girls from official sources of support or medical care on a college campus, the path toward an abortionist is embarked upon regularly by large numbers of young women every day.

What is the medical definition of abortion?

> Abortion . . . is the induced termination of pregnancy before the normal fetus has attained viability, or the capacity for life outside the womb. The word applies only to *intentional* termination as opposed to *spontaneous* abortion, which occurs when fetal growth is impaired, and frequently referred to as *miscarriage*.

> The standard hospital technique of abortion is known as a dilation and curettage, or a "D and C." The patient, anesthetized to eliminate all pain, is protected against infection by antibiotics and rarely kept in the hospital for more than one night.

> First, the cervix is dilated or stretched to permit the use of curette . . . a tiny metal instrument shaped like a rake [with which] the surgeon . . . removes the embryo, alternating curette and forceps until the uterus is clean.

> If an abortion has to be performed after three months of pregnancy, the standard technique is a hysterotomy, or miniature cesarian, requiring a small, longitudinal incision in the lower abdomen.[24]

Lader reports that a D and C costs from $100 to $500 dollars depending on the social status of the patient and the hospital entered. A hysterotomy ranges from $200 to $500 dollars.[25] Reduced to medical terms, an abortion is a simple scraping of the uterine wall with a sharp instrument to remove pieces of live

[23] See Schur, *op. cit.,* pp. 14–22.
[24] Lader, *op. cit.,* p. 18.
[25] *Ibid.*

flesh full of blood during pregnancy and the source of nourishment for the unborn child. The same operation is performed routinely for correcting postmenopause blood-spotting and checking for uterine cancer. A hospital abortion is, ". . . one of the simplest and safest of all operations . . . it is safer to have a hospital abortion than to have a baby." [26]

The question of abortion is not exclusively medical but also a moral one, that is, under what conditions will this operation, and those on whom it is willingly performed by experienced people, be labeled "good" or "evil." An abortion is the consequence of biological processes, aleatory social processes, ecological factors, location in a social structure and a sequential process of transformation of self and other definitions.

In summary, the college campus provides the necessary social, ecological, and demographic conditions which "produce" pregnancies. It contains a system of social control which filters the larger conventional morality and acts to limit access to certain demanded services to some categories of persons and stigmatizes and criminalizes their behavior. The consequent infrastructure is a secret one, maintained as such as a result of the nature of the knowledge shared and by pluralistic ignorance. The infrastructure is "unknown" or "invisible" until a search begins. Following a description of the methodology employed, we will discuss the girls' view of the contingencies of the search.

METHODS AND TECHNIQUES

Several of my students wrote descriptions of their own or others' experiences in abortion-seeking, the "abortion subculture," or attempted abortions.[27] In connection with these papers and in the course of later research, ten informal interviews were gathered with girls who had undergone abortions.[28] One student sim-

26 *Ibid.,* pp. 17–18.

27 I would like to thank Quent Reader, Mary Ellen Carlin, Judith Dauer Wickline, and Ann Shaw for writing these papers and several other students who provided me with suggestions for carrying out the research.

28 These protocols were gathered by the persons listed in note 27.

ulated the role of a pregnant coed over a three-month period.[29]
We constructed a simple but durable "cover story." She was pregnant by a boyfriend (her actual boyfriend was known to be off
campus) and was looking for leads to an abortionist. In most public conversations she claimed that she was looking for an abortion
for a friend, a credible cliché story which was used to protect her
own self-esteem during the course of the study.

Embarking on the study, she shared feelings of mixed fear,
guilt and anxiety expressed by the interviewed girls.

> My first difficulty was the threat of rumor. Because I live in a
> sorority house with forty other girls, the possibility of rumor of me
> actually being pregnant was always present. Although this rumor
> was not a tremendous threat to my self-concept, it was a unique
> situation in which to find myself. Another problem that I en-
> countered in my study was the fact that some people that I knew
> had abortion contacts were reluctant to talk with me. . . . I knew
> two people that had assisted other girls in obtaining abortions. I
> naturally felt that these girls would be excellent sources of informa-
> tion. Unfortunately, when these people discovered that I was doing
> an abortion study, they were hesitant to talk with me or give me
> the names of their contacts.

At first, she was afraid to raise the topic in conversation; she felt
that if she was too open with her problem of being pregnant and
seeking an abortionist she would diminish the verisimilitude of
the experiment. That is, she felt that a pregnant coed would not
indeed be so open with friends. So, she tried another tact.

> I assumed that a pregnant girl would first attempt to gain a lead
> to an abortionist through friends that she knew had received an
> abortion or that had knowledge of an abortionist. Later in my
> study I realized that if I were to make a sufficient number of abor-
> tion contacts . . . I would be forced to more open discussion of
> my problem with larger groups of people.

---

[29] I would like to thank Ann Shaw for this heroic duty. In addition, she
served as general research assistant on the project. She handled the embarrassment and rumor with great sophistication. One of the discoveries we made
was that if one claims to be looking for an abortion for a "friend" the statement is suitably ambiguous to protect oneself and at the same time permit
others to feel compelled to help. It is not clear whether they "really" believed
the story or not.

From that time on, she began to talk with friends and acquaintances about sexual behavior on campus, specifically about pregnancies and abortions. From these unthreatening situations, she obtained many leads.[30]

Our aim was to "replicate" a portion of the Lee study (see footnote 1) based on a question which asked the women to list persons they had asked for information on how to arrange an abortion, or for the address of an abortionist. Lee asked each girl to describe her relationship to each person named, why they were chosen and what help they provided.[31] After arrangements were made, that is, an appointment made to see the physician, my colleague called and cancelled, explaining that she and her boyfriend had decided to be married.

She sought contacts leading to an abortionist and kept field notes on the social chains (contacts and those to whom she was referred). Her procedure was to follow a chain until it terminated or until she was able to make an appointment with an abortionist. The fieldworker kept careful field notes on each person asked who was able to provide information which lead further. For each contact, one of three outcomes was possible: (1) a facilitating lead going directly to an abortionist, (2) a facilitating lead which led to another person in the chain, which kept it "alive," or (3) a terminal person, or "dead end." All the persons who were not terminal initially (an unfortunate loss of data, for it is clear that in this study there were many such names) were recorded. Each set of contacts was considered a social chain. A completed social chain was one in which contact was made with an abortionist, or more specifically where an appointment was made for her to see the abortionist. An incomplete social chain was one which terminated after at least one lead and which did not result in an appointment.[32]

---

[30] She found that many people, especially males, felt somehow obligated to present a facade of knowledge when asked for abortion-relevant information. Many of the leads she received in such situations were false.

[31] See Lee, *op. cit.*, p. 177, Appendix. The entire questionnaire is reproduced in this appendix.

[32] See Lee's very original and interesting development of the idea of a social chain from which these ideas are drawn, *op. cit.*, chs. 5 and 8.

THE SEARCH

Our data are limited on some of the stages and are more adequate on others. Our most definitive facts bear upon the actual search for and contacting of an abortionist. Four stages were discovered using the interview materials, through the simulated search by a girl posing as a "pregnant coed," and in the very important work of Nancy Howell Lee: *The Search for an Abortionist,* Chicago: The University of Chicago Press, 1969. Each stage takes as a focus the *essential feature* of that stage: (1) The initial defining process (What does it mean?), (2) Constructing alternatives (What does on do?), (3) Contacting help (How to do it?), and (4) A resolution of the search (When is it over?).

The Initial Defining Process

Conception results within a diversity of male-female relationships. The focus of this stage is on the recognition of the signs of pregnancy *after* conception. Since most women normally menstruate approximately every twenty-eight days, failure to menstruate as expected is usually the first clue. This initial defining process seems to take place within two weeks after the failure is first noticed. At that point, girls begin to question their normalization of the sign. Some of the girls mentioned that it was an almost everyday thought since they had begun regular intercourse. The irregularity of their periods made it difficult for a few girls to detect pregnancy with certainty.

The critical feature of transforming the problem of a missed period into pregnancy involves an actionable definition, or a conception of the signs as indications of pregnancy. To some extent, this hinges on the tendency for the woman at this point to focus upon her body, as one autobiographical account reported: ". . . obsessed as I was with the world within me." This same account suggests that some girls experience very little uncertainty at this time, transforming the signs almost immediately into pregnancy:

> I suppose it was terrible most of all because it was a time of such uncertainty, of waiting. Though what uncertainty? I knew I was pregnant, just as I never thought I was when I wasn't. My body

told me. My breasts. Everywhere. My skin. The heaviness throughout. Running to the john. The feeling of containing the whole
world in my belly.[33]

The action implications of an unwanted pregnancy arose from
the usual feeling that the girl was not prepared or willing to em-
bark on motherhood (all of the girls were unmarried and none
planned to marry the father at the time). This closed off half the
alternatives listed in the tree in Figure 1, leaving abortion, legal
or illegal, bearing the child for adoption, or keeping the child.

Searching for an abortion is a time-bound process. Nancy
Howell Lee summarizes the problem:

> Whether or not the abortion seekers are aware of it, there is an
> effective time limit operating on the search for an abortionist.
> Most abortionists refuse to accept cases in which the pregnancy is
> advanced beyond the twelfth week, when induced abortions be-
> come more difficult and dangerous to perform. Since the pregnancy
> shows no signs before two weeks, and is rarely confirmed before
> five or six weeks, those seeking abortion usually have less than six
> weeks in which to make a decision, locate the abortionist, raise
> whatever money is necessary, and have the abortion carried out.[34]

The stage of defining the signs as pregnancy is often followed by a period of very high anxiety. This is the point of re-
constructing the meaning of the act of intercourse, the girl's
identity and self, and projecting the possible consequences of an
abortion. Following the narrowing of the meanings of the pregnancy, the second stage of constructing alternatives begins.

Constructing Alternatives

The central problem of this stage is "What to do?" The immediate social environment of friends and medical services is critical.
One of the girls who obtained an abortion at a Rocky Mountain
Women's College with a reputation as a liberal arts school for
daughters of fairly wealthy families reported:

---

[33] "I didn't have the baby, I had the abortion," in Charles H. McCaghy,
James K. Skipper, Jr., and Mark Lefton, eds., *In Their Own Behalf: Voices
From the Margin* (New York: Appleton-Century-Crofts, 1968), p. 12.

[34] Lee, *op. cit.*, pp. 6–7.

The health center at this school is equipped with birth control devices of all types, free of charge, and one of the doctors will give abortions provided that the girls have enough money. This is a perfect set-up for an abortionist—rich girls who are able and willing to pay almost anything to keep their families from finding out. [She] had a very expensive abortion and ended up having to get a part of the money for it from parents and from [the interviewer].

In contrast, as stated previously, the Midwestern university campus on which this research was conducted is unwilling to take responsibility for pregnant coeds, married or unmarried, abortion aside. Students know the pill is available on campus from one or two of the health service doctors, but there is no public policy making contraceptive information generally available. The counseling center and the health center are defined as agents of the administration, and as one girl put it, "Everyone knows that if you go to the Counseling Center, everyone can get at your records."

In this situation, the health center sees primarily "miscarriages," or self-induced abortions.[35] Only one of the girls reported going to the campus health center for either verification of the pregnancy or for other medical examination.

The construction of alternatives eliminates help from local sources, and makes an open possibility of the search outside or on the campus. The alternatives possible emerge from the *interpersonal networks* in which the girls were implicated. These are in turn patterned by the relationships of the girl to her peers, to those from whom she wished to conceal the pregnancy and her intentions, and her relationship to the biological father. We are concerned with the subjective interpersonal networks in which the girls were implicated, following Stebbins' definition.[36] An in-

---

[35] One physician with whom I was discussing this study said, "I hope that you'll interview some of the girls we get coming in here bleeding after abortion attempts."

[36] See Stebbins, *op. cit.* This definition is ambiguous enough to include sociometric choices, actual interactions, and normative or idealized statements. In other words, the meanings of the relationships to participants is not a necessary part of the definition. These networks should be distinguished from the networks which radiate out from the abortionist into a potential population.

terpersonal network, in brief, is a subjective and expanded version of the definition of the situation which takes into account the ways in which it comes to mediate, for a *group* of linked persons, the "social structure" of objective social facts.

We discovered, in line with this sensitizing construct, that the informal identities which patterned the networks were not random.[37] Most central in this stage were the father and close female friends. The supportive nature of the father was not clearcut in our small sample, but female friends, the most important members of the girl's social network, were central and supportive. All but two of the women in the Lee sample obtained abortions (two induced their own), which suggests that the unanimity of opinion which they found among those consulted is probably a necessary condition to the accomplishing of abortion.[38] Unfortunately, there is no comparative data for women who fail, women who choose other alternatives, or women who decide to keep the child.[39]

However, from the general comments of the girls and the literature, it is clear that the major networks are those based on the female sex-role. Specifically, the girl is defined as the locus of social control in the dating and courtship situation, while the male is expected to be the "aggressor." The double standard surrounds both the control and stigmatizing processes: pregnancy is seen as the result of the female's failure to take precautions, as her unwillingness to protect herself, as a wish for self-destruction, and so forth.[40] As Vincent pithily observes: "The female tends to *use sex* (or sex enticements, in the larger sense) *as a means*—to dates, companionship, an expense account, upward mobility, and possible marriage. The male tends to date, provide the companionship, pay the bills, court, express love—*as a means to sex.*[41]

[37] Lee, *op. cit.*, Table 14, p. 55.

[38] *Ibid.*

[39] The most useful data are found in Vincent, *op. cit.*

[40] Coeds who are sexually assaulted are often unwilling to report these events in part because they suggest the failure of the female to control the male and are threatening to her self-esteem, C. Kirkpatrick and E. Kanin, "Male Sex Aggression on a University Campus," *American Sociological Review* 22 (February 1957): 52–58.

[41] Vincent, *op. cit.*, p. 78.

The outcome of these bargains, when they result in unwed pregnant girls, make visible several aspects of the sexual mores of the society. The total effect in the case of the abortion search is potential stigmatization of both the male and the female in the broader "normative context." Vincent perceptively summarizes this state of affairs in his evaluation of the *ex post facto* label of "exploiter" applied to the male:

> . . . the *ex post facto* description of the unmarried father as an exploiter is less a censuring of his *sexual misbehavior* (since it is primarily the female's responsibility to avoid illicit sexual unions), and more a censuring of his *role misbehavior*—i.e., his failure to assume the traditional masculine role of protecting the female. Having illicit sexual relations and becoming pregnant are primarily the. female's "areas of fault." Failing to protect her and not shielding her from shame (by marrying her) when she becomes pregnant are primarily the male's "areas of fault." [42]

Responses of the girls regarding the role of the male in the definitional and search stage ranged from being very supportive, providing money, arranging the entire matter, being moderately supportive, to total removal from the situation. Most of the men involved apparently, however, were helpful, especially as indicated by the continuity of the relationships after the abortion.

The identities of the female frequently constrain her from consulting other people who might be of aid and comfort, especially parents. Most of the girls felt that this fact, along with money, was the most difficult aspect of the entire experience.[43] Some girls in this study, however, were assisted by their parents.

The actual search for help began as the result of a drift into a situation which was defined as having no other solution.

Contacting Help

The central problem of this stage is "How do I do it?" It parallels the problem faced by anyone with a self-defined problem with which he seeks to cope, whether it be medical, legal, social,

---

[42] *Ibid.*, p. 81.
[43] Lee, *op. cit.*, pp. 141–142.

or religious. Recent studies of the relationships between self-defined significant problems and requests for professional help clearly show that a wide range of intermediate processes often unrelated to professional definitions of seriousness and need pattern the use of services.[44] Location in a *social structure* (class, race, culture, ethnicity), *resources* and the *type of problem* pattern help-seeking. In the case of the search for clandestine services, the added dimension of immorality or illegality also patterns the process. The control of service by the legal restriction of access restricts information.

Lee estimates that the distribution of abortion-relevant knowledge is quite widespread. Yet, because of the attrition of the information (abortionists move, retire, are imprisoned, desist, and die) and the unwillingness of some people to discuss such matters with others, Lee estimates that very few women actually have useful information which will lead another to an abortion.[45] Conversations with students and fieldwork by others suggests that knowledge about abortion and abortionists is a case of "pluralistic ignorance." There is a fair amount of knowledge distributed among students, but they are unaware of the extent of others' knowledge. Several of the fieldworkers in this study remarked about this. They were consistently surprised at how easy it was to acquire "abortion-relevant" information from friends, relatives, and professors. They thought they were among a few people sensitive to these facts. Each persons sees himself as having private, personal information, unshared, and perhaps of little use to his "moral" friends. The results of the simulated search for an abortionist in this study suggest that the problem of attrition does not exist in an acute form on this campus. Lee's description of a "successful searcher" aptly fits the girls interviewed as well as the "pregnant coed" who undertook the search: ". . . socially

[44] See E. Freidson, "Client Control of Medical Practice," *American Journal of Sociology* 65 (January 1960): 374–382; I. K. Zola, "Culture and Symptoms," *American Sociological Review* 31 (October 1966): 615–630; and Charles Kadushin, "The Friends and Supporters of Psychotherapy: On Social Circles in Urban Life," *American Sociological Review* 31 (December 1966): 786–802. A good summary is Mechanic's *Medical Sociology* (New York: Free Press, 1968).

[45] Lee, *op. cit.*, ch. 8.

skillful women with contacts with a wide range of people who accept abortion as legitimate, who don't all know each other and who had previous experience with abortion, should find it fairly easy to arrange a satisfactory abortion." [46] One of the girls who interviewed others who had had abortions summarized her five interviews:

> In view of the fact that all of the girls to whom I spoke are college coeds, I can speak with a great deal more authority as to how contacts are made [with an abortionist] and how the arrangements are carried out. I would like to make it quite clear that it is relatively easy to find a girl who has the name of an abortionist.

The girl who assumed the role of the pregnant coed set out to perform a "natural experiment" to investigate several features of the abortion search, two of which are discussed in this stage— the *availability* of abortion services and the *time* it takes to make the arrangements which make an actual abortion a near certainty.

Lee found that more than half the women found an abortionist within a chain having less than two intermediaries (mean = 2.83, median = 2.0).[47] The results of this study, involving only eight chains, are shown in Table 1.

The three completed chains in this study all involved physicians in a nearby metropolis, confirming the myth and Lee's findings that "the abortionist is out of town." [48] All of the girls interviewed in this study had abortions performed out of town in such widespread sites as Baltimore, Maryland, Chicago, Illinois and Detroit and Ann Arbor, Michigan.

The circumstances of the first completed chain (#4) demonstrate that, with some luck, it is actually quite easy for a person

---

[46] Nancy Howell Lee, "Acquaintance Networks in the Social Structure of Abortion," published as Lee, *op. cit.*, Harvard University Department of Social Relations, Ph.D. dissertation, 1968, p. 185. One of my colleagues, confronted with a student who claimed he could not take a final exam because he had been thus far unable to arrange an abortion for his girlfriend, decided to try himself to locate an abortionist within twenty-four hours. At the time he had no prior clues. He succeeded.

[47] Lee, *ibid.*, Table 17, p. 69.

[48] Lee, *ibid.*, p. 94.

TABLE 1. SOCIAL CHAINS DISCOVERED IN THE SIMULATED ABORTION SEARCH

1. Girl Friend 1⟶ Her Husband (Termination: refused to ask a friend due to a confidential relationship)

2. Girl Friend 1⟶ Her Husband (Termination: friend at work *was* asked, but quit coming to work)

3. Male Student 1⟶ Male Student 2⟶ His brother (Termination: no longer knew the phone number or contact)

4. Girl Friend 2⟶ Dr. A. *Completed Chain*

5. Girl Friend 3⟶ Girl Friend 2⟶ Dr. A. *Completed Chain*

6. Professor ⟶ Female Classmate ⟶ Male Contact ⟶ Dr. B. *Completed Chain*

7. Professor ⟶ Female Classmate (same as in #6) ⟶ Male Contact (Dennis Day) ⟶ Investigator ⟶ Girl Friend 4⟶ Male Contact (Dennis Day) ⟶ Dr. B. *Completed Chain* (A check on Chain # 6, reported in full in Appendix A)

8. Male Student 3⟶ Male Student 4 (Termination: did not have the expected information)

The investigator, Ann Shaw, was the initiator in each case.

without abortion knowledge to locate the necessary information in time of need:

> . . . I was discussing my problem with my friend C——. She listened with interest as I told her about the study. Then she told me that she had the name of a [large metropolitan area] doctor that would perform abortions. She explained that all that was necessary was to make an appointment with him, and bring a sufficient amount of money to cover the cost of the operation. I followed this contact by calling the doctor's office only to discover that the doctor did not accept appointments but took patients as they came.

Chains 4 and 5 resulted in appointments with the same doctor. While talking to another friend about her problem, she received the name of the same doctor. She later discovered they had both obtained it from the same mutual friend, C——.

The average number of people involved in obtaining the appointment in the case of the completed chains was close to the Lee estimate of two to three. It may be somewhat easier to obtain an abortion on a college campus with a high rate of interaction and movement. One chain was completed in five days, following a lead I encountered, which I then forwarded. The fieldworker obtained the name of a person who was the intermediary for a physician on the following day, Friday, and she was able to set an appointment for an abortion on the following Monday. Chain 4 is more difficult to discuss since the doctor took people on a first-come-first-served basis. According to interviews, there are two types: the long search, often out of state, and the relatively easy search, leading to the closest urban area or one of its satellite cities. Of course, the major factor may well be the time involved, if travel is necessary. The local problem pregnancy clinic which advises some girls to obtain abortions after interviews, has arrangements for girls in London and passes out an instruction sheet. There are also rumors that local travel agencies can arrange an abortion trip in either Japan or Sweden.

A further question addressed by fieldwork and relevant to contacting help, was the possible existence of an "abortion subculture," similar to the hippy or drug subcultures on campus and existing at large. It was expected, because of the demand for the service, the possibly large numbers of young men and women on the campus who had been through the search themselves or with or for others, and the prohibition of service at the Health Center, that a "shadow world" of this sort might exist. No evidence bears out this hunch.

Lee discovered a number of women whom she calls "abortion specialists," women who because of political-ideological reasons or because of their own extensive experiences had established lists of names for assisting abortion-seekers. These persons served as links between the abortionist and the searcher. Several such persons were discovered in the course of the research, one being a student in my deviance class.

Although these abortion specialists exist, they are not a subculture for they are unknown to each other, and probably they do not even constitute a network. There is no evidence of an abortion subculture with shared values, norms, interaction patterns and roles growing out of a shared problem. The network is mobilized virtually anew by each searcher. Although the research did not address this question, it is likely that pluralistic ignorance insulates against widespread information diffusion. Further, the transitory and "unique" nature of the event, for young college girls at least, may allow them to insulate themselves sufficiently so that they do not define themselves as being deviant. That is, they do not view themselves as having a deviant character, but only as committing a deviant act which does not lead to a change in substantial self.[49]

Once a firm contact is made, the conditions necessary for the resolution of the search have been fulfilled.

The Resolution of the Search

The search can be resolved in a number of ways.[50] Our interest is in "fixing what you feared," a search which culminated in an abortion, where the end was recognized when the operation was completed.

Contacting an abortionist seems to be a middle-class matter; that is, most abortions, legal or illegal, are performed on middle-class women.[51] Consequently, the impression conveyed to women is one of respectability justified with the medical rhetoric.[52]

[49] A substantial self is the totality of the individual's self-evaluations while a situated self is a self-evaluation which does not extend beyond limited interactional encounter. See Jack Douglas, *The Social Meanings of Suicide* (Princeton: Princeton University Press, 1967), pp. 280–283. For an analysis of changes in self and identity, including attention to the relationship between substantial and situated self, see Donald W. Ball, "Self and Identity in the Context of Deviance: The Case of Criminal Abortion" in *Perspectives on Deviance*, ed. Robert Scott and Jack Douglas (New York: Basic Books, forthcoming).

[50] It is quite possible that a study could develop comparisons of "successful" and "unsuccessful" seekers, those who failed at the last minute, those who decided to marry, those who gave up and had the child, etc. These are all resolutions.

[51] See Schur, *op. cit.*, pp. 21–22, and Lee, *op. cit.*, pp. 28–29.

[52] See Donald W. Ball, "An Abortion Clinic Ethnography," *Social Problems 14* (Winter, 1967): 293–301, and Schur, *ibid.*, pp. 32–33.

Physicians contacted by interviewers and by the fieldworker engaged in tactics which allowed the impression of respectability to be fostered and which, at the same time, protected them from legal difficulties. One physician, according to an informant, works exclusively out of the university studied. The first step involved in reaching him is to telephone. It is not sufficient to talk to his nurse; the physician himself must talk with each girl. If the girl makes the mistake of mentioning the word "abortion," or anything suggesting it, such as being "in trouble," the doctor promptly hangs up the phone. Once the doctor comes to the phone, the coed must identify herself as a student at ——— University with "a problem." She must then make an appointment to see the doctor. Once there, the operation is carried out in the office.

In another reported case, the girl simply had to call the doctor's office and explain to the nurse, who is involved in the abortion practice, that she has a problem similar to "Sue's problem," a girl known to the coed and the physician as one of his abortion patients. The word "abortion" is never used, but the nurse is alerted by the word "problem." When the potential client comes to the physician, she explains in his office that she desires an abortion. Another physician followed the pattern of the first, but simply asked women to come in and have the abortion performed that same day in the office.

Another physician maintained a contact man who gathered by phone the following information from girls requesting an abortion: hometown, age, student status, student number, estimated length of time pregnant, date of last period, reaction to any drugs, access to money, address, phone number, and a tentative date for meeting the contact man. In the case of contact with the "pregnant coed," (Chains 6 and 7), whenever hesitation or fear was expressed, the contact man was reassuring. He claimed that the doctor he represented was the only person in the area who could provide the service, claimed that the physician performed safely over 200 abortions a year and was a skilled, professionally trained gynecologist. When the girl persisted in asking questions, he became very authoritarian, asserting forcefully the value and high quality of the service. The second or "checking" exchange (Chain 7) with this contact man was very revealing, and is contained in full in an appendix.

When the appointment was made with this physician, the exact location was kept from the girl until the day of the operation. Although she was to undergo the operation at 8:00 P.M. Monday, the contact man explained that he would not inform her of the meeting place until 5:30 P.M. that day. Although the boyfriend would be permitted to take her to the location, he would not be allowed further after the first rendezvous. A similar ritual is reported in the autobiographical account mentioned above. Secrecy was an aspect of all the arrangements of which we are aware.

The cost of the abortions quoted or rumored on the campus ranged from $80 (midwife) to $300 as quoted by several persons, and one at $450.[53] On two occasions, a figure of $700 to $750 was quoted to the fieldworker (Chains 6 and 7). She commented on this: "I feel that perhaps the high cost of the services . . . could be explained by the fact that I told [the doctor's contact man] that money would be no problem. Thus, he called back the next day to inform me that the operation would cost between $700 and $750." The same figure was quoted the second time it was mentioned that money would not be a problem. This indicates that prices are on a sliding scale and that the contact man is free to obtain his fee at whatever level the traffic will bear.

The concern of this preliminary report is not the actual abortion; however, some of the after-effects of the abortion are relevant to the search, and a possible contribution to the study of deviant behavior. The two most common problems were those of the perceived illegality of the act and facing friends who were informed of the search.

Although there was acute awareness of the illegality of the operation they underwent, there was very little guilt feeling among the girls interviewed. With few exceptions, they had *neutralized* the effect of the abortion and felt that it was the

[53] Lee cites a range of $60 to $1,150, with a mean of around $300, *op. cit.*, Table 26, p. 92.

only expedient thing to do under the circumstances.[54] There seemed to be little psychological effect on the girls, although they only discuss it with their close friends (the time since the abortion varied from one to two years). None of them expressed the feeling that they were "deviants." Several girls who were contacted in the course of the study who were "abortion specialists" likewise felt no stigma as a result of their having helped other girls to obtain needed help in times of crisis. These are limited generalizations, tentatively advanced, that need to be further explored. They do, however, suggest the need for a greater precision in the study of labeling of self and others and the conditions under which it occurs, when it is effective, and when it can be neutralized.[55]

No women were found who reacted in a political fashion, that is, reacting and defining abortion as a political act as described by Lee.[56] Lee obtained her sample by leaving the questionnaires in planned parenthood offices, obtaining assistance from advocates of abortion law reform and through birth control clinics. Consequently, she may have attracted women with political definitions for their acts.

SUMMARY AND CONCLUDING REMARKS

An abortion is the product of concerted social action which makes an "invisible service" available. The nature of abortion is not determined solely by biology or medicine but by the interdigitation of social, biological, and legal facts and social-psychological definitions and meanings. This preliminary report, drawing on the natural history approach, suggests several areas requiring further research. The lack of legal medical services on

---

[54] On neutralization, see Gresham Sykes and David Matza, "Techniques of Neutralization: A Theory of Delinquency," *American Sociological Review* 22 (December 1957): 664–670, and James M. Henslin, "Guilt and Guilt Neutralization: Response and Adjustment to Suicide," in *Deviance and Respectability*, ed. Jack D. Douglas (New York: Basic Books, 1970), pp. 192–228.

[55] I have addressed this issue theoretically in *Explaining Deviance* (New York: Random House, forthcoming).

[56] *Op. cit.*, pp. 111–112.

the campus and the campus system of social control produce a "shadow world" of services which can be tapped. Although an abortion subculture does not exist on this campus, a number of "abortion specialists" apparently do, and there is no appreciable difficulty in obtaining an abortion if the seeker is diligent, skillful and a bit lucky. Some women may have resources, social, psychological or economic, which insultate them against a deviant self-conception in the face of their illegal actions, that is, having an abortion. It may be that although abortion-relevant knowledge is secret (not widely shared) except in crisis, giving it is a sign of social support for the searcher and thus insulates her from stigma. From the point of view of those who provide the information it may be considered immoral not to provide information which will prevent further stigmatizing consequences. An abortion may be seen as less "deviant" than bearing an illegitimate child. The nature of the information flow itself may be *protective*—for by giving the information one admits to himself that not sharing secret knowledge would create even additional "deviant" consequences. The abortion is a lesser evil. The exchange of information also affirms to the searcher that she is being supported in an expedient journey which may minimize her exposure to further stigmatizing reaction. Perhaps because of the secrecy of information, the "normal" causes of the pregnancy, and the lack of public labeling, this is a useful example of "situational deviance." These questions require further exploration within the context of "labeling theory," a partial framework for this paper.

APPENDIX

Case Study of Social Chain Number 7

by Ann Shaw

As I was interested in studying the uniformity of the techniques of a contact man involved in an abortion referral network, I decided to repeat the contact process of social chain number 6. In order that the contact man would not recognize any similarities between my connections with him last spring and this term, I asked my roommate, Mary Smith, to call him and ask for an abortion under the assumed name of Cindy Kampman, while I listened to the conversation on another extension.

First Conversation—Thursday afternoon.

Mary asked to speak with Dennis Day. Male on other end of line acted slightly confused, and then repeated the name "Dennis Day" in order to make sure that the caller was sure with whom she wanted to speak. He then said "yes" as if Mary was to explain her reason for calling. When Mary explained that she would speak with no one but Dennis Day, the male said that he was Dennis Day. Mary explained that she was Cindy Kampman and she had been referred to him by Ann Shaw. She said that she needed an abortion. Dennis asked Mary to halt for a moment. He left the phone, came back, and asked her to start over (as if he were writing down all the information). Mary repeated that she was Cindy Kampman and that she was from Flint. Dennis then recalled Ann Shaw (girl who decided to get married). He then asked Mary if Ann had told her anything about the price of the operation. Mary said money was no problem but she thought that Ann had said about $750. Dennis agreed and repeated "money no problem" (as if writing it on information sheet). Next he inquired about her student status. She explained that she was a student at ——— and enrolled in summer school. He asked her student number. When Mary gave only five numbers (a mistake), he said that the number could not be her real number. Mary said she would rather not give her number. He then asked if she were definitely a ——— student, and asked if she were living in "Collegeville" this summer. Mary answered "yes" to these questions. He asked her how far along she was. Mary said "two months." He asked if she were allergic to any drugs—"No." Mary then questioned him about the physical dangers. Dennis explained that it would be a safe D and C. He asked how soon she would like the operation. Mary said "Monday or Tuesday." Dennis said that he would have to make the arrangements and call her the following day. When Mary suggested 9:00 A.M., he said that 9:00 A.M. would not give him enough time. It was agreed that 2:00 P.M. would be the best time. Mary gave him her phone number.

Second Conversation—Friday 9:00 A.M.

Dennis called and asked for Cindy. I answered and said that she would not be back until 2:00 P.M. He questioned my relationship to Cindy. I said that I was Sandy, her roommate. He then became very authoritarian and asked if Cindy were indeed a student of ——— this summer. I said she was only carrying a few credits and perhaps wasn't listed in the student directory. He said he would call back at 2:00 P.M.

As Mary became frightened, it was decided that I would talk to Dennis at 2:00 P.M.

Third Conversation—Friday 2:00 P.M.

Dennis called and asked for Cindy. I explained that Cindy was frightened and would not talk with him. He then said with a tone of authority that he knew that Cindy Kampman was a fictitious name and no such student had ever been enrolled in ———. I said that she had given a false name because of her fear and embarrassment. Also, I explained that I was sure that his real name was not Dennis Day. At this point he became very upset and said that he could not offer his services unless we were honest with him. He said that in this type of operation "security measures" must be very tight. I agreed, but said that I hoped that he could understand Cindy's feelings and position. He agreed, but said that he must have a name of someone he could trust. He did not really care about Cindy's name, but he did need one reliable name—such as Ann Shaw. He then questioned me about Ann Shaw; that is, was Ann a real person, did she marry, where did she now live? He explained that if he really wanted to know Cindy's real name, he could easily discover under whose name the phone was listed. After this he lowered his voice to its normal tone and explained that "they" were the only people in the ——— area who could offer such services. Everything else was closed down. He reported that this abortion would be done by a registered gynecologist who performed over 200 abortions per year. He explained that "they" were in the position to turn people down. Also, he had previously only had one other case of an untruthful applicant. I said "Cindy was her real name and that she was still interested." He agreed to talk with her Monday—but she must tell the truth.

Because of the fear that Dennis might discover that the phone was listed under Ann Shaw, it was decided not to extend this social chain to its most complete stage. It was agreed that I would call him Monday and explain that Cindy did not wish to go through with the abortion.

Monday 6:00 P.M.

I called home of Dennis Day—no answer.

Fourth Conversation—Monday 7:00 P.M.

Dennis called and asked for Cindy. Sam, Mary's cousin, answered and explained that Cindy was not home. He did not talk with Dennis as he did not know what he was supposed to say.

Before the next conversation with Dennis Day another call came to our apartment. The male voice asked for ———, Mary's nickname and ——— (our other roommate). When Sam said that both girls were away the male caller said that he was Dennis and would call back. At this point we were very much afraid that Dennis knew our real names and our apartment address. Therefore, it was decided that Sam would call Dennis Day. (One week after this incident we were informed by our old friend Dennis, an old neighbor, that he had called Monday evening. Thus, it was our friend Dennis, and not Dennis Day).

Fifth Conversation—Monday 8:00 P.M.

Sam called and asked to speak with Dennis Day. Dennis answered that he was Dennis Day. Sam explained that he had not talked with him on the earlier call as he had been confused by the names of the "dames" he had mentioned. Sam said he did not know them. Sam went on to explain that he was Cindy's boyfriend and that they had decided not to go through with the operation. Dennis said, "They called me, I didn't call them." Sam replied, "O.K., Goodbye."

SEX BY FORCE

Forcible Rape: A Comparative Study of Offenses Known to the Police in Boston and Los Angeles

DUNCAN CHAPPELL, GILBERT GEIS,
STEPHEN SCHAFER, LARRY SIEGEL

This paper represents an attempt to examine and to interpret a random sample of cases of forcible rape known to the police in Boston and Los Angeles, two cities which generally are regarded as supporting quite distinct styles of life. The ethos of Boston, for instance, is said by John Gunther to be epitomized in the act of a censor who insisted that a line in the play *Life With Father* be changed from "Oh, God," to "Oh, fudge." Gunther notes further of Boston that "There is nothing in the country to rival it for a kind of lazy dignity, intellectual affluence and spaciousness, and above all a wonderful acquired sense of responsibility for its own past. Of course, it suggests rather than overstates. Indeed, the quality of understatement characterizes much in Boston life." [1]

Los Angeles, on the other hand, appeared to Gunther in his cross-country tour of America to be an area of "petroleum, crazy religious cults, the citrus industry, towns based on rich *rentiers,* the movies, the weirdest architecture in the United States, refugees from Iowa, a steeply growing Negro population, and devotees of funny money." [2] In Los Angeles, according to the

[1] John Gunther, *Inside U.S.A.* (New York: Harper & Brothers, 1951), p. 518.
[2] *Ibid.,* p. 4.

anthropologist Ashley Montagu, "the very fact that the sun shines continuously, that the air is warm, comfortable, and only occasionally cold, attracts individuals who are interested primarily in creature comforts." [3] Montagu remarks, in a piece of rhetoric not unrelated to alleged precursors of the criminal offense of forcible rape, that "a high positive correlation is likely to exist between a devotion to physical comforts and a lack of interest in the spirit, the essential qualities of humanity." [4]

The comparative focus of the present paper is designed to circumvent the more elementary pitfalls inherent in investigations confined to a localized geographic area. The literature of criminology is replete with illustrations of generalizations confined in space which fall asunder when extrapolated onto an alien scene. Thus, for instance, we have on a simple level the perplexing conclusion of Wolfgang, on the basis of a Philadelphia study, that murders are committed primarily by stabbing,[5] a conclusion strikingly different from that of Morris, whose study, conducted at about the same time, found that in Boston shooting was the method of homicide more often used than all other means combined.[6] Simultaneous and coordinated study might readily have cleared up questions regarding whether the divergent findings represent variations in definition or data collection or whether they are the product of differing patterns of criminal homicide. If the latter were true, further efforts could have been directed toward an explanation of the inconsistency.

In a similar, and rather more important, vein, Cohen ques-

[3] Ashley Montagu, *The American Way of Life* (New York: G. P. Putnam's Sons, 1966), p. 190.

[4] *Ibid.* Further notation of the point is readily available. For instance: "Though no one has really done a thorough investigation of the matter, the casualness about sex . . . is said to permeate large segments of Los Angeles society" (Howard S. Becker, "Deviance and Deviates," *The Nation 201* [September 20, 1965]: 119). And observe the free associational antithesis between Boston and Los Angeles by a psychiatrist discussing draft evasion: "Life in Canada cannot be that different from life in the United States. While Toronto is different from Boston, it is probably less different than Los Angeles is . . ." (Willard Gaylin, *In the Service of their Country: War Resisters in Prison* [New York: The Viking Press, 1970], p. 5).

[5] Marvin E. Wolfgang, *Patterns in Criminal Homicide* (Philadelphia: University of Pennsylvania Press, 1958), pp. 83–84.

[6] Albert Morris, *Homicide* (Boston: Boston University Press, 1955), p. 15.

tions some of the interpretative conclusions of studies of juvenile gang behavior in the United States by noting that foreign research indicates that gangs, as they are known in America, are rare in Italy and that, where such gangs do exist, they seldom attack other adolescents, but rather direct their activities against adults. "If this is true," Cohen suggests, "the tendency for delinquents to coalesce into gangs and for gangs to war on other gangs, so common in our country, is not necessarily implicit in the idea of delinquency." [7] As a final and fundamental illustration, we might note the skepticism expressed by English criminologists regarding widely supported programs for reducing crime in the United States. Such programs concentrate on alleviating human misery—poverty, discrimination, and similar social sores. But, say English scholars, such conditions have been strikingly improved in recent times in Great Britain; nonetheless, the crime rate continues to rise in dramatic fashion.[8]

In essence, then, the comparative approach offers a method for avoiding ethnocentric conclusions and uni-cultural, idiosyncratic interpretations of such conclusions.[9] It is responsive, in this respect, to the fundamentally scientific inquiry of the statistician who, when asked by a colleague, "How is your wife?", wanted to know: "Compared to what?"

The use of comparative material, however, has many pitfalls of its own, some of which may invalidate or seriously bring into question whatever advantages the approach offers. For one thing, procedural and definitional variations between jurisdictions regarding the behavior to be examined must be controlled. For another, it is very difficult to determine which elements of a culture can be said to account for discerned variations in the examined behavior. It is also difficult without further study to maintain steadfastly that a general culture is equivalently shared by all members of a polity. It is perfectly possible, for example, that Los Angeles and Boston, while very different locales, may

[7] Albert K. Cohen, "Sociological Research in Juvenile Delinquency," *American Journal of Orthopsychiatry* 27 (October 1957): 783.

[8] Leon Radzinowicz, quoted in *The New York Times,* September 17, 1967.

[9] See further Nils Christie, "Comparative Criminology," *Canadian Journal of Corrections* 12 (January 1970): 40–46.

include within them groups of persons—such as the rapists—who are more similar to each other than they are reflections of the cultures in which they commit their crimes. Or it may be that the alleged variations in the cities' cultural climates is no more than a collection of stereotypes, or perhaps a statement only of the way of life of the more visible or more powerful segments of the populations of the two areas. These items—and others which we shall explicate in greater detail below—make cross-cultural conclusions and their interpretation inordinately hazardous undertakings. Nonetheless, possible gains from such a procedure—first in terms of speculative insights and later in terms of the refinement of such insights—make it an attractive scientific enterprise.

The Search for Hypotheses

A reasonably satisfactory explanation for variant rape rates ought to be able to be educed from consideration of the sexual climate of a given setting. Published research sheds some light on discrete items which appear to be related to rape rates. Sociological studies, for instance, agree that rapists tend to be young, unmarried and, at least in terms of those imprisoned,[10] to suffer unusually from physical handicaps.[11] The psychiatric material concentrates on the view that rape is fundamentally an act of aggression and that its sexual component is primarily sadistic.[12] The sadistic component of sexual behavior, however, represents largely a function of social definitions of sexual behavior rather than a matter intrinsic in intercourse itself. So, too, being young and unmarried are conditions variantly viewed in

[10] The best study of rape is Menachem Amir, "Patterns in Forcible Rape with Special Reference to Philadelphia, Pennsylvania, 1958 and 1960" (Ph.D. diss., University of Pennsylvania, 1965). The dissertation was made available to us through the courtesy of Marvin Wolfgang of the University of Pennsylvania. See also, Paul H. Gebhard, John H. Gagnon, Wardell B. Pomeroy, and Cornelia V. Christenson, *Sex Offenders* (New York: Harper & Row, 1965), p. 193; John M. Macdonald, "Rape," *Police 13* (March–April 1969): 42.

[11] John L. Gillin, *The Wisconsin Prisoner* (Madison: University of Wisconsin Press, 1946), p. 129.

[12] See, for example, Manfred S. Guttmacher, *Sex Offenses* (New York: W. W. Norton and Company, 1951), p. 50.

diverse cultures, and they produce different kinds of conduct as a consequence of the definitions accorded to them.

Most published material regarding forcible rape concentrates upon the dynamics of the situation between offender and victim and their personal characteristics rather than upon social and cultural circumstances and their possible connection with the rate at which the offense occurs. Rape is often seen as a tribute to the virility and aggressiveness of the perpetrator, a theme notable in Greek literature, where rape tends to be an explicable, although somewhat unfortunate, event in the lives of heroic figures and gods, such as Paris and Zeus.[13] In western societies, rape also tends to be viewed as an omnipresent latent impulse in male nature. It is on the basis of his sudden awareness of his own drive toward rape, for instance, that Levin claims to have at last understood Nathan Leopold's urge toward murder.[14] Rape is also commonly viewed as the just dessert of an overseductive but undercompliant female. It is part of entrenched belief as well that rape is not without certain satisfactions to some victims, who are presumed to respond erotically to a show of sexual force. "He fought her as a raped woman might struggle," John Updike writes in *Couples,* "to intensify the deed."[15] Only infrequently—and then usually only in gang rapes—is the offense viewed from the perspective of an injured victim. The case of Maria, Hemingway's heroine in *For Whom the Bell Tolls,* is an outstanding example. "When we picked the girl up . . . she was very strange," one of the men says of Maria. "She would not speak and she cried all the time and if any one touched her she would shiver like a wet dog."[16] Compassionate treatment of gang rape can be found as well in Algren's *Never Come Morning;* Selby's *Last Exit from Brooklyn;* and Wasserman's play, *The Man of La Mancha.* Depictions of individual instances of rape are notably rare in contemporary literature, however.

[13] See, for example, Hans Licht, *Sexual Life in Ancient Greece,* trans. J. H. Freese (London: Panther Books, 1969), pp. 209, 214.

[14] Meyer Levin, *Compulsion* (New York: Simon and Schuster, 1956), pp. 492–494.

[15] John Updike, *Couples* (Greenwich, Conn.: Fawcett, 1968), p. 81.

[16] Ernest Hemingway, *For Whom the Bell Tolls* (New York: Charles Scribner's Sons, 1940), p. 28.

Anthropological evidence is most persuasive in support of the view that the number of rapes committed, the manner in which rape is carried out, and the persons involved in it are tied to the social and sexual climate of an area. There are some societies, for instance, in which rape is virtually unknown. The Arapesh of New Guinea, according to Margaret Mead, know nothing of rape beyond the fact that it is the unpleasant custom of the Nugum people to the southeast of them. Arapesh people, Mead reports, do not have any conception of male nature which would make rape understandable to them.[17] On the other hand, the Gusii, a tribe located in the Kenya Highlands, show a rape rate that is conservatively estimated to be four to five times that in the United States, with the dynamics of rape among the Gusii providing insight into the manner in which a culture can elicit an aggressive sex offense. Marriages, for instance, are viewed as intersex contests, involving force and pain-inflicting behavior, largely because the male has to obtain a bride from an adjacent tribe, traditionally viewed as an enemy of his own. Girls resist sexual intercourse with their husbands and berate them ceaselessly about their sexual competence. There is also a good deal of teasing behavior among the Gusii, as LaVine's ethnographic statement indicates:

> Gusii girls who have no desire for sexual relationships deliberately encourage young men in the preliminaries of courtship because they enjoy the gifts and attention they receive. Some of them act provocative [sic], thinking they will be able to obtain the desired articles and then escape the sexual advances of the young man. . . . An aggressive conclusion is particularly likely if the girl is actually married. In the early stages of marriage brides spend a good deal of time in their home communities visiting their parents. Such a girl may . . . pretend to be unmarried in order to be bribed and flattered. . . . No matter how emotionally and financially involved in her a young man becomes, the bride is too afraid of supernatural sanctions against adultery to yield to him sexually. After she fails to appear at several appointments . . . he may rape

[17] Margaret Mead, *Sex and Temperament in Three Primitive Societies* (New York: New American Library, 1950), pp. 80–81.

her in desperation the next time they meet, and she will report the deed.[18]

In regard to the United States, at least two related hypotheses might be employed to explain the relationship between sexual mores and rape rates. The first would suggest that the more restricted and rare are opportunities for cooperative heterosexual performance (given a reasonably intense stress on such performance and some chance to engage in it) the higher the rape rate is apt to be. In such terms, forcible rape represents an almost classic response along the lines of Merton's paradigmatic representation of deviation, standing as a behavior emerging in the face of compelling pressures toward a kind of action combined with the absence of legitimatized opportunities for such action.[19] It is just such a supposition that underlay the recent observation by an Austrian writer that the decline in bestiality could be related to "larger opportunities for heterosexual contacts." [20] The Merton-derived view, stated simply, would maintain that the more sexually permissive a society, the lower its forcible rape rate.

We did not find this position persuasive, however, and came to our data with a hypothesis which maintains that the forcible rape rate should be higher in a social setting in which their exists a *relatively* permissive sexual ethos than one in which heterosexual contacts are less readily available because of cultural prohibitions—assuming, of course, that all other relevant items were equivalent in the two settings. It is believed that the relative frustration of the male is significantly higher in the more permissive setting than in the less permissive situation. The hypothesis argues that a rejected male in a nonpermissive setting is

[18] Robert R. LaVine, "Gusii Sex Offenses: A Study in Social Control," *American Anthropologist 61* (December 1959): 983.

[19] Robert K. Merton, *Social Theory and Social Structure,* rev. ed. (Glencoe, Ill.: Free Press, 1957), ch. 4.

[20] Roland Grossberger, *Die Unzucht mit Tieren,* reviewed in *British Journal of Criminology 9* (April 1969): 199. Similarly, it has been maintained that the closing of brothels in 1959 in Queensland, Australia, is related to a subsequent increase in rapes. See R. N. Barber, "Prostitution and the Increasing Number of Convictions for Rape in Queensland," *Australian and New Zealand Journal of Criminology 2* (September 1969): 169–174.

more able to sustain his self-image by allegating that it is the setting itself that is responsible for any sexual setback he suffers. Women are inhibited, church rules are too oppressive, parents too strict, or laws too stringent—any of these conditions may be used to "explain" an inability to achieve a desired sexual goal. In the permissive setting, the rejected male becomes more hard-pressed to interpret his rejection. We would argue that forcible rape represents a response arising out of the chaos of a beleaguered self-image.

It may be suggested, of course, that in the permissive settings there are apt to be fewer potential rapists because there will be by the nature of things fewer rejected males. It is our belief, however, that in its present stage, despite growing sexual permissiveness, the culture of the United States keeps a significantly large number of men from achieving desired sexual relations both in its permissive and nonpermissive regions. In addition, we believe that cultural prohibitions reduce frustration in many instances by inhibiting a certain number of ideas about sexual conquest.

An explication of our view appears from the behavior of men in the homosexual bars in San Francisco. Contrary to popular belief, they do not engage in a spontaneous round of pick-ups, despite the fact that almost all have gathered to form sexual liaisons. Rather there is a great deal of reticence and holding back with very tentative approaches. Hoffman explains the behavior in terms of the exclusive value homosexuals place on physical attractiveness, downgrading in the process other criteria which have some suasion in heterosexual relationships, criteria such as wealth, humor, education, and occupation:

> If they are rejected in making a conversational opening, this is interpreted [probably correctly] to mean a rejection of that crucial part of themselves, namely, their desirability as a sexual partner. Hence, their self-esteem is very much at stake and they have a great deal to lose by being rejected . . . a rejection by a desired partner is a rejection of the only valued part of one's identity in that world.[21]

[21] Martin Hoffman, *The Gay World: Male Homosexuality and the Social Creation of Evil* (New York: Bantam Books, 1969), pp. 55–56.

It is well known, of course, that homosexuals have a high homicide rate, growing out of sexual quarrels between partners.[22] We would interpret this, in terms of our hypothesis, as an indication of the relative unavailability to homosexuals of rationalizations to account for rejection. We would rely on the same reasoning to anticipate a high rate of forcible rape in a permissive city, such as Los Angeles is said to be, compared to a nonpermissive city, such as Boston is said to be.

In addition to the total rape rates in the two settings, there were other clues we sought from the police data which we thought might provide additional insight into the comparative patterns of rape. We were looking for, although we did not find, variations in the amount of oral sexual behavior, for both offender and victim, as a possible indication of distinctions between the cities in motivations for rape. We thought that perhaps age and race differences might shed some initial light on cultural aspects of rape in the two jurisdictions. The time—both in the day and during the week—in which most rapes occurred, the sites upon which they occurred, and the manner in which they took place were also regarded as offering possible leads for further inquiry. If, for instance, Boston (as it did), tended to show higher rates of rape in the warmer months, perhaps, future studies would be well advised to hold seasonal matters constant and attempt to look further into other correlates of forcible rape.

The Reported Totals of Rape

The differences between the reported forcible rape rates in Boston and Los Angeles are striking. In 1967, the *Uniform Crime Reports* of the Federal Bureau of Investigation indicated that the forcible rape rate for the Los Angeles-Long Beach Standard Metropolitan Area was 35.4 per 100,000 population. This was the highest rate in the United States. It was almost two and a half times the rate for the nation as a whole, and compares in that year with rates of 24.2 in Chicago and 17.6 in New York.

[22] See, for example, Manfred S. Guttmacher, *The Mind of the Murderer* (New York: Farrar, Straus & Co., 1960), p. 83.

The comparable rate for Boston was 7.7 per 100,000—almost one half the overall rate for the United States and one fifth that of Los Angeles.[23]

The figures in the *Uniform Crime Reports* also show that forcible rape makes up a quite different proportion of the so-called index (i.e., serious) crimes in the two cities. In Boston, forcible rape (126 cases in 1967) constitutes about one-half of one percent of the index crimes (homicide, forcible rape, robbery, aggravated assault, burglary, larceny of fifty dollars or more, and auto theft). In Los Angeles (1421 rape cases) the offense accounts for slightly more than one percent of the total number of index crimes. The discrepant forcible rape rates, therefore, are not a function of different prevailing rates of crime in the two jurisdictions, but are specific to the offense itself.[24] The 1967 figures, in addition, are not idiosyncratic manifestations of a single year, but rather reflect long-standing differences between the forcible rape rates reported from Boston and Los Angeles.[25]

Raw Material: The Police Reports

To search for an explanation of the discrepancies in the forcible rape rates of Los Angeles and Boston, the writers examined in some detail a random sample of police reports on forcible rape cases in the two cities during 1967. This sample—136 cases from Los Angeles and 46 from Boston—was made available to us by the National Commission on the Causes and Prevention of Violence.[26] These were the cases upon which the tallies of forcible rape forwarded to the F.B.I. were founded.

Our first concern centered upon the accuracy of the reports themselves and, most importantly, upon their comparability. The alleged unreliability of original materials that form the basis for

[23] Federal Bureau of Investigation, *Uniform Crime Reports,* 1967, Table 5.
[24] *Ibid.,* Table 57.
[25] See *Uniform Crime Reports* for years before 1967.
[26] These reports were extracted by the Commission from a national sample of reports of five categories of crime—murder, manslaughter, rape, assault, and armed robbery—provided by 17 municipal law enforcement agencies to permit the study of patterns of criminal violence throughout the country.

the neat tabular presentations of the *Uniform Crime Reports* is a common allegation among criminologists.[27] As far back as 1931, the National Commission on Law Observance and Enforcement (the Wickersham Commission) had commented caustically on "the unsystematic, often inaccurate, and more often incomplete statistics available for this country." [28] Thirty-six years later, the President's Commission on Law Enforcement and Administration of Justice was no less appalled by the state of official statistics on crime. "If it is true, as Commission surveys tend to indicate, that society has not yet found fully reliable methods for measuring the volume of crime," it was noted, "it is even more true that it has failed to find such methods for measuring the trend of crime." [29] Particularly revealing was a compilation by the Commission of instances in which changes in reporting procedures between 1959 and 1965 resulted in increases in reported crime in eleven major cities of between 26 and 202 percent.[30]

Criticisms of reported criminal statistics, however, have not delved deeper than the official figures that appear in the *Uniform Crime Reports*. Challenges were based on the wide variations between figures for certain crimes in the jurisdictions which reasonably should have showed similar patterns or on wide discrepancies from year to year in particular jurisdictions where no likely explanations for such discrepancies could be found. The present paper represents, to our knowledge, the first attempt to determine the credibility of raw materials from which the reported figures on crime are taken.

Instructions supplied to police departments by the Federal Bureau of Investigation request that an offense should be classified as forcible rape or attempted forcible rape if it involved

---

[27] See, for example, Marvin E. Wolfgang, *"Uniform Crime Reports:* A Critical Appraisal," *University of Pennsylvania Law Review 111* (April 1963): 708–738; Albert Biderman, "Social Indicators and Goals," in *Social Indicators,* ed. Raymond A. Bauer (Cambridge: M.I.T. Press, 1966), pp. 68–153; Robert M. Cipes, *The Crime War: The Manufactured Crusade* (New York: New American Library, 1968).

[28] National Commission on Law Observance and Enforcement, *Report on Criminal Statistics* (Washington: Government Printing Office, 1931), p. 34.

[29] President's Commission on Law Enforcement and Administration of Justice, *The Challenge of Crime in a Free Society* (Washington: Government Printing Office, 1967), p. 27.

[30] *Ibid.,* p. 25.

actual or attempted sexual intercourse with a female forcibly and against her will.[31] This definition excludes specifically cases of statutory rape, in which no force was employed and the victim was under the legal age of consent or otherwise was legally incapacitated from agreeing to participate in the act. Sodomy and incest offenses are also eliminated by definition from the forcible rape category.

The classification rules, therefore, are reasonably clear. It is another matter, however, to apply the rules carefully and uniformly around the nation, where the exigencies of daily police operations are not directed toward niceties of classification, since such activity holds out little promise for easing the work burden. Nor, for that matter, is the F.B.I. able to exert any real suasion or provide much immediate guidance to an operating agency.

Beyond this, the offense of forcible rape is one whose commission is unusually involved in various kinds of spurious considerations. Victimization surveys indicate that probably three and a half times as many offenses of forcible rape go unreported as come to police attention;[32] and this figure may itself be an underestimation since respondents are apt to manifest the same close-mouthedness in the face of interviewers that led them in the first instance to keep to themselves the details of their experience. In addition, reports to the police of forcible rape are frequently found to be false or, at least, highly exaggerated. The *Uniform Crime Reports,* for instance, notes: "As a national average 18% of all forcible rapes reported to police were determined by police investigation to be unfounded. In other words, the police established that no offense actually did take place. This is caused primarily due to the question of the use of force frequently complicated by prior relationship between victim and offender.[33]

Finally, there exists considerable discretion for a law enforcement agency to interpret variantly the behavior of the victim, the offender, and the police officer himself before deciding

[31] Federal Bureau of Investigation, *Uniform Crime Reporting Handbook* (Washington: Government Printing Office, 1966), p. 17.

[32] President's Commission on Law Enforcement and Administration of Justice, *op. cit.,* p. 21.

[33] Federal Bureau of Investigation, *Uniform Crime Reports* (1967): 13.

whether or not the behavior should be classified as forcible rape, regarded as totally unfounded, or placed into another category of crime.[34] The problem is not that such procedures are erratic. If they were, the similar approaches across the nation would at least make the data comparable. The difficulty is that individual departments develop localized methods of dealing with various kinds of cases, methods which are distinctly different than those employed elsewhere, and persist with such idiosyncratic approaches so that the kinds of acts reported as a given offense from one site refer to very different forms of behavior than those reported from another area.

The Boston and Los Angeles Data

The truth of the preceding observations becomes strikingly evident the moment the ingredients of the police reports on forcible rape from Los Angeles and Boston are examined. A considerably more embracive definition of what constitutes forcible rape obviously prevails in Los Angeles as contrasted to Boston, and it is not unlikely that it is this definitional quirk which year after year serves to place Los Angeles far above the remainder of the nation's cities in its reported rate of forcible rape. Indeed, in Los Angeles virtually any instance in which a person appears to be seeking "sexual gratification"—to use the term favored by that city's detectives—is apt to be classified as a forcible rape.

Two cases illustrate this point. In the first, a twenty-five-year-old man persuaded two sixteen-year-old girls to accompany him into a public park. In the park, he proceeded, according to their statement, to tickle each of the girls on the stomach and knees for about five minutes. Subsequently, the young girls complained to the police. When police officers apprehended the man, he was asked, among other things: "Did you come in your pants?" His answer was: "Yes, but I didn't use my hands. I did

[34] A number of interesting illustrations of the influence law enforcement officers have upon the ultimate decision as to the appropriate sexual offense which will be charged against the offender appear in Jerome H. Skolnick and J. Richard Woodworth, "Bureaucracy, Information and Social Control: A Study of a Moral Detail," in *The Police: Six Sociological Essays*, ed. David J. Bordua (New York: John Wiley and Sons, 1967), pp. 99ff.

it on my own." The "sexual gratification" motif of the crime, rather than any attempt or likely attempt at sexual intercourse, was apparently the rationale for its inclusion among the forcible rape cases reported from Los Angeles.

The second case, not dissimilar, involved a man who inched near two young girls on a busy suburban street, then pinched one of them on the bottom. A police officer, who had been watching the encounter, immediately arrested the man. In his statement, the offender indicated that he frequently engaged in this sort of activity. His main satisfaction from it, he said, derived from frightening the girls. His case was also listed under the heading for forcible rape.

Instances such as the foregoing never appear in the sample of forcible rapes in the files of the Boston Police Department, although we may assume that similar kinds of activity go on there as well as in Los Angeles. For their part, the Boston police include as forcible rape a number of cases in which very young females—girls of eight and nine—are molested in parks by equally immature boys. Sexual intercourse does not take place, and perhaps could not have taken place. Again, it seems likely that a number of such cases occur in Los Angeles, but the files on forcible rape there do not contain them, probably because they are handled by the juvenile division and classified under the more amorphous rubric of "delinquency."

The style and quality of police work in Boston and Los Angeles in regard to forcible rape cases merits mention. The Boston reports, in general, tend to be much more terse and formal than their counterparts in Los Angeles—perhaps this constitutes a bit of testimony regarding the divergent cultures of the two cities themselves. Each Boston report is "respectfully submitted" by the investigator for the review of his superiors. The Boston police reports, too, reflecting perhaps the puritan tradition said to be immanent in the city, are notably laconic and vague about the details of what had occurred between the victim and the alleged offender. Preliminary moves on the part of each are described, the setting is detailed. Then, according to the typical Boston report, the culprit fell upon his victim and "raped her."

In contrast, the Los Angeles documents tend to be in the nature of Dostoevskian endeavors, with a goodly amount of Mickey Spillane added. The verbal preliminaries of street encounters that end in actual or attempted rape are often detailed word for word. "I'm going to fuck you," is, for instance, a routine bit of pre-rape conversation, at least according to the complainants. "This is for you, you God damn whore, you prostitute. I've heard about you," another offender is quoted as saying. Bras, capris, and other garments are often ripped asunder, and the attack on the victim—at least in Los Angeles—is apparently carried on with a fair bit of gusto.

The detailed, descriptive nature of the Los Angeles material at least offers the researcher a fair opportunity to delve into the possible motivations involved in the rape cases and to obtain an inkling of the prior interaction and relationship between victim and offender. Officers describe with some precision the victim's condition at the time she is being interviewed, and with some shrewdness they probe for inconsistencies and contradictions in the complainant's version of events. The "officialese" of the Boston reports, on the contrary, carries the impression that the richness of the events has been, perhaps rather summarily, pressed into a preordained formula.

For our purposes, neither the Los Angeles nor the Boston procedures offered much encouragement for sophisticated comparative study. It is patently obvious that what each department regards as kind of case to be classified as forcible rape and forwarded to the *Uniform Crime Reports* for tabulation as such is far from equivalent. It is apparent, too, that even were the events included in the sample data comparable, the discrepant attention paid to various kinds of details of the offenses in Boston and Los Angeles makes item-by-item comparisons impossible along a number of seemingly fundamental dimensions.

The need for standardized police reporting methods for the entire nation seems so obvious to us, particularly after our sessions with the Boston and Los Angeles data, that the absence of such measures, given the nature of public and political concern about crime, appears almost incomprehensible.

The Patterns of Rape

In regard to the materials with which we were working, we can only echo the lament that Barbara Wootton put on record after her overview of major criminological research of recent times: "Poor quality of our data is an obstacle to progress," she noted. "We are constantly obliged to use the materials that happen to be available as distinct from that which would ideally have been both relevant and adequate." [35]

Our analysis was undertaken only after a considerable effort to render the materials more comparable by eliminating cases that seemed to fall far short of what most persons would reasonably regard as meeting the criteria provided by the F.B.I. for classification as forcible rape.[36] This procedure resulted in our discarding thirty reported forcible rapes from Los Angeles; to us, these cases seemed clearly to be at best mild instances of frottage or other kinds of nuisance behavior, and not suitable for listing as forcible rape. We did not discard any cases from Boston, retaining even the two that involved juveniles. This outcome did not represent, however, a testament to the greater ability of the Boston police to follow F.B.I. rules, but rather to their habit of rendering their reports in so bland and unrevealing a manner that it was difficult to find grounds on which to differ—or to agree. Nobody can dispute, for instance, a statement noting: "He fell upon her and raped her," although he might look quizzically at: "After drinking together for several hours at the Moonlight Bar, the couple returned to her apartment. She said he was in the process of raping her when her husband, who accompanied her to the police station, returned and interrupted him, forcing the alleged offender to flee hastily."

The following items, among the many that we compared,

[35] Barbara Wootton, *Social Science and Social Pathology* (New York: Macmillan Co., 1959), pp. 308–309.

[36] All Los Angeles reports were submitted to two independent observers. Each was asked to discard only those cases which he felt could not be classified as attempted rape. Any cases which both observers discarded were removed from the sample.

demonstrated statistically significant differences in regard to forcible rape offenses in Los Angeles and Boston:

1. More rape offenses were committed during weekends in Los Angeles than in Boston (see Table 1).

TABLE 1. PERIOD OF THE WEEK DURING WHICH CRIME WAS COMMITTED

	L.A.		Boston	
Period of the week	*No.*	*%*	*No.*	*%*
Weekday	50	46	30	65
Weekend	58	54	16	35
Total	108	100	46	100

$$X^2 = 3.90 \quad \text{Sig } 0.5$$
$$n = 154$$
$$df = 1$$

2. Rape offenses in Los Angeles were distributed with relative evenness over the twelve months of the year. In contrast, Boston showed a clear seasonal trend, the majority of rapes occurring between May and September, with peaks in May and August (see Table 2).

TABLE 2. SEASONAL DISTRIBUTION OF OFFENSES

	L.A.		Boston	
Seasons	*No.*	*%*	*No.*	*%*
January–April	37	34	10	22
May–August	35	33	26	57
September–December	36	33	10	22
Total	108	100	46	100

$$X^2 = 7.84 \quad \text{Sig } .05$$
$$n = 154$$
$$df = 2$$

3. Rape offenses were much more likely to be committed by more than one person in Los Angeles than in Boston (see Table 3).

TABLE 3. ACCOMPLICES TO CRIME

	L.A.		Boston	
Number of accomplices	*No.*	*%*	*No.*	*%*
No accomplice	58	54	33	72
Accomplice	50	46	13	28
Total	108	100	46	100

$$X^2 = 4.3406 \quad \text{Sig .05}$$
$$n = 154$$
$$df = 1$$

4. A higher proportion of offenders in Los Angeles than in Boston were black or Mexican-Americans, though this result was no more than a reflection of the differing distributions of ethnic groups within the two communities. In 1960, Los Angeles reported a black population of 13.5, compared to 9.8 in Boston, but the Mexican-Americans, although regarded in Los Angeles as a distinct group, are counted, as they should be, as part of the "white" population by the Census Bureau, and their numbers are usually only roughly estimated by reference to "surname" tabulations by demographers (see Table 4).

5. Boston showed a significantly higher percentage of rape offenses in which the offender was a total stranger to the victim (see Table 5).

Variations in the ages of rape victims and, when known or estimated, the ages of the offenders were rather similar in both cities. Thirty-five percent of the victims in Boston were under 21 years of age and 37 percent of the Los Angeles victims. However, 61 percent of the Boston victims were under 30 as compared to almost 75 percent of the Los Angeles victims. In regard to offenders, 74 percent of the Boston and 80 percent of the Los Angeles group were reported to be under 30, although 30 percent

TABLE 4. RACE OF OFFENDER

Race	L.A.		Boston	
	No.	%	No.	%
White	26	24	17	39
Black	67	63	26	59
Other	14	13	1	2
Total	107	100	44	100

$$X^2 = 5.98 \quad \text{Sig .05}$$
$$n = 151$$
$$df = 2$$

TABLE 5. RELATIONSHIP OF OFFENDER TO VICTIM

Relationship	L.A.		Boston	
	No.	%	No.	%
Stranger	60	56	39	91
Acquaintance	48	44	4	9
Total	108	100	43	100

$$X^2 = 15.38 \quad \text{Sig .01}$$
$$n = 151$$
$$df = 1$$

of the Boston group compared to 20 percent of the Los Angeles group were under 20. Thus, more young victims were in Los Angeles, and more young offenders in Boston. The age patterns of the two cities, it might be noted, are quite similar. The median age in Boston during the 1960 census was 32.9 and that in Los Angeles 33.2. Los Angeles had slightly more persons in the younger age brackets (30.5 percent under 18, compared to 28.7 percent in Boston), but not to an extent adequate to account for the discrepancies in the rape statistics. Boston had a slight edge in the number of potential rape victims, registering 52 percent of its population as female compared to 51.7 for Los Angeles.

The higher percentage of young rape victims in Los Angeles suggests that an explanation for the variations in rape rates might fruitfully be sought in sexual climates. Certainly, by American definition younger women represent more desirable sexual objects, creatures whose possession is urged upon the adult male population insistently, especially in a site such as Los Angeles with its reputation for hospitality to starlets and nymphets. The disproportionately higher number of rapes occurring during weekends in Los Angeles suggests further the possible relationship between the offense and the "party" climate, which might impel rape through cultivation of implicit sexual promise coupled with explicit sexual denial. The seasonal variations, noted in Table 2, add further testimony to the oft-noted relationship between warm weather, human proximity, and the commission of personal crimes. Be it short tempers or short skirts, correlates of hot temperatures, the summer months obviously create rape conditions in Boston, while the more uniformly balmy climate in Los Angeles leads to a more even yearly distribution of rape offenders.

Finally, the considerably greater number of accomplice offenses in Los Angeles would seem to point to the "social" nature of the behavior, a product of group definitions of "proper" sexual performance rather than of individual deviations. In the same manner, the strikingly higher number of offenses involving "acquaintances" in Los Angeles, indicated in Table 5, would seem to add to the possibility that the west coast city possesses specific cultural characteristics that contribute to its high rape rate. Rape in Los Angeles is inflicted upon known persons, in relationships possessing rather more symbolic and interrelational content than those represented by the "stranger" rapes reported so much more often from Boston.

There were a number of general impressions derived from the data that could not be tested statistically because of the failure of the reports uniformly to take cognizance of the items. We gained the impression, however, that more victims in Boston than in Los Angeles received serious injuries during the course of the rape offenses, though very few victims in either place (according to our preconceptions) were reported to have been injured.

In general, it appeared that in Boston rape was more likely to be committed by an offender who had broken into and entered an apartment and then confronted his victim or had seized his victim in some deserted street or alley. It would have been interesting to determine whether this first pattern, similar to that employed by the much-publicized Boston Strangler, also characterized the city's rape offenses in the period before the Strangler's activities were known. In Los Angeles, rape more often seemed to involve an automobile whose occupants sighted a female walking or waiting for public transportation and then either forcibly abducted her or offered her a ride and later committed the rape offense. In Los Angeles more than in Boston, it also was apt to be true that the offender and the victim had met and conversed either at a bar or at a party prior to any sexual involvement.

Résumé and Interpretation

What light, then, does the comparative material from Boston and Los Angeles shed on the offense of forcible rape as committed in two divergent settings?

Among other things, of course, it fulfills our expectation that the more permissive city rather than the more restrictive city reports the higher rape rate. Police policies and police efficiency and reporting irregularities may mitigate, however, some of the sharp distinctions between the Boston and Los Angeles rates, but it appears that they would not likely reverse the findings. It would be necessary, however, to translate the best figures available into age-specific rates, besides introducing other regularizing refinements, before they may be regarded as definitive materials, truly indicating the actual differences in the behavior they are supposed to reflect.

The other findings lead into deeper speculative waters, where the eddies are apt to be intellectually treacherous. We would suggest, mildly, that each of the discrete findings offers some hint that the cultural character—as well as the ecological nature—of Los Angeles might well play an important part in conditioning the rate of forcible rape. Such a statement does not, of course, preclude explanations that offer supplementary insight. Jane Jacobs, for example, in her discussion of the impact of the quality of city life on crime rates, has also singled out Boston and Los Angeles for comparison. She finds that neighborhoods such as the North End in Boston show extremely low crime rates because they are marked with a vivid, flowing street life, in the face of which surreptitious acts cannot readily take place. Los Angeles, she finds, encourages crime by its anonymity and its long stretches of sparsely settled territory.[37]

The suggestions of Jacobs, as well as the views put forward earlier in this report, underline a number of pressing needs in regard to research about sex offenses. For one thing, the basic data must be improved immeasurably, so that not only identification items but also data responsive to particular hypotheses concerning rape can be fairly tested. From our viewpoint, we would particularly be interested in comparative studies between, for instance, climatically congruent cities such as Phoenix and Los Angeles, and ecologically similar settings such as Boston and, perhaps, San Francisco. It is only when such materials become available that we will be able to reach fully substantiated explanations of the relationship between social conditions and criminal offenses such as forcible rape.

[37] Jane Jacobs, *The Death and Life of Great American Cities* (New York: Random House, 1961), pp. 30–37.

OCCUPATIONS AND SEX:

WHERE THE OCCUPATION
INVOLVES SEX

Sex and Cabbies

JAMES M. HENSLIN

Each occupation has its problems and compensations which influence the lives of the members of that occupation, and, in so doing, also influence the type of occupational culture that results. Thus, if one is going to understand the world of the workers in some occupation, one must understand the occupational factors which those workers define as problematic and those factors which the workers define as compensatory. Such an understanding can be gained by examining the influence of these factors in their lives. By *problems* I am referring to the job demands or requirements of a given occupation that the workers themselves define as making life difficult for them. By *compensations* I am referring to those aspects of the occupation that the workers define as being beneficial to them, the reward aspects of the occupation that, in the workers' perception, make the occupation worthwhile. Such compensations, quite obviously, go beyond the pay check and the official fringe benefits.[1] They include the "fringe benefits" that

[1] Most of the literature on occupations underplays the importance of the problems that occupations present to workers. For studies that do analyze occupational problems as being important to the members of the occupation studied, see: Howard S. Becker, *Outsiders: Studies in the Sociology of Deviance* (New York: The Free Press, 1963), where the conflicting expectations of the professional musician and his audience concerning the type of music to be played is discussed; Howard S. Becker, Blanche Geer, Everett C. Hughes, and

are never written up in a job description or mentioned by the hiring personnel, the benefits that are built into the occupation because of the very nature of that occupation. With cabbies such "fringe benefits" include the opportunity to live an expressive life-style, spatial mobility, sociability with passengers, "hitting it big," and camaraderie with fellow cabbies. In this paper I shall focus on just one "fringe benefit" that cabdrivers enjoy—that of sex.

Over a period of approximately six months, I drove a cab in the city of St. Louis. When I applied for the job, I posed as what I was—a student needing part-time work—and throughout my

---

Anselm L. Strauss, *Boys in White: Student Culture in Medical School* (Chicago: The University of Chicago Press, 1961), where differing expectations by the faculty and students of the amount of learning to be done is analyzed; Ely Chinoy, *Automobile Workers and the American Dream* (New York: Random House, 1955), for a discussion of alienation on the assembly line and its importance for the worker's adjustment to factory life; Raymond L. Gold, "In the Basement—The Apartment-Building Janitor," in *The Human Shape of Work: Studies in the Sociology of Occupations,* ed. Peter L. Berger (New York: Macmillan Co., 1964), pp. 1–49, where conflicts between the tenant and the janitor due to status and material disparities and adjustments to these are analyzed; George C. Homans, "Status among Clerical Workers," *Human Organization 12* (January 1953): 5–10, where a status problem of employees is analyzed; and especially William Foote Whyte, *Men at Work* (Homewood, Ill.: Richard D. Irwin, Inc., 1961), where much emphasis is placed on the importance of understanding occupational problems.

This same underemphasis is also present when occupational sociologists analyze occupational compensations. Taylor, for example, makes the statement that "relationships among colleagues may constitute one of the most important conditions of work . . . ," (p. 315) but, having said this, when he deals with "occupational remuneration and rewards," he analyzes primarily the "official" fringe benefits of occupations. Additionally, Taylor's class bias comes through strongly when he defines colleagueship as a "special occupational situation involving deep intellectual stimulation plus an integrity of meaning" (p. 413). Unfortunately, he never seems to get down to the actual compensations of occupations as perceived by the members of the occupation themselves. With cabdrivers, for example, colleagueship is extremely important, but it does *not* at all seem to involve what Taylor means by intellectual stimulation. It means something entirely different to them, some understanding of which I hope is communicated to the reader through this paper. See Lee Taylor, *Occupational Sociology* (New York: Oxford University Press, 1968). For an attempt to get at the worker's world in both problems and compensations, see Peter G. Hollowell, *The Lorry Driver* (London: Routledge and Kegan Paul, 1968).

employment neither the management nor my fellow workers knew that I was studying this occupation. Accordingly, the data for this paper were gathered by covert participant observation and supplemented by unstructured interviews with cabbies. In doing this research I used a hidden tape recorder to tape conversations with passengers, management, and fellow cabdrivers. A major advantage of using participant observation to study such a group is that the sociologist is able to gain the subjective perspective. Participant observation allows the researcher to understand the occupation, both its problems and its compensations, from the viewpoint of the actor himself. By experiencing the life-styles of his subjects, their occupational problems, their occupational compensations, and in a direct sense experiencing the social forces that sometimes painfully impinge and press down upon the cabdriver, the sociologist is able to understand why certain things are defined as "normal" or "expected." He is able to see what the various aspects of the cabdriver's life situation mean to the cabdriver himself. The researcher, through participant observation, is able to understand why certain things are *shared* with fellow occupational members and why a common outlook builds up toward various aspects of life. He is able to become a part of the "common culture" of the occupation. Participant observation allows the researcher to grasp this subjective perspective so that one does not only know *what* the symbols are within the world being studied but also learns the *meaning* of those symbols for the members of the occupation itself. In this way we are able to picture accurately the cabdriver's world as he sees it, even being able to grasp the cabdriver's motivations as he interacts within that world that is so peculiarly his.

    Covert participant observation allows the researcher to study his subjects with minimal interruption of the interaction-flow of those subjects. Through covert participant observation the researcher enters into the lives of his subjects and observes at firsthand the *process* of interaction as it occurs within a natural setting. Because the researcher is "one of them," he is granted access to interaction as it naturally occurs. He is present as his subjects express their attitudes and knowledge, tell their jokes, play their games, and engages in other interactional aspects of their world, as well as personally experiencing the actual physical fulfillment of the occupational requirements of driving the cab. The researcher personally *participates* in the life of the people he is studying, and, directly experiencing the things that cabbies talk about, he is able, through these experiences, to grasp the significance or meanings of these events for their lives.[2]

In the cab company I studied, cabbies rent their cabs on a shift basis and do not need to report to the company during their shift. This allows an expressive life-style because of the unaccountability of time and the ready accessibility of cash. In such a company, as long as the cabbies can meet their "pro" (rental fee) and gasoline expenses when they "turn in," the company does not ordinarily concern itself with what they do during their shift. This means that if a driver so wishes he can drive until he has enough money for a few beers in his favorite tavern, that he can drink until his money runs out, and that he can then drive some more. This also means that if a cabdriver likes to gamble he can follow "floating crap games"[3] throughout the city or stop and play poker for several hours.[4] It also means that the cabdriver is provided with "unbounded time" to pursue sexual opportunities available to him.

What follows, then, is a presentation and analysis of the role of sex within the occupation of cabdriving as experienced through covert participant observation. We shall begin by analyzing the cabdriver's role in the exploitation of sex, in selling sex on the job, and in the extorting of a "tax" from persons wanting to engage in sexual acts in his cab. We shall then turn to an analysis of how the cabdriver is himself sexual, both by having sex on the job and by being sexually oriented.

---

[2] For more information on this point, see James M. Henslin, "Observing Deviance in Four Settings: Research Experiences with Cabbies, Suicides, Drug Users, and Abortionees," in *Observing Deviance,* ed. Jack D. Douglas (New York: Random House, 1971).

[3] A "floating crap game" is one which is held over a period of time but is not held at a single address. To decrease the likelihood of being raided by the police, the participants move from place to place, for example, to different apartments or hotel rooms.

[4] For an analysis of gambling activities by cabdrivers, see James M. Henslin, "Craps and Magic," *The American Journal of Sociology 73* (November 1967): 316–330.

EXPLOITING SEX: SELLING SEX ON THE JOB

The reputation of cabdrivers for soliciting customers for prostitutes is both worldwide and well earned. The city of St. Louis is a fairly closed city to prostitution, that is, the association between cabdrivers and prostitution is slight, and what association there is, is under cover—under cover to the extent that cabdrivers do not ordinarily talk about it among themselves in their work groups. Yet, there is a connection, and some cab companies have more of a reputation for an active participation in prostitution than do others.[5] One company, for example, has such a notorious reputation among the cabdrivers that some drivers are reluctant to drive for this company because of the suspicion to which they would fall heir. There is another cab company that appears to have little or no reputation for such association. The company for which I drove, Metro Cab Company (a pseudonym), is somewhere between the two—the connection exists, but it is slight and surreptitious.

There was a time when St. Louis had a publicly known and legally tolerated red light district, as well as many burlesque "joints" and bars with prostitutes openly operating out of them. Today, however, St. Louis enforces a law that imposes the threat of a $500 fine, from two to twenty years in the state penitentiary, and the loss of the vital taxicab driver's license to any cabdriver who solicits patronage for prostitutes. Since this law is enforced by vice squad officers who pose as "liners" (passengers wanting prostitutes), and the cabdriver has few cues to tell him whether his passenger is a "legitimate liner" or an agent of the vice squad, the risk is high and the resultant connection is slight.

How a Driver Learns About Prostitution

In an "open" city a new driver will probably be routinely instructed about his place in the communication network of pros-

[5] For an analysis of cabdriving within the confines of an "open" city, see Edmund W. Vaz, "Metropolitan Taxi-Driver: His Work and His Self-Conception" (M.A. thesiss, McGill University, 1955).

titution as he learns what is expected of him as a cabbie. (See, for example, the conversation with a cabbie on pages 200–205.) Even in a "closed" or a "tight" city, other drivers communicate certain information about prostitution. For example, the driver who said to me: "I got a liner after you left last night." I said, "A liner—what's that?" He replied, "A guy wantin' some pussy. I made seven bucks off him." In a "tight" city, such learning of cabbie terms and cabbie attitudes takes place by means of informal communication. Other than learning directly or indirectly from other cabdrivers about prostitution (assuming that he does not already know from his own experience as a member of the city where the houses of prostitution are, which bars have "B" girls, and the like), he learns these things in the course of his regular occupational activities.

The cabdriver learns much about his passengers in the course of his interaction with them, and because prostitutes and their clients ride cabs, he learns much about prostitutes and their "johns" as he performs his routine tasks. Some of this knowledge is gained by verbal revelations from the passenger: other knowledge is communicated by the "social situation." For example, the "place-from-which" the passenger has come and the "place-to-which" the passenger is going often tell the driver much about his passenger's past and/or future activities. As an example of this latter type of unintended communication consider the following:

> I was dispatched to the ——00 block of Enright. When a cabdriver receives a "street name and number" as his order, he figures that at least 90 percent of the time it will be a residence, either a single or multiple dwelling.[6] In this particular case it turned out to be a residential area, but my location was two apartment buildings joined by a sort of enclosed breezeway with a red neon sign saying "——— Hotel."
>
> I went into the hotel to locate my passenger and was confronted with what at first looked like the typical lobby of a small rundown hotel. There were lounging chairs to the left, and to the

[6] For an analysis of the orders dispatched to cabdrivers, see George Psathas and James M. Henslin, "Dispatched Orders, and the Cab Driver: A Study of Locating Activities," *Social Problems 14* (Spring 1967): 424–443.

right were mailboxes and a switchboard behind a counter on which was a registry. Behind the counter were three black women, two of whom appeared to be in their twenties and one in her forties, all watching television. They were all wearing dark dresses which were pulled up above their knees. The oldest one asked me what I wanted, and she called upstairs to a room and informed someone that his cab was there. She told me he would be down in a few minutes. I later received validation of my idea about "what sort of" hotel this was by checking with other drivers.

In this case the *"place-from-which"* communicated much to me about the passenger's activities—I concluded that he was a "liner after the event."

The point is that before this contact with this passenger at this location I did not have any idea that a house of prostitution existed in this neighborhood; *in the course of his ordinary occupational duties the cabdriver becomes associated with this form of deviance.* He does not have to seek it out; the nature of his job gives him an inherent connection with it.

There are other ways that the driver in his normal routines learns about the ecology of prostitution. For example,

I took a passenger to the 3400 block of Delmar, but I was unable to change his five dollar bill. Since he was going to a bar, I went with him to get my change. A white woman in her early twenties, wearing nylons held by a garter band just above her knees and what I can best describe as a flaring, pastel orange "prom" dress, a dress similar to that worn by high school juniors and seniors to their proms, was sitting sideways in a booth with her legs propped up in the seat. ·

I had never been in this bar before and would not have known about the "B" girl-prostitutes working out of it if my cabdriving activities had not brought me to it.

The *"place-to-which"* also communicates to the cabdriver much information about passengers' activities, both "normal" and "deviant." Obviously, if a male passenger were going to the hotel on Enright, the cabdriver would draw certain conclusions about his intended activities. However, the "place-to-which" also communicates information in a much more subtle manner, as in the following example which combines three sources of information, the "place-from-which," the "place-to-which," and the passenger's own statements:

> About 1 A.M. I was dispatched to an apartment building. My passenger was a tall, attractive, well-dressed, honeycomb coiffured woman of about twenty. The "place-from-which" she was coming was just on the Negro side of the dividing line that bounds the ghetto from the rest of the city. The "place-to-which" she was going was an all white area of small, lower middle-class homes.
>
> The "fit" of the known elements was not right—the "place-from-which," the "place-to-which," and the time of night. After some tentative questioning, she told me that she was a call girl on her way to a "john." She asked me to hustle for her, stating that several other cabdrivers were. She said that she received twenty dollars a visit, and that although most girls gave ten of this to the pimp, she paid only eight dollars.[7] She told me how to put "johns" in contact with her at the ——— Bar and Motel where she would be each Monday through Saturday night from nine to about twelve.

This call girl also illustrates a common feeling or expectation on the part of the general public concerning cabdrivers and prostitution. She expected, since I was a cabdriver, that I would be interested in her proposal. The liner feels the same way, "If you're a stranger to the city and want a girl, where do you go? To the nearest cabdriver, of course." And often the cabdriver is more than willing to procure a girl for approximately a five dollar fee plus the amount on the meter. This expectation comes out strongly in the following conversation with a passenger (P = passenger and D = driver):

> I had a "walk-up" from the Deb Stand. He was a white male of about twenty-five.
>
> P: I know you guys don't like to talk about business,[8] but I been trying to find a girl over here I used to know—a long time ago. I don't know, maybe you know her. Her name was Diane Jenkins.

[7] Her meaning was that she, by means of this differential payment, was in a status above those who paid more. This corroborates previous findings on prostitution by researchers such as Murtagh and Harris concerning the hierarchy among prostitutes. See, for example, John M. Murtagh and Sara Harris, *Cast the First Stone* (New York: McGraw-Hill Co., 1957).

[8] "Business," in the sense in which he used it, meant pimping.

D: Diane Jenkins.
P: She's a blond, about 5'9". Brown eyes, real dark complected. She was a prostitute.
D: She was a prostitute?
P: Yeah, She worked down on —. She worked with a guy run a ——— cab— his name was Harry.
D: Harry?
P: Yeah, I guess that was it. A dark Italian fellow.
D: No—where did she work out of?
P: Out of the Stardust Room and out of the Owl Restaurant. . . . She'd sit in there with the guys, by herself, you know.
D: What?
P: She'd pick up some guys in there by herself.
D: Yeah. Does she still work out of the Stardust?
P: I don't know. I haven't seen her for about six months. I been looking for her.

After the passenger got out of the cab, he walked around to the driver's window and said:
P: If you hear anything about her—I ride the cabs a lot—let me know, will ya?
D: OK. I'll probably see ya around then.
P: Yeah. Her name is Diane Jenson. She's 5'9". She might be a little bit older now. She might have changed her name, too. I don't know.
D: Yeah.

This man, as did the call girl and as do liners, assumed that since I was a cabdriver, he could tie into "a common body of expectations and shared understandings" concerning prostitution. It did not matter to him that he did not know me or that he had never even seen me before because the relationship with prostitution, in his estimation, did not depend upon the individual cabdriver but was inherently related to the occupation itself. His introductory statement also illustrates this: "I know you guys don't like to talk about business," which means that, although he does not know me personally, since I am in the occupation of cabdriving, I must be pimping as a part of my regular work activities. He expected that I would be so familiar with prostitution that I should be able to identify this particular prostitute, or, if not, that I would probably meet her at some point in my cabbie activities and would then be able to bring him into contact with her.

This expectation is, of course, not limited to the public but is often shared by cabdrivers themselves. When a cabdriver who has such understandings begins to drive in St. Louis, the "reality shock" can take a rather humorous turn, as:

> I was dispatched to the Crown Bar at 2 A.M. on a Saturday morning. My passenger turned out to be a tall, slender white male of about thirty-seven who also drove for Metro. He was very talkative. After we arrived at his home, we talked for about fifteen minutes more. He mentioned a particular driver who always works in one certain area, which is unusual for our drivers to do, and said that he thought he was "hustling." I then asked:
>
> D: I wonder how many guys hustle . . . I think this one guy down in Gaslight does . . .
> P: Well, if you ever get—I understand—now I used to do it down at home—used to drive cab down home and did it, and we— Nothin' wrong with it, shit! We go hustlin' and get around an' makin' money and everybody—
> D: Where was that?
> P: West Virginia—and everybody—everytime you take a guy down there, the gal she'd pay you so much, you know, if he stayed an hour or two, and if he stayed all night she'd pay you that much more, and she'd call you back an'— Man! I was talkin' to a guy— two guys—the other night—two cabdrivers says, "No! You don't do that up here!" They catch you up here, hustlin' a broad— what the fuck is it? Five hundred dollar fine, I think, and a year in jail, something like that.
> D: Is that right?
> P: Oh, yeah! They're stiff up here! They'll lower the fuckin' boom on ya when . . .
> D: Uh huh.
> P: Yeah, if they even *think* you're hustlin', they'll—they'll follow ya an' watch ya. They catch ya—boy, they'll lower the fuckin' boom on ya. Now I didn't know this, ya see. I thought, "Well, shit!" I mean, I— 'Course I haven't driven this long, I figured, "I don't know where anythin' is." But if I did, I'da been hustlin'. I didn't know the difference, see. They says, "Man!

Oh, man! Don't hustle in this city—in this city, no!" They said, "If you—even if it means ten, fifteen bucks to ya' just forget it. 'Cause man! They catch you with them cocksuckers," they said, they said, "They'll throw you in there for a fuckin' year!" They give you a five hundred dollar fine—'course you may get suspended—may have to spend thirty days—but you'd sure spend thirty days for the five hundred dollar fine. And fuck that! For what? For fifteen dollars?! Or maybe five. Huh uh! Not old dad. But I didn't know this, see, I thought, I thought shit! You'd hustle, ya know, on the side, and nobody'd say nothin'. They say they, they got a couple crews out watchin' us. Ya hustle the wrong guy, boy!

D: From the company?

P: No, no! Shit no!

D: Oh, the police.

P: Yeah.

D: Yeah! Oh, yeah! I imagine. I imagine they send guys out probably to try us, to try out cabdrivers.

P: I mean, they, they may, who knows, they may even send, a, a woman out, tell her to get four, five drinks before she goes out—so she'll be in the mood, ya know, an'—she, she don't never gets drunk, but she gets in the mood and so you can smell it on her and all this shit, an' she'll hustle ya and see what your, watcha got goin', see, and talk to ya. You'll talk to her naturally, quick, quicker'n ya would anybody else, see. Then they—an' she gets the goods on ya, she calls in an' fuck you're gone.

D: Hmm.

P: You're out of a fuckin' job, an' they'll fire your ass right now! You're done fired an' a five hundred dollar fine (laughs) and six months in jail. Oooh, Man! It ain't worth— So that's why—that's why they put this pressure on ya. See, uh, they don't want ya doin' it so they put the pressure on. Now, if you're goin' to chance it, you can chance it, but not me.

D: Well, some guys chance it. There's no doubt about . . .

P: Oh, yeah. But shit!

D: Maybe . . .

P: But, yeah, well, here—here's the thing. Now, if it was a twenty-five dollar fine, well, ya think I wouldn't chance it? Why, I'd be hustlin' every day! Day and night. What the hell's twenty-five dollars. I mean, I'd probably go three or four years and never get caught. So I get caught! I'm makin' an extra hundred an' fifty, two hundred dollars a week. So I get caught! Costs me twenty-five dollars.

D: Yeah.

P: But I don't give a shit if I'm hustlin' for—if I'm makin' two thousand dollars a week. You mean to tell me that I'm gonna get caught and go up for thirty days, or maybe ninety days, lose my fuckin' license an' everythin'. Huh uh!

D: Lose your job.

P: It ain't worth it!

D: Hey, what, uh— How did that work when you were in West Virginia? What did the— Did the girls pay you so much each time? Or was it . . .

P: No. No. We'd take 'em, no, we'd take 'em down— See I knew, I knew all the gals that run these places.

D: Yeah.

P: Negroes worked for 'em. See? They had a deal with the cab company. Ya take 'em down there, see. A guy come in town and say, "Hey, where can I—where can I get a gal?" "Oh, I'll take ya right down. What d'ya want, a colored or white, either one?" "Oh, give a— I want a white one." See? (D: Yeah.) So I take him down to this place, an'— Well, her name was Marie. I knew Marie, see. I go up and say, "Hey, I got a customer for ya." So she'd say, "Well, I'll call ya back." An' that's all. Ya get in your cab and leave. An' then about— If, if the guy stayed, if the guy stayed an hour, or two hours, she'd call ya back in about three hours. She'd say, "Hey, uh, is number so and so there?" She says, "Send him down. I want to talk to him." An' ya go down there an' ya pick your money up. She pay ya in cash. She never did— She didn't took ya. What she owed ya, she paid ya.

D: Well, how did . . .

P: An' then if, then if ya was goin' off duty, or the guy wanted to stay all night, she'd say, "Well, I'll catch . . ." She'd call the dispatcher an' say, "Well, I'll catch 'em tomorrow." An' if, the next day ya always had trips down there. Ya go down there an' she'd say, "Hey! The man stayed all night. I owe you three dollars." And she'd pull it out and give it to ya.

D: Ya got three bucks for if he stayed all night?

P: No, it was— If, if he stayed for fifteen or twenty minutes or an hour or somethin' like that, ya got, ya got a buck, buck and a half.

D: Uh huh.

P: Maybe two. I don't know. An' if he stayed all night— Now if he stayed all night, I think it was— I think ya got five. If he stayed all night, she give ya five. But she paid it! Never worry about that.

D: Hmm. Well, she called the dispatcher— The dispatcher was in on it an' everythin', huh?

P: Yeah. Yeah.

D: The whole company . . .

P: An' you're supposed to, you're supposed to scratch the dispatcher's back a little bit, too. See . . .

This conversation brings out beautifully the difference that an "open" and a "tight" city makes for the cabdrivers' position in the communication network of prostitution. In an "open" city the whole cab company might be tied into prostitution, including the dispatcher and management, with most of the cabdrivers' livelihood being received from this commerce, while in a "tight" city, although the connection between cabdriving and prostitution is not severed, it becomes a matter of whether an individual driver is willing to run the risk.

One final example illustrates both the assumption of some passengers concerning the cabdrivers' association with prostitution and the opportunities that sometimes confront the cabdriver to become formally involved in this activity:

I took a second-shift worker to the General Motors assembly plant on north Union. He asked me if I had any connection with women, and said, "You know, we've got 2500 to 3500 men working there, and they want some fast ass they can have and then forget, some nice clean stuff. Most of 'em are married so it's got to be clean stuff, you know? I've got a job that takes me all over the plant. How about arranging something? I know the guys that can be trusted. You find the women." [9]

Obviously, if this man's story were on the level, such an arrangement between him and a cabdriver could be extremely lucrative. Since this employee would make the contacts with the "johns," the problem of members of the vice squad posing as customers would be eliminated, and the cabdriver would be furnish-

[9] This conversation was written from memory shortly after it occurred, rather than being taped as were the others.

ing women that he knew could be trusted. Such an association could go undetected for a long time, and with such a huge number of potential "johns," many cabdrivers may very well accept such an offer.

These examples illustrate that *it is impossible for the cabdriver not to be in direct contact with deviance*. At the very minimum the cabdriver serves as a means of transportation for "johns" to and from houses of prostitution and for call girls to and from their "johns." The passenger gives the driver an address. The driver has no business asking what his passenger intends to do when he gets there. The cabdriver, whether he wants to be involved or not, by the very nature of his occupation serves as a vital link in the communication network of prostitution.

As these examples illustrate, pimping is a built-in temptation for cabdrivers since they come into contact with both "liners" and prostitutes and possess the transportation for bringing them together. This can be viewed as a compensatory aspect of the occupation, since the incomes of cabdrivers are extremely limited—these drivers, although working a twelve-hour day netted only fifteen to eighteen dollars per twelve-hour shift. Since he can collect from the prostitute approximately 40 or 50 percent of her fee and also collect for the metered trip from the "liner," pimping offers financial rewards that can be considerable. Moreover, he is sometimes able to collect an additional fee from the "liner" for cooperating with him. The risks, of course, are similarly great, including the threat of prison and the loss of the cabdriver's license. For drivers who do not regularly pimp, but who occasionally come across an eager "liner" that they perhaps hesitatingly serve, this deviance lets them "make it big" on a given shift. But because St. Louis is a "tight" city, this is a subject that is seldom discussed by these men, and, when they do so, it is in hushed tones and only among a select group of men who know one another well.

Sometimes the compensations that an occupation provides its members are given in the form of discounts, for example, discounts on food to checkers in the supermarket or clothing to salesmen, and so forth. Interestingly, cabbies also are provided with a "discount"—a discount not in cab fare, but with prostitutes. This works in the following way: a prostitute arranges with a cabdriver to recruit clientele for her, to direct "liners" to her. For this service she usually pays the driver 50 percent of the fee she charges the "liner." The driver, in turn, can use the services of the prostitute himself, paying her fee minus his commission, thus receiving a 50 percent discount! It has also been reported to me that in certain other cases he is allowed to "sample the merchandise" before deciding to hustle for a particular woman. Again, there aren't many occupations that provide such "fringe benefits." [10]

EXPLOITING SEX: "USE TAX" FOR SEX

Just as "liners" and prostitutes provide an opportunity for extra income, so do sexual acts that take place in the cab. When he is aware that his passenger(s) intends to use his cab for an illegal act, the cabbie, in extracting what I am calling his "use tax," waits until the passenger(s) is in a compromising position and then announces to him that he must "pay through the nose" to secure the driver's cooperation. These situations generally involve persons engaged in some sexual act. One driver reported that he waits until the individual(s) has begun the act, then announces that the passenger(s) must pay or he will take him to the police. Specific examples of this form of extortion include situations in which passengers engaged in genital-genital sexual intercourse, oral-genital relations, homosexual relations, and bestiality.[11]

The New York cabdriver whom I interviewed on this subject had a mirror that looked like an American flag, so that from the passenger's seat one could not recognize it as a mirror. He monitored his passenger's activities, and if they engaged in acts of deviance, he would charge them for this special use of his cab. For example, one day he had three lesbian passengers:

[When he saw that one was going to "go down" on another, he stopped his cab and said:] Wait a second. I don't give a damn

[10] Another occupation that also frequently provides its members with access to this same "optional fringe benefit" is bellhopping.

[11] This section is based on an extensive taped interview with a New York cabdriver on June 24–25, 1966.

what you do back there, (but) it's not a hotel. If you want it to be a hotel, I want ten dollars an hour plus that meter. The one that I am talking to says, "Okay, get goin'." I look at the clock to see if it's quarter after or eleven o'clock, and I take off. And I take the highway, and I ride, and ride, and ride, and I'm watching through the mirror. And they're eating it back there. All three of them go down with each other, and they're eating it. I watch in that mirror, and I got a hard on. Well, anyway, to make a long story short, when I got through, I think I had driven four hours with her . . . and I got forty dollars plus I think I had thirty dollars on the meter. So she gave me seventy dollars.

Another form of sexual deviance this cabdriver reported that he used as a basis to extort passengers was the following:

I picked this woman up with a dog. She had a big sized poodle dog, you know. The poodle's about that big, you know. About that high. "Driver, will you take me to the park? I want to walk the dog." I said, "Yeah. Sure." I figured nothing. There's plenty of them that do it. I take 'em for a ride to the park, and they walk the dog. So I picked them up, and I take them to the park. She got out and walked the dog a little bit, you know. She got back in the cab, and she says, "Uh, take me back to the (hotel)." I said, "Okay." . . . I got my mirror working, and I'm watching her and the dog. And all of a sudden I see her spread, and the dog is eating. I stopped in a nice position where the dog goes right off. I caught her in a moment where she's dyin' back there. I turned around. I said, "Lady, a hundred dollars before I move another foot, or to the station house (police station) I go." She got twenty dollars, handed it to me. I just drove slowly around the park . . . so there's a couple extra pennies for me, you know. But if you ever get caught, they hang ya.

This driver, in his many years of hacking, had had three experiences with female passengers and dogs. One of the others was the following:

I was working at night, and I picked up this woman with a German Police Dog . . . And I picked her up, and she wanted to go—I forget where, somewhere on the west . . . and all of a sudden I happened to hear something moving but good. I took a look, and there's this dog. I said, "OH! What's going on here?" I stopped the car, and said, "Hey! I've had everything! Fags, dogs, but I never seen a dog screwing a woman." I said, "This is it!" She said, "Look, after we're through, we'll talk." I said, "No." She said, "I'll sic the dog on you." I said, "You'll sic shit! I'll throw you out on the highway there." [This respondent related that he was not afraid of the dog because of the glass partition separating the driver's and passenger's seats and that he was then able to extort thirty dollars from her.]

Finally, this driver related one more incident:

I never will forget. I picked up an old guy one time. He had a girl he'd picked up out of a show, one of those little nightclubs on the east side, you know. They got her real hot and bothered. And he told her, he said, "I can't get it up." So she says, "Eat it." So I was watching in my mirror and he's going down and just as he's about to go into it, I hit the brake. His head went forward and back. Nearly broke his neck. He said, "Why, what did you do that for?" I says, "You're not going to ride in that, think you're going to enjoy yourself back there and you're going to pay that meter and that's all I'm going to get." He says, "How much?" I said, "Well, put something in there" (in the driver's outstretched hand). So he put a ten, put another ten, then he put two tens, and I said, "Ah, go ahead. Have fun." . . . So uh, when I took him where he was going, she got out, and I took him to the hotel, and I think I had five dollars on the clock. So he said, "Well, I gave it to you." I said, "You've got five dollars on the meter. Five dollars or I'll call a cop." He paid me the five dollars.

Instances of deviant sexual acts serving as a basis for extortion because they are performed in a cab are rare. These examples all were related by a single driver who has enjoyed a rich and varied occultional life in driving a cab in New York City for over twenty years. During this period he has been maximally exposed to such interactions. Needless to say, in true American entrepreneurial fashion, he has made the most of his opportunity.

BEING SEXUAL: HAVING SEX ON THE JOB

Cabdrivers tell a lot of stories to each other about the opportunities that they have for sexual relations with female passengers. They tell stories about women who are "on the make" and even women who want to "take it (the fare) out in trade." At least one of these incidents that cabbies relate to one another appears to have entered the status of "myth," the story of the woman who gets in the cab, and, while the cab is moving toward her destination, undresses entirely, changing into a completely different outfit. Others are more situationally specific, such as the following (not recorded, written from memory soon after it was told):

> I had the strangest thing happen to me last week that has ever happened in the fourteen years I've been driving cabs. I picked up this guy and a broad at [Place], and he stopped at [Place], and she waited in the cab while he went inside. She was good lookin', about twenty-five. She had her dress up to here (gestures to mid thigh) and I'm lookin' in the mirror and then I turn around to look. She sees me lookin' but don't say nothin'. I see something dark under there. Figure maybe it's her pants. I start talkin', but she don't say nothin'. Just writes on a pad. Probably couldn't write anyhow. Anyway I get tired of tryin' to look and talk, and I turn around and sit and almost fall asleep when this guy comes back. He was gone about half an hour, and the meter was tickin' away.
>
> When he gets back, he says, "Hey! Did she show you her pussy when I was gone? She's got a nice one!" Here I'd been tryin' all that time to see it, and he says that!! I said, "No," and he lifts up her dress and she didn't have on no pants. That dark spot I saw *was* her pussy!!! She had it shaved back to about here [gestures with his fingers to indicate that about a half inch of pubic hair remained on either side of the vulva]. She closed her legs, and he says, "Naw. Let him see it," and he pulled her legs apart. There I am lookin'. Then he starts playin' with her pussy, and she opened them wide. He played with her pussy all the way to the hotel. Man! You shoulda seen that porter's eyes bug open when he opened the door [at the hotel]. I never seen a man's eyes get so big.
>
> "I told my wife what happened, and was she ever pissed!"

Another driver related this incident to me (O = observer):

> D: Son of a bitch! Know what happened tonight?
> O: No, what?
> D: Picked up this woman at [Street] and she wanted to go to [Place]. Drove through Forest Park, and while we were driving through the park, she said, "You know, I could just climb up in the front seat and rape you!"
> O: She didn't?!

D: Yeah. I said, "Well, lady, it wouldn't exactly be rape. I might help you a little bit." "Would you!?" she said. I said, "Oh, yeah. But I wouldn't do anything in the cab. If you want to stop at a hotel, that's OK."

O: Did you?

D: No. She didn't want to go to a hotel. I sure as hell am not going to do anything in a fuckin' cab. Some fuckin' cop comes by and . . .

O: Yeah.

Not all drivers appear to be afraid of engaging in sexual relations with passengers in the cab, as indicated by one driver who in an after work group talked about a nymphomaniac passenger, saying:

D1: That's Sue—that gal I was telling ya about, that nympho I had in my cab—after I fucked her she had me ready to go again— after I—and I was fuckin' real good—I couldn't get her to go into a motel—she wanted to fuck in the cab—when she got in that back seat she got on top of me—I fucked 'er twice layin' down—she took me to a deserted spot out there in the county —she got on top of me, and then I got finished fuckin' her again—she said, she said, she got her nuts off—she still by god had her fucking legs spread apart and was finger fucking herself. She still hadn't had enough. You know what she told me—

D3: Well you take a—— l——

D1: She told me, she said, "You can give anybody my telephone number." She said, "I'll take 'em all as long as they come out here," she said. "The bigger the cocks are," she said, "the better I like them." She was a good looking bitch, too, boy.

D3: Now you is talking about a come-freak. I mean that's a woman that just likes to come. You know what I mean?

D1: She told me that she just couldn't be satisfied—she said that she couldn't be satisfied.

D3: Oversexed!

D2: White liver!

D3: The woman was oversexed!

D1: Yeah, white-livered woman. White liver.

D3: Well she—

D1: She almost tore me up!

D3: A woman like that will kill your goddamned ass!

Communicating Sexual Availability

Now it is needless to add that a large number of cabbies would love to have had this woman as their passenger. It is, of course, questionable whether this woman actually exists or not. Cabbies have certainly developed "cabbie myths," myths that aid them in their occupational adjustment, myths that remove some of the boredom and tediousness of the occupation, myths that make their passengers appear exciting and that provide them with a feeling that "perhaps the next passenger will be one like that." Are such stories only mythical, or is there an objective base to them? I do not know whether the particular stories that are told have an objective base or not, but I do know from experience that cabdriving does provide an opportunity for a varied sex life. Cabbies, as they go about their routines of transporting passengers, occasionally do come across women on the make, and the low supervision of cabbies by management provides them with the time to take advantage of their "opportunities" if they so desire.

The cabdriver receives many calls to bars, and frequently his passenger turns out to be a female. She is often unaccompanied, and sometimes she is interested in a man. This interest varies in degree from the woman who is "open" to a sexual encounter if the male were to make an overture through the woman who lets it be known that she is interested in such an encounter to the woman who insists that the encounter occur.

As discussed earlier see pages 198–200), the primary location (place-from-which) and the secondary location (place-to-which) communicate much to the driver about his passenger.[12] This covert or unintended communication includes messages about the probability of the passenger being "open" or "not open" to a sexual encounter. The primary location that signals to the driver the greatest likelihood of such an encounter is a house of prosti-

[12] For an analysis of how these locations communicate trust or distrust to the driver, see James M. Henslin, "Trust and the Cab Driver," in *Sociology and Everyday Life,* ed. Marcello Truzzi (Englewood Cliffs, N.J.: Prentice-Hall, 1968), pp. 138–158.

tution or a hotel or apartment building out of which he knows call girls work. A situation which communicates this same type of information and is much more common to these drivers' experience is a woman leaving a bar alone. This immediately signals to the driver an increased possibility of a sexual encounter. (Note the qualification of being "alone.") Certain primary locations, on the other hand, even though a woman is alone, signal that she is probably not available for such an encounter, for example, her home or a church. This is not to deny the possibility of such encounters in these latter cases, simply that they communicate to the driver less likelihood of such an encounter. The secondary location works in exactly the same way. A woman going to a bar by herself or to a cheap hotel communicates the potential of sexual "openness" to the driver, but going home or to church communicates that she is "closed" to this encounter. Related to this is the prior activity of the woman, for example, evidence of drinking is taken as increasing the possibility of "openness."

Aside from the locations, it is interesting how women themselves signal to drivers that they are available for a sexual encounter. There is a hierarchy of such responses ranging from sitting behavior to overt sexual actions (see Figure 1). The way in which people do things communicates to others something about themselves, such things as who one is, one's purposes or intentions, and whether one is "open" or "not open" to an encounter.[13] Sitting behavior, the way one sits, also communicates something about the self. Thus a woman can sit so as to tell others that she is alert or tired, concerned or unconcerned, prudish or sexy, available or unavailable for an encounter, and so forth. A woman passenger, just by the way she sits, can communicate that she is sexually available to the driver. She can do this, for example, by choosing to sit in the front seat rather than the back, or if she does sit in the back, by sitting with her legs apart and hiking up her dress and keeping it hiked up even when the driver

[13] Communicating to others by our gestural behavior is called "sign activity" by Erving Goffman. He gives an interesting analysis and conceptualization of sign activity in his book, *The Presentation of Self in Everyday Life* (Garden City, N.Y.: Doubleday Anchor Books, 1959), pp. 1–16.

FIGURE 1. A CONTINUUM ILLUSTRATING THE SIGNALING OF SEXUAL AVAILABILITY OR SEXUAL NONAVAILABILITY BY A FEMALE PASSENGER TO A MALE CABDRIVER *

SIGNALS MAXIMUM SEXUAL AVAILABILITY

7. Physical Contact:	Grabs driver Rubs against driver
(Direct):	"Take it out in trade." "Want to come in for a drink?" "You got something in mind?" "I'd like to see you again."
6. Verbal Behavior:	"Can you take me back?" "I'd sure like a drink." "I'm all alone."
(Indirect):	Emphasis on certain words Tones and inflections
5. Looking Behavior:	Desirous Invitational Sexy Much eye contact
4. Sitting Behavior:	Skirt hiked Legs apart Sits in front Leans forward
3. Dress:	Revealing clothing
2. Drinking Behavior:	Drunk Been drinking
1. Accompaniment:	Alone

0. ZONE OF NEUTRAL BEHAVIOR

1. Accompaniment:	Accompanied
2. Drinking Behavior:	Not been drinking
3. Dress:	Concealing clothing
4. Sitting Behavior:	Sits in back seat Sits back in seat Legs tightly together Skirt tight around knees
5. Looking Behavior:	Minimum eye contact "Ordinary" looks
6. Verbal Behavior:	"Normal" tone, inflection and emphasis
7. Physical Contact:	Avoids direct contact

SIGNALS MINIMUM SEXUAL AVAILABILITY

looks back. She can also lean forward, paying special attention to what he is saying. The opposite of this is to sit with her knees close together and with her dress wrapped tightly about her legs, or in this age of miniskirts, with an object, such as a newspaper, placed demurely over her knees. This, of course, in the absence of contradictory information at least, communicates being "closed" to this type of encounter.

A woman can also communicate sexual accessibility by "looks." She can look at the driver in a way that they both, being socialized into the same culture, have learned to interpret as an "invitational," "sexy," or "desirous" look. When he receives such a look, the driver knows that he is being looked at as a sexually desirable man, not as a driver.[14]

She can also communicate sexual-encounter openness by verbal gesture. Some of these invitations are subtle, but others are not so subtle. Those that are subtle include the tone of voice used, for example, a "sexy" tone, or an inflection that takes otherwise ordinary statements and words or phrases out of the ordinary and gives them new meaning. The following is an example of a subtle approach:

> On a dispatched order I picked up a female passenger of about nineteen. Upon giving her destination, I asked if it was her home, and she replied, "No, it's a residence. I'm all alone—sad to say."

---

* The continuum in Fig. 1 contains only responses personally experienced or reported by other drivers. To accurately apply to other settings and other interaction situations, for example, a bar, a street corner, a classroom, these responses would need to be modified by deletions or additions. There are probably various other gambits (e.g., a lingering touch when paying the fare, telling a suggestive joke) that are used in the cabdriving situation, but these have neither been experienced by the author nor reported by other drivers. Locations, as mentioned in the text, can be very important in such communications, but they are not included in the figure. Finally, these responses do not usually occur in isolation, but in combination.

14 David A. Ward and Gene G. Kassenbaum in *Women's Prison: Sex and Social Structure* (Chicago: Aldine Publishing Company, 1965), p. 146, mention an interesting example of "looking" behavior, that practiced by lesbians: "Girls are approached in the same way a man approaches a woman. He looks at her and the way she looks back gives him the clue as to further action. She looks at you like she wants you, a look of desire."

Somewhat less subtle is the following:

> I was dispatched to an apartment. The woman said that she had
> to go to the grocery store and added, "But I sure would like to
> stop off and have a drink first." This was said in such a way that
> it was apparent that the woman would have been happy if the
> driver had suggested that they stop for a drink.
>
> Later this same woman made the comment that when she was
> through with the groceries she would have to have someone drive
> her home. Again, this was said in such a manner as to indicate that
> she wanted the driver to come back and take her home. What
> would happen when they arrived at ther home was implicit in her
> statement.

Note that this is not a bar patron, just a woman on her way to
the grocery store. This is another occupational compensation in
the area of sex: the driver interested in such things *never knows
when* the opportunity will present itself. This possibility and uncertainty adds interest to each order he receives. There is a strong
game-like element in being dispatched to locations where one
does not know for certain what is awaiting.

Sometimes such passengers become even less subtle and more
direct, as in the following:

> A woman had been telling me about her activities at a friend's
> house, and I asked, "You going home now?" She replied, "Yeah,
> unless you got something else in mind." When I didn't respond
> verbally to her invitational statement, she added still more directly,
> "You got something else in mind?"

> A Black passenger on her way to Union Station was very
> friendly, telling me about her childhood, her employer, her neigh-
> bors, and her enlightened racial attitudes. When she paid her fare,
> she said in a low voice, "I'm coming back Sunday night, and I sure
> wish you'd be here to pick me up. I'd like to see you again."

Another common way of demonstrating sexual availability
is for the woman to invite the driver in for a drink. Drivers frequently report this happening to them, and my experiences support their statements. The most direct invitation I ever received
was an insistence that I come in for a drink after I had said that
I wasn't interested. This lady finally stated that she would not

pay her fare, but that I could "take it out in trade." Since this event gives direct support to cabbie anecdotes (to which one might otherwise be inclined to give little credence) indicating at least a factual base, although they may become elaborated on in their telling, I shall quote the incident in some detail:

At 9:50 P.M. on a Saturday night I was dispatched to a bar called the Bottoms Up. As I walked towards the bar, the bartender came out of the door supporting an intoxicated, faded redhead of about sixty who was unable to walk by herself. I helped her down the curb and with the bartender's help got her into the cab.

She gave me an address that was probably a sixty-five cent trip and said that she wanted to stop for a six-pack at a certain liquor store on the way. When we got to the liquor store, she asked me to go in and buy it, and I agreed. When I asked for the money for the beer, she told me to buy the beer with my own money, and I told her I couldn't do that. After some discussion, she said to skip the beer and take her home.

When we were about two blocks from her home, she said she wanted the six-pack. I drove her back to the same liquor store, and she again wanted me to use my money. I refused. She then made the comment that she didn't trust me with her ten dollar bill, adding that she was going to get out here and that she wasn't going to pay the meter. After some discussion, she agreed to pay the fare, and since the meter had been running all this time, it was now up to $1.15. She started to get out in this run-down neighborhood, and since there were several males standing on the corner watching this drunk waving her ten dollar bill, I thought she probably wouldn't last long, and I said, "No, don't get out. I'll go get it." She again repeated that she didn't trust me with her ten dollars, and I said, "Well, look, here's a five dollar bill. You give me the ten, I'll give you the five, and I'll only have five dollars of yours." She did this, and I bought the beer, giving her $3.90 in change.

When we approached the area of her apartment, she instructed me to go the wrong way on a one-way street, and I refused. She then started to get out of the cab while it was still moving, and I said, "No, wait until I stop. I'll pull up to this gas station, and you can get out."

When I pulled into the gas station, which was closed, she asked, "Do you want to come up for a drink?" I gave a negative reply and asked her to pay her fare which was now $1.75. She asked, "How much would it be if you came up for a drink?" I said, "Just pay me the $1.75." She then said, "I won't pay it, but you can take it out in trade." I said, "Just pay me the $1.75." She said, "I'm not going to do it," and she got out of the cab.

I got out, too, and blocked her way so she couldn't go by me. We argued for a while, with her saying, "You can take it out in trade, but I'm not going to pay you," and me saying, "Look, Lady, just pay me what you owe me." She then walked around me and into her apartment building.

In this, one of the strangest incidents that happened to me while driving a cab, the dispatcher finally sent the police to collect the fare. She refused to pay, even after the police broke into her apartment. She consented only after one of the officers agreed to return to her apartment and take her to bed after he got off duty.

In one sense, the most direct way of signaling sexual availability is when the woman goes beyond certain ways of sitting, beyond looks, beyond tones and inflections, beyond verbal invitations and even beyond verbal insistence, to a physical approach, actually touching the driver in some way. For example, one driver reported in an after work group that his female passenger, who was sitting in the back seat, grabbed him around the neck and started kissing him. He said that he had to tell her to stop because he couldn't see to drive. This is an extreme case, and when I first began driving a cab I disbelieved stories concerning available sexual partners; after having driven a cab, I would say that even if this particular reported incident may be exaggerated or may not be based on an actual event, it is within the framework of drivers' experiences.

As a sort of postscript to this section, I should add that it is sometimes the case that the cabdriver finds that which is sexually available to him not quite to his liking, as is humorously illustrated by the following incident related by a driver in an after-work conversation:

D1: Did you ever have a guy get in your cab and call you honey?
D2: Honey?
D1: Yeah.

D2: Yeah, I have. Whenever that's happened, I open the door and and tell him to get the fuck out of there!

D1: I was driving down Union and Delmar about two o'clock this morning, and this woman hollered, "Taxi." I wouldn't have stopped at that time in the morning, but I saw it was a woman, so I stopped for her. At least I thought it was a woman. And she gets into the cab, and she turns out to be a guy all dressed up like a woman. He said he didn't want to go anyplace, and I asked why he called "Taxi" then. He said he didn't want a taxi but wanted some "peter." I told him he wasn't going to get any here!

BEING SEXUAL:
A GENERAL ORIENTATION

As appears to be common with lower-class, male-dominated occupations (as perhaps with any male-dominated occupation—and, I might add, perhaps with female ones as well), these cabdrivers are highly sexually oriented. They will, for example, take the slightest opportunity to give a sexual interpretation to behavior. For example:

When I related to a driver that I had just taken a woman who had strep throat and some additional infection to a doctor who told her that her throat was full of sores, he laughed and said, "She musta got holda some guy that had the clap, and got a hair caught in her throat. That'll do it."

Even the simplest interaction can be given sexual meaning, and frequently is by these men, as:

When I was in the garage for "down time," I was eating a cookie that was still left from my lunch. One of the garage men said: "That's really something. You're just going to eat in front of me, huh?" I said, "No. Here, have one," offering him a cookie. He replied, "A cookie? No. I'm a meat eater." He said this in such a way as to leave no doubt that he was referring to homosexuality.

These drivers also use a standardized form of greeting that has an overt sexual content. In two such standardized greetings the question is usually asked by a driver already in the drivers'

room and the answer is given by a driver entering the drivers'
room:

> D1: "Well, it's Joe. You gettin' any lately?"
> D2: "What do you think?"
>
> D1: "Well, it's Joe. You still eatin' pussy?"
> D2: "Why not?"

There is some variation in the form, but basically they follow
the above pattern. In every case the reply is followed with general laughter by the drivers.

"Formal" jokes are also told in this group. I am differentiating the anecdotal kind, a "joke," from informal behavior on
the physical and verbal level, "joking." Cabbie jokes deal primarily, almost exclusively, with sex. The topics of the above
two standardized greetings frequently appear in the jokes these
men tell. Most of their sexual jokes could be described as "direct" and to the point.[15] The laughter from joking and jokes, of
course, serves to increase the cohesion in this group of cabdrivers.

Their conversations also frequently center on sex. These include joking about the sexual prowess and exploits of various
drivers, and they especially enjoy telling about job-related sexual incidents. Just as this occupation furnishes its workers with
easy access to sexual objects, as analyzed above, so this same access provides them with the raw materials from which they are
able to form the stories they revel in telling in the work groups.
Thus, just as the direct experience of sex is a compensation in
this occupation,[16] so is the indirect experience through telling
and listening to such adventures.

[15] There isn't much about cabdrivers' jokes that is subtle. This seems to
be in keeping with their whole style of life. To the middle-class ear, many
of their jokes might be considered "crude" or vulgar. This is not to imply
that the middle class does not tell jokes about sex, but that the type of sexual
joke enjoyed and the language employed are class-related phenomena. Since
the middle class has greater education and a markedly different style of life,
one might expect that the language of middle-class sexual humor would be
less colorful and that there would be greater emphasis upon puns and
aspects of the language itself.

[16] The form of this sexual compensation in which these drivers seem to
take the greatest delight concerns female passengers who will let the cabdriver
make love to them while the meter is running. Such incidents have been
reported by these men, but I have no direct evidence of their occurrence.

These men also play physical games with each other, one of which has a rather overt homosexual content, the game of "goosing." [17] In the "goosing game," one driver will "goose" another (poke him in the anus), and the "goosed" driver will jump. Frequently, he, in his turn, will "goose" the "gooser." This game can continue for some time, with much verbal exchange between the two men and with many expressions of amusement on the part of the drivers witnessing the game. Although the game of "goosing" contains overt homosexual elements, I do not think that we need search for covert explanations such as latent homosexuality to explain the game since, besides whatever physical pleasures are derived, the game appears to be played primarily for the benefit of the spectators. In other words, it is a game "played for an audience," representing behavior in which the players probably would not engage if they were alone.

CONCLUSION

Because these cabbies are of the same sex, possess similar educational backgrounds, share similar incomes, and live in the same urban area, they have similar ideas, attitudes, beliefs, and behavior patterns. In addition, they belong to the same occupational subculture which, in turn, leads to further shared values, similarities in speech, in problems, in hopes, in frustrations, and in life's opportunities. As members of both the same culture and subculture, cabbies have developed similar attitudes and responses to occupational and other life situations, and they freely communicate their ideas and attitudes, interacting with one another in a manner that is both spontaneous and expressive.

One means by which cabbies express solidarity with one an-

[17] These games seem to be common among lower-class males in certain occupational settings. I have witnessed them also at the General Electric factory in Ontario, California, where they were frequently played. It was rumored at GE that a rule was passed against the "goosing game" after one worker played it using an air hose and injured his role partner. One can also witness this game among service station attendants, automobile repairmen, and mechanics. In these groups, for one who becomes known as "goosey" (i.e., one who overtly responds by a jump and a scream), life can be rather miserable as fellow workers continually choose him as their object.

other is by way of relating occupational sexual incidents. The drivers view these sexual anecdotes from the same perspective, express the same attitudes and share the same humor. Through sexual anecdotes cabbies communicate to one another that, although there are many disadvantages to their job, there are also certain advantages that few other jobs provide. Such anecdotal sharing provides vicarious pleasure and builds positive expectations concerning the work situation.

Not only are cabbies able to be sexual with one another in their humor and in their stories, being able, in a primary group, to frankly and expressively interact and exchange a sexual content of attitudes, values, and humor, but their occupational situation is such that it both provides sexual opportunities and affords the luxury of pursuit of those same opportunities. The "sexual overlay" of orders, that is, the uncertainty of and the possibility of a particular order holding a sexual surprise or covert sexual "pay-off," provides a certain amount of "gaming excitement" for a job that is otherwise so deprived and depriving.

Additionally, cabdriving provides major opportunities for exploiting sex. The most common is that of prostitution, where the cabdriver serves as middle-man for deviance, and is paid for putting "johns" or "liners" in contact with prostitutes. In cities that are lenient toward prostitution, such pimping activities can easily constitute the major source of remuneration for the cabbie. This can also be the case in "tight" cities, but here the risk is high, and such symbiotic activities need remain covert, being shared primarily among select groups of trusted fellow drivers. In either type of city, serving as a middle-man in prostitution is a distinct possibility for cabbies not only because of the opportunities for engaging in pimping, but also because of the otherwise ridiculously low remuneration for driving a cab.

The other type of exploitive sex engaged in by cabbies, levying a "use tax" as cab rental for sexual acts performed by passengers, is much rarer than is pimping. Being a behavior that would be approved by most cabbies, but also, being rare, it is one that many cabbies would not be presocialized into, and they would, accordingly, not know the proper extortive techniques.

If it is true for us that we all live in a sexual world, or that our world is sexual, it is perhaps even more so for cabbies. However, sex for cabbies does not usually have the finely honed veneer and finesse as sex frequently does for the middle and upper classes of America. Sex for cabbies is an open and regular part of life, perhaps crude from other points of view, but perennially present in both his occupational duties and in his interactions in work groups, being primarily viewed by cabbies as something to be grabbed as compensatory pleasure for an otherwise extremely difficult and degrading life, or as something to be compensatorily exploited.

Police and Petting:
Informal Enforcement
of Sexual Standards

MARVIN CUMMINS

Among the characteristics of modern societies often noted by sociologists is the tendency to provide formal, legal codes that can
be applied to govern the relations and behaviors among the members of these societies. In truth although these codes nowhere
govern the range of actual behavior, they provide the legal structure that may be invoked in situations where initiation by public
reactions or by agents of social control dictate. The development
of large-scale, bureaucratized political states is predicated upon
an extensive machinery of legal order, a machinery widely ranging in its formal and informal application.

The arena of potential legal action surrounding the typical
day-to-day social behavior is vast. Most of the social relationships
within our American society are underwritten, at least at minimal
levels, by legal codes that prescribe necessary components or proscribe certain patterns of social relationships.[1] Marriage in the
eyes of the law obliges a husband, however much he dotes upon

This work was fully supported by the National Institutes of Mental
Health under Training Grant #6630. I received numerous helpful criticisms
on an earlier draft from John Goering, James Henslin, and George Psathas.

[1] See Max Weber, *On Law in Economy and Society*, ed. Max Rheinstein
(New York: Simon and Schuster, 1967), especially chapter 6 entitled, "Forms
of Creation of Rights." A summary discussion of the matter can be found in
Edwin Schur, *Law and Society* (New York: Random House, 1968).

his mate, to provide her also with a living. The failure to do so is sufficient legal grounds in most states to dissolve the relationship. On the other hand, violations of the state's criminal codes abridge the otherwise guaranteed relationship between the citizen and the state. Felonious convictions disqualify an individual from his political rights as a citizen.

The area of sexual relations, too, is girded by legal prescriptions for sexual behavior. The legal system contains a body of codes limiting the modes and conditions of sexual behavior. The codes mirror specific historical and class norms of sexuality, mostly predating the evolution in sexual attitudes and behaviors that is popularly known as the "sexual revolution." Moreover, the gap between actual behavior and public standards, either in laws or in conventions, has been documented and publicized by social research.

Even with the comparatively strong reliance upon legal control in modern societies, there is not universal agreement that the state should legislate and enforce particular sexual standards for its members. Most obviously, this issue has surfaced in England and America in the controversy over whether or not homosexuality between consenting adults should be considered illegal. But the general issue of the establishment and enforcement of morality by the state is a matter attacked both abstractly by legal scholars and behaviorally by youth groups establishing their own, contracultural life-styles. Among the intellectual analysts the legal controversy has been debated in terms of whether there are (1) an established morality shared by the "common man" in large, heterogeneous societies, and (2) a danger to the general morality of society if private moralities are given license.[2] Behaviorally, the life-styles embodied in the hippie communities, and other young, radical collectives have been guided by self-defined moralities for life in general and sexuality in specific[3] in direct con-

[2] The controversy can be found in the companion volumes: H. L. A. Hart, *Law, Liberty, and Morality* (New York: Random House Vintage Books, 1966); and Patrick Devlin, *The Enforcement of Morals* (New York: Oxford University Press, 1965).

[3] To insure that none takes these as "new," let me hasten to point out the repeated attempts at radical moralities in American history. John Humphrey

frontation to the middle-class standards which they reject as the repressive "hang-ups" of an older generation. Either intellectually or behaviorally, in its most abstracted form the question involves two basic sociological dimensions: the position of sexuality in society and the use of formal structures to control behavior.

Sexual behavior is an exchange relationship by virtue of being a social relationship. Its elements are constituted by the situational and relational factors that go into all social behavior: normative definitions, reciprocal patterning, affective components, ecological structures, and others. According to the legal structure, there is a legitimate market of exchange—courtship and marriage and an illegitimate market—prostitution, homosexuality, and so forth. The exchange of sexual relations can take place on either market. Despite the absence of full consensus, the modern political state has been employed to control the illegitimate market of sexual exchange.

The characteristic of establishing illegal forms is a set of defining criteria under the law. One sociologist, Stanton Wheeler, has suggested that the legal standards that govern sexual relationships involve four aspects.[4] First, the law regulates the permissible *degree of consent* in the relationship. The legal structure, based as it is on the idea of individual will, recognizes varying levels of consent, as well as the ability to formulate such consent. Second, the law limits the *nature of the object*. The realm of legal sexual relations has traditionally been restricted to intercourse between married partners. From that point the law has variously proscribed by race, sex, age, kinship categories, and other factors those persons who could be potential sexual partners. Third, there are legal restraints around the *nature of the sexual act*. Heterosexual intercourse has been the only sexual act recognized as acceptable by the American legal structure.

Noyes' *History of American Socialism* traces some of the radical communities that tried unusual moral and communal arrangements. John Humphrey Noyes, *History of American Socialism* (New York: Dover Publications, Inc., 1966).

[4] Stanton Wheeler, "Sex Offenses: A Sociological Critique," *Law and Contemporary Problems* 25 (Spring 1960): 258–278.

Fourth, as Wheeler notes, the law restricts the *setting in which the act occurs*. Privacy is one, even if not the dominant, factor in determining whether or not sexual behaviors are legally acceptable.

There is a continuum, then, of legally permissible aspects of sexual relations and activities. From the legally "normal" sexual relations to the illegal and "unnatural" acts, there is a wide range in the conditions suggested by Wheeler. But it is the legal structure that can define the limiting characteristics, and thereby it is the control agents of the legal system that are empowered to check and prohibit many sexual activities. That fact means that the police force is given the occupational mandate as potential enforcers of these sex-regulating laws.

Most obviously, policemen are known for their involvement in the hardcore areas of illegal sexual activities, those involving prostitution, rape, homosexuality, and passive sexual deviations. Social scientists have documented the routines of policemen enforcing the laws against illegal sexual activities. Jerome Skolnick, for example, has described how policemen on duty in police vice squads—often known as "pussy patrols"—attempt to suppress prostitution.[5] Skolnick shows how policemen, frustrated by the fact that sexual relations are exchange relations and therefore salable, try to apprehend street prostitutes as they go about their business. In another study William Westley illustrated the attitudes of policemen toward male homosexuals.[6] Westley found that policemen indicated a willingness to use illegal force as a policy device to punish or deter homosexuals. But these studies focus on the clearly illegal sexual activities and on the problems of enforcement in areas where the sexual behavior was unmistakably accepted as illegal.

Less described are the contacts of the police with the legal or with the marginally illegal sexual activities. The police meet, as a matter of course, many lovemaking and sexual activities, and

[5] Jerome Skolnick, *Justice Without Trial* (New York: John Wiley & Sons, 1967), ch. 5.

[6] William Westley, "Violence and the Police," *The American Journal of Sociology 59* (July 1953): 34–41.

beat patrolmen commonly "happen" onto such activities. There is a considerable amount of lovemaking sexual behavior that takes place in secluded, public areas and thus within the physical rounds of the police officer's work, if not clearly within his legal domain. In the remainder of this paper I shall describe routine police encounters with couples in various stages of sexual, lovemaking. This description is based upon fieldwork carried on as a participant-observer riding with beat patrolmen and specifically with the encounters witnessed and the discussions about the treatment of lovemaking couples.

Lovemaking, sexual activities themselves form a continuum, varying from innocent hand holding all the way to "perverted" acts. They vary from clearly legal to clearly illegal sexual exchanges. The potentiality of illegality does provide a mandate for police officers to scrutinize lovemaking behavior in public places. And, since these lovemaking activities do involve a variety of sexual activities, police officers encounter a whole range of sexual behaviors, some legal, some illegal, and some ambiguously situated, culturally and legally. Petting is one such behavior, as is premarital sexual intercourse, if one judges legality not only by statute but by enforcement too. In these areas the current standards are indeterminate. As one prominent family sociologist has summarized the matter, ". . . in previous American generations, there was social consensus that premarital sexual relations were immoral, and those who indulged knew this. Today that consensus is divided." [7] But the role demand dominates the policeman's operations more than simply his attitudinal prediliction.

However, the factor to be noted about lovemaking activities is less their legal status and more their ecological distribution. Sexual activities are both culturally and legally defined as private activities. Whether legal or illegal, "normal" or "perverted," the presumption is that these activities are carried on in settings that promote intimacy and that bar external invasion. The rou-

[7] J. Richard Udry, *The Social Context of Marriage* (New York: J. B. Lippincott, 1966), p. 169.

tine exposure of beat policemen to sexual activities is less a matter of legal violation than of the ecology of public-private spaces.[8]

For the police officers, then, legal norms play a small part in dealing with these activities since the situational context tends to preempt the criminal assumption. Despite the fact that the law might prohibit many of these behaviors, few policemen would attempt to take such cases to the prosecuting attorney or to the courts for enforcement. That is not to say, of course, that police officers would ignore all violations simply because they took place in these settings. But even though the possibilities of forcible or statutory rape or other violations do exist, lovemaking activities are treated as localized, constant activities, to be dealt with primarily as a matter of occupational routine.

The police meet these lovemaking sexual activities in a variety of locations, in alleyways, hallways, abandoned or little-used buildings, and most especially in parked cars. The common police calls for "suspicious auto" or for "suspicious persons" often turn out to be people engaged in lovemaking behaviors. A not atypical complaint is this one from an irate resident: "The kids have been parking over on Blair Street, the next one over, and throwing their rubbers around. . . . The word's out that that's a good place to park. They're throwing beer cans around and everything." Furthermore the police officers become aware that among these complaint calls there are mixed elements of piousness and vicarious relish, just as one police officer noted about a regular female caller: "She's a horny old bitch. She calls about once a week with these long, detailed stories about the kids diddlin' on her grass."

But not all of the patrolmen's contacts come through public complaints, for routine police patrolling also brings the police officer into contact with lovemaking couples. The parked car provides many people, particularly the young who lack control over other areas, one of the few regions of privacy.[9] The love-

---

[8] Arthur L. Stinchcombe, "Institutions of Privacy in the Determination of Police Administrative Practice," *The American Journal of Sociology 69* (September 1963): 150–160.

[9] A point made by Hubbard Taylor Buckner in "The Police: The Culture of a Social Control Agency" (Ph.D. diss., University of California, Berkeley, 1967).

making activities that occur in secluded portions of public places notably involve this population of the nonwealthy young who do not have their own areas of privacy. For lovemaking activities, which lack approval from parents or other adults, these people are forced out of privately controlled areas into isolated public spaces.[10] There is, then, a systematic but unacknowledged distribution of couples, primarily young, parked in cars for the distinct purpose of lovemaking activities.

The police come into contact with these parked cars partly from complaints, as suggested above, but more from patrol work. The location of this parking is reasonably constant and is comprised of locations that can meet the demands for privacy. These locations include dead end streets, streets in parks, cut-off side streets, and abandoned or poorly developed roads, none of which carry much traffic or provide any throughway. These "lovers' lanes" are chosen apparently for a forbidding quality that keeps even the stray motorist from wandering into such territory. The accommodation patterns that develop around the use of such areas works to the advantage of those policing the area, for the maintenance of typical lovemaking sexuality makes the area inhospitable to "deviant" sexual activities. It is in the interest both of lovers and the police to insure that such locations do not get a bad name. Learning these parking areas, then, is part of learning the beat for the novice patrolman. The knowledge of such locations is passed on from officer to officer, and as rookie policemen are broken in they are quickly introduced to these areas.[11]

Within the physical areas the cars themselves are treated by police officers as giving off signs of the lovemaking activities. The relative degree of penetration into the region is taken as indicative of the degree of sexual involvement. Cars parked along the

---

[10] In contrast to the popular assertion that the automobile has increased sexual activities multifold, one also must ask where such activities took place prior to the use of the automobile.

[11] In the latter stages of the research, the author himself inadvertently contributed to the socialization of a new policeman. One night riding patrol a young officer was talking about the "spots" and commented, "I guess X Road is the place for just about the whole county." I replied, "Yeah, that and Y Road." The junior officer said, "Where's Y Road? I never heard of that one!"

peripheries are presumed to be involved in milder activities, while those fully cached in the area, perhaps even secluded off the roadways, are taken as more thoroughly involved. Furthermore, the shadows of heads above the horizon of the car seats, a running motor, steamed-up car windows, and even the age and make of the car are taken as symptoms of the fact of typical lovemaking, sexual activity.

The norm of privacy surrounding sexuality is strong enough that policemen must not only learn where the parking takes place but how to approach a parked couple. For the police officer is most certainly invading the space and activities of others, and those activities are accepted as private. Justifiable causes for approaching the car can be invoked, if need be, to legitimate the encounter, and the police officer has several possible justifications: "You're parked down here where anybody could pull up and block your car and jump you." "Somebody's been parking up here and throwing out their beer cans."

The remote possibility of a girl being raped, the possibility of minors with alcohol or drugs, the vulnerability of the parked couple, or even the questionable character of the partners, all combine in low probabilities to justify the policemen's disruptions of these lovemaking activities. The justifications are also applicable for the officers themselves, as well as for the disrupted couple: "I once caught a burglar getting a jump here. You know even a burglar's gotta get a little now and then."

The initial approach can be handled in a variety of fashions, a matter reinforced by the indistinct legal status of the activity. Most police officers approach a parked car with headlights and perhaps a spotlight, although the police subculture suggests that some policemen drive up on cars without any lights in the attempt to "catch 'em in the deed." [12] And, likewise, the officers can use varying lengths of time to get out of the police car and up to the parked car; and again by fumbling for flashlight or hat or some other delaying behavior, policemen allow the couples a momentary reprieve. The restraints of intimacy provide

[12] And those officers who follow the "sneaky" routines are identified by themselves and their fellow officers as low-down, indicating even then that there is a recognition that the right of privacy is being invaded.

an interpersonal check on a situation that could prove overly embarrassing to the policemen themselves.

In that brief period between the time that the lights first illuminate the parked car and the time that the officer begins to discuss the situation with the couple, or most usually with the male partner, there is a flurry of activity to restore the scene to at least tolerable levels of decorum. The attempt to regain the situation for the couple means to get into a separated, upright position on the car seat with a quick rearrangement of hair-dos and of loose articles of clothing and to assume a nonchalant composure, despite the obvious embarrassment that pervades the situation. Illustrative is this conversation after an officer had shown his spotlight into the window on the driver's side of the car and the man rolled down his window and yawned:

"You been sleeping?"

"Yeah, just about asleep."

"Who's that?" the officer asked looking at the bare, female legs stretching across the passenger's side of the car."

"Oh that. That's Trixie."

In the quick few seconds that the couple is attempting to recover, the relative state of undress and the position of the couple provides the officer with a picture of what he thinks has been taking place prior to the time of his arrival.[13] To attempt to deal with the situation, either for legal or harassment purposes, the police officer strengthens his position if he can witness some feature of the event before it disappears. Prone or upright, behind the steering wheel or away from it, in the front or back seat, these positional features are taken as indicators of exactly what has been going on. The degree of undress, unfastened buttons or zippers, or loose articles of clothing in the car also give evidence for the police to make summary estimates. Typical observations by police officers include:

---

[13] The officer's presence also may redefine the event, just as that of any other observer. It is possible, for example, to transform sexual intercourse into rape by having a policeman drive up on the event, a fact that patrolmen are well aware of when they listen to female complaints.

When the light hit the window, they were arched straight over the top of the front seat.

There they were in the back seat with her skirt completely off and the other couple right there in the front seat.

Man, they were *bare-assed*, both of 'em. Just as bare as they could be.

While the police officer may be discreet, he does not necessarily avoid the exposure that goes with intervening in lovemaking activities. Experience teaches the patrolman that at any given stage of the lovemaking routine, the girl is more likely than her male partner to be disrobed. Despite the disinterested presentation that the police officer gives in handling the situation, he is unlikely to overlook the visual accessibility that goes with intruding into the scene. One example illustrates the pattern. After pulling up to a parked car and shining the spotlight in, the officer walked up to the driver's side and looked in. He told the driver, "Get out of the car," and a girl remained behind with her slacks halfway between her knees and waist. The officer flashed his flashlight onto the back seat and under the front seat on the driver's side. He pulled back out of that side of the car, dryly said to the girl, "Go ahead and pull up your pants," and walked around to the other side of the car to check under the front seat there. After leaving, the policeman commented: "She wasn't too bad. A little chunky, but not too bad." Again the police subculture manifests signs that police officers have been known to maximize the exposure and the embarrassment by routing couples out of their car to parade their nudity.

The policeman comes to process the set of symptoms that he gathers in each encounter as the activity *per se*. He does not seek to establish what was going on, and in fact he uses questions about the event as rhetorical devices to further illustrate the discrediting. The sanctioning begins with the policeman's operations that presume that the couple has been engaged in reproachful activities.

For most couples the policeman's presence is sufficiently guaranteed by his occupational role and by their awareness of the general lack of approval for their behavior, and they accept the patrolman without protest despite his interruption into their intimacies. In a smaller number of cases the policeman or the couple shows the need to account for his presence. As noted above, there are several possible justifications that the officer may use. The most frequent approach seems to be the one stressing the danger in parking, the vulnerability of the couple because of physical isolation and psychological-physical preoccupation. But the norm is clearly for the couple to accept the police officer's presence. The police subculture is replete with stories of couples that continued to carry on their behavior despite the police officers' presence. One officer recalled that as he shone his flashlight into a car and knocked on the driver's window a couple continued sexual intercourse without interruption: "What are you doing?" the officer asked. "You know damn well what we're doing!" came back the reply. Whatever the accuracy, the interest in these pieces of lore is precisely in the fact that the couple did not even stop to acknowledge the presence of the police officer.

The officer normally addresses himself to the male partner of the couple. The police officer treats the male as though he were the responsible partner and spokesman for the couple, a fact that fits with any legal concerns that the officer may have. So too, the patrolman can himself stay free of suspicion by keeping away from the female partner, especially if she should be in inopportune circumstances. But additionally, the officers showed an awareness of the differential level of emotional involvement for the male and the female partners. Toward the females the officers display an almost paternal approach. Clearly related were the officers' own, after-the-fact acknowledgments of the disruption of the emotional intimacies:

> You feel bad when she's a good looker. You know the guy's probably worked a long time to get her out there.

> One thing about that broad. I don't think he'll have any trouble getting her started again.

Given his estimate of the couples' activity, the patrolman follows a simple routine. He first makes an estimate of the similarities of the characteristics of the partners, especially of their age: "I just stop 'em to make sure they're old enough or to see that there's not an older guy with a young broadie." The primary stated concern, therefore, is with the youthful female, for the policeman is part of the broad system of legal paternalism and his occupational obligations are rooted in that fact. If the two partners in the couple are in their twenties or older, the patrolman shows little inclination to press the typical situation: "I always tell the older ones to move on and get a motel." The maturity for the policeman reduces the consent problem associated with legal violations, but furthermore it increases the officer's apprehension about resentment to his interruptions, for the policeman knows that his authority produces greater intimidation among the younger groups.

But age is not the only characteristic that the officer considers. Like the rest of the public, policemen have the implicit and explicit notions of an appropriate match in couples in terms of age, beauty, class, neatness, and other factors. Surfacing of these can be seen in the following comments of policemen:

> She was a cute thing, well dressed and everything. And he's a wrangy kid from the other side of the river.

> Is that your girl, Billy [a boy known to the officer]? She's all right for an ugly like you.

The more seriously an officer views the activity, the more likely he is to remove the couple from their car. (In terms of seriousness it is difficult to separate law enforcement from harassment based on nonlegal factors.) In minor situations the police officer will simply talk to the couple as they remain seated in their own car. In more involved relationships he is more likely to talk to the pair by transferring them to the police car. And, in those few cases where the patrolman believes there is something serious, perhaps even worthy of legal treatment, he will separate the partners and talk to them one at a time in the police car. Policemen strongly believe in the ecology of interrogation both for the sake of inducing fear and for information, obviously not independent features.

The patrolman asks for identification of some kind, especially a driver's license, or at least for the names, ages, and addresses of the partners. If the officer decides that the couple is overly involved or otherwise suspicious, he may proceed to take down complete "pedigree" information on each person in the form of "field interrogation reports," short forms used in police departments to indicate contacts with disreputable persons. The use can either be for recording the questionable person or activity, or it can be used for reinforcing the shame for those whom the officer thinks that it will serve as a proper deterrent or punishment. And, indeed, the official recording is a source of anxiety for those "caught" by the police officer. The partners see additional problems if their activities become a matter of public record. As one girl asked during such an interrogation: "I hope these don't get reported? I wouldn't want my boyfriend to find out I was down here."

Of course, not all couples are cooperative. But this is one time when the policeman knows that moral shame can be an efficient weapon of control. It is the couple that has been caught in some presumed violation of sexual standards, where sexual morals are the major index of the character of the female. For all practical purposes the police officer holds the apparent power of public disclosure of private sexual exchanges. This means that shame is the primary tool which the officer can use in such situations and that it can be used to divide the partners of the activity. So the officer has only to turn the focus of hostility of uncooperative couples upon the partners themselves. As a patrolman explained: "If they give me a ration (of protest), I just say, 'Hey, if you thought anything of this girl, you wouldn't bring her out here to park.'" It is fairly obvious for most couples that the quickest way to escape the embarrassment of the situation is to go along with the officer.

There is considerable variation in the reactions of the police officers to the parked couples, usually imparted in the parting comments of the officer to the couple as he releases them. Despite the age and occupational factors that would be expected to produce more strict views toward sexuality, the recurring contact with such couples mitigates the patrolman's response. While not impossible, it becomes increasingly difficult to display effective disapproval toward the commonplace. This produces cross pressures that result in mixed reactions to these sexual activities. Typical responses include:

> I suggest that you leave here now and work on developing some *modesty.*

> I'm not condemning what you're doing. You gotta find a better place to go, though. In fact, you know where the Court Motel is?

In effect, the officers' individual reactions are only different degrees of censure. For even though the individual patrolman indicates that he personally feels no disapproval for these lovemaking activities, the general pattern of policemen stopping these activities is in itself an accusing process. As pointed out above, the sanctioning is comprised in the assumption of sexuality as discreditable conduct and thus subject to police scrutiny. This assumption is credible in this situation in a large part because of the similarity in form of legal and illegal sexual behavior. The contact with the police is, then, a moral if not a legal condemnation for those so involved.

SUMMARY

This account of routine police encounters with lovemaking sexual activities can be reasonably taken as descriptive of the specific interaction process that sociologists call the labeling of deviance.[14] In this case there is an elaboration of the locating and the inspecting aspects of the labeling process. There are regularized temporal and spatial patterns of lovemaking sexual activities, and regularized patterns of reaction and constraint by control agents, the police officers. This example, specifically, involves the intersection of two areas of marginality, for neither is the lovemaking taken as deviant nor acceptable, nor are the efforts at control taken as official nor peculiarly individual.

The interaction description shows the elementary features,

14 See Howard S. Becker's books, *The Other Side: Perspectives on Deviance* (New York: The Free Press, 1964) and *Outsiders: Studies in the Sociology of Deviance* (New York: The Free Press, 1963).

however, of labeling activities as deviant. There does exist a systematic routine of officials that aims at seeking out and making preliminary examination of the activity in question. The interaction sequence that develops around these phases enforces the shame associated with the behavior, even though the enforcement is not official and the behavior may not be illegal. Couples are "caught." They are subjected to the assumption of shame without any external legitimation for their activity and without any subculture, legitimate or deviant, to support them.

The context of the label is limited in this case simply to the police contact itself. There is no attempt to specify and legitimate the character of the deviant act, nor to provide corrective recourse to the behavior. Unlike much that is treated as deviant, the policeman is treating behavior or its immediate symptoms rather than recounted versions of the behavior. The control of the reality of the situation, in part, stems from the limited access to defining the situation. Only the police officer and the couple have access to the situation.

At this stage of the labeling, then, the police officer can afford to treat all cases as guilty, for the formal criteria of legal guilt are not relevant at this stage. In the eyes of the legal system there has been no significant contact, no deviation worthy of treatment. For those involved, however, it is enough that the symptoms of their offense should be elaborated to them to reinforce their degradation. The morally compromising sphere of sexuality makes the presumption of the situation weigh heavily against them. The policeman need only cite the physical facts of the setting, the contact, the positions, the degree of undress as intimidating factors that expose the partners. And it is primarily the physical terms that are treated by the policeman, and these physical features allow the activities to be treated in sexual terms rather than in emotional terms. To these physical symptoms are added the status attributes of the lovers, all of which itemize the personal character of their shame.

The interaction processes must be understood within the framework of the marginality of norms for sexual behavior, for the standards defining premarital petting and intercourse are not clear. The young Americans view the adult generation as restrictive and intolerant of their sexual activities. As the fore-most scholar of American premarital sexual behavior concludes, ". . . regardless of the individuals' own level of permissiveness, he tends to view his parents as low on permissiveness and his peers as high on permissiveness." [15] Police control of lovemaking sexuality is a consistent experience, then, with the general adult disapproval of sexual activities among the young.

Thus, sexual behavior is dealt with by a covertly disapprov-ing structure. These activities remain condoned. Legally, and probably parentally, these lovemaking activities are less disci-plined than denied. Their very indefiniteness allows for the ex-ercise of control based on shame. This very structural ambiguity makes those who participate in these lovemaking activities sub-ject to the possibility of "victimization" by harassment by the police.[16] There is limited recourse to police encounters when the young cannot admit these activities to disapproving parents.

Likewise, the application of formal control, as enforced by the police, is marginal by virtue of its semi-official nature. The scope of law enforcement concerning sexuality is indistinct, es-pecially when the commercial and "perverted" aspects are set aside. Sexual regulation traditionally has been closely linked with family structures of control. While it is not a unilinear function, there is justification for saying that there have been shifts away from informal family controls to formal, institutional controls. With the development of an autonomous dating and courtship pattern, there is a decrease in family control over sex-ual behavior, and law enforcement has taken up some of that gap by informally regulating sexuality in public areas.

In one sense, it should come as no surprise that the police should take on the job of overseeing the sexuality of the young, for the police assume that youth activities in general fall within the natural domain of police work. The lack of political re-taliatory power and the high occurrence of law violations among

[15] Ira Reiss, *The Social Context of Premarital Sexual Permissiveness* (New York: Holt, Reinhart and Winston, 1967), p. 137.

[16] See an analogous description of the exploitation of homosexuals in Edwin Schur, *Crimes Without Victims* (Englewood Cliffs, N.J.: Prentice-Hall, 1965), pp. 82–85.

the young makes them the ready object of police scrutiny.[17] Police intervention into youthful lovemaking sexuality gets implicit support from the public demands of police calls, from the occupational subculture of fellow officers who carry on the practice, and from the legal codes constraining sexual behaviors. At the same time, there are few corresponding restraints in this informal enforcement.

So too, do the police take responsibility for the activities that occur in public spaces. The fact that these behaviors may be hidden away in secluded locations makes them even more suspicious. As densities and space usages increase, the police have assumed more and more responsibility for the surveillance of public areas. The possibility of obtaining privacy in public spaces would appear to be diminishing, especially as the cry for "order" on the streets increases. The warrant for police surveillance of suspicious persons and places continues to include informal sanctioning of activities socially defined as morally questionable.

[17] See James Q. Wilson, "Dilemmas of Police Administration," *Public Administration Review* 28 (September–October 1968): 407–412.

Dramaturgical Desexualization: The Sociology of the Vaginal Examination

JAMES M. HENSLIN

MAE A. BIGGS

INTRODUCTION: PROBLEMATICS
OF GENITAL EXPOSURE

Genital behavior is problematic in American society. Americans in our society are socialized at a very early age into society's dictates concerning the situations, circumstances, and purposes of allowable and unallowable genital exposure. Exposure of the genital area of infants is not as problematic as that of adults, but, at least for the middle and upper classes in America, such exposure takes place primarily in the presence of family members or individuals assigned such tasks as diapering and other aspects of child care. Infants are unconcerned about who sees their genitals, but parents do not seem to share this view, and they socialize their children into associating feelings of shame, guilt, and modesty with the genital area. While there are social class differences of which we know very little, for the most part it does not take many years until the youngster becomes extremely conscious of the proprieties concerning his (or her) genitals, and things previously of no concern to him become prob-

Our thanks to Erving Goffman for commenting on this paper while it was in manuscript form. We have resisted the temptation to use his suggested title, "Behavior in Pubic Places."

lematic, such as going to the bathroom in the presence of others or exposing items associated with the genital area, e.g., underwear.

After an American female has been socialized into rigorous norms concerning society's expectations in the covering and privacy of specified areas of her body, especially her vagina, exposure of her pubic area becomes something that is extremely problematic for her. Even for a woman who has overcome this particular problem when it comes to sexual relations and is no longer bothered by genital exposure in the presence of her sexual partner, the problem frequently recurs when she is expected to expose her vagina in a nonsexual manner to a male. Such is the case with the vaginal examination. The vaginal examination can become so threatening, in fact, that for many women it not only represents a threat to their feelings of modesty but also threatens their person and their feelings of who they are. Because of this threatening aspect of the structured genital exposure of the vaginal examination, some women keep putting off vaginal examinations, and it is not uncommon for women to wait until they are in their last trimester of pregnancy before coming in for their first prenatal examination.

With such problematics, including the whole related area of emotions being associated with the genital area through the learning of taboos, the vaginal examination becomes an interesting process, representing a structured interaction situation in which the "privates" no longer remain private. The interaction occurring here is unique since we who are so "up tight" about genital exposure, allow males to examine the genitals of our females, both the married and the unmarried, the young and the old, and we even pay them for inserting their index and middle fingers into the vagina. That we would structure such interrelationships and interaction in such a way is not only interesting in and of itself, but the interaction that takes place in this structured relationship is also interesting from a sociological point of view. What happens during such interaction? Since a (if not *the*) major concern of the persons involved is that all the interaction be defined as nonsexual, with even the hint of sexuality being avoided, what structural restraints on behavior operate?

How does the patient cooperate in maintaining this definition of nonsexuality? In what ways are the roles of doctor, nurse, and patient performed such that they conjointly contribute to the maintenance of this definition? It is on questions such as these that this paper will focus.

In analyzing the vaginal examination, we shall use a dramaturgical model (Goffman 1959), following the patient from the time she enters the doctor's office until the time she leaves, analyzing her role in relationship to that of the other major role-players, the doctor and the nurse. In doing this, we shall develop an ethnography of the vaginal examination, delineating the major acts by which the problematics of the vaginal examination are handled (see Figure 1), detailing the specific roles played by the doctor, nurse, and patient in cooperatively desexualizing the interaction.

This analysis is based on a sample of 12 to 14,000 vaginal examinations. The female author served as an obstetrical nurse in hospital settings and as an office nurse for general practitioners for fourteen years, giving us access to this area of human behavior which is ordinarily not sociologically accessible. Based on these observations, we have divided the interaction of the vaginal examination into five major scenes preceded by the pre-prologue and prologue and followed by an an epilogue and post-epilogue. We shall now examine each of these bounded interactions in order.

PRE-PROLOGUE:
THE PRE-PATIENT PHASE

In the waiting room the woman engages in such activities as reading, conversing with other patients, and/or dealing with paramedical personnel such as the doctor's secretary and receptionist. The waiting room is not reserved for patients only, but a whole cadre of persons use this room, such as drug detail men (representatives of drug companies), salesmen of medical equipment, and relatives and friends of patients.

The interaction is characteristic of that which ordinai

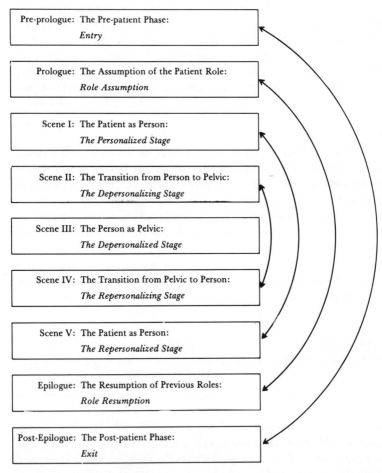

Figure 1. The Depersonalization and Repersonalization Process of the Vaginal Examination: Scenes of the Dramaturgy, with Their Title (in italics), and the Stages of Personalization.

occurs between strangers who are in a bounded setting where the focus of activity is centered not on interacting with others within that bounded setting but on waiting for future action to unfold, for example, waiting for a play to begin or a train to arrive. Interaction between strangers within the waiting room as they await their interaction with the doctor is marked by superficiality, being confined primarily to remarks about the weather or current events or to that which is elicited by external signs such as children ("What a darling baby!"), bandages, slings, or casts ("Oh, I see you've broken your leg."). Interaction in the waiting room is also marked by choice, that is, persons in the waiting room need not verbally interact with one another if they do not wish to. The waiting room is set up in such a way as to maximize noninteraction or noninvolvement if that is what a person desires. By using the magazines, books, and newspapers contained in the waiting room, a person who wishes to avoid interaction with others is able to do so by sustaining a minimal main involvement. Thus, by using these props she is able to avoid appearing disengaged and declares that she is not open to interaction initiated by others; yet she is able to immediately discard such "involvement" when her name is called and she is summoned to assume the patient role (Goffman 1963: 51).

Significantly, in this pre-patient phase the individual holds onto the identity she had when she entered. Although she is preparing for a change in identity, she does not at this time have to depart from the identity that she brought in with her, as she must in the interaction scenes that follow. She is still a full person, remaining a sexual being. We shall now examine her progressive depersonalization and desexualization through role playing as the dramaturgy of the vaginal examination unfolds.

PROLOGUE: ASSUMPTION OF THE PATIENT ROLE

The pre-patient phase ends when the nurse calls out the individual's name, both summoning her to move from the waiting room into the medical area and officially summoning her to assume the role of patient. Contrary to interaction in the pre-prologue, the individual's behavior from this point on is no longer optional. Roles are now sharply delineated or differentiated, with the medical personnel playing the dominant or superior role and the patient taking the complementary subordinant role. After calling the patient's name, the nurse says, "Would you please follow me?" She then walks to the scales and says, "We would like to get your weight first," or, "Would you please step on the scale?" This simple direction given by the nurse establishes the role hierarchy, placing the patient in the role of a subordinate who follows directions, and the medical personnel in the role of superordinates who are in charge of this and the interactions that follow.[1]

After the patient is on the scale, the nurse records the weight on the patient's record and announces the weight to the patient. The patient typically reacts in one of the following ways: she will either give some form of agreement or assent, such as, "That's right," "That's what I weigh at home," or, "I didn't know I had gained that much"; or she will express disagreement, such as, "Your scale is wrong," "That's not what I weigh at home," or, "Are you sure this is balanced right?" Such reactions appear to reflect the connection in the patient's mind between her weight and her self-concept and indicate her assumption of a subordinate role in allowing this aspect of her person to be officially recorded.

Since the doctor has been taught from his early days in medical school that information concerning the patient's weight must be obtained routinely, he has ritualized this information-gathering process such that he obtains it on all patients, regardless of their medical problem. Thus, weighing the patient has a

[1] Actually, giving access to one's weight is optional, although it is recognized as such by few patients. Almost all patients allow the medical personnel to gather this information, but a small minority refuse to let the doctor take their weight. Although there is disapproval on the part of the medical staff, such noncooperative persons are still allowed to play the patient role. Of the several thousand patients in this sample, only three or four persons adamantly refused to allow their weight to be taken. Without exception, these were extremely obese women. In other cases where the women did not want to be weighed, the nurses were able to maneuver them into permitting it.

manifest function (Merton 1957), that of obtaining information about the patient for a medical record which will guide the doctor in making diagnoses, prescriptions, and prognoses, this information being important for certain patients, such as those who are pregnant, those who have been involved in weight problems, or those who have a history of heart and/or kidney problems.

Beyond this manifest instrumental function, however, there lies a latent supportive function, that of assuring the patient that she is in good medical hands, that her doctor is performing as he is supposed to, and that he is meeting those expectations that the patient has developed through her previous experiences in similar situations. Beyond these functions, the ritualization of the "weighing-in" serves an additional latent function, that of role-legitimization. By looking at weight-taking as role-legitimization, we can see the weighing process in relation to the total performance of the vaginal examination. Although at first there may appear to be but a slight connection between taking the patient's weight and the vaginal examination itself, there is a more integral connection. A woman's weight is intimate. It is something that she ordinarily does not publicize, something that she keeps to herself, something that she may perhaps communicate only to personal friends, something that she may even lie about, often tending to minimize her weight so as to meet some typical American ideal. Because an American woman believes that she is supposed to match some idealized standard, or to approximate it in some way, she is concerned about who has knowledge of her weight and in what way it reflects her approximation to this standard. Accordingly, her self-concept, her ideas about herself as a person, is involved in the weighing process. She takes the results of weighing as an indication of a judgment about her self. As such, she is ordinarily secretive with this information, but in this situation the doctor is defined as one who can legitimately have access to this information, as one who can direct the nurse to gather this information.

Interaction during this prologue to the main performance delineates the medical personnel as those who gather information about intimate details of the patient's life and the patient as one who cooperates in giving such information. By legitimizing such role-playing, the coming performance of the vaginal examination and the "intimate-but-not-intimate," the "sexual-but-not-sexual," interaction with the doctor is legitimated. This legitimation, which is so important to the smooth playing out of the drama, is accomplished by the single maneuver of weighing the patient. If the doctor can legitimately gather such privileged information about the patient, the role relationship of doctor-patient becomes firmly established, making it easier for him to gather information about her pelvic region as well. Thus, the act of weighing the patient takes on significance beyond the physical act when we view it in the context of role assumptions for the vaginal examination.[2]

Following the weighing of the patient, the nurse escorts her into the doctor's office-examination room. "You may be seated," she says, indicating the chair by the desk, "The doctor will be with you shortly." With this statement the nurse has announced the conclusion of the prologue. She then exits, and the first scene is ready to be played.

SCENE I: THE PERSONALIZED STAGE: THE PATIENT AS PERSON

The setting for the vaginal examination, the region in which Scenes I through V are played, may be delineated into two areas (see Figure 2). Although there are no physical boundaries employed to demarcate the two areas, highly differentiated interaction occurs in each area. Area 1, where Scenes I and V are played, includes that portion of the "office-examination" room which is furnished by a desk and two chairs. Area 2, where Scenes II, III, and IV are played, is furnished with an examination table, a swivel stool, a gooseneck lamp, and a sink with a mirror above it. In each area differential interaction takes place. In Area 1 (Scenes I and V) the patient is interacted with by the doctor as a full person, while in Area 2 (Scenes II, III, and IV)

---

[2] It should be noted that the meaning of the weight-taking process differs from situation to situation. Here, we are analyzing only the meaning of this process as it relates to the vaginal examination.

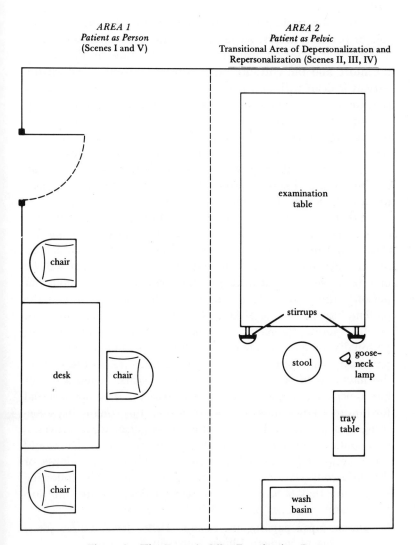

AREA 1
Patient as Person
(Scenes I and V)

AREA 2
Patient as Pelvic
Transitional Area of Depersonalization and
Repersonalization (Scenes II, III, IV)

examination
table

stirrups

stool

goose-
neck
lamp

desk

chair

chair

chair

tray
table

wash
basin

Figure 2. The Doctor's Office-Examination Room.

the individual is transformed from a full person into an object, into a "person-possessing-a-pelvis," and in Scene III even into a "pelvis-that-incidentally-belongs-to-a-person." We shall now examine in detail the dramaturgical process of depersonalization and desexualization.

After the prologue in which the woman has assumed the role of patient, the first scene of the vaginal examination begins, a scene that is set off from previous interaction by the exit of the nurse and the entrance of the doctor, a scene in which the patient is dealt with as a person. The interaction flow of Scene I is as follows: (a) the doctor enters the "office-examination" room; (b) greets the patient; (c) sits down; (d) asks the patient why she is there; (e) questions her on specifics; (f) decides on a course of action, specifically whether a pelvic examination is needed or not; (g) if he thinks a pelvic is needed, he signals the nurse on the intercom and says, "I want a pelvic in room (X)"; (h) he gets up, and (i) leaves the room.

What we mean when we say that during this scene the patient is treated as a full person is that the courtesies of middle-class verbal intercourse are followed, and, in addition to gathering medical information, if the doctor knows the patient well he may intersperse his medical questions with questions about her personal life. When the doctor enters the room, he greets the patient, usually saying either, "Good morning (afternoon)," or "Hello," adding the name of the patient. If he knows the patient personally, he addresses her by her first name, but if he does not personally know her, he uses her last name, even in cases where she has been his patient for over twenty years. When a doctor has a personal relationship with the patient, it is not unusual for him to ask her about her personal life, thus conducting something of a nonmedical conversation. This personalized conversation contains elements very similar to a conversation that would occur between friends seeing each other after a time lapse or that of a conversation between friends at a party. The following interaction that occurred during Scene I demonstrates the doctor's treatment of his patient as a full person:

> Doctor (upon entering the room): "Hello, Joyce, I hear you're going to Southern Illinois University."

Patient: "Yes, I am. I've been accepted, and I have to have my health record completed."

The doctor then seated himself at his desk and began filling out the health record that the patient gave him. He interspersed his questions concerning the record form with questions about the patient's teaching, about the area of study she was pursuing, about her children, their health and their schooling. He then said, "Well, we have to do this right. We'll do a pelvic on you." He then announced via the intercom, "I want to do a pelvic on Joyce in room 1." At that point he left the room.

This interaction sequence is typical of the interaction that occurs in Scene I between a doctor and a patient he knows well. When the doctor does not know the patient well, he does not include his patient's name, either her first or last name, in his announcement to the nurse that she should come into the room. In such a case, he simply says, "I want to do a pelvic in Room 1," or, "Pelvic in Room I." The doctor then leaves the room, marking the end of this scene.

SCENE II: THE DEPERSONALIZING STAGE: TRANSITION FROM PERSON TO PELVIC

When at the close of Scene I the doctor said, "Pelvic in room (X)," he was in effect announcing the transition of the person to a pelvic. It is a sort of advance announcement, however, of a coming event because the transition has not yet been effected. The doctor's signal for the nurse to come in is, in fact, a signal that the nurse should now help with the transition of the patient from a person to a pelvic. Additionally, it also serves as an announcement to the patient that she is about to undergo this metamorphosis.

The nurse then enters this setting and assumes the role of "pelvic preparer," making the transition as smoothly as possible by readying the woman to play a passive cooperative role, by preparing the props and setting the scene for the doctor's re-entrance for the vaginal performance. The nurse, in effect, serves as a stagehand for the performance which is to follow. She also serves as a stage director in the doctor's absence, expediting performances so as to maximize the number of patients the doctor can handle in a day. To do this, she minimizes her interaction with the patient during this scene.

The interaction flow which accomplishes the transition from person to pelvic is as follows: Upon entering the room, the nurse, without preliminaries, tells the patient, "The doctor wants to do a vaginal examination on you. Will you please remove your panties?" While the patient is undressing, the nurse prepares the props, positioning the stirrups of the examination table, arranging the glove, the lubricant, and the speculum (the instrument which, when inserted into the vagina, allows visual examination of the vaginal tract). She then removes the drape sheet from a drawer and directs the patient onto the table, covers the patient with the drape sheet, assists her in placing her feet into the stirrups, and positions her hips, putting her into the lithotomy position (lying on her back with knees flexed and out).

We shall now analyze in detail certain aspects of the interaction that takes place during Scene II that demonstrate the problematics of preparing one's self for a nonsexual genital presentation.

Meaning of the Doctor's Absence

The doctor's exiting from this scene means that the patient will be undressing in his absence. This is not accidental. In many cases, it is true, the doctor leaves because another patient is waiting, but even when there are no waiting patients, the doctor always exits at the end of Scene I. His leaving means that he will not witness the patient undressing, thereby successfully removing any suggestion whatsoever that a striptease is being performed. From the patient's point of view, the problem of undressing is lessened since a strange male is not present, and when the doctor returns, only a small and particularized portion of her body will be exposed for the ensuing interaction. The *time lapse* between the doctor's announcement to the patient that she will have a pelvic examination performed on her and his return to perform that examination, the time during which the nurse prepares her for this transition, not only provides time for the transition to occur, but it also provides time for her to psychologically adjust to the transition. Thus sexuality is removed from the undressing, and when the doctor returns, as we shall see, he is no longer dealing with a person, but he is, rather, confronted by a "pelvic."

Preparatory Washing

It is ordinarily the case that middle-class American women thoroughly cleanse themselves prior to visiting a doctor, usually even "dressing up" for their appointment. They are concerned about the presentation of self that they will make, and in the case of a vaginal examination, they are concerned about the "presentation" of their genital area. Not only are middle-class persons in our society concerned about cleanliness in general, but the medical profession represents or symbolizes aseptic standards to the nth degree. Expecting, then, the highest aseptic standards from the medical profession, when they become role-players within the medical setting, they attempt to fit in with or match these standards. When it is the vagina that is to be examined, it is then the concern of most middle-class women that the vagina meet the standards of cleanliness of the one who will be doing the examining.[3] To meet such expectations, these women prepare their physical selves very carefully prior to the examination. In some cases, the patients verbally specify their concern and preparation, such as the patient who said: "I figured he would do an exam on me this time. I took a bath right before I came here just in case." It would also appear that olfactory aspects of the "presentation" of the self in the vaginal examination are also a consideration in the patient's preparation since some

---

[3] It appears that doctors generally dislike performing vaginal examinations on prostitutes and, in some cases, on lower-class women, in part, perhaps, because these women sometimes do not approximate or strive toward the same standards of asepsis as do middle- and upper-class women. Sometimes doctors are "less gentle" with such patients and "less concerned" about the patient's feelings during the examination. Henslin had this reported to him by women on welfare concerning the coldness and callousness of doctors performing vaginal examinations in public health settings, while Biggs has observed this same behavior in a public health clinic.

of them powder their vaginal area, perhaps in anticipation of their part in the performance.

After the nurse requests that they remove their panties, approximately 50 to 60 percent of the women ask if they can go to the bathroom. There are several possible reasons that this occurs at this particular point of the interaction sequence. Possibly due to the nervousness and excitement of anticipating the vaginal examination, bladder tension is increased which leads the patient to fear that she might lose bladder control during the examination. It is also possible that going to the bathroom is a precautionary step in yet a second way, by emptying the bladder she minimizes discomfort during the coming examination. Another possibility is that the patient, in her concern about the presentation of her genital area, desires to leave for a moment so that she can wash herself once again before the examination. The patient usually brings this subject up by asking, "Can I go to the bathroom?" or, "Is it all right to go to the bathroom?" rather than asking, "Where is the bathroom?" Since she frequently accompanies her question with a request for a towel, it appears that she is asking if there is sufficient time to go to the bathroom, to perhaps wash herself in preparation for the examination, without disrupting the interaction flow.

The Problem of Underclothing

Undressing and nudity are problematic for the patient since she has been socialized into not undressing before strangers.[4] Almost without exception, when the woman undresses in Scene II, she

___

[4] With a society that is as clothing conscious and bodily conscious as is ours, undressing and nudity are probably problematic for almost everyone in our society from a very early age. It is, however, probably more problematic for females than for males since males ordinarily experience structured situations in which they undress and are nude before others, such as showering after high school physical education classes, while females in the same situation are afforded a greater degree of privacy with, for example, private shower stalls in place of the mass showers of the males. Jim Hayes has given us a corroborating example. In the high school of 4,000 students that he attended in Brooklyn, swimming classes were segregated by sex. Male students swam nude in their physical education classes, but female students wore one-piece black bathing suits provided by the school. One can also think of the frequently traumatic, but required, en masse nudity experiences of males in military induction centers; such experiences are not forced upon our female population.

turns away from the nurse and the door, even though the door is closed. She removes only her panties in the typical case, but in some cases undressing includes removing only a girdle, in some girdle and panties, while in others pantyhose and slacks are removed. A small number of the patients also remove their shoes.

After the patient has removed her panties and/or girdle, the problem for her is what to do with them. Panties and girdles do not have the same meaning as other items of clothing, such as a sweater, that can be casually draped around the body or strewn on furniture. Clothing is considered to be an extension of the self (Gross and Stone 1964), and in some cases the clothing comes to represent the particular part of the body that it covers. In this case, this means that panties represent to women their "private area." The patient's problem as to what she should do with her panties is not because of what the other person actually thinks when he sees the undergarments (in this case the doctor when he comes upon the scene), but, rather, what the patient imagines the doctor will think when he enters the room (Cooley 1902). Comments made by patients that illustrate the problematics of panty exposure include: "The doctor doesn't want to look at these," "I want to get rid of these before he comes in," and, "I don't want the doctor to see these old things."

Some patients seem to be at a loss in solving this problem and turn to the nurse for guidance, asking her directly what they should do with their underclothing. Most patients, however, do not ask for directions, but hide their panties in some way. The favorite hiding or covering seems to be in or under the purse.[5] Other women put their panties in the pocket of their coat or in the folds of a coat or sweater, some cover them with a magazine, and some cover them with their own body on the examination table. It is rare that a woman leaves her panties exposed somewhere in the room.

[5] From a psychiatric orientation this association of the panties with the purse is fascinating, given the Freudian interpretation that the purse signifies the female genitalia.

In some examination rooms, the problem of where to put the undergarments is solved by the provision of a special drawer for them located beneath the examination table.

The Drape Sheet

Another problematic area in the vaginal examination is what being undressed can signify. Disrobing for others frequently indicates preparation for sexual relations. Since sexuality is the very thing that this scene is oriented toward removing, a mechanism is put into effect to eliminate sexuality—the drape sheet. After the patient is seated on the table, the nurse places a drape sheet from just below her breasts (She still has her blouse on.) to over her legs. Although the patient is draped by the sheet, when she is positioned on the table with her legs in the stirrups, her pubic region is exposed. Usually it is not necessary for the doctor to even raise a fold in the sheet in order to examine her genitals.

Since the drape sheet does not cover the genital area, but, rather, leaves it exposed, what is its purpose? The drape sheet depersonalizes the patient. It sets the pubic area apart, letting the doctor view the pubic area in isolation, separating the pubic area from the person. The pubic area or female genitalia becomes an object isolated from the rest of the body. With the drape sheet, the doctor, in his position on the low stool, does not even see the patient's head. He no longer sees or need deal with a person, just the exposed genitalia marked off by the drape sheet. Yet, from the patient's point of view in her prone position, her genitals are covered! When she looks down at her body, she does not see exposed genitalia. The drape sheet effectively hides her pubic area *from herself* while exposing it to the doctor. With this, we have a beautiful example of a mechanism that effectively covers the pubic area for one actor while exposing it to the second.

Noncooperativeness

The smoothness or the flow of the intersection is based on the presumption that all actors will fulfill their roles. If, of course, any actor balks at some point, this has the potential of at least disrupting the performance. That such disruptions are rare is excellent testimony that the actors have been well socialized into their respective roles. However, it sometimes happens, though it is extremely rare, that in this second scene a patient balks in cooperating with the transition from person to "person-possessing-a-particular-region." For example:

> A woman of seventy was informed that she would have to have a vaginal examination. She went into the examination room and was told to remove her panties. She refused to do so. After the nurse patiently insisted that she do so, she said that she was wearing more than one pair of panties because it was cold. She said that she would remove one pair but she didn't see any reason to remove the second pair. She took off the first pair, a longer pair of panties. After much coaxing and reassurance that she would be draped, she finally consented to remove her second pair of panties.

In the second case:

> A woman in her sixties came in for a vaginal examination. She refused to remove her panties, insisting that if the doctor was going to examine *her* that the nurse would have to cut a hole in her panties—a hole just large enough for the doctor to get to her. The nurses coaxed the woman, trying to get her to remove her panties, but she absolutely refused. She finally relented and consented to being examined, but she first took the nurse's scissors and cut a section from her panties. She was then placed on the table with her panties on, and the doctor, not without some humor, ended up performing the vaginal examination in this way.

It should be emphasized that these are the only two such refusals that showed up in this sample of 12 to 14,000 vaginal examinations, and in each case the doctor succeeded in performing the examination.

Thigh Behavior

American girls are given early and continued socialization in "limb discipline," being taught at a very early age to keep their legs close together while they are sitting or while they are retrieving articles from the ground (but, see Suttles 1968: 67 for possible ethnic differences). They receive such cautions from their mothers as, "Keep your dress down," "Put your legs together," and "Nice girls don't let their panties show." Evidence of socialization into "acceptable" thigh behavior shows up in the vaginal examination while the women are positioned on the examination table and waiting for the doctor to arrive. They do not let their thighs fall outwards in a relaxed position, but they try to hold their upper or midthighs together until the doctor arrives. They do this even in cases where it is very difficult for them to do so, such as when the patient is in her late months of pregnancy.

Although the scene has been played such that desexualization is taking place, and although the patient is being depersonalized such that when the doctor returns he primarily has a pelvic to deal with and not a person, at this point in the interaction sequence the patient is still holding onto her sexuality and "personality" as demonstrated by her "proper" thigh behavior. Only later, when the doctor reenters the scene will she fully consent to the desexualized and depersonalized role and let her thighs fall outwards.

After the props are ready and the patient is positioned, the nurse announces to the doctor via intercom that the stage is set for the third scene, saying "We're ready in room (X)."

SCENE III: THE DEPERSONALIZED
STAGE: THE PERSON AS PELVIC

A Double Dyadic Encounter or
Face-to-Pubic Interaction

The interaction to this point, as well as the use of props, has been structured to project a singular definition of the situation and to maintain this definition. The definition that has been projected, of course, has been that of legitimate doctor-patient interaction, and, specifically, the nonsexual examination of a woman's vaginal region by a male. In support of this definition, a team performance is given in this scene (Goffman 1959: 104). Although the previous interaction has been part of an ongoing team performance, it has been sequential, leading to the peak of the performance, the vaginal examination itself. At this time, the team goes into a tandem cooperative act, utilizing its resources to maintain and continue the legitimation of the examination, and by its combined performance reinforcing the act of each team member. The doctor, while standing, places a plastic glove on his right hand, again symbolizing the depersonalized nature of the action—by using the glove he is saying that he will not himself be actually touching the "private area" since the glove will serve as an insulator. It is at this point that he directs related questions to the patient regarding such things as her bowels or bladder. Then, while he is still in this standing position, the nurse in synchronization actively joins the performance by squeezing a lubricant onto his outstretched gloved fingers, and the doctor inserts the index and middle fingers of his right hand into the patient's vagina while externally palpating (feeling) the uterus. He then withdraws his fingers from the vagina, seats himself on the stool, inserts a speculum, and while the nurse positions the gooseneck lamp behind him, he visually examines the cervix.

Prior to this third scene, the interaction has been dyadic only, consisting of nurse and patient in Scene II and doctor and patient in Scene I. In this scene, however, the interaction becomes triadic in the sense that the doctor, nurse, and patient are simultaneously involved in the performance. The term triadic, however, does not even come close to accurately describing the role-playing of this scene. Since the patient has essentially undergone a metamorphosis from a person to an object—having been objectified or depersonalized, the focus of the interaction is now on a specific part of her body. The positioning of her legs and the use of the drape sheet have effectively made her pubic region the interaction focus, not only demarcating the pubic region as the focus of interaction but also blocking out the "talklines" between the doctor and patient, physically obstructing their exchange of glances (Goffman 1963: 161). Interaction between the doctor and the patient is no longer "face-to-face," being perhaps now more accurately described as "face-to-pubic" interaction. What would otherwise be a triadic encounter has been successfully transformed through the use of props to a double dyadic encounter. This, at the minimum, is an interesting and highly effective use of props and space.

Breasts as Nonsexual Objects

Projecting and maintaining the definition of nonsexuality in the vaginal examination applies also to other parts of the body that are attributed to have sexual meaning in our culture, specifically the breasts. When the breasts are to be examined in conjunction with a vaginal examination, a rather interesting ritual is regularly employed in order to maintain the projected definition of nonsexuality. This ritual tries to objectify the breasts by isolating them from the rest of the body, permitting the doctor to see the breasts apart from the person. In this ritual, after the patient has removed her upper clothing, a towel is placed across her breasts, and the drape sheet is then placed on top of the towel. Since the towel in and of itself more than sufficiently covers the breasts, we can only conclude that the purpose of the drape sheet is to further the definition of nonsexual interaction. Additionally, the doctor first removes the sheet from the breasts and exposes the towel. He then lifts the towel from *one* breast, makes his examination, and *replaces* the towel over that breast. He then examines the other breast in exactly the same way, again replacing the towel after the examination.[6]

The Nurse as Chaperone

That interaction in Scene III is triadic is not accidental, nor is it instrumentally necessary. It is, rather, purposely designed, being another means of desexualizing the vaginal examination. Instrumentally, the nurse functions merely to lubricate the doctor's

[6] In contrast to this we should note that an Electrocardiography and Basal Metabolism Technician in the U.S. Navy who ran electrocardiographs on over 200 female patients at Great Lakes Naval Hospital and Pensacola Naval Hospital from November 1968 to April 1970 reported to Henslin that the majority of patients preferred having the drape sheets removed from their breasts rather than having the technician "feel" for the electrode position. One doctor also instructed his male technicians to remove the drape sheet in order to accurately place the electrode. Major differences between this situation and the breast examination we are reporting on should be apparent: in ours the "feeling" is instrumental, the way in which the examination is carried out; in the electrocardiography situation the "feeling" due to draping is incidental to the examination and undraping eliminates a male technician from "feeling" the patient's breasts.

fingers and to hand him the speculum. These acts obviously could be handled without the nurse's presence. It becomes apparent, then, that the nurse plays an entirely different role in this scene, that of chaperone (Shibutani 1961: 388), the person assigned to be present in a male-female role relationship to give assurance to interested persons that no untoward sexual acts take place. Although the patient has been depersonalized, or at least this is the definition that has been offered throughout the performance and is the definition that the team has been attempting to maintain, the possibility exists that the vaginal examination can erupt into a sexual scene. Because of this possibility (or the possible imputation or accusation of sexual behavior having taken place), the nurse is always present.[7] Thus even the possibility of sexual content in the vaginal examination is ordinarily denied by all the role-players. It would appear that such denial serves as a mechanism to avoid apprehension and suspicion concerning the motivations and behaviors of the role-players, allowing the performance to be initiated and to smoothly continue to its logical conclusion.[8]

The Patient as a Nonperson
Team Member

With this definition of objectification and desexualization, the patient represents a vagina disassociated from a person. She has

[7] In one instance drawn to our attention by a female reader of this paper, the doctor insists that·his nurse *not* be present during his vaginal examinations—at least this is his behavior when he examines her.

It is interesting to note that even the corpse of a female is defined as being in need of such chaperonage. Erving Goffman, on reading this paper in manuscript form, commented that hospital etiquette dictates that "when a male attendant moves a female stiff from the room to the morgue he be accompanied by a female nurse."

[8] Compare what Goffman (1959: 104) has to say about secrets shared by team members. Remember that the patient in this interaction is not simply a member of the audience. She is a team member, being also vitally interested in projecting and maintaining the definition of nonsexuality. Another reader of this paper reports that during one of her pregnancies she had a handsome, young, and unmarried Hungarian doctor and that during vaginal examinations with him she would "concentrate on the instruments being used and the uncomfortableness of the situation" so as not to become sexually aroused.

been dramaturgically transformed for the duration of this scene into a nonperson (Goffman 1959: 152). This means that while he is seated and performing the vaginal examination, the doctor need not interact with the patient as a person, being, for example, neither constrained to carry on a conversation nor to maintain eye contact with her. Furthermore, this means that he is now permitted to carry on a "side conversation" with the person with whom he does maintain eye contact, his nurse. For example, during one examination the doctor looked up at the nurse and said: "Hank and I really caught some good-sized fish while we were on vacation. He really enjoyed himself." He then looked at his "work" and announced, "Cervix looks good; no inflammation—everything appears fine down here." Such ignoring of the presence of a third person would ordinarily constitute a breach of etiquette for middle-class interactions, but *in this case there really isn't a third person present*. The patient has been "depersonalized," and, correspondingly, the rules of conversation change, and no breach of etiquette has taken place.[9]

The patient, although defined as an object, is actually the third member of the team in the vaginal examination. Her role is to "play the role of being an object"; that is, she contributes her part to the flow of the interaction by acting as an object and not as a person. She contributes to the definition of herself as an object through studied alienation from the interaction, demonstrating what is known as dramaturgical discipline (Goffman 1959: 216–218). She studiously gazes at the ceiling or wall, only occasionally allowing herself the luxury (or is it the danger?) of fleeting eye contact with the nurse. Eye contact with the doctor is, of course, prevented by the position of her legs and the drape

---

[9] In this situation a patient is "playing the role" of an object, but she is still able to hear verbal exchange, and she could enter the interaction if she so desired. As such, side comments between doctor and nurse must be limited. In certain other doctor-patient situations, however, the patient completely leaves the "person role," such as when the patient is anesthesized, which allows much freer banter. In delivery rooms of hospitals, for example, it is not uncommon for the obstetrician to comment while stitching the episiotomy, "She's like a new bride now," or, when putting in the final stitches, to say, "This is for the old man." Additionally, while medical students are stitching their first episiotomy, instructing doctors have been known to say, "It's not tight enough. Put one more in for the husband."

sheet.[10] Not quite as well under her control, it seems, are her hands. Frequently a patient will grasp the sides of the examination table, clutch the edge of the sheet, or tightly clench her hands if she has them folded across her abdomen (cf., Ekman and Friesen 1969). Such behavior betrays her as still possessing "person-ality" in this interaction situation.

But she is cooperating in offering the definition of herself as an object, as a desexualized and depersonalized being, and since objects neither speak nor make eye contact, the patient ordinarily does not.[11] The patients are usually able to sustain their characters quite consistently, restraining their emotional involvement and presenting images of self control (Goffman 1967: 37).[12] It is sometimes the case, however, that patients communicate "out of role" (Goffman 1959: 169) and utter such expressions as "My God!" when the speculum is inserted or some part of the examination is painful.

A Case of Role Failure

Although these role-players almost always play their roles well, and the interaction almost inevitably proceeds without hitch, occasionally the patient does not cooperate and play the role of object. To better contextualize the usual acceptance of the depersonalized role of object, we shall quote in some detail an *atypical* case of performance disruption through the noncooperation of a young, unmarried post-hymenotomy patient: [13]

10 See the analysis of the sociological function of eye contact as given by Georg Simmel in his *Soziologie,* as cited in R. E. Park and E. W. Burgess, *Introduction to the Science of Sociology,* 2nd ed. (Chicago: University of Chicago Press, 1924), p. 358, or in Goffman (1963: 93).

11 This generalization is limited. One friend, upon reading this, stated that she talks to her doctor during this time.

12 It is perhaps excellent testimony to the patients' self-control and communication in character that not even a single instance of expelled flatus was observed in these 12 to 14,000 vaginal examinations.

13 A hymenotomy is a surgical procedure by which the hymen is incised to enlarge the vaginal opening. Such a procedure is sometimes called for when the hymen is thicker or covers more area than usual and first sexual intercourse would be extremely painful.

The doctor enters the room and says, "When is that wedding going to be?" He pulls on his glove.

The patient turns her head to the wall and mumbles, "The fifth of February."

Doctor: "You should be completely healed by then." As the doctor starts to approach the patient, she moves back on the table away from him.

Nurse: "Gerry, please bring your hips down."

Doctor: "Come on, Gerry, bring your hips down."

Patient: "I can't. It'll hurt."

Doctor: "I'll be as careful as possible." The patient moves her hips down to the edge of the table. She closes her eyes tightly and tightly grips the edges of the table. The doctor inserts his fingers and begins the examination.

Doctor: "Relax, Gerry, relax."

Mother: "Come on, Gerry, he can't examine you if you act that way." The patient begins moving her head from side to side. The doctor starts to insert the speculum. The patient again moves her hips away from the doctor.

Patient: "I can't! I can't!"

Doctor: "Please relax so I can insert this speculum."

Mother: "Gerry! Quit acting like that!"

The patient again moves her hips to the edge of the table. The doctor carefully and slowly inserts the speculum.

Patient: "My God! You're tearing me apart! Give me something to bite on! Mom! Give me some gum!" (Patient is shaking her head from side to side very rapidly.) The mother reaches into her purse, removes some chewing gum, unwraps a piece and places it in the patient's mouth. The patient rapidly chews the gum. The nurse moves up to the abdominal area of the patient.

Nurse: "Gerry, please try to relax. It will be so much easier for you." The patient places her right arm over her eyes. Then she reaches out and grabs the nurse, digging her fingernails into the nurse's arm.

Patient: "He's ruining me! I can't stand it!" She continues to shake her head from side to side.

Doctor: "Gerry, I'm just trying to help you. This will be very helpful to you after you get married."

Patient: "I don't see how. It hurts too much."

Mother: "I'm sorry, doctor."

Doctor to Mother: "She's in good condition now. She'll take a normal sized speculum without difficulty." He withdraws the speculum and removes his glove. "I don't think I'll have to see her again—that is, unless she has difficulties later on."

Doctor to Patient: "O.K., Gerry, get dressed." The doctor touches her on her shoulder and says, "I want to have a long talk with you about your wedding." The patient closes her eyes and brings her arm over her eyes. The doctor then leaves the room.

Fortunately for the success of the interaction flow such a refusal to accept the role of object—to be unresponding and uncomplaining—is rare. Almost always the projected definition of dramaturgical depersonalization is not only offered by the involved medical personnel but is also both eagerly accepted and cooperatively role-played by the patient.

After the doctor tells the patient to get dressed, he leaves the room, and the fourth scene is ready to unfold.

SCENE IV: THE REPERSONALIZING STAGE: THE TRANSITION FROM PELVIC TO PERSON

During this stage of the interaction the patient undergoes a demetamorphosis, dramaturgically changing from vaginal object to person. Immediately after the doctor leaves, the nurse assists the patient into a sitting position, and she gets off the table. The nurse then asks the patient if she would like to use a towel to cleanse her genital area, and about 80 percent of the patients accept the offer. In this scene, it is not uncommon for patients to make some statement concerning their relief that the examination is over. Statements such as "I'm glad that's over with" seem to overtly indicate the patient's recognition of the changing scene, to acknowledge that she is now entering a different scene in the vaginal drama.

During this repersonalizing stage the patient is concerned with regrooming and recostuming. Patients frequently ask if they look all right, and the common question, "My dress isn't too wrinkled, is it?" appears to indicate the patient's awareness of and desire to be ready for the resumption of roles other than vaginal object. Her dress isn't too wrinkled for what? It must be that she is asking whether it is too wrinkled (1) for her resumption of the role of person and (2) her resumption of nonpatient roles.

Modesty continues to operate during this scene, and it is interesting that patients who have just had their genital area thoroughly examined both visually and tactually by the doctor are concerned that this same man will see their underclothing. ("He won't be in before I get my underwear on, will he?") They are now desiring and preparing for the return to the feminine role. They apparently fear that the doctor will reenter the room as they literally have one foot in and one foot out of their panties. They want to have their personal front reestablished to their own satisfaction before the return of this male and the onset of the next scene. For this, they strive for the poise and composure that they deem fitting the person role for which they are now preparing, frequently using either their own pocket-mirror or the mirror above the sink to check their personal front.

During this transitional role patients indicate by their comments to the nurse that they are to again be treated as persons. While they are dressing, they frequently speak about their medical problems, their aches and pains, their fight against gaining weight, or feelings about their pregnancy. In such ways they are reasserting the self and are indicating that they are again entering "person-hood."

The patient who best illustrates awareness that she had undergone a process of repersonalization is the woman who, after putting on her panties, said, "There! Just like new again." She had indeed moved out of her necessary but uncomfortable role as object, and her appearance or personal front once again matched her self-concept.

After the patient has recostumed and regroomed, the nurse directs the patient to the chair alongside the doctor's desk, and she then announces via intercom to the doctor, "The patient is dressed," or, "The patient is waiting." It is significant that at this point the woman is referred to as "patient" in the announcement to the doctor and not as "pelvic" as she was at the end of second scene. Sometimes the patient is also referred to by name in this announcement. The patient has undergone her demetamorphosis at this point, and the nurse, by the way she refers to her, is officially acknowledging the transition.

The nurse then leaves the room, and her interaction with the patient ceases.

SCENE V: THE REPERSONALIZED STAGE: THE PATIENT AS PERSON ONCE MORE

When the doctor makes his third entrance, the patient has again resumed the role of person and is interacted with on this basis. She is both spoken to and receives replies from the doctor, with her whole personal front being visible in the interaction. During this fifth scene the doctor informs the patient of the results of her examination, he prescribes necessary medications, and, wherever indicated, he suggests further care. He also tells the patient whether or not she need see him again.

The significance of the interaction of Scene V for us is that the patient is again allowed to interact *as a person within the role of patient.* The doctor allows room for questions that the patient might have about the results of the examination, and he also gives her the opportunity to ask about other medical problems that she might be experiencing.

Interaction between the doctor and patient terminates as the doctor gets up from his chair and moves toward the door. This signals the end of the interaction with that particular patient, and the patient responds by leaving the room, marking the end of this scene.

EPILOGUE: THE RESUMPTION
OF PREVIOUS ROLES

From the doctor's office the patient goes to the receptionist where she pays her fees and makes her next appointment if it is indicated. She has moved into full person phase of the interaction, with her patient role no longer taking priority in her multiple role set. Recognition of the patient as a person is evidenced during the interaction of the epilogue not only by such things as her requesting that she be sent a bill instead of paying cash for her visit, requesting that a particular insurance form be completed, or even asking the receptionist to call her a taxi, but also by her requesting that a suggested appointment time be changed due to either a conflict with previous appointments, lack of transportation on the suggested day, or because she might be out of town, and so forth. Thus, she is now able to interact as an individual, and at this point in the dramaturgy she is able to give her "other identity" preference if she so desires. *Her nonpatient roles directly affect the interaction at this point.* In the epilogue she is not only treated as a patient but also is recognized and interacted with as a person who has multiple roles with concomitant and conflicting responsibilities.

POST-EPILOGUE: THE POST-PATIENT
PHASE

This section is unimportant for our analysis and is mentioned only for the sake of closure. At this point the individual has moved entirely out of the patient role and has assumed her full previous identity. As she exits from the medical area into the waiting room to either await transportation or to leave the building, she once again is a "full person" and has the choice whether or not to interact with others in the waiting room. Whatever choice she makes is dependent upon her resumed full identity, since she has now discarded her patient role.

CONCLUSION: DESEXUALIZATION
OF THE SACRED

In concluding this analysis, we shall briefly indicate that conceptualizing the vagina as a sacred object yields a perspective that appears to be of value in analyzing the vaginal examination. Sacred objects are surrounded by rules protecting the object from being profaned, rules governing who may approach the "sacred," under what circumstances it may be approached, and what may and may not be done during such an approach (Durkheim 1965: 51–59). If these rules are followed, the "sacred" will lose none of its "sacredness," but if they are violated, there is danger of the sacred being profaned.

In conceptualizing the vagina in this way, we find, for example, that who may and who may not approach the vagina is highly circumscribed, with the major person so allowed being one who is ritually related to the possessor of the vagina, the husband. Apart from the husband (with contemporary changes duly noted),[14] except in a medical setting and by the actors about whom we are speaking, no one else may approach the vagina other than the self and still have it retain its sacred character.[15]

Because of this, the medical profession has taken great pains to establish a routine and ritual that will ensure the continued sacredness of the vaginas of its female patients, one that will avoid even the imputation of taboo violation. Accordingly, as we

[14] The other major exception appears to be a same-sexed relative or friend, but only in exceptional circumstances such as illness, when such a person is actually playing the nurse role.

Additionally, it should be noted that we appear to be undergoing a cultural change which is redefining and broadening permissible persons or relationships. For example, currently such approaches by the fiancee would seem to run less risk of violating the sacred than at earlier periods in our history. The same is true for other male-female relationships depending a good deal on education, age, and social class membership.

[15] It is perhaps for this reason that prostitutes ordinarily lack respect: they have profaned the sacred. And in doing so, not only have they not limited vaginal access to culturally prescribed individuals, but they have added the further violation of allowing vaginal access on a pecuniary basis.

have herein analyzed, this ritual of the vaginal examination allows the doctor to approach the sacred without profaning it or violating taboos by dramaturgically defining the vagina as just another organ of the body, disassociating the vagina from the person, while desexualizing the person into a cooperative object.

REFERENCES

Becker, Howard S.; Geer, Blanche; Hughes, Everett C.; and Strauss, Anselm L. *Boys in White: Student Culture in Medical School.* Chicago: The University of Chicago Press, 1961.

Cooley, Charles Horton. *Human Nature and the Social Order.* New York: Charles Scribner's Sons, 1902.

Durkheim, Emile. *The Elementary Forms of the Religious Life.* New York: The Free Press, 1965. (1915 copyright by George Allen and Unwin Ltd.)

Ekman, Paul, and Friesen, Wallace V. "Non-Verbal Leakage and Clues to Deception." *Psychiatry 32:* 88–106, 1969.

Goffman, Erving. *The Presentation of Self in Everyday Life.* Garden City, N.Y.: Doubleday, Anchor Books, 1959.

Goffman, Erving. *Behavior in Public Places: Notes on the Social Organization of Gatherings.* New York: The Free Press, 1963.

Goffman, Erving. *Interaction Ritual: Essays on Face-to-Face Behavior.* Chicago: Aldine Publishing Company, 1967.

Gross, Edward, and Stone, Gregory. "Embarrassment and the Analysis of Role Requirements." *American Journal of Sociology 70:* 1–15, 1964.

Merton, Robert K. *Social Theory and Social Structure.* New York: The Free Press, 1957.

Shibutani, Tamotsu. *Society and Personality.* Englewood Cliffs, N.J.: Prentice-Hall, 1961.

Suttles, Gerald D. *The Social Order of the Slum: Ethnicity and Territory in the Inner City.* Chicago: University of Chicago Press, 1968.

We did not come across the following source until this book was in page proofs, but it should be consulted for its points of similarities and differences: Joan P. Emerson, "Behavior in Private Places: Sustaining Definitions of Realities in Gynecological Examinations," in *Recent Sociology No. 2: Patterns of Communicative Behavior,* ed. Hans Peter Dreitzel (New York: The Macmillan Company, 1970), pp. 74–97.

OCCUPATIONS AND SEX:
WHERE THE OCCUPATION IS SEX

Stripteasing:
A Sex-Oriented Occupation

JAMES K. SKIPPER, JR.
CHARLES H. McCAGHY

Several occupations have as their common goal the profitable sale of sex or sex-related materials. Pimping and prostitution come most readily to mind, but there are also great numbers of people involved in the production and sale of pornography and of a multitude of items designed to enhance sexual satisfaction. In addition, there are occupations dealing with more vicarious sexual experiences within the area of "live entertainment": go-go girls, topless and/or bottomless dancers, and stripteasers. For students of sexual behavior there is a paucity of knowledge concerning these occupations with the possible exception of prostitution. It is the purpose of this paper to help alleviate this lack by providing information about stripteasers: the estimated 7,000 women in the United States who earn a living by removing their clothes in a suggestive fashion before paying audiences (Jones 1967).

The main focus of this paper concerns the sexual aspects of the occupation. Specifically, we will describe and discuss strippers' attitudes toward sex and toward their occupation, the nature of stage performances, and strippers' involvement in off-stage

We would like to express our appreciation to David Gray for his assistance during the data collection stage of this research. We would also like to thank Betty Jeanne Ruano and Joan L. Skipper for their constructive criticism of earlier drafts of this manuscript.

deviant sex behavior. In order to place this material within perspective, we will also briefly review strippers' physical and background characteristics, plus the career process by which they became involved in the occupation.

Nature of the Research

The data were derived from a field study of stripteasers in which both observational and interview techniques were utilized. The principal research site was a midwestern burlesque theater belonging to the "eastern wheel." At the time of this study, this circuit consisted of eleven theaters, some of which have now closed, in ten cities east of the Mississippi River. Each theater employed a different group of touring strippers each week.

The theaters are operated by a firm located in New York City. Through a central booking agency, also located in New York City, the girls sign contracts to work the circuit for specified periods of time, usually several months. Three or four girls, with two or three comics, travel as a show and spend seven days in major cities and less time in smaller cities. However, there is considerable intermixing of girls so that one group is seldom together for long periods of time. Each theater has its own local manager, but with the exception of the "headliner" or star feature, he has little control over which strippers will be sent to him and at what time. The strippers are required to belong to a union, the American Guild of Variety Artists. The minimum wage on the theater tour in 1968–69 was $175 per seven-day week. The strippers also receive traveling expenses (train fare) but not room and board. The booking agency automatically receives 5 percent of each stripper's wages.

With the permission and support of the local theater manager three male researchers [1] viewed stage performances at no expense, and had access to the backstage dressing room area before, during, and after afternoon performances. They were introduced to each touring group of strippers by the stage manager, a female whom the girls trusted. After the stage manager presented them as "professors from the university who are doing

[1] The researchers consisted of the authors of this paper and a psychologist who assisted with the interviewing.

an anthology on burlesque," the researchers explained that they were interested in how persons became stripteasers, and what they thought about stripping as an occupation. From this point, the researchers bided their time with small talk and general questions to the girls about their occupation. The purposes of this tactic were to make the girls more comfortable and to allow the researchers to survey the field for respondents. In this manner casual contacts and interviews were conducted with approximately 110 performers. However, the primary data for this report were gathered through in-depth interviews with thirty-five strippers.

Although no systematic method of selecting respondents from each touring group was used, an attempt was made to obtain a range of ages, years in the occupation, and salary levels. There were only four outright refusals to be interviewed, one coming after the girl had consulted with a boyfriend. In six cases no convenient time for the interview could be arranged because the potential subjects were "busy." It was impossible in these instances to determine whether the excuses really constituted refusals. In general, the researchers found the girls eager to cooperate, and far more girls wanted to be interviewed than could be accommodated.

The interviews, lasting an average of an hour and a half, were conducted in bars, restaurants, and, on occasion, backstage. Although difficult at times, the interviewing took place in a manner in which it was not overheard by others. In all but one case two researchers were present. Interviews also were conducted with others, both male and female, whose work brought them in contact with strippers: the theater manager, stage manager, union agent, and sales persons selling goods to strippers backstage. The interviews were semistructured and designed to elicit information on the background characteristics of strippers, their process of entering the occupation, and their attitudes toward various aspects of the occupation.

Background Characteristics

The women interviewed who strip for a living on the eastern burlesque circuit come from a wide range of social classes and religions. However, they do have some important common characteristics. In terms of physique, when compared with the average American woman age twenty to thirty, the strippers are taller, heavier, have larger hips, and much larger busts.[2] Typically, they are Caucasian and were born and raised in standard metropolitan areas of over 100,000 inhabitants. Almost 90 percent of the girls were firstborn in their family of orientation. During their early childhood they received little affection from their parents, especially from the father who had usually left the home by the time the girls were in their teens. The strippers tended to reach puberty and develop secondary sex characteristics at an early age. Apparently, at this point in life the girls sought the company of others outside the home, in all likelihood to meet their need for affection. They had little difficulty in attracting men, probably because of their early sexual development. In the short run, their relationships with men outside the family were pleasing and satisfying and led to coital experience by age sixteen. By age eighteen they had left home, usually through marriage. In almost every case these marriages ended in divorce.

Occupational Choice of Stripping

Almost all the girls entered the occupation under fortuitous circumstances involving economic need. Few of the girls considered stripping as a way of making a living until shortly before their debut. Only a handful knew anything about the occupation until involved in it. Although most of the girls began stripping with little anticipatory socialization and with little or no training, in most cases they previously had held jobs which required display of their bodies to the general public: dancers, singers, go-go girls, jugglers, "gimmick girls," artists' models, waitress-bar maids, and show-type hat check girls in night clubs.

The data lead us to believe that the career sequence for most

[2] In 1968 a scientific anthropometric survey of women between the ages of twenty and thirty was conducted for the apparel industry to provide information on which to base garment sizes (*Cleveland Plain Dealer*, November 10, 1969). Our finding is based on data from this study compared with the strippers' reported measurements. For elaboration see: Skipper and McCaghy, 1970: 394–395.

strippers involves three important contingencies. The first concerns the use of exhibitionistic behavior for private gain. The girls became aware of their own sexual attractiveness at an early age and used it in an attempt to attract men and gain affection outside the home. For most, the utilization of sexual attractiveness also carried over into their choice of jobs prior to stripping. It is our hypothesis that when an opportunity to strip was available for these girls, their adolescent and employment experiences predisposed them to look upon an occupation involving display of the body as an acceptable economic alternative.

The second contingency concerns the opportunity structure. All subjects were residing in cities which had clubs or theaters which employed strippers, and they all had the necessary physical attributes to qualify as strippers. Furthermore, in almost all instances a friend, employer, agent, or acquaintance suggested stripping to them as a legitimate occupational choice, and many encouraged and supported them during the early stages of their career. It is our opinion that this social support from trusted persons was crucial for facilitating the transition into stripping.

The final contingency is the sudden awareness of easy economic gain. The subjects' discovery that they could immediately make more money stripping than in any other available legitimate occupation proved to be crucial in convincing them to alter career plans. For all girls in the sample, the monetary aspect still remains the most important occupational reward.

Occupational Stereotype

As the level of general education in the United States continues to rise, an individual's occupation becomes an increasingly significant variable in evaluating and locating his place in society. The public's judgments about an occupation may not always be based on objective considerations of tasks performed, however. Instead, the public either may be misinformed about the actual work accomplished or, for one reason or another, may choose to evaluate an occupation from a different perspective or criterion. Individuals within an occupation, of course, not only have better knowledge of work accomplished but may justify their existence from perspectives or on criteria not considered legitimate by the public. Consequently, these individuals' judgments concerning the social worth of their occupation may be quite different from that of the public's.

Nevertheless, individuals' attitudes about their occupation are bound to be affected by what they believe other people think. This would seem to be especially true if they perceive societal response to be essentially negative. Stripteasing, as an occupation, presents such a case: many strippers' attitudes toward their occupation are adjustments to a perceived negative stereotype.

What image does the public have of strippers? Although data are meager, indications are that "conventional" society sees little to commend them. In a survey of seventy-five college students we discovered a definite negative image of stripteasers. To the question, "What type of women do you think make their living by stripping?" the following words and phrases were representative of student replies: "hard women," "dumb," "stupid," "uneducated," "lower class," "can't do anything else for a living," "oversexed," "immoral," and "prostitutes." In a study concerning nudity in art training, Jessor and Donovan (1969) provide data from 155 non-art university students and 122 of their parents showing that stripteasers are given a lower occupational ranking than such traditionally low-status types of work as: janitor, artist model, and professional gambler. D'Andre (1965) summarizes the stereotype in the following fashion:

> In the laymen's view the stripper is an underworld figure who inhabits the dark places of the urban community. She is thought to consort with various hoodlums, hustlers, drug addicts, pimps, prostitutes and other disreputable characters who populate the "tenderloin area of the large city." The notion is probably widespread that exotics are persons who shift back and forth from prostitution, posing for pornographic photos and stripping, depending upon the shifts in economic conditions. The patently sexual stage names adopted by strippers contribute to the stereotype of them as markedly unconventional persons. Most of them assume names such as Stark Naked, Vampira, Beddy Fox, Helen Bedd, Tempest Storm, Irma the Body, Satin Doll, Frosty Winters, Blaze Starr, and Exotica.

While this stereotype is overly harsh in its portrayal of the stripper, as we will demonstrate later, in certain respects it is not far from reality. However, what is important here is to understand that strippers are aware of their public image and adjust their own image to it.

All but three girls in our sample felt that the average person thought the worst of stripteasers and their occupation. The following are typical of their beliefs:

> Yes, most people seem to think stripping is a low-down dirty way to make a buck.

> Because you are a stripper people think that you automatically will indulge in some type of perverse sexual activity.

> A lot of people believe if you take your clothes off and do a little act with it—it is immoral.

> The public thinks strippers are some kind of an object, not human beings having human qualities. People are continually interfering with your privacy. They make vulgar remarks to you. Call you up at night and send you dirty letters and proposition you.

Reactions to the Stereotype

Among the strippers there were three quite different reactions to the stereotype. *First,* about 20 percent of the sample *agreed* with the negative public image. These girls appeared to have much in common with the type of prostitute which Jackman, O'Toole and Geis (1963) describe as "alienated." They were ashamed of their occupation and of themselves, their main rationalization being that they stripped strictly for the money. Since it was difficult for them to favorably define behavior which is generally condemned by conventional society, they perceived themselves as having adjustment problems, and they had definite negative self images. The following remarks are typical of their attitudes toward the occupation:

> Stripping *is* dirty. There is a little dirty streak in anyone who strips.

> Stripping is like a narcotic: once you get started it's hard to break the habit. I have tried and tried but I can't stop.

> I hate burlesque with a passion—everything about it. The girls are
> rotten to the core. If I had to do it over again I would continue in
> school and get my degree.

The above attitudes were accompanied by:

> I am nothing but a sinful stripper.

> I know I am a bad girl. I suppose I will go to Hell someday.

> I am afraid I am going to get kicked out of the church and maybe
> go to Hell.

Goffman has commented that when one's deviance is not
readily apparent: "The issue is not that of managing tension
generated during social contacts, but rather that of managing
information about his failing" (1963: 42). These strippers offer
a clear example of this type of behavior. The perceived stigma
associated with stripping is so strong with this group that they
make every attempt to conceal their involvement in the occupation, even from family members. As one girl put it, "I would
simply fall apart if my mother knew I stripped." The usual ploy
is to convince the family that they are dancers, singers, or in
some form of more "legitimate" entertainment. In public they
avoid admitting to anyone that they are strippers. At times they
do not even call themselves entertainers, but make up an unrelated occupation instead, such as secretary or receptionist. When
checking into a hotel they register under their real name rather
than revealing their occupation by using their exotic professional
name. Finally, we observed that when these strippers left the
theater they were dressed very conservatively or, in two cases, a
bit on the shabby side. They wore little or no makeup. Once on
the street they blended in with everyone else, and it would have
been impossible to recognize them as strippers. This is in sharp
contrast to the majority of strippers whose manner and dress in
public strongly suggest that they are show girls of one sort or
another. To use Goffman's (1963) terms, in the former case exotic
dress is perceived as a "stigma symbol" while in the latter it is
seen as a "prestige symbol."

The *second* reaction to the negative public image common
to about 30 percent of the strippers was to flatly *deny* it had any
validity. They reacted as victims of what Lemert has called "pu-

tative deviation"—"that portion of the societal definition of the deviant which has no foundation in his objective behavior" (1951: 56). These denials often took the form of simply insisting that strippers are not prostitutes, homosexuals, fast women, drug addicts, or any other kind of deviant. In effect, these strippers perceived themselves as being no different from any other working girls. They viewed stripping as a legitimate form of entertainment. To them, performing on stage was part of show business, and they were proud to be part of it. Several of these subjects claimed that more sexual deviation, or "hanky panky" as they sometimes put it, goes on among secretaries, teachers, and nurses than among strippers. As one stated: "Stripping on stage is quite a lot different than a secretary 'shacking up' with her boss every weekend."

The *remaining* strippers (roughly 50 percent) *rationalized* the stereotype, expressing an agreement with some components of the stereotype but claiming that no question of morality was involved. Their justifications closely approximated the kinds of rationalizations that Sykes and Matza (1957) label "techniques of neutralization," especially "denial of injury" (whether or not anyone is hurt is a matter of interpretation) and "condemnation of the condemners" (those who condemn are hypocrites).

They admitted that they or many of their colleagues engaged in prostitution and/or lesbian activities. Furthermore, many of them frankly enjoy a variety of bed partners: "If I like a guy I sleep with him." They professed a *laissez faire* normative code toward sexual activities: "If you are not hurting anyone, how can it be bad?" We noted a deep resentment in these strippers toward anyone who criticized their activities: "If it does not involve them, it is none of their damn business what I do." In addition, several of this group felt that many "respectable" people were hypocritical: on the one hand they publicly condemn sexual deviation, while on the other they privately engage in it.

Occupational Ideology

Unlike the strippers who admitted the validity of the negative stereotype, both those who denied it and those who rationalized it had positive self-images. They appeared to have fewer prob-

lems in adjusting to the occupation. It was from this group especially that we discovered a rather well-developed ideology in
which the girls appeared to firmly believe.

The *stripper ideology* centers around concepts of entertainment and service to both the community and the individual. In
terms of the *entertainment orientation* the girls' justification for
participation in the occupation may be stated quite simply: the
burlesque show, of which stripping is part, is a time-honored and
legitimate form of show business. People come to see the shows
to be entertained the same way they go to see movies, stage shows,
or football games. Strippers are performers with the same motivations, needs, and rewards as any other performers, be they
actresses or ice skating queens.

The *service orientation* of the ideology is more complicated
than that of the entertainment aspect, and it needs elaboration.
First, it must be understood that while performing, strippers
often witness reactions from the audience which actually shock
them. Because of lighting conditions strippers on stage are unable to see clearly beyond the first few rows. From these rows
they are continually treated to acts rivaling their own performance: male exhibitionism and masturbation. The strippers are
very conscious of this phenomenon and characterize a large proportion of their audience as "degenerates." The term "degenerate" turned up so often in our interviews that it must be
considered an integral part of the stripper argot.[3] Although strippers understand that many "respectable" people attend their
performances, such persons are usually seated beyond the first
rows, out in the dark where they are not easily seen. Thus, the

[3] Strippers do not use an extensive occupational argot unique to themselves. Much of it is borrowed from show business in general. Yet there are
a few terms which have a special meaning within the business. The term
"degenerate" is one of these. Others which will be referred to in this paper
include: (1) *bird*—female genitalia, (2) *birdwatcher*—males in the theater audience whose main interest in the shows is watching for the "bird" to appear,
(3) *flashing*—the lowering of the G-string so that the pubic area is displayed,
(4) *floor work*—that portion of a stripper's performance done sitting, kneeling
or lying on the floor, (5) *holding their own*—masturbating in the theater audience, (6) *strong act*—a performance which contains a high degree of overt
sexual content or *dirty work*, (7) *a strong city* is one in which strippers are
permitted to perform strong acts.

girls are preoccupied with the "degenerate" portion of the audience. Given this perspective, it is not difficult to understand that the strippers believe that they provide a service by allowing such individuals an outlet for their sexual needs in a manner which does not harm society. For example:

> Strip shows allow a lot of people to get their sexual kicks without hurting anybody. It keeps peeping toms off the street, and helps protect people from getting molested.

> A strip house in the community can help release peoples' tensions and prevent things like rape and sexual assaults.

> We perform a real service to the community. The people who come to see us are mostly sexually frustrated or degenerate, you know. They are unable to take out normal desires in normal ways, and thus, they come to the theater to look at it. If they did not do this, they would be doing immoral acts outside like rape and molesting young girls and things like that.

One stripper professed that if legal shows were not available, the same services would be provided underground:

> If burlesque houses were abolished, you would find the same things in private and small groups. There would always be girls who would be willing to do it. In general, it protects women by having it all out in the open.

Strippers' feelings toward the first rows can only be described as ambivalent. On one hand, strippers are not particularly sympathetic toward these "degenerates," but on the other hand, these same "degenerates" play important functions for strippers as well: as just discussed, they provide a raison d'être; for many strippers, interaction with them is an integral part of their performance; and "degenerate" or not, these are *regular* paying customers. So while strippers do not appreciate their presence, it is questionable whether they could do without them.

Strippers' services are useful not only for the denizens of the front rows, however. They also provide a remedy to other males for whom circumstances have precipitated problems:

> People come to see stripping to obtain a form of substitute com-

panionship. Someone might be temporarily lonely where a wife or friend might be ill or in the hospital and come to see the show as a substitute or fantasy relationship.

Several subjects also pointed to the often neglected voyeuristic function of their occupation. As one of the more articulate strippers in our sample put it:

> Males have an overwhelming need for visual sex. This need is independent of physical sex. The American female has little understanding whatsoever of the male's need for visual sex. Many males will even buy their wives sexy garments and frilly underclothes and nightgowns which the women see no reason for wearing, so they go into the drawer, and they are never worn. That is why men go to strip shows and buy girlie magazines.

Another claimed:

> Men are funny. They get a big kick out of seeing women dressed up in frilly undergarments and acting sexy. It is a thing with them. You are men; you know what I mean. After a woman gets married for a year or two, she thinks she has got it made. She thinks she does not have to do it anymore. She only looks pretty when she is going out, you know, for other people but really not her husband. That is why so many men come to see us. Then they go home and dream of us while they are making love to their wives. If the average housewife ever wised up, we would be out of business. But they won't.

Finally, one girl felt that strippers even performed an educational service to women: "Women come to strip shows because they are curious. Not about the girls, but to get ideas. They come to see what really turns men on."

It appears, then, that the ideologies of strippers concerning the role of their occupation can be roughly classified as: (1) strictly legitimate entertainment, (2) a sexual catharsis for elements of society, and (3) a sexual educational service. The extent to which these rationales reflect reality is relatively inconsequential. More important is that they enable a large proportion of the girls to avoid a negative self-concept which the opinions of conventional society fosters: Society can believe what it wants, but their performances mean more than the pursuit of a buck in a dirty business.

It is interesting to note that the stripper ideology in many respects is similar to that of another sex-oriented occupation—"call girls." However, Bryan (1966) found little evidence that the call girls personally endorsed their occupational ideology. From our observations, we suspect that strippers may differ from call girls in this respect since many of the girls in our sample did endorse their occupational perspective.

The Performance

We are not aware of any estimates as to the percentage of the American public which eventually finds its way into a burlesque theater. Whatever the number, no doubt many are disillusioned if they have relied on Hollywood's portrayal which includes a large pit orchestra, sumptuous settings, and performers who not only "striptease" but display a spectrum of entertainment talents. Perhaps these did characterize the burlesque of yesteryear. But aside from the comics, who are vestiges of burlesque's golden age, the often attractive girls' costumes, and the beauty of nakedness, today's burlesque sells little to bedazzle the ear or eye.

Many acts, aside from those of the headliner or star feature, are simply exercises in divesting to the legal minimum with the emotion of a robot. What many of the girls lack in talent, they refuse to make up in enthusiasm. Among most headliners and others with talent and/or enthusiasm, the performances may be considerably embellished, but the outcome is never in question: what authorities will allow is displayed with aplomb. The product is sex with varying degrees of icing and, notwithstanding claims of humanitarian service, undressing before a roomful of men is a routine job.

In describing the stripping performance, it is helpful to use a typology or system of classification. We are aware that performances may be analyzed on a number of different levels; however, for our purpose, two variables are sufficient: the content of performance and the extent of the performer's interaction with her audience. By "content" we refer to the extent to which the performance is dominated by sexual activity or by "entertainment" in the form of singing, dancing, magic act, etc. Content will be considered in terms of a triad: predominately *sexual,* predominately *entertainment,* and a *combination.* Audience interaction refers to the amount of banter and exchange of risqué anecdotes between the performer and her audience; it will be dichotomized as either high or low. Logically, there are six possible types of performance:

1. Sexual—high interaction
2. Sexual—low interaction
3. Combination—high interaction
4. Combination—low interaction
5. Entertainment—high interaction
6. Entertainment—low interaction

Of these possibilities, one did not occur during our observations: entertainment—high interaction. This absence of one of the low sexual content performances may be at least partly due to the degree of permissiveness in the city which served as the primary research site.

The enforcement of obscenity laws in the state where the strippers were interviewed is usually left up to local officials. This results in considerable variation in interpretation of what is obscene among the cities which have burlesque theaters. The city in which the research was conducted is more permissive than most in its interpretation of the law. In the argot of the occupation, it is known as a "strong" city. Performers are allowed to bare their breasts completely and are permitted to "flash," that is, lower the G-string so that the pubic area is displayed. Although the G-string may be lowered to the knees or ankles, its complete removal apparently is considered obscene. With but few exceptions the local management requires the strippers to "flash."

Of those performances observed, the one least appreciated, judging by audience applause or verbal response, was entertainment—low interaction. They comprised about 5 percent of the performances we viewed. Typical of this type was the stripper who performed a quasi-magical act. Wearing a long cape over her costume as she pranced around the stage, she would turn her back to the audience and remove a piece of clothing. The garment she took off seemed to vanish in thin air. The climax of her act was the removal and disappearance of her bra. At no time did she remove her panties, hence not even her G-string was shown.

The second least frequent type of performance was that which involved a combination of sexual and entertainment content with low audience interaction. This type of performance seemed somewhat more appreciated by the audience and comprised about 10 percent of the acts we viewed. A prime example of this type of performance is the girl who comes on stage dressed in a beautiful gown and singing a popular song. Then on the spur of the moment and without formality she takes off all her clothing and flashes her "bird."

One of the two most frequent types of performances was sexual—low interaction. Approximately 30 percent of the performances were of this type. It was most typical of girls with well-developed busts. For example, as one girl with a forty-eight inch bustline stated: "I don't try to project any type of image. I just parade my tits around. It is as simple as that. I don't even have to flash much."

An equally frequent (30 percent) but more appreciated type of performance had predominately sexual content with high audience interaction. Unlike the performance described above, in this type the tease is as important as the strip. Sometimes the girl carries on a conversation with the whole audience, but usually she directs her remarks at selected individuals in the first two rows. As one girl told us, "You try to find a couple of good 'birdwatchers' and go to work on them." The conversation and gestures are attempts at sexual provocation. By conventional standards they would be classified as vulgar and obscene. However, they do seem to have an effect on the men in the first few rows. It was our observation that the highest frequency of "holding their own" among these men occurred during acts with high sexual content combined with high audience interaction.

The final type of performance, a combination of sexual and entertainment content with high audience interaction, was most applauded by the audience. Approximately 25 percent of the performances we viewed fitted this type. They were larger, longer, and more costly productions, usually involving elaborate gowns and/or props. In almost all cases, girls in this type of performance were "headliners," the stars of the show, and were well paid for their work. Characteristically, the girls tried to project an image: a little girl look, subtle sophistication, jungle woman, a lady from Spain, and so forth. The performances also included a large segment of what in stripper argot are termed "floor work" and "prop work." These refer to the use of the floor or props (e.g., hosiery, a snake, a chair, a couch) as part of the act. "Floor work" and "prop work" usually are used exclusively by the head-liner in a touring group.

Representative of this type of performance was the stripper who portrayed a sophisticated Spanish lady. She entered the stage garbed in a spectacular eighteenth-century Spanish costume complete with tiara and fan. While the band played Spanish music, she performed several Spanish dances while occasionally chatting with the audience in Spanish. During this portion of the act, lasting several minutes, she removed only her cape. During the next several minutes, while in constant conversation with the audience, she seductively removed all her clothing except the G-string. The last segment of the performance was devoted to "dirty work." The climax came when while sitting in a reclining chair facing the audience, she let the G-string fall to her ankles, spread her legs and suggestively gestured to the audience.

Deviant Acts Off Stage

Contrary to the stereotype, we discovered little evidence that stripteasers are engaged in a wide range of deviant activities. With the exception of one girl who claimed to have a boyfriend in the Mafia, none of the strippers admitted knowing anyone who was remotely connected with organized crime. Two girls appeared to be in the early stages of alcoholism, but in general strippers appear to use alcohol in moderation if they drink at all. We found no evidence of drug addiction, nor did the use of marijuana appear to play a significant role in the stripper subculture. Thus, in these areas of nonsexual deviance, we found little evidence to support the public stereotype. Only a few of the girls stated that they had posed for pornographic "art" pictures or played in stag and "beaver" films. However, we did find sizable portions of the strippers involved in prostitution and homosexual activities.

The restricted sample and relatively brief contact with the strippers did not allow us to ascertain directly the extent of their involvement in sexual deviation. However, we were able to gauge the salience of such behavior in the occupation by asking the strippers to estimate what percentage of their occupation engaged in such activities. For prostitution, the estimates ranged from 50 to 100 percent. From self-admission we have evidence that at least 18 subjects in the sample (over 50 percent) had at one time or another practiced prostitution. One girl told us: "You cannot be in this business for six months without becoming a prostitute."

A male closely related with burlesque for twenty years related to us:

I never met a stripper who would pass up a chance to turn a couple of easy tricks. It is good money, $50 to $150 a John these days, and they don't pay taxes on it. Besides it is a lonely business. When they get through work, they have a choice of going back to a crummy hotel room or going out on the town—the clubs I mean. For most of these girls, they have got to be with people; they go nuts being alone. So they live it up at night.

At the same time there is evidence that not all strippers are enthusiastic about the opportunity for prostitution:

I don't like the girls who use stripping as a vehicle for prostitution. It gives the occupation a bad name, and furthermore it drives down the price managers will pay you. The managers say, for example, "I will pay you $200 a week for playing here, but you probably can pick up $350 a week turning tricks." What happens then to the girl who says, "Well, I don't want to turn tricks?"

It is our estimation that a large percentage of the girls, perhaps as many as 75 percent, have at one time or another engaged in prostitution. However, of the strippers we interviewed working in the theater circuit only six (17 percent) of the sample were systematically involved in prostitution. Two of the girls claimed that in 1968–69, at $35 to $100 a trick, they made more money in prostitution than they did by stripping.

When the respondents were questioned on the extent of homosexual activities among strippers, their estimates ranged from 15 to 100 percent of the girls being at least bisexual in their orientation. However, the majority of the responses indicated that between 50 to 75 percent of the girls had, on occasion, engaged in homosexual liaisons while in the occupation. We also have evidence, mostly self-admissions, that nine of the thirty-five respondents (26 percent) had themselves engaged in homosexual behavior while in the occupation, although in no case did we request such information or have prior evidence of the respondents' involvement. We did attempt to include subjects in the sample whom we suspected were maintaining stable homosexual relationships. Our efforts were unsuccessful. In several instances strippers known to be traveling with unemployed and unrelated female companions refused to be interviewed. In each case their excuse was the same, "I just don't have the time."

Although we were unable to fix an exact proportion of strippers who had been involved in lesbian behavior, it was clear from the respondents' estimates and discussions that such behavior is widespread in the occupation. The estimates of 50 to 75 percent are well above Kinsey's findings that 19 percent of his total female sample had physical sexual contact with other females by age forty (1953: 452–453). This difference is further heightened when we consider that a large majority of our sample (69 percent) were or had been married; Kinsey found that only 3 percent of married and 9 percent of previously married females had homosexual contacts by age forty (1953: 453–454).

It is interesting to note that the vast majority of the girls do not appear to have had lesbian experiences before entering the occupation. From the discussions with the strippers, it became evident that much of such behavior could be attributed to occupational conditions. Those conditions specifically supportive of homosexual behavior in the occupation of stripping are as follows: (1) isolation from affective social relationships, (2) unsatisfactory relationships with males, and (3) an opportunity structure allowing a wide range of sexual behavior. Since this particular subject is dealt with in detail in another paper (McCaghy and Skipper 1969), it will only be summarized here.

The demands of the occupation place obstacles in the way of the strippers establishing and maintaining firm affective relationships even on a temporary basis. Their work restricts them to the theater from 1 P.M. to 11 P.M. (even later on Saturday nights) except for a two and a half hour dinner break. After the last show the girls go either to a nearby night club for entertainment and/or to make contacts for prostitution, or to their hotel rooms to watch television. Characteristically, they sleep until shortly before the 1 P.M. show. This type of life severely limits the range of relationships the strippers might otherwise have. The most universal complaint among strippers on tour is the loneliness they experience. For reasons of which the strippers either were unaware or did not care to verbalize, the girls in a touring group rarely do things together outside the theater. In itself, this loneliness would not necessarily lead to homosexual activities, for the isolation is from females as well as males. However, when strippers discover that contacts with males are not only limited, but often not very pleasurable, lesbianism may become an attractive alternative.

Throughout the course of the interviews we noted the strippers' disillusionment with males. Many of them had bitter memories of fathers from whom they received little attention and affection. Others recalled unpleasant initial sexual experiences, two of the girls even claiming to have been raped before age fifteen. Of the twenty-four girls in the sample who had ever been married, twenty (82 percent) had experienced at least one divorce. Their use of the term "degenerate" to describe the majority of males in the burlesque audience is also indicative of their disillusionment with males. When strippers do establish relationships with males, they often end in disappointment. Frequently the girls become involved with rough, unemployed males who are only interested in a financial or sexual advantage. There is also evidence that the girls meet more than their share of what one of our respondents called "pimps, leeches, or weirdos." Under these circumstances, relationships with lesbians are perceived as more pleasurable than relationships with exploitive males. However, one should not get the impression that most strippers are anti-male or that they have severed all contacts with males. In fact, most of the girls hope to get married again. The "career" homosexual is the exception among strippers; the majority may be most accurately described as bisexual.

The third occupational condition contributing to lesbian activities is the opportunity structure allowing for a wide range of sexual behavior. Partly as a consequence of their occupation, strippers have a very liberal and permissive attitude toward sex. Their tolerance level of homosexual behavior is very high. Like prostitution, little or no stigma is attached to homosexual behavior. For strippers the current cliche is applicable—what two consenting adults do in privacy is their own business. Thus, if a girl decides to be gay, she can be assured that she will not be ostracized by the majority of her stripping colleagues.

Discussion and Summary

This presentation mainly has been a descriptive account of: the physical and background characteristics of stripteasers; the career process by which they become involved in the occupation; their attitudes toward sex and their sex-oriented occupation; the nature of their stage performances; and their involvement in off-stage deviant behavior.

Realizing the small and nonrandom sample on which this study is based, we suggest the following tentative generalizations:

1. *Stripteasers are not recruited randomly from the general population; they share certain common physical and social background characteristics.* In physical build they are taller, heavier, and have larger hips and busts than the average woman in their age group. Strippers characteristically come from large metropolitan areas, were firstborn children who received little parental affection, matured physically at an early age, experienced early coital experience, and left home by age eighteen, usually by a marriage which eventuated in divorce.

2. *There is a discernible pattern in the occupational choice of stripping.* Entrance into the occupation occurs under fortuitous circumstances involving economic need. There is little training or anticipatory socialization, except for previous jobs which required display of the body. Three contingencies appear important. First, the girls had a history of exhibitionistic behavior for gain. This may have predisposed them to view an occupation involving display of the body as an acceptable economic alterna-

tive. Second, they were all living in metropolitan areas which contained stripping establishments. In addition, the opportunity was suggested, supported, and sometimes facilitated by persons whom the girls trusted. The third contingency was the girls' sudden awareness of the easy economic gain they would receive from stripping.

3. *The attitudes of strippers toward themselves and their sex-oriented occupation are greatly influenced by their perception of the public's negative image of their work.* Three different reactions were apparent from our research. The first is acceptance of the negative stereotype: this in turn results in a negative self-image, problems of adjustment, and attempts to keep their work secret from others outside the occupation. The second reaction is to deny the stereotype by insisting that strippers do not participate in any more deviant acts than the general public. The third reaction consists of admitting that while aspects of the stereotype are true, any question of morality or propriety is irrelevant since the behavior is a private matter and does not harm others.

4. *Many strippers have a relatively well-developed ideology.* Some believe the occupation has an entertainment function; others believe it acts as a sexual catharsis for certain segments of society, and is a source of sexual education for some individuals.

5. *Although strippers' performances vary in form and detail, they essentially involve little aside from sexual content.* While acts differ in the amount of talent displayed, beauty of costumes, interaction with the audience, etc., it is the sexual content that is at the heart of the performance. For many of the girls, their performances are devoid of any emotion and are presented with impersonal detachment from the audience.

6. *The stereotype of strippers as persons who engage in a wide variety of deviant acts appears unwarranted. There is evidence, however, that strippers participate to a large extent in two types of sexual deviance: prostitution and lesbianism.* Participation in deviant sexual acts is probably related to the permissiveness and tolerance toward all sexual matters inherent in the occupation. In addition, other aspects of the occupation contribute to the incidence of lesbian behavior: isolation from affective so-

cial relationships of any type and obstacles to maintaining lasting and satisfactory relations with males.

REFERENCES

Bryan, James. "Occupational Ideologies and Individual Attitudes of Call Girls." *Social Problems 12* (Spring): 441–450, 1966.

D'Andre, Ann Terry. "An Occupational Study of the Strip-Dancer Career." Paper read at the Pacific Sociological Association Meetings, Salt Lake City, Utah (April, 1965).

Goffman, Erving. *Stigma: Notes on the Management of Spoiled Identity*. Englewood Cliffs, N.J.: Prentice-Hall, 1963.

Jackman, Norman, Richard O'Toole, and Gilbert Geis. "The Self-Image of the Prostitute." *The Sociological Quarterly 4* (Spring): 150–160, 1963.

Jessor, Clinton, and Lewis Donovan. "Nudity in the Art Training Process: An Essay with Reference to a Pilot Study." *The Sociological Quarterly 10:* 355–371, 1969.

Jones, Libby. *Striptease*. New York: Simon and Schuster, 1967.

Kinsey, Alfred C., Wardell B. Pomeroy, Clyde E. Martin, and Paul H. Gebhard. *Sexual Behavior in the Human Female*. Philadelphia: W. B. Saunders Co., 1953.

Lemert, Edwin M. *Social Pathology*. New York: McGraw-Hill, 1951.

McCaghy, Charles H., and James K. Skipper, Jr. "Lesbian Behavior as an Adaptation to the Occupation of Stripping." *Social Problems, 17* (Fall): 262–270, 1969.

Skipper, James K., Jr., and Charles H. McCaghy. "Stripteasers: The Anatomy and Career Contingencies of a Deviant Occupation." *Social Problems 17* (Winter): 391–405, 1970.

Sykes, Gresham, and David Matza. "Techniques of Neutralization: A Theory of Delinquency." *American Sociological Review 22* (December): 664–670, 1957.

The Prostitute:
Developing a Deviant Identity

NANETTE J. DAVIS

INTRODUCTION

The movement into prostitution is frequently explained by harsh childhood experiences leading to emotional inadequacy or sex-role confusion [1] or, from the deviant's viewpoint, by accounts of "atrocity tales" which justify the "fallen" state.[2] My participant observation of youthful female offenders in a training school for a three-month period in 1965, however, suggests that situational and cognitive processes tend to be the dominant influences in

This study is based on an unpublished Master's thesis, "Prostitution and Social Control: An Empirical Inquiry Into the Socialization Process of Deviant Behavior," (1967) University of Minnesota, under the direction of Professor David A. Ward.

The writer wishes to express appreciation to James M. Henslin, Peter K. Manning, Bernard N. Meltzer, John Petras, and Ira Reiss for their helpful comments.

[1] Greenwald used a psychoanalytical framework in his study of twenty call girls. Emotional disturbances and sex-role confusion were cited as characteristics that predispose females to prostitution. Harold Greenwald, *The Call Girl* (New York: Ballantine Books, 1958).

[2] Erving Goffman, *Asylums* (New York: Doubleday & Company, 1961), p. 151.

this behavior.[3] Since most of the institutionalized girls I encountered had similar backgrounds and social experiences, and yet only a few had become prostitutes, a more fruitful explanation could focus on those interpersonal processes and self-definitions that help to define the deviant role.

My earlier intent was to study the first phase of learning deviant behavior and the initial enactment of that behavior. By concentrating on the self-reported experiences of adolescent prostitutes, I had hoped to determine the characteristic forms of experiences that may predispose persons to this behavior. The subsequent expansion of this study to include the later ordering of events leading to a career in prostitution was influenced by (1) the possibility of gaining a larger sample than was possible by focusing only on the early offender, and (2) the theoretical concern with secondary deviation,[4] or the labeling process, by which people react to the consequences of having been labeled deviant by others.

[3] The sociology of prostitution has had scant research. Mention should be made, however, of certain works, some of which adopt an orientation different from the one considered in this paper. Kingsley Davis' theoretical work in this area has focused on the condemnation of prostitutes in industrial societies. The prostitute, Davis argues, engages in a primary contact in a secondary relationship which not only profanes the sacredness of the sentimental relationship, but also as a basis for income, leaves uncontrolled the social effects. Kingsley Davis, "Sexual Behavior" in *Contemporary Social Problems*, 2nd ed., ed. Robert K. Merton and Robert A. Nisbet (New York: Harcourt, Brace & World, 1966), pp. 322–372. A short survey of the literature may be found in: Travis Hirschi, "The Professional Prostitute," *Berkeley Journal of Sociology* 7 (1962): 37–48. James Bryan, who utilized a career orientation in his study of prostitutes, offers research on the socialization and ideology of thirty-three call girls. James K. Bryan, "Apprenticeships in Prostitution," *Social Problems 12* (Winter 1965): 287–297; and "Occupational Ideologies and Individual Attitudes of Call Girls," *Social Problems 13* (Spring 1966): 441–450.

[4] Lemert has distinguished "primary deviation" which is polygenetic, arising as it does from a variety of social, cultural, psychological, and physiological factors, from "secondary deviation." The latter term refers to the socially defined responses people make to the facts of their deviance. Only secondary deviance, in Lemert's analysis, has implications for the status and psychic structure of an individual. Edwin M. Lemert, *Human Deviance, Social Problems, and Social Control* (Englewood Cliffs, N.J.: Prentice-Hall, 1967), p. 40.

This paper will examine the changing motivation [5] of the prostitute as this reflects the degree to which a person has internalized a deviant self-conception in response to informal labeling, public branding and subsequent stimatization. Legal reactions to deviance, often considered to be the most significant factor in the etiology of deviant careers, do not necessarily have such an effect on the individual's self-conception. In fact, such criminalization proceedings may be viewed as irrelevant or, sometimes, as status enhancing. Informal reactions to deviance, conversely, may be the crucial factor in self-identifications. The imputation of deviant motives by intimate associates, such as parents, hustler associates, pimps, and others to whom the individual has a strong emotional bond may lead the girl to incorporate a deviant version of the self. The movement into the career will be elucidated by a stage analysis,[6] which permits an evaluation of the motives of the women at different levels of role commitment. The three stages to be delineated are: (1) Stage I—the process of drift from promiscuity to first act of prostitution, (2) Stage II—transitional deviance, and (3) Stage III—professionalization.

The source of data for this exploratory study is provided by a jail sample of thirty prostitutes from three correctional institutions (reformatory, workhouse, and training school) in Minnesota. Included are seventeen white women, twelve Negro

[5] The social psychological conception of motivation used here emphasizes that motives may be considered as "typical vocabularies having ascertainable functions in delimited societal situations." C. Wright Mills, "Situated Actions and Vocabularies of Motive," *American Sociological Review 5* (December 1940): 904–913. The contemporary dominant vocabularies of motives, says Mills, are individualistic, sexual, hedonistic, and pecuniary, an ethos I might add that is well adapted to the motivational structure of professional prostitutes.

See also, Scott and Lyman in their analysis of "accounts." These are statements—excuses or justifications—made to explain untoward behavior and bridge the gap between actions and expectations, thus neutralizing questionable acts. Accounts function as a "manifestation of the underlying negotiation of identities." Marvin B. Scott and Stanford M. Lyman, "Accounts," *American Sociological Review 33* (February 1968): 46–62.

[6] Becker uses a "stages" analysis for marihuana users in: Howard S. Becker, "Becoming a Marihuana User," *American Journal of Sociology 59* (November 1953): 235–242.

women, and one Indian woman. The age range was fifteen to thirty-four, with an average age of twenty-one.[7] All of the thirty women were legally classified as "common prostitute," although only twenty-four of the thirty informants reported that they were professional prostitutes. The women operated at the "street-walker" level of prostitution, that is, lounging in bars or on streetcorners and openly soliciting clients. High levels of spatial mobility were typical patterns for this group. Data were elicited through structured interviews, with emphasis, however, on the informants' verbalized statements. The interviews averaged one and one-half to two hours in length. Official records also were used. Further, informal data were gained through participant observation as noted above.

STAGE I: THE PROCESS OF DRIFT FROM PROMISCUITY TO FIRST ACT OF PROSTITUTION

The first phase of deviance is characterized by a process of drifting from promiscuity to the first act of prostitution. The data suggest that a delayed self-definition as deviant is more probable among these prostitutes than among those who have an informed choice of social roles. Early commitment to prostitution because of purported pathologies, either psychological or social, is not supported by this evidence. Rather, there is a "drift into deviance," [8] with promiscuity initially used as a status tool,[9] but later becoming defined by the individual as having consequences for the foreclosure of alternative career routes. This process of drifting into deviance will be analyzed by examining: (1) the age at

---

[7] Clinard reports that the average age of the prostitute is seventeen to twenty-four years, the peak of physical attractiveness for women. Marshall B. Clinard, *Sociology of Deviant Behavior*, 2nd ed. (New York: Rinehart and Company, 1966).

[8] David Matza, *Delinquency and Drift* (New York: John Wiley & Sons, 1964).

[9] These findings are similar to those of Thomas' study of motives for promiscuity. W. I. Thomas, *The Unadjusted Girl* (Boston: Little, Brown & Co., 1937), p. 244.

first sexual experience and of self-definitions of promiscuity, (2) the girl's perception of her childhood and adolescent years as leading to a self-conception as "different" or as a "troublemaker," (3) the drift from promiscuity to the first act of prostitution, and (4) the roads to recruitment by which the individual is inducted into the behavior.

Age at First Sexual Experience

The women in this sample were ordinarily initiated into sexual experiences at an early age. The mean age at which they first had sexual intercourse was 13.6, with a range of seven to eighteen. Rape experiences, reported by two women, account for the lower age level (seven and nine years, respectively). Three other informants noted traumatic sexual experiences with brothers, stepfather, or father, at age twelve or under. Nineteen of the thirty women report they had sexual intercourse by age thirteen, although almost one-half of the white girls had experienced intercourse by age twelve.[10] The most characteristic pattern was coitus with a boyfriend, typically, five or six years older than the girl. Four informants were sexually initiated by another girl with heterosexual relations occurring within a year after such lesbian contacts. The "technical virginity" pattern typical of the middle class female was not in evidence here. First sexual contacts typically involved sexual intercourse, with only one girl reporting an initial petting experience.

Preconditions for those characterized by "early sexuality" are: (1) high levels of familial permissiveness led to association with older males at parties, neighboring houses, or street pick-

[10] Kinsey's data indicate that female premarital coitus was relatively rare in the early teens with about 3 percent of the total sample having had coital experience by age 15 (pp. 287–288). Further, slightly less than 5 percent of the total sample *have had* homosexual experiences by age 15 (see Figure 82, p. 452). Kinsey's sample, however, has limitations in that it is largely based on data from middle-class and upper-status females. It does not include histories of women who have had penal institutionalization. Such a group "is much more promiscuous in its premarital activity" according to their calculations (p. 292). Alfred C. Kinsey, Wardell B. Pomeroy, Clyde E. Martin, and Paul H. Gebhard, *Sexual Behavior in the Human Female* (Philadelphia: W. B. Saunders Co., 1953).

ups, (2) familial social control was often lacking or inconsistent, (3) peer group norms encouraged early sexuality, and (4) sexuality was associated with freedom (a movement away from a disliked family), or conversely, security (the certainty of male companionship). Three girls, on the other hand, did not experience their first sexual intercourse until age seventeen or eighteen. Those having this "late sexuality" experienced these typical conditions: (1) sexual matters were taboo areas in the family, (2) the mother was highly protective, exerting strong religious and familial controls with consequent little freedom of opportunity in early adolescence, and (3) a rebellion pattern eventually developed in opposition to the rigidity of the controls.

Almost all of the women (twenty-eight of thirty) report that their first sex experience was either meaningless or distasteful, for example, "It was nothing," "I did it just to please him," "I really didn't like it," "I disliked it," "It was awful," "I was scared," "It made me sick." A need for conformity seems to be the most salient motive for this first sexuality, as:

> I did it just to belong. Everybody was doing it.

> I was the only virgin in the crowd (age fifteen). Five of my girl-friends had kids at sixteen.

A lack of sex education for the younger girl explains, in part, the negative evaluation: "I was young then. I really didn't know what it was about. I didn't learn until I was fourteen what it was about. I learned sex here (at the training school)."

The promiscuous pattern which developed for most girls (three women had early pregnancies which were followed by marriage, with promiscuity and prostitution occurring *after* these events) seems to reflect associates' expectations, the desire to attract males ("The boys were always hot after me"), and an opportunity structure which facilitated the behavior.

Perception of Childhood and Adolescent Years

The promiscuous pattern may provide one condition which can lead to informal labeling ("bad" girl, "easy mark") and subsequent stigmatization by parents, teachers, and conventional associates. But other circumstances may arise, prior to or following this sexual behavior, which also modify the self-conception. These women perceived their childhood and adolescent years as marked by negative or degrading interactions with society, as the following data briefly indicate:

1. Familial instability was typical for almost all of the white girls (sixteen of seventeen) and two-thirds (eight of twelve) of the Negroes. Such instability included a drunken, violent or absentee parent (usually the father), extreme poverty, or families larger than the parents could cope with. Conditions within the family were eventually brought to the attention of neighbors, welfare board, or court. Such attention was defined as humiliating or demoralizing.

2. More than half of the informants (eighteen of thirty) have spent one year or more of their childhood (under twelve) in foster homes, living with relatives, or in other separations from the nuclear family.

3. Almost all of the informants (twenty-eight) report that parents, neighbors, and/or teachers considered them "troublemakers," "slow learners," or generally inadequate in relation to expectations.

4. The Negro women (nine of twelve) especially, reported "unfair" treatment by white teachers or students, inability to gain and/or hold a job, and frustration in cases where self-improvement was attempted.

5. *Twenty-three of the thirty* informants reported that they had been sentenced to a juvenile home or training school as adolescents for truancy, incorrigibility, or sex delinquency. Such early institutionalization was not necessarily in Minnesota.

Such background events should be viewed from the perspective of the labeling process as possible *typical* or *contributing* conditions by which a deviant identity can emerge. The significance of these events, however, is in the situated meanings which impose on the girl, a self-definition of unconventional or "troublemaker." In the interactional processes with significant others (parents, teachers, neighbors, and friends), the girl achieves an identity as one who is "different." She is a person who is expected to behave in unconventional ways. Absenteeism from school, chronic disobedience at home, and later, promiscuity, categorizes the girl as difficult, if not impossible to control. Low family cohesion with consequent weak affectional ties between parents and daughter leads the girl to seek street associates who will support the informally labeled degraded status.

Yet, the expressed motives of the promiscuous girl tend to approximate the standardized attitudes of the general youth population. In other words, until imprisonment, the rationale for promiscuity, and initially for prostitution, is a hedonistic concern for fun, new experiences, excitement, and a response to peer group expectations. Sex as a status tool is exploited to gain male attention. The adolescent urge for liberation from the confines of the family and controls of school and job leads to involvement in drinking parties or hustler groups, wherein differential identification with sophisticated delinquents occurs.

The Drift from Promiscuity to First Act of Prostitution

Regardless of the age at which the girl first experienced intercourse, there then followed a *"drift"* or *"slide"* [11] *process from promiscuity to prostitution,* with the girl first prostituting herself in late adolescence (mean = 17.3 years). There was a range, however, of fourteen to twenty-five years. The early age of prostitution was facilitated by a definition of the deviant situation as similar to sexual promiscuity—excitement and desire for male attention. However, the "pickup" pattern no longer has intrinsic appeal ("I just was laying up for the sake of laying up") while the sex-with-money act, an instrumental behavior, is viewed as a normal response to peer norms, and an indication of emancipation, both social and financial. For example:

[11] The word "slide" is used advisedly. Many (fifteen of thirty) of the women retrospectively report highly negative attitudes following the first prostitution experience. These self-reported demoralizing effects of the behavior could indicate that the women had internalized the conventional norms of degradation associated with prostitution. Another explanation for the frequently observed negative reactions is the problem of interviewer bias. See Daniel Katz, "Do Interviewers Bias Poll Results?" *Public Opinion Quarterly 6* (1942): 248–268.

It was either jump in bed, and go with every Tom, Dick, and Harry, and just give it away, so I decided to turn tricks instead. . . . The money was so easy to get.

I wanted freedom and opportunity. It was the excitement, too. . . . I wanted things everyone else had.

Information of age differentials for first sexual experience and entrance into prostitution is summarized in Table 1.

TABLE 1. MEAN AGE AT FIRST SEXUAL EXPERIENCE AND AT ENTRY INTO PROSTITUTION

Present Mean Age of Group (N = 30)		Mean Age at First Sexual Experience		Mean Age at Entry Into Prostitution	
* Total group	21.0	Total group	13.6	Total group	17.3
Negro	23.3	Negro	13.8	Negro	18.3
White	19.3	White	13.7	White	16.8
Training school girls	16.4	Training school girls	12.3	Training school girls	15.8

* The statistical breakdown represents overlapping categories. Thus, the "training school girls" category (twenty-three institutionalized during adolescence) includes both the white and Negro groups.

My data strongly suggest that the movement from casual delinquency to the first phase of defined deviance is facilitated by the policy of confining deviants to correctional institutions. The adolescent girl who is labeled a sex offender for promiscuity or "mixing" (white girls associating with Negro males) may initially experience a conflict about her identity. Intimate association with sophisticated deviants, however, may provide an incentive to learn the hustler role ("The girls told me about it—I was such an avid listener."), and thus resolve the status anxiety by gaining prestige through association with deviants, and later, experimentation in the deviant role. Frequent and predictable escapes from the open institution are common.[12] Lines of communication be-

---

[12] Informants report that, on the average, they were "runaways" about twice a year from the training school.

tween urban vice neighborhoods and training school inmates as-
sures the escapee of finding accommodations during a "run."

As an outlaw, the girl cannot seek the security of parents or
the home neighborhood. Thus, isolated from conventional associates or activities, and dependent on deviant contacts for financial and social support, the girl may come to define the situation
as one that inevitably leads her into enacting the deviant role, as:

> I ran away from the institution. I went and visited my girlfriends.
> I was out of the institution about a month, just loafing around. I
> talked to some friends of mine who were hustlers. Someone sug-
> gested I try it. I had been sponging off everybody. I got sick of
> sponging. I'd sleep here one night, and there another.

> I was on run. You just normally can't get a job then—so I tried
> this (prostitution). It was an easy way to get money.

> I had run away (from the training school). I had no money or any-
> thing. I went walking the street. I had run away before. The older
> girls (institutionalized associates) told me about it.

The data suggest that the earlier age at which the training
school girl encounters the deviant opportunity (15.8 years of age
as compared with 21.3 years for nontraining school females) may
be a function of early promiscuity, arrest, detention, and subsequent anticipatory socialization into the prostitution role.

Roads to Recruitment

Adolescent institutionalization, then, often prior to the actual
commitment of a deviant act, may act as a structural condition
which facilitates the learning of a deviant role. Induction into
the career, on the other hand, proceeds through alternative
routes, chief of which are: (1) response to peer group expectations, (2) involvement in a pimp-manager relationship, and (3)
adolescent rebellion.

Response to *peer group expectations* undoubtedly provides
the major avenue to recruitment ("It's the environment. Everyone is doing it."). Associating with hustlers, "party girls," or
pimps, while viewed as prestigious, can only be maintained by

"trying out" the behavior. Clearly, for twenty-eight of the thirty informants, differential identification with deviant associates accounts, in part, for the movement into prostitution.

> I was on run . . . I didn't get up until 3 P.M. I was staying with my boyfriend. He was unemployed. He was planning to set me up [for prostitution]. We had been talking about it. I took long precautions . . . A friend helped me out. Everything happened so fast. It was kind of like prearranged for me. Crazy! We were staying in a hotel with lots of pimps, prostitutes and faggots living there. The first time was at the World's Series. I was dressed like a normal teenager.

> The girls I ran around with did it (hustling). I never thought about it one way or another.

Involvement in a *pimp-manager relationship* provides a typical method of entrance for some under-age girls (eight informants). In other instances, the pimp may not have initially arranged the first contact, but he typically appears relatively early on the scene to direct the girl's activities. The uninitiated girl views the pimp relationship as a means of security in an otherwise rejecting world. "I always had a need to belong. . . . A pimp moves in, and he sees you're attractive, and he sees you want to belong. Pimps are the most understanding. They're the least educated persons, though. I thought my pimp was my knight in shining armor." Certainly, the pimp represents a sophisticated model of the hustling world to the young girl. One informant, who first prostituted at age fourteen, recalled: "I was staying with this one man . . . one of the better pimps in ———. He was classy. I met him down at the ——— restaurant. I was on run. I went out on the street by myself. . . . My pimp even set up the apartment."

The pimp's ability to "set the girl up" by arranging clients is a measure of the girl's arrival on the deviant scene. One informant, whose first experience was such an arrangement, recalled how the system operated.

> I was living with a girlfriend . . . She wasn't a hustler—and started going with this one boy. He introduced me to this pimp. He asked

> me if I would [hustle]. I was against it, but they all said how easy
> it was. I went to this pimp's house. I was a call girl. There were
> three of us [hustlers]. The pimps would come in. They got all the
> contacts, and they'd say to the tricks, "Lookee here. I got these
> girls, see," and he'd line up the tricks. Then he'd say to the girls
> that there was a trick in this hotel, and you'd go to a room number.

Another girl commented that the pimp used alternate techniques
of violence ("He hit me on the head when I said no") and per-
suasion: "He told me, 'I can put you in big business. You won't
have to hustle hard.' I saw the girls and how they did it. It was
like a dream."

Adolescent rebellion operates for girls who have experienced
oppressive familial controls (six women), forming another typical
pattern.

> Well, I started hustling, I suppose, because the party group I ran
> around with were always talking about it. My mother had always
> picked my friends. She wouldn't allow any bad influences—the
> square friends only, the goody-goody club activities at church. My
> parents were very old-fashioned. They didn't drink or smoke, and
> were very church-going. But when I got in with this group, it was
> really different, man!

The rebellion pattern is reinforced if accusations of perceived
promiscuity by a suspicious parent induce the girl to experiment
with street life. The labeling process is clearly indicated in these
informants' retrospective observations:

> They accused me of running around. They kept saying, "If you're
> staying out this late, you're indulging in something, or will in-
> dulge in something in the future."

> I did it because I was rebelling against the folk's authority. I be-
> lieved I was better than they said I was. But I was doing just what
> they said I was.

Dominant Motives
During the First Stage

Underlying these main roads to recruitment into prostitution are
curiosity and a desire for new experience, defined idleness, iden-

tification with hustler norms, and a strong present-time orientation.

Curiosity and access to new experiences (or "kicks") acts as a dominant motive to the naïve girl who seeks esteem from the hustler group. "I was unemployed at the time, just hanging around with a group. I wanted some excitement—kicks, you know."

Remarks such as, "It was the glamor and game of it," "I did it just for the fun of it," "There's a lot of excitement to that—the cops on you and everything," indicate a perception of deviance as part of the excitement and risk of street life. As such, a self-definition as deviant is not yet incorporated into the self-conception.

Defined idleness is the typical pattern for most women (twenty-three of thirty). Separations from family, school, job, or other conventional activities characterizes this first deviant phase. For the runaway training school girl, prostitution may relieve the dullness of an otherwise undirected existence.

> I was sixteen and on the run, just loafing around my girlfriend's house. One of my girlfriends gave me the pointers, so I decided to try it.

> I had run away—like I was lost or something. I had been walking the streets all day, and at 6 P.M. I met this guy. I was really looking for love and attention, but not necessarily the men.

Identification with hustler norms undoubtedly accounts for the frequently expressed (twenty-seven of thirty) money rationale. However, economic deprivation is not the dominant element for most girls. Only two women, for instance, expressed intense financial need because of child support. Independence, isolation from conventional supports, and the lure of "easy" money, were major considerations.

> I was on run—no job or anything. I was by myself. It was about 8. I went out, went downtown. My boyfriend worked in the ——— Hotel. He called me up to say that he had a man who had fifty dollars to get a girl, and so there it was. I got forty-five dollars the first night—for four men. Everyone was doing it, anyway. Then I walked back downtown, and had three more, and then went back to my apartment.

A strong present-time orientation characterizes the younger girl particularly, who conceives of the act as satisfying immediate needs only, without considering long-range implications.

> The first time I did it was to buy a present for my boyfriend. The next time just to have some spending money. I've been asked to hustle lots of times. I know all the gimmicks, and how to do it . . . all that stuff.

> I was going to school and I wanted to go to this dance the night after. I needed new clothes. I went out at ten o'clock and home at twelve. I had three tricks the first time, and fifteen dollars for every trick.

Whatever the mode of recruitment, or the dominant motives involved, this study shows certain common elements present at this state of deviant involvement. These generally include: informal labeling which early categorizes the girl as unconventional or "troublemaker"; isolation from conventional family, friends, or associates; response to deviant associates' expectations; and expressed need for economic self-sufficiency while "on run" or probation. Such motives indicate that : (1) episodic involvement, or a *drift into deviance,* is characteristic of prostitutes and is related to hedonistic and short-term concerns; and (2) stigmatized persons may respond to a morally degraded status by seeking associates who may reward the deviant behavior.[13]

STAGE II: TRANSITIONAL DEVIANCE

Twenty-one of the thirty women interviewed experienced an "occasional" or "transitional" stage of deviance. Of the nine other labeled prostitutes, four repudiated the role after three or more deviant episodes, while five women moved directly into full-time

---

[13] A deviant subculture is only one of many types of adaptation to the deviant role; others may include: a social movement, individual deviance, suicide, cycles of abstinence and relapse. Goffman, for instance, nicely illuminates various strategies the stigmatized person may develop: Information control as in name-changing, "passing," maintaining physical or social distance, covering, and self-disclosure. Erving Goffman, *Stigma* (Englewood Cliffs, N.J.: Prentice-Hall, 1963).

deviance. The transitional stage lasted an average of six months (with a range from two weeks to four years). It could be viewed as an on-the-job learning period, but one in which the girl typically postpones self-definition of the deviant status.

Motivational ambivalence during the transitional phase creates a zig-zag pattern of deviance for most prostitutes. They vacillate between conventionality and deviance. The conventional life, for instance, is not yet denied. Some girls make verbal commitments to stop, or even attempt to return to home, school, job or to set themselves up in an apartment with conventional associates. Conventional motives involve expressed reluctance to move into the act because of fear of discovery, interracial contacts, or belief that such conduct is immoral. ("It's not the right thing to do. I would get a bad reputation.")

Table 2 indicates certain conventional commitments of these women during the transitional period. In many instances, the behavioral commitment was very brief (a job lasting two weeks, or a movement from living with conventional associates to living with a boyfriend or pimp, with such arrangements of short duration only). For others, however, there was an attempt to establish a more stable pattern. Seven Negro women lived at home with their mothers and/or children during most of this period.

TABLE 2. CONVENTIONAL COMMITMENTS DURING THE TRANSITIONAL STAGE

	N = 21 *
School attendance	4
Full- or part-time job	7
Living at home	10
Living with husband and/or children	5
Living in an apartment with other girls who are not hustlers	4
Living alone in an apartment	7

* Categories overlap; hence N = more than 21.

During this phase they indicate indecision and confusion regarding their role. By hustling only occasionally, not more than two or three times a week, or engaging in prostitution "only when I wanted to," or "sometimes when I'm lonesome," or for "just something to do," the individual perceives that she is in control of the situation and delays a self-definition as deviant.

It is apparent here that the drift into deviance by specific actions rather than by an informed choice of role and status occurs through *normalization of the act*.[14] Postponement of the deviant identity may occur through rationalizations appropriate for promiscuity—the desire for male attention.

> There's so many of them out there (potential clients). The older guys went for my shape. "You've got a beautiful ass" they'd tell me. I liked some of the compliments, but some of the dirty ones (obscene phrases) I didn't. It was always the older ones that complimented me.

> I'm a person who likes to walk. There's nothing wrong with picking somebody up while you're walking. I always like walking around at night, and girls will be tempted. Girls like the offer. They like to see what the guy is going to say.

The "gaming" element, which revolves around the excitement of the "pickup" and independence on the street, is also linked to a promiscuous, rather than deviant, orientation. The promiscuous girl with conventional in-group supports may not define herself as a prostitute at this point.

In certain cases role ambivalence may even lead to repudiation of the "trial" role after a few experiences (four informants). Negative experiences with a client, pimp, or policeman, for instance, may lead her to reject the role. Inadequate motivation is a typical condition leading to role failure in many areas of life. It was expressed by one seventeen-year-old informant who had hustled on-and-off for about a month before her career had been interrupted by jail:

> Hustling—I don't get no kicks from it. I wouldn't go out and do it for a living. There are better ways to make money. I couldn't go

---

[14] Motives and/or rationalization act to normalize or neutralize the deviant status. Gresham M. Sykes and David Matza, "Techniques of Neutralization: A Theory of Delinquency," *American Sociological Review 22* (December 1957): 664–670.

through everything a prostitute goes through. I really don't have the guts for it. A prostitute picks up anyone off the street, and gets money for it. The tricks I had it with I did it just for sex, but not for me—not the whole self. I knew I couldn't make a career out of it. When you don't care about the guy, sex isn't for that.

Sex with affection, uncontaminated by money, still operates as a norm for the deviant dropout.

Their continuation in this sexually deviant behavior, on the other hand, is contingent on strong economic motivation (twenty-one women), loneliness (three), and/or expressed entrapment because of pimp control (six). For two girls, drug addiction acted as an inducement for continuation of the deviant role. Continuation in the deviant role is further contingent on an adequate learning period uninterrupted by police harassment or jail sentencing. Unlike the call girl, who frequently learns the deviant role under the tutelage of an experienced prostitute,[15] the streetwalker is often a "loner," and consistently exposed to the vicissitudes of street life. Development of adequate coping mechanisms is requisite if she is to continue.

Delayed definitions of the act as immoral, degrading or repulsive (fifteen women report intense dissatisfaction or disgust with the situation) can no longer be postponed if situations occur that force unequivocal perception of a deviant self. Self-discovery, for instance, may be inevitable for some prostitutes when the pimp's behavior shifts from lover to exploiter, and for example, nightly money quotas become the primary condition for the relationship ("I was just another one of his hustlers."). The individual validates the degraded self by seeking group supports, as in a permanent move into an apartment with a hustler or pimp.[16] Another typical experience is contact with the police, court, or jail, where the label "common prostitute" is assigned. After the

[15] See James F. Bryan, "Apprenticeships in Prostitution," *op. cit.*

[16] The prostitute's problem of maintaining a consistent self-image because of stigmatization is analyzed by Jackman, O'Toole and Geis: Interaction with significant others or absorption in a fantasy world are two alternatives which mitigate self-denigration. Norman R. Jackman, Richard O'Toole, and Gilbert Geis, "The Self-Image of the Prostitute," *The Sociological Quarterly* 4 (Spring 1963): 150–161.

legal confrontation, public exposure proceeds in rapid order.[17] Listing the girl's name in the paper, or passing the information to parents from "inside" sources, implies that, as a consequence, the girl soon renounces the pretence of conventional commitments. At this point, she may cut herself off from family and conventional others' support. Informants report such responses to the labeling procedure:

> They sent me up for something I didn't do, so I might as well do it. I wasn't afraid of anything.

> Society is really uninformed. They don't put themselves to the trouble to understand. There are lots worse things besides prostitution that happen. Society isn't helping at all. There's not a chance to be decent. Society has put the brand on us.

Personal integrity at earlier phases of the career had been maintained by secrecy regarding the deviant behavior. Role segregation breaks down, however, if the woman has internalized the streetwalker's myth—"once a girl is on the streets, everyone knows what she is." For example, "At first I was scared. The news gets out so fast. Everyone knows when a girl's on the streets a couple of nights. I thought about stopping, you know, but I just went on."

The individual *normalizes the deviant status* through the learning of satisfactions and through access to rewards. Hustling becomes a way of absolving the individual from failures in the larger society and an escape from responsibilities. A deviant vocabulary of motives arises, indicating that earlier pressures that may have hindered movement into the career no longer persist— or that the individual has learned to accommodate stress. As one informant pointed out:

> I always wanted to get away from it (hustling). I'd hide the money to get relaxation. But it was good money, and I was a better prostitute than most. It really wasn't what I wanted, but I got high and then I was o.k. During this time I was best with my parents. I was

---

[17] Public branding, as Schur suggests, may automatically and retrospectively effect crucial modifications in a person's identity. Edwin M. Schur, *Crimes Without Victims* (Englewood Cliffs, N.J.: Prentice-Hall, 1965), p. 5.

charming to them, and gave things to them. I had a million other good qualities, but I couldn't see then that I was doing anything good.

For this respondent certain conditions facilitated the deviant identity: a high level of competence in the act, narcotics which blurred the effects of the negative definitions, and satisfaction in providing financially for her family.

For a few prostitutes interviewed, there is an immediate movement into regularized deviance (five women). Factors facilitating early self-definition as deviant are: total identification with deviant associates *before* the first deviant act, pimp control, and/ or no expressed negative attitudes (fear, disgust, guilt) regarding the act.

In-service training for this streetwalker group during the transitional period includes: (1) willingness to satisfy a broad range of client requests, requiring certain social and sexual skills; (2) elimination of fears regarding clients who are defined as "odd" (sadomasochists); (3) adaptation to police surveillance and entrapment procedures; (4) avoidance of drunken clients, or those unable or unwilling to pay; and (5) substitution of a "business" ethic for the earlier one of "gaming" or excitement concerns. If socialization is lacking in these areas, the woman may continue to define herself as an "occasional" or "part-time" prostitute only (nonprofessional). Or she may continue to endure an identity crises that is only temporarily relieved by short-term movements into conventional life—marriage, job, or family obligations, or by jailing ("I got what I deserve.").

STAGE III: PROFESSIONALIZATION

The final stage of deviant involvement is the unequivocal perception of a deviant self. Behavior becomes regularized, and the self-conception revolves around sex as a vocation.[18] Deviance is

---

[18] Prostitution is defined by Polsky as the granting of nonmarital sex "as a vocation." Ned Polsky, *Hustlers, Beats, and Others* (Chicago: Aldine Publishing Company, 1967), p. 193.

no longer viewed as a segmental part of the self. The prostitute identity permeates the behavior system which incorporates deviance as a pattern. Expressed motivations indicate accommodation to the status. Abatement of conflicts follows the discovery that "the life" is difficult, but not one of disgrace. Professionals report, for instance, that the work is a "drag," "tedious," "boring," "scary," "dirty," and a "trap." Typically, the girl has been beaten, forced to perform indignities, sickened from narcotics, or worked seven days a week under a pimp's control. Furthermore, the hustler life is highly mobile, affecting personal relationships, which are often highly superficial and tenuous. The sustaining ideology internalized from hustler associates, however, tends to define the "square" life as impossible at this point, while extolling the rewards of prostitution.

> I'm in it for money. Sure, I started another job, but it doesn't do any good. I can't cope with square people. I get fed up. So I went back into the life. I have independence in the game—no responsibility. No one tells me what to do.

> I can't be satisfied with being poor . . . I have everything that money could afford. I personally am able to afford any nightclub or any party.

> They're [prostitutes] really different. They've been put into institutions—got out into the game. They've got pimps. If you're on a regular job, you're a nobody—just a square. But sell your body, and then you're somebody.

Prestige follows the acquisition of money (even though most earnings are turned over to the pimp), giving them access to expensive clothes and furniture, elaborate hairdos, and costly entertainment. Some prostitutes even assert that prostitution is a transitional career, leading to "something better" such as dancing, modeling, singing, and so forth. When confronted with chronic disillusionment, the hustler *normalizes behavior* with such rationalizations as "Society needs us," "Johns are suckers anyway," "Society is hypocritical," "We're just minding our own business—it's a job like any other," "I only do it for my pimp." The denial of responsibility is a frequently stated motive, as: "I make 100 bucks a night. Most of it goes to the pimp. We have an understanding with our pimps. My guy thinks I'm more qualified than most. He just needs that $100 a night. He's money crazy, my man is. He would leave me if I didn't fork it over."

The hustler ideology supports an impersonal view toward men ("I see men as customers—or tricks"). This ideology also defines males as having an unlimited sex drive. It defines the prostitute as one who provides an outlet that prevents the male from exploiting his wife sexually.

A man often gets stuck in a marriage. Out of tradition he stays in. He has respect for his wife, but he's not satisfied sexually. He needs this sex, or he'll be mentally insane. They know life, these men. They have their self-respect. They don't want sex to interfere in their lives . . . He needs sex—he goes wild for it.

Men don't know when to stop when they go to bed with a woman. They want to continue all night. They want to be a hog about it. That's why married men are out after hustlers.

Continued interaction with men as clients, not as persons, leads some prostitutes to define males as unsatisfactory for sex purposes. Even the pimp becomes interpreted as "just another trick" when the individual defines the relationship as contaminated by business concerns. As males become defined as unsatisfactory sources of sexual gratification, some prostitutes turn to females for this gratification.

Prostitutes who express strong negative feelings toward clients ("men are dogs") develop a preference for lesbian relationships (thirteen of twenty-four professionals expressed preference for sex with women). Homosexuality is facilitated by: (1) frequent imprisonments, whereby lesbian contacts are made, (2) impersonal or degrading confrontations with clients, and (3) hustler norms which emphasize the rewards of female sex relationships ("I haven't met a man yet that could satisfy me."). For example, "I prefer women because johns are no good sexually. A woman is more tender. If the wife-in-law (the pimp's other woman) wouldn't have sex together with me, then I'd just get another hustler. The pimp doesn't really care."

Bisexuality is a typical accommodation in cases wherein two or more hustlers share an apartment and a pimp. "Most hustlers are bisexual. They're living with a husband or pimp, but they have sex with women." Further, bisexuality is viewed as adaptive for the prison role.[19] "When I'm in jail, I have a woman. I play the passive role. I do it for the companionship it brings."

Expressed motives regarding pimps, however, are generally favorable. In-group consensus reflects the sustaining belief that pimps support and maintain the deviant role. Hustler norms that reinforce the identity include a strong money motive, hostility to clients, and a counter morality—motives which neutralize the heavy social stigma.

In this sample there are different types of prostitution based on differences in: (1) reference group orientations, and (2) life styles. The reference group dimension suggests three accommodations.[20] (1) The *hustler subculture* (fourteen of twenty-four women). This group involves identification with the hustler world of prostitute, pimp, homosexual, and the "rackets." The life-style is typified by irregular living patterns (high mobility, frequent change of pimps or other hustler associates), with sporadic dependence on alcohol or drugs. Interaction with conventional persons is very limited (if it exists at all). Hedonism and a strong present-time orientation is especially operative. (2) The *dual-worlds culture* (seven women). Internalization of both the hustler culture (by night) and the middle-class culture (by day) leads to a separation of referent others and activities. Accommodation to certain middle-class norms may entail maintaining a home with children or supporting parents (especially for Negro women), self-improvement (golf lessons or library visits), and acquiring the status symbols associated with success. (3) The *criminal subculture* (five women). Referent others are often involved in full-time criminal careers. Regular drug use may require systematic stealing, from clients or others, and shoplifting, which may lead to

[19] Analysis of the homosexual adaptation in the women's prison has been explored by David A. Ward and Gene G. Kassebaun in *Women's Prison—Sex and Social Structure* (Chicago: Aldine Publishing Company, 1965).

[20] Jackman, O'Toole, and Geis, *op. cit.*, have identified three orientations of prostitutes, based on interviews with fifteen women (1) criminal world contraculture, (2) dual worlds, and (3) alienation.

assault or felony charges being leveled against them. Consequently, there is frequency of jailing for this group. Contranorms are particularly operative for this group.

Prostitutes, as with other groups in society, are differentially ranked, with call girls having more contact with affluent clients and generally having a higher life-style than streetwalkers.[21] Prostitutes may be similar to other occupational groups in an industrial society in that the intelligent, productive, or highly skilled person may acquire the material trappings of success, while the less able or low-skilled individual may realize only limited occupational achievement. These prostitutes interviewed evidenced a range of life-styles from affluence to poverty commensurate with their market value. Most of these women, however, were only marginally successful because: (1) although they are high earners, their pimps or legal fines absorb most of the income, and (2) capital is usually invested in short-run gains—wigs, costumes, and entertainment, with few if any savings or other monetary accumulations.

Generally, the consequences of stigmatization may lead to further mechanisms of deviant adaptation for this prostitute group, as in the elaboration of the role to include such secondary activities as "jack-rolling" (taking the client's wallet, often with the help of a male accomplice), shoplifting, drug addiction, homosexuality, and assault (two women of the sample were convicted for "knifing" their clients).

DISCUSSION AND CONCLUSIONS

On the basis of interviews with thirty streetwalkers, this paper has attempted to explore some typical conditions leading to a career in prostitution. Changes in the behavior system were analyzed through delineation of the motivational changes at various career stages.[22] The assumption is that the verbalized motives the

21 Bryan, *op. cit.*, and Greenwald, *op. cit.*

22 Hackler conceives of deviants as passing through three stages: (a) the new deviant who still endorses conventional norms and has a conventional self-conception, although he perceives that others anticipate deviance; (b) the

individual adopts with changes in status and role indicate that these streetwalkers do introject the negative labels consequent from the stigmatization process. This process may be triggered not only by the formal criminalization proceedings but also by those interactions wherein the person undergoes a drastic change in her self-conception.

The theoretical implications of this preliminary study are concerned with the criminalization of deviance, or the social act of public branding, as a crucial step in the individual's progress toward a criminal career. Such an approach stresses the significant ways in which deviance comes to be shaped by the attitudes and actions of others.[23] The concept of "secondary deviance," enunciated by Lemert, offers one of the more systematic approaches to the problem of labeling, which, it is assumed, acts to reinforce a deviant self-conception. The crucial variable in secondary deviance, in Lemert's analysis, is the official, public reaction—as in prosecution and conviction—which leads the actor to incorporate a deviant version of the self and to organize his behavior system around such a self-conception.

Lemert's view of the significance of the social response of legal agents in effecting changes in the offender's self-conception appears to require certain modifications. Attention should be directed to the role of significant others who crucially influence the individual's responses to the definitions made by legal and other formal agencies.

Further, while Lemert's analysis is useful in eliciting some

---

evolving deviant who would not as yet endorse deviant norms, but would have a deviant self-concept and perceive that others anticipate deviant behavior; and (c) the confirmed deviant who would have internalized deviant norms, have a deviant self-concept, and perceive that others anticipate deviant behavior. James C. Hackler, "Predictors of Deviant Behavior: Norms vs. the Perceived Anticipations of Others," *The Canadian Review of Sociology 5* (May 1968): 92–106.

[23] Societal reaction in cases of deviation does not have a single sequence or pattern. Lemert indicates three possible end-products of community reaction: (1) acceptance and integration of the variant behavior, (2) unstable equilibrium or symbiotic relationship between the aberrant and the normal, and, (3) complete rejection of the deviance. Edwin M. Lemert, *Social Pathology* (New York: McGraw-Hill, 1951), p. 59. Also see his section on "Prostitution and the Prostitute" in the same study (pp. 236–280).

typical or contingent conditions involved in the self-definition of deviance, his analysis tends to assume a greater universality of rules than actually prevails. In a pluralistic society, deviance is highly relativistic behavior. Contradictions in definition and treatment of deviants, for instance, are especially obvious in the transactions between prostitutes and legal officials. Age and race of the offender, visibility of the offense, prior institutionalization of the woman, the offender's link to other criminal groups, and the degree of community tolerance, are all variables involved in the legal definition. Such ambiguity in rules and sanctions implies that while the labeled person may be ambivalent about the deviant status and may endure consequent identity crises, there is no necessary movement toward a total deviant identity. Casual experimentation, even though officially labeled deviant, need not lead to a sustained pattern of deviant behavior. Instead, the crucial factor may be the imputation of motives by persons who act as positive referent others (parents, pimp, hustler associates, or regular client, for instance).

Prostitution, however, may offer a more salient case for labeling theory because of powerful social sanctions against sex-norm violations, especially when committed by members of the lower social strata. Segregation of adolescent sex deviants (a typical pattern among these women) leads to a loss of status in the conventional world and provides intimate contact with highly sophisticated sex offenders, whereby anticipatory socialization into professional deviance is possible.[24] Further, the enactment of the streetwalker role, unlike that of the call girl, is a highly visible and public evidence of deviance. Clothing, speech, gesture, stance, and other symbols validating the self announce to both clients and authorities the woman's identity.[25] Frequent prosecution and

[24] Albert Reiss, for example, points out that "from a sociological point of view, juvenile institutional populations are the most experienced in sex behavior of any subgroup in the population." The single-sex institution actually fosters highly deviating sex practices. Albert J. Reiss, Jr., "Sex Offenses: The Marginal Status of the Adolescent," in Simon and Gagnon, *op. cit.*, pp. 43–77.

[25] As Stone has pointed out, appearance is at least as important for the establishment and maintenance of the self as is discourse. Gregory P. Stone, "Appearance and the Self," in *Human Behavior and Social Processes*, ed. Arnold M. Rose (Boston: Houghton Mifflin Co., 1962), pp. 86–118.

jailing often result from such salience, further reinforcing the self-definition as "outsider."

Social problems research in this area could focus on the network of social relationships (with pimps, clients, and police) that both facilitate and, often, determine the sexual, occupational, and social roles of the prostitute.

HOMOSEXUALITY

Homosexuality in Prison

GEORGE L. KIRKHAM

A newspaper article or sensational magazine story sometimes focuses brief public attention on the subject of homosexuality in prison. Beyond such ephemeral interest, which usually follows in the wake of a jail or prison scandal, society evinces little interest in the sexuality of those of its members who have been temporarily banished through imprisonment. The entire problem of prison homosexuality thus remains characterized by widespread ignorance and confusion. Even the more basic issue of why the subject warrants being labeled a "problem" is unclear. In an era which witnesses an increasing tolerance of all forms of sexual behavior, it is maintained by some that concern over prison homosexuality derives from nothing more than a residue of Victorian, heterosexual bias; on the other side, moralists and prison reformers attempt to portray American prisons as being "rife with degeneracy." Panaceas, such as "conjugal visitation," are often advocated or opposed with little understanding of the nature of homosexuality in prison. It seems clear that there is a need to objectively examine the entire phenomenon against the unique subcultural backdrop which is represented by the prison.

Basic to any consideration of the structure and dynamics of prison homosexuality is an understanding of the total impact which prolonged confinement in a world without women has upon adult males in our society. Everywhere in the contemporary American prison one finds overwhelming evidence of what Sykes has labeled the "pain of heterosexual deprivation." [1] Perhaps this frustration, which attends the "figurative castration" of prison inmates, is most apparent in the conversation and humor of prisoners. The new employee or visitor to prison is immediately struck by the extent to which "sex" is a dominant motif in the thought and communication patterns of inmates. A rich sexual argot, many terms of which are unintelligible to the outsider, is to be found in all prisons. New words enter the lexicon of both inmates and staff, where they redefine the meaning of sexual phenomena through the subcultural eye of the beholder.

It has been suggested many times that being without women is by far the most difficult aspect of imprisonment for most men. Certainly, the loss of liberty, the requirement to live in a restricted and insecure environment, and the absence of certain goods and services are frustrating to all prisoners; yet, it is the complete unavailability of sexual and social relations with women which is almost intolerable for the average man in prison. As Victor Nelson, a man who spent twelve years in prison, has poignantly written, "But to be starved for month after weary month, year after year . . . this is the secret quintessence of human misery." [2] The prison inmate must somehow adapt to and endure the complete absence of heterosexual intercourse at a social class level where the frequency of marital coitus often averages six or seven times a week.[3] The stoic middle-class ethic of "deferred gratification" finds little acceptance among men whose lives have largely been characterized by an impulsive and hedonistic pursuit of sexual gratification. In addition to facing prolonged—sometimes indefinite [4]—physical frustration, the prisoner

[1] Gresham M. Skyes, *The Society of Captives* (Princeton: Princeton University Press, 1958), p. 456.

[2] Victor Nelson, *Prison Days and Nights* (Boston: Little, Brown & Co., 1933), p. 143.

[3] Alfred C. Kinsey *et al., Sexual Behavior in the Human Male* (Philadelphia: W. B. Saunders Co., 1948), p. 529.

[4] Heterosexual deprivation is perhaps most difficult to endure in those states which employ the so-called "indefinite" sentence system. Where broad minima and maxima exist in penal statutes, the prisoner is painfully aware

must also adjust to what is perhaps an even more painful reality: the complete unavailability of even social contact with women. A man who has become accustomed to validating his masculinity through regular interaction with members of the opposite sex may suddenly find his ego-image in grave jeopardy once a prison sentence consigns him to an all-male world. As Sykes states, ". . . the inmate's self-image is in danger of becoming half complete, fractured, a monochrome without the hues of reality." [5]

As if such sexual and psychological "pain" were not already sufficiently stressful for men whose backgrounds amply attest to an inability to adaptively handle frustration, the memory of woman is kept painfully alive by a multiciplicity of stimuli. In addition to the sexual themes so common in prison humor and conversation, and the sub-rosa body of pornographic literature which is always in circulation,[6] the mass media play an important role in aggravating the prisoner's psychosexual condition. Television, radio, newspapers, motion pictures—all combine to provide unrelenting titillation by keeping inmates exposed to the sexually charged atmosphere which characterizes contemporary American society. Mail and visits from wives and girlfriends, only exacerbates the frustration which men in prison must endure daily. The result of all this is a kind of green pastures syndrome which engulfs the prison community and serves to keep its members constantly preoccupied with unobtainable sexual objects. Sex, as Tappan notes, ". . . becomes disproportionately important for men in prison." [7]

It is truly paradoxical that the same humanitarian innovations which have improved the overall lot of most prisoners in recent years have also had the dysfunctional effect of intensifying

---

that his release could take years; the absence of a clear "definition of the situation" with respect to sentence time leaves him to the capricious whims of his captors.

[5] Sykes, *op. cit.*, pp. 71–72.

[6] For a discussion of prison pornography and its effects, see Charles E. Smith, "Prison Pornography," *The Journal of Social Therapy I* (April 1955): 126–129, and S. B. Zuckerman, "Sex Literature in Prison," *The Journal of Social Therapy I* (April 1955): 126–132.

[7] Paul W. Tappan, *Crime, Justice and Correction* (Pennsylvania: Maple Press, 1960), p. 678.

their sexual frustration. Prior to the advent of congregate penology and widespread penal reform, generally wretched physical conditions prevailed in many American prisons. During this period the attention of prisoners was largely focused on the lowest level of what Maslow terms a "natural need hierarchy." [8] Most prisoners were so preoccupied with securing a modicum of edible food, adequate clothing and shelter that "sex" paled to relative insignificance alongside these more prepotent physical needs.

In contemporary American prisons the pendulum of need fulfillment may be said to have come full swing from its position at the turn of the century. The average prisoner, in addition to having most of his important physical needs met, is also provided means for gratifying higher, aesthetic needs. As Lindner observes, "The essential wants and needs, even the basic rights, if there are such things, are satisfied. Food, clothing, shelter, books, movie theatres, recreation, employment—the list is never ending and always on the increase—are obtainable." [9] Prisoners who are cold and hungry are scarcely concerned with sex, but when these same men are given well-balanced meals, comfortable clothing and other creature comforts, they become predictably vulnerable to sexual frustration.

At the same time that prisons were becoming physically less austere places, there was a shift in penal philosophy and practice from the isolation of prisoners from one another—the so-called "separate system"—to congregate confinement: inmates began to work, eat and cell together. With these two developments —improvement of overall physical conditions and the opportunity for interaction among prisoners—the stage was set for the emergence of a complex inmate social system, an important segment of which would center around the problem of adapting to sexual frustration.[10]

[8] Abraham H. Maslow, *Motivation and Personality* (New York: Harper & Brothers, 1954), pp. 146–154.

[9] Robert M. Lindner, *Stone Walls and Men* (New York: Odyssey Press, 1946), p. 456.

[10] The gradual "shift in penal philosophy and practice" from isolating prisoners to permitting increased interaction—which permitted development of a complex inmate social system—was something which paralleled the movement away from the so-called "Pennsylvania or separate system" to the

Granted the fact of prolonged heterosexual deprivation, there exist only three possible adaptations open to members of the inmate community: sexual abstinence, masturbation, or involvement in institutional homosexuality. The individual reactions of abstinence and masturbation warrant only brief consideration here, since the problems which arise from "sex in prison" are primarily sociological products of the interaction of inmates with one another. Suffice it to say that an inmate may take the ascetic task of complete abstinence during his incarceration, or the more common one of regular or sporadic masturbation. Successful self-imposed continence is usually associated with an extremely short sentence and rigidly internalized notions of the inherent evilness of both masturbation and homosexuality. While it is true that individual differences in age and physiology enable some inmates to serve even long periods of confinement without any sexual outlet, the pressures on the average prisoner are such that he engages in at least periodic masturbation. As Ellis states, "All authorities agree that the great majority of men in prison masturbate." [11]

Homosexuality represents a third possible reaction to the deprivation of heterosexual intercourse. Situational homosexuality is believed by many to be widespread in American prisons, a conviction which is doubtless largely fostered by a tendency on the part of sensational writers to grossly exaggerate the actual incidence of the phenomenon; even veteran prison administrators,

---

Auburn ("silent system"), or what is known as "congregate confinement" in the United States. The Auburn system involved a radical departure from the old system of complete, round-the-clock separation of prisoners from one another. By permitting congregate or group labor during the day, Auburn opened the door to what has become a steadily increasing level of social interaction between inmates in American prisons. As inmates begin to talk, eat, work, and cell together, a prison subculture emerges—and with it the "homosexual problem." Prior to Auburn, which opened in 1816, the austere "separate system," as its name implies, so isolated men from one another that only the most rudimentary social system may be said to have existed. The history of this gradual shift from isolation to congregate confinement is well documented in Tappan, *op. cit.*, pp. 601–611.

[11] Albert Ellis, "Masturbation," *The Journal of Social Therapy I* (April 1955): 143.

such as San Quentin's former Warden Duffy,[12] often argue that the majority of inmates engage in homosexual acts while incarcerated.

Actually, the number of inmates who participate in any form of homosexual behavior while imprisoned is relatively small when compared to the vast majority of prisoners who adapt to sexual frustration by masturbating.[13] However, the constricted microcosm of steel and concrete that is the prison lends such an exaggerated visibility to homosexual activity that both inmates and staff are inclined to misperceive its extensiveness; yet this fact does not diminish its sociological importance. If a sufficient number of men define widespread homosexuality as a reality, the consequences in thought and action will be comparable to those which would obtain if this were really the case. The small number of prisoners who engage in institutional homosexuality comprise a subterranean world, a kind of subculture within a subculture, which has profound consequences for the entire prison community. A homosexually oriented system of values, norms, argot and statuses is so inextricably interwoven with the larger inmate social structure as to render the subject of sex between men an inescapable reality of daily life for all prisoners. Homosexuality in prison becomes something with respect to which every man must constantly define himself as long as he is incarcerated.

A careful definition of terms must precede any serious discussion of homosexuality in prison. This is so because the words "homosexual" and "homosexuality," when used by prison in-

[12] Clinton T. Duffy, *Sex and Crime* (New York: Doubleday & Co., 1965), p. 29.

[13] I mean here that not only sensational writers, but professional penologists as well, misperceive the actual extensiveness of prison homosexuality. One can find in a literature both very high and very low estimates. However, on the basis of questionnaire responses of a stratified random sample of 150 inmates, and the statements of many institutional homosexuals who were in a favorable position to estimate the amount of homosexuality, I conclude that a relatively small number, although a highly visible minority, is actually involved. In my random sample of Soledad's tri-facility (three separate prison units in one compound), 80.7 percent agreed with the statement, "I think that masturbation is far more common in here than sex acts between inmates," 64 percent agreed with the statement, "I would say that very few inmates in here get involved with sex acts with other inmates," while 18.4 percent were undecided and only 17.5 percent disagreed.

mates, assume a special subcultural significance. In free society these expressions are highly pejorative and emotionally charged stigma symbols; as such, they are often applied indiscriminately and interchangeably to anyone thought to have engaged in erotic activity with a member of his own sex. Most people do not distinguish between individuals in terms of the motives and circumstances which underlie their homosexual acts; rather, all persons are uniformly stigmatized as "homosexuals," or, more colloquially, as "queers" and "fruits."

Homosexuality in prison is quite a different matter. Inmate society makes many complex distinctions between both acts and actors when evaluating any sexual activity which involves two or more prisoners. Like the Eskimo, for whom the word "snow" has little meaning by itself because of so many possible contexts in which it may be employed, "homosexual" must be related to a complex value system in order to acquire meaning to the prison inmate. To categorically label any prisoner who engages in a homosexual act "a homosexual" would seem as absurd to him as the failure to do so would seem to the average person. He would wish to know a great deal about the actors and the act before reaching a conclusion.

Members of inmate society exempt certain of their peers who indulge in homosexuality while incarcerated from the odious ascription of a "homosexual" status. There exist two criteria, both of which must be fulfilled, for an inmate to escape such stigmatization: (1) the homosexual act or acts must represent only a situational reaction to the deprivation of heterosexual intercourse, and (2) such behavior must involve a complete absence of emotionality and effeminacy—both of which are regarded as signs of "weakness" and "queerness." An inmate who engages in homosexual activity must present a convincing façade of toughness and stereotypical "manliness" in order to escape being defined as a homosexual. It is only because of the unrelenting "pain" of being totally deprived of sexual contact with women, something which is felt by all men in prison, that inmates are willing to take into consideration situational determinants of homosexuality. They therefore make a sharp distinction between homosexual behavior which is preferential and that which is believed to be only a substitutive response to heterosexual deprivation.

All inmates who become involved in homosexuality are ascribed particular hierarchical positions in prison life by their peers; predictably, these men reveal in their attitudes and behavior the fulfillment of the role expectations which correspond to such statuses. The tendency for each status to involve a definitive cluster of values, folkways, and mores, which clearly differentiates it from other statuses, has led some writers on the subject to approach it in terms of a tripartite typology of homosexually-involved inmates. Expressed in the prison vernacular, these three types of statuses are: (1) The "queen" or "fag," (2) the "punk," and (3) the "wolf" or "jocker." [14] Too often, however, such analyses have taken at most an isolated snapshot of prison homosexuality. An attempt will be made here to link these three argot statuses to the larger inmate subculture and to explain why the phenomenon of homosexuality represents such an important daily reality for the majority of nonhomosexually involved prisoners.

I studied the inmate population of a major California medium security prison—the Correctional Training Facility, Soledad—while I was employed there over a two-year period as both a Student Professional Assistant and, later, as a Correctional Counselor. In gathering data for this period, I employed several methods: analysis of case files of homosexually involved inmates; examination of incident reports relating to homosexual acts and actors (many of these yielded information on the subcultural nature of "homosexual violence" and "pressure cliques"); and, thirdly, I developed a forty-three-item questionnaire using a Likert Scale which was designed to tap attitudes of the general inmate population with respect to various kinds of institutional homosexuality, as well as information on masturbation, abstinence, and so forth. This questionnaire was administered to a random sample of 150 Soledad inmates, and I analyzed the responses in terms of racial-ethnic status, marital status, age, offense, time served, and the particular institution—there being three separate prisons at Soledad.

---

[14] This typology of homosexually involved inmates is lucidly presented by Sykes, *loc. cit.*

The "Queen" or "Fag": Preferential Homosexuality

The expression "queen" is used by both inmates and staff to refer to the inmate who closely approaches the popular stereotype of the "flaming faggot," the classically effeminate homosexual. It is believed that the queen engages in prison homosexuality solely out of a preference for male sexual partners. The behavior of such an inmate, rather than being rationalized as a situational reaction to being deprived of women, is felt to be merely the logical continuation of a preexisting pattern of "righteous homosexuality." Even if women were available, inmates aver, the queen would continue to play a "passive" homosexual role; nor is his homosexuality felt to derive primarily from either a desire to secure prison amenities, or protection, though these motives are recognized as sometimes being of secondary importance.

While prison queens form the smallest category of homosexually involved inmates, they are quickly identifiable solely on the basis of their overt appearances and mannerisms. Exaggerated limp-wristed effeminacy, a bizarre caricature of real femininity, serves to set them apart from the majority of inmates who engage in homosexuality. In every nuance of appearance, attitude, and behavior, the queen seeks to make "herself" attractive to a heterosexually deprived population of men as the closest approximation to a much desired but unobtainable sexual object: Woman. Queens, who are usually referred to in the feminine gender by both inmates and staff, usually adopt nicknames which are unequivocally feminine; not infrequently, the selection of names such as Dee-Dee, Chee-Chee, and Peaches, betrays a sardonic mockery of females, which is also apparent in dress and other mannerisms. Even the casual visitor will easily notice the queen's "swishy" gait. If necessity is truly the mother of invention, then the queen has done well in using what the environment offers in approaching a feminine appearance: back pockets are torn out of tight prison denims to make them form-fitting, makeshift cosmetics are fashioned from smuggled medical and food supplies, and jewelry is produced in hobby shops. Hair is grown as long as officials will tolerate, and eyebrows and whiskers often plucked. Like "her" counterpart in free society, the institutional "drag queen" is easily recognized.

The ostensible contempt and ridicule with which members of the inmate population speak of the queen belie the fact that "she" actually enjoys the position of a scarce object of high functional utility; for with the passage of time in prison, the flagrant differences which exist between male and female reach such a point of situational convergence for many sexually deprived men that the queen possesses a very real substitutive appeal. As one inmate confided, "Some of them look and act so damn much like real women!" The queen's effeminacy thus often evokes a memory and longing for females, a longing which sometimes leads otherwise exclusive heterosexual men to seek sexual relief from the queen.

The genesis of the queen's effeminate homosexuality almost always is to be found in events which occurred prior to imprisonment. The noninstitutional etiology of the queen's homosexuality is suggested by the argot saying, "Queens are born. Punks are made." [15] The queen's distinctive effeminacy often involves strong components of narcissism and exhibitionism. This compulsive need to be noticed by others as conspicuously "feminine" is apparent in the following excerpt from a voluminous autobiography entitled, *Life History of Lily Bond, The Redhead:*

> I used to dye my hair blonde and let it grow long, just as if I were a real woman. My wardrobe included a mink coat, a choker, a double set of wedding and engagement rings, and a very expensive suit that was more than seventy-five dollars . . . it hasn't been so awfully long since I was in slacks and blouse, shoes, slip, and panties. . . . I was just wondering what people would say if they could see two or three female "boys" coming from C.I.M. [California Institution for Men] all decked in panties, slip, etc. . . . Lay here on my bunk and wonder why they didn't put two bunks in a cell.

[15] *Ibid.*, p. 96.

It is common to find strong elements of fetishism and transvestism in the psychopathology of prison queens. Even the more
serious gender aberration of transsexualism is sometimes apparent, as suggested in another statement by a queen: "I'd much
rather live a girl's life than a man's, because you have much more
fun. . . . In fact, if I had the money, I would take the chance
of an operation to become a woman. I would give my right leg
to be born a girl now . . ." (Author's file).

The queen's scarcity in prison, usually enables her to be
highly selective in choosing sexual partners. Exceptions to this
occur, however, in the case of older, less attractive queens. One
such individual boasted to the writer of having established a sexual liaison with an inmate less than half her age, a claim which
was openly and immediately denied by several of her peers, who
were present; they derisively maintained that she couldn't find
anyone to "go down with," let alone a younger inmate.

Usually the queen will enter into a number of prison sexual
liaisons which perhaps are best described as approaching serial
monogamy. The use of the term, marriage, to describe these
evanescent liaisons is no misnomer, for such relationships often
reveal many of the elements common to heterosexual marriage.
The queen brings to a marriage a desire for esteem, security, and
affection, as well as for sexual gratification. She will usually continue the relationship for only as long as a preponderance of
these needs are fulfilled. Like the heterosexual marriage, there
is usually a stringent demand for sexual fidelity in such relationships. The violation of this marital form may bring in its wake
violence, even murder. It is true that the proclivity for exhibitionism and flirtation which is common among queens has more
than once led to institutional homicide, when combined with the
strong emotional investment so often found in prison marriages.
As one queen, serving a life sentence for murdering her homosexual partner, confided: "No one else had better not interfere,
for it is very dangerous."

The following excerpt from a letter written by a queen to
her partner illustrates well the charged emotional atmosphere
which often exists in prison marriages:

Dear Danny:

You see, I have never been able to be a good woman to you because I always knew that you never cared that much for me. I did not know, however, that you did not respect me. That hurts me more than anything. I have read your letter a dozen times, and each time I do I break out crying. I love you and nothing could ever change that. I wish you would give me the chance to be a good woman to you, but I guess it's too late. I pray that you and I can work something out, then, instead of hurting each other. Will you do this for me, darling? Be good, honey, and I do love you.

Love Forever and a Day
Love Always, Johnnie [Author's file]

Another "kite," or prison note, written by a spurned queen, suggests that dissolution of a marriage may be imminent: "Why did you defy me, Bobby? Why didn't you let me go into the wing? Keep that punk out of your face! You used to tell me how you kept them out of your face, so what's so special about this one?" (Author's file).

Despite the general proscription of infidelity, two marriage partners may arrive at an agreement whereby the queen will prostitute herself to other inmates in return for certain goods and services. One inmate "pimp" exhorts his spouse: "Look sweetheart, I need some cigarettes bad. If this fool doesn't want to play, drop him and find another damn fool. Get busy and get some cigarettes over here because your husband isn't going to smoke that state shit!" (Author's file). Some prison queens are able to amass considerable institutional affluence through selective prostitution; obviously such activity also may serve the latent function of providing variety in sexual partners as a means of gratifying the queen's narcissism.

The brittle marriage of the queen results from a tacit, symbiotic contract in which she agrees to provide another inmate, usually known in prison parlance as a "wolf" or "jocker," with both sexual gratification and status among his peers as a "daddy." The "jocker," in addition to reciprocating sexual favors, acts as a protector and provides the queen with a measure of security in a highly predatory environment. The symbiosis thus revolves primarily about sex and security. Security, in the form of physical protection, is particularly important to the weak and effeminate queen. It is for this reason that most queens move from marriage to marriage, seldom terminating one relationship unless another is immediately available. By thus remaining always with a strong "daddy," she becomes relatively immune to the institutional phenomenon known as "sex pressuring" (coercion into homosexual activity). An unattached queen is constantly liable to sexual assault by lone predators, gang rape, and coercion into indiscriminate prostitution. Without a protective marriage, as one queen put it, ". . . the traffic gets too heavy to bear." While a married queen may occasionally be "hit on" (approached for sexual favors), the knowledge that any aggressive overture may elicit a reprisal from her "daddy" serves to largely insulate her from the fate which befalls other weak and sexually vulnerable inmates.

The "jocker" or "wolf" who "takes a queen" must be able to convincingly demonstrate toughness and strength to his peers. Most enter such relationships with only the manifest goal of securing substitutive sexual gratification; sometimes, however, an element of latent homosexuality in the "wolf's" personality surfaces, as is suggested in the following excerpt from a letter written by one such inmate to his "wife":

Darling . . . Angel . . . Sweetheart . . . I need you, baby, and I want you bad. You are making me feel like I do when I am around my wife, Roberta. But I can tell you this, sweetheart, she never made me feel the way I do right at this minute . . . Sleep tight, my darling, and when you dream, keep everyone out of them but you and me. [Author's file]

As an especially "swishy queen" skips from marriage to marriage, she may leave in her wake a series of beatings and stabbings, spread veneral disease, and occasionally produce riots. Such an inmate, as Lindner states, ". . . is every bit as dangerous as a stray female in prison." [16] It is for this reason that queens who are especially provocative and who fail to settle down in a non-disruptive pattern of serial monogamy are often isolated from the main body of prisoners in a "queen's row" or other specialized unit of an institution; yet, while the queen occasionally cre-

16 Lindner, *op. cit.,* p. 464.

ates serious custodial problems, she usually does not produce nearly the volume of trouble that may be attributed to the two other argot types.

The "Punk": Canteen and Pressure

Those members of the inmate community who are regarded by their peers as "punks" occupy a status which is the very nadir of prison life. With the possible exception of the "rat," or informer, the punk is uniformly the most despised of inmates, a pariah who occupies at most a precarious position on the margin of inmate society. Unlike the queen who openly chooses a life of passive homosexuality and even embraces the stigma of effeminacy as desirable, the punk is hated because his involvement in prison homosexuality is believed to result from either personal weakness in the face of pressure or from a mercenary willingness to sacrifice his manhood for certain goods and services. As Sykes states:

> But even though the punk does not exhibit those mannerisms characterized as feminine by the inmate population he has turned himself into a woman, in the eyes of the prisoners, by the very act of his submission. His is an inner softness or weakness; and from the viewpoint of the prisoners, his sacrifice of manhood is perhaps more contemptible than that of the (queen) because he acts from fear or for the sake of quick advantage rather than from personal inclination.[17]

Of perhaps greatest importance in understanding the hostility which is meted out to the punk is the realization that, by failing to live up to the cardinal tenet of the inmate code to "be a man," he raises anxieties in all prisoners over their own ability to successfully resist involvement in prison homosexuality. It is possible to discern two subcategories of institutional punks; in the language of the prison, these are (1) the "canteen punk," and (2) the "pressure punk."

[17] Sykes, *loc. cit.*

The Canteen Punk

Inmates who are ascribed membership in this status are believed to engage in homosexual acts out of a desire for personal aggrandizement. They are men whose homosexuality represents an attempt to mitigate the frustration which results from being deprived of certain goods and services; thus canteen punks form a class of prison prostitutes who perform fellatio and submit to pederasty in return for gratuities such as candy, cigarettes, money, or personal favors. As such, they represent a sexual outlet which is available to the inmate who desires homosexual release, but who is unable either to win a queen or to successfully coerce a weaker inmate into performing homosexual acts without cost. The "canteen punk's" counterpart in free society is the youthful male prostitute who frequents certain areas of large cities. The canteen punk, like the queen, essentially capitalizes upon his substitutive appeal in a world without women. A further point of similarity is the fact that the canteen punk may deal with only particular inmates in return for securing their protection from homosexually aggressive peers.

The number of inmates who elect to engage in such passive homosexuality, without preexisting homosexual tendencies, is indeed small. In most cases, confinement in prison will eventually bring latent homosexual impulses to the surface; often an inmate who is initially raped by a group of predatory peers, or "ripped off," will, as the saying goes, "get to liking it." Such a person may rationalize future voluntary sexual activity on the ground that, since he has no alternative except to adjust to homosexuality, he may as well profit from it. While effeminacy is seldom apparent in the punk, a few metamorphose into queens with the passage of time in prison.

The Pressure Punk

This category includes most of those who are disparagingly referred to by inmates and staff as punks. The "pressure punk" is one who submits to a homosexually passive role because of either threatened or actual physical force. As a group, such inmates are predominantly younger, less "prisonized" [18] individuals who have been singled out as "weak" by more sophisticated and sexually aggressive peers; usually, such men evince little or no prior history of homosexual behavior.

There exist two subcultural routes to this lowly status in the prison community. Sometimes a man enters prison with a "punk jacket." The dynamics of this process are often as follows: a rumor, often completely false, is circulated by one or more inmates at the institution that a prisoner who is scheduled to arrive has already been "ripped off" or "turned out" at the county jail or the prison transferring him; often this is done with the cooperation of inmate clerks at the other end, who have placed a pre-arranged pen mark or other symbol on the prisoner's file card to denote that he can probably be successfully "pressured" for sex. Soon word spreads throughout the institution, through an amazingly intricate communications system, that the inmate in question is "stuff," or a "broad." By the time the new prisoner arrives, the matter of the truth or falsity of this belief will be sociologically irrelevant. This entire process may be set in motion by nothing more than a "hunch" based upon an inmate's youthful or weak appearance. Sometimes, however, it results from a calculated desire on the part of others to even up a score for some real or imagined wrong committed outside the prison.

Whatever the reason, an inmate defined as amenable to sexual "pressure" will be tested by sexually predatory prisoners for the purpose of verifying his "punk" status as a preliminary to securing homosexual favors. The burden of proving that he is not a "pressure punk" rests entirely with the new inmate.

In other cases, an individual plays a more active role in his own victimization. Prisoners have an expression that "you bring pressure on yourself," by which they mean that failure to meet the normative expectations which attach to "being a man" in

---

[18] The expression "prisonization" was originated by Donald Clemmer, *The Prison Community* (New York: Holt, Rinehart and Winston, 1958) to denote the extent to which an inmate has taken on, or internalized, the value system of the prison.

prison may render one particularly vulnerable to the sexual aggression of peers. It is because of a lack of "prisonization," acculturation to the complex norms which regulate social behavior in the prison, that the new inmate often inadvertently brings sexual pressure on himself. This is true not only of men who have never before been in prison, but also of the youth facility "graduate"; often such inmates make the grave social error of carrying the swaggering, boisterous actions and "delinquent" appearance—which conferred prestige among a younger group of prisoners—into the quite different milieu of the adult person. Where the prison social system prescribes serving time quietly, "doing your number by walking slow and drinking plenty of water," the youthful newcomer's loud laughter, horseplay, and "ducktail" haircut makes him stand out like the proverbial sore thumb. It is a deficiency in institutional socialization which makes him ready prey for sexually predatory "wolves" or "jockers."

A very real *rite de passage* confronts all new arrivals at the adult male prison. Unless a man is a well-known returnee or has friends or "homeboys" who will help define him as a "solid con" to other prisoners, he may be in serious trouble. An inmate who lacks such resources, and who does not possess a sufficient level of prisonization to enable him to navigate in a normatively acceptable manner, will very often have to run a terrifying gauntlet of sexual "pressuring" at the hands of other prisoners.

From the moment a new busload of inmates arrives at the prison, institutional "jockers" make a careful review of all "fish," or newcomers, in the hope of discovering which men will likely prove vulnerable to sexual coercion. Inmates who are regarded as potential pressure punks often will be first approached in the yard or cellblock with a friendly offer of goods or services. The new inmate, alone and frightened in a strange environment, is all to eager to accept the offer of assistance, candy or cigarettes, from the man who appears to know his way around. Because of his lack of familiarity with prison life, he does not realize that a "real con" never accepts anything from another prisoner—goods or services—without a clear statement of what is expected in return. He likewise fails to grasp that the acceptance of favors under such circumstances is regarded by those proffering them as tantamount to a willingness to reciprocate in the currency of homosexual behavior.

Another common means of ensnaring the unwary "fish" is the invitation to enter a card game, or other gambling activity—which is predictably crooked—for the purpose of getting him into debt. The "fish," who usually has nothing to gamble with, at first is told that he can owe until canteen draw; however, suddenly he is deeply in debt and his fellow gamblers are no longer willing to wait until commissary time for settlement of the debt. As Lindner states:

> When the showdown arrives and payment is demanded, he [the pressure victim] may be unwilling to come across. Then a startling transformation comes over his benefactor and erstwhile friend, and the harassed neophyte finds himself backed against a wall with a knife pressed to his stomach, and he hears the demand to "fuck or fight." [19]

The approaches of bribery and gambling are often expediently bypassed if an inmate is regarded as especially weak and frightened. Such men are often bluntly informed to submit to homosexual acts or else! One young inmate was approached less than five minutes after his arrival by a prison "jocker" who stated, "Listen, you need a 'daddy' and I'm it!"

Many inmates who capitulate to such demands enter prison as exclusive heterosexuals; however, the fact that a man may have no homosexual tendencies, and may even have a wife and family on the "streets," in no way insulates him from the depredations of prison "pressure artists." The fact that sexually aggressive inmates are often able to back up their demands with impunity is responsible for the "punking" of many such inmates.

Successful homosexual pressuring is made possible by certain tenets of the so-called "inmate code." This system of subcultural folkways and mores is accorded lip support by most inmates in the presence of their peers out of fear of being thought less than a "real con." The code proves singularly dysfunctional for the new and friendless inmate who is not familiar with the

[19] Lindner, op. cit., p. 454.

nature of prison life. Two maxims of the code, "don't rat" and "do your own time," serve to effectively isolate him from the assistance of either staff or fellow inmates. In the event of "sex pressure," the code, in demanding that such an inmate "be a man" and stand his ground at all costs, proscribes running to other prisoners as "sniveling" and "weak." A "real man" must resist pressure, fight, if necessary, even at the risk of serious injury or death.

Other inmates avoid those of their peers who are being subjected to sex pressuring; they refuse to help either out of fear of suffering the same fate or because of a very real danger of being beaten or even killed for interfering. Nor can the inmate under pressure go to staff for help because of the proscription against "ratting." A man who violates this sacrosanct tenet of the code will be forced to "lock up" in protective custody in order to escape violence at the hands of fellow prisoners. In addition to being called a "p.c. punk," that is, protective custody, such an inmate will suffer the added onus which accompanies the status of "rat." If the punk is jeopardized by the taboo against "ratting," his aggressors are protected by it. "Wolves" and "jockers" are able to wield sanctions ranging from threats to cold-blooded murder with the confidence that virtually no one will inform on them out of fear of being labeled a "rat." The code exhortation to "do your own time" also serves to reinforce the unwillingness of other inmates to become involved in the punk's problem. The subcultural belief that the pressure victim "brings it on himself" out of weakness or stupidity enables other prisoners to rationalize their noninvolvement in preventing behavior which they actually disapprove of. Fear, resulting from the well known process of "pluralistic ignorance," effectively keeps prisoners from communicating their real sentiments to one another.

Even inmates who have never been subjected to sexual pressures live in constant fear of being "ripped off" by aggressive peers. Strict public adherence to the inmate code and the formation of a mutual aid pact with a few friends are defensive measures which are employed by most prisoners in the hope of averting "pressure."

The pressure punk is a "situational homosexual" in the strict-

est sense of the expression. While he typically does not see himself as a "queer," such an inmate faces the formidable task of
integrating into his self-image a new identity which has literally
been forced upon him. He must somehow deal with the humilia-
tion which attends being passed around like a prostitute among
other men, and he must adapt to the derisive remarks which are
daily meted out to him by the only reference group on his horizon. His own lower-class socialization, which places a premium on
"toughness" and "manliness," condemns him to great inner tur-
moil. In the eyes of his peers, the punk is little more than an
article of commerce. He may not escape from the shackles of this
lowly status without incurring the wrath of his masters; indeed,
the knowledge that his oppressors stand ready with blade and
metal pipe to enforce compliance with their sexual demands
keeps the punk trapped in a quagmire of shame and self-hatred.
Illustrative of the contempt with which the punk usually comes
to regard himself was the statement of one inmate, who, when
asked if he would consent to an interview, stated, "No, I don't
want anyone to know what I am in here!" Another prisoner, long
regarded by his peers as a pressure punk, emotionally burst out
during a group therapy discussion, "These people (other inmates)
think I'm a sissy, but I'm not. I'm a man."

Pressure punks are usually "owned" by one or more of the
predatory groups of "jockers" which exist in prison. In addition
to being used for homosexuality by the "pressure clique," the
punk is often forced by such groups into prison prostitution or
to "burn," that is, rob, the cells of other inmates. These groups
of "wolves" or "jockers," each of which may range in size from
three or four to twenty or more inmates, divide the proceeds of
such activity on a businesslike basis. Sometimes the clique, or
one of its members who has come into sole ownership of a "punk,"
will sell him to another group or individual, a "good punk"
bringing perhaps fifteen to twenty cartons of commercial cigarettes. The ignominy of repeatedly being sold is sometimes
intolerable for the inmate punk. One such prisoner, revolting
against what he called "being sold like an animal," attacked and
seriously injured one of his "jockers." Afterward, he confided,
"I was afraid they [pressure clique] were going to sell me again,

as I was just sold for twelve cartons." Like the queen, a punk may form a symbiotic alliance with a strong "jocker" in the hope of escaping homosexual assaults and control by pressure cliques.

The "Wolf" or "Jocker": Loners and Pressure Cliques

Under certain circumstances a homosexually involved inmate may be defined by his peers as a "wolf," "jocker," or "daddy." These expressions each refer to a single status which involves a minimum of stigmatization. Men who are placed in this category by the inmate community are not regarded as "real homosexuals," since their behavior is felt to be the result of heterosexual deprivation, and conspicuously lacks effeminacy and emotional attachment.

The wolf or jocker plays the stereotyped "male" role in sexual activity. He views himself, and needs to be viewed by his fellow inmates, as "a man"; and within prison to be "a man" and still engage in homosexual acts one must present an image of exaggerated toughness and unequivocal masculinity. The jocker, by consistently wielding force over or raping his sexual partners, maintains for himself and others a perception of his behavior as basically masculine under the circumstances. The more violence that surrounds his sexual acts, the closer the jocker comes to actually engaging in an emotionless act of rape, thereby escaping both homosexual anxiety and the imputation of "queerness" by his peers. Compared to the queen, the wolf represents the opposite side of a coin of bizarre gender caricature: the Marlboro Man juxtaposed against the frail *femme fatale*.

The "jocker's" personality and background are usually characterized by an impulsive and hedonistic concern with securing personal gratification. When combined with the psychopathy which often pervades his personality, imprisonment in a world without women leads him to adopt a "take sex where you can get it" philosophy. While the jocker ostensibly has a strong preference for heterosexual partners, homosexual intercourse means little more to him than the difference between intravaginal and intra-anal penetration. He usually evinces little if any concern for the attitudes or feelings of his partners, whether they are heterosexual or homosexual. The sex history of such an inmate is usually, as Lindner observes, ". . . non-selective, transient, and adventitious." [20] While most prisoners disapprove of his behavior, the jocker usually escapes the public scorn and derision which are meted out to punks and queens. A notable exception to this, however, is the jocker who "takes a queen." Other inmates are aware of the emotional elements likely to be involved in such a relationship, if only because of the nature of queens. Rather than being regarded by peers as consistently playing the maculine sex role, jockers who marry queens are often believed to "flip-flop," that is, sometimes play a passive sex role. Prisoners have a saying, directed toward such liaisons, that "when you make the team, you agree to play any position." One will sometimes hear jibes, such as "Who's playing the daddy tonight?" derisively flung at the jocker who has "courted and married a queen." The possibility of homosexual panic appearing is very real for the would-be masculine jocker who finds himself becoming emotionally involved with a queen.

Prison queens and canteen punks make the sardonic comment that "this year's business is next year's competition," which has reference to the common downward mobility of some wolves or jockers. The jocker is painfully aware that the slightest suggestion of weakness, or emotional involvement in homosexual relations—the smallest chink in his armor of tough masculinity—may instantly topple him to the lowly status of "punk." He constantly must face the possibility that someone will successfully challenge the legitimacy of his claimed status. It is because of this that most prison jockers do not operate as loners; instead, such men usually form predatory alliances with other wolves. The manifest reason for the existence of such groups is the belief that extortion of homosexual favors requires the "muscle" of more than one inmate if it is to be successful; however, the formation of such groups actually serves the latent function of providing security for individuals who often are quite frightened themselves. For the jocker who is running scared, the best defense is a good offense.

[20] *Ibid.*, p. 458.

The homosexual problem in prison, as Kinsey observes, is largely to be equated with ". . . the control of men who are particularly aggressive in forcing other individuals into homosexual relations." [21] The inability to effectively control prison pressure cliques proves both frustrating and embarrassing to the staff of a correctional institution. The files of many inmates who have been raped, beaten, and even sometimes killed, by groups of pressure "artists," are often filled with letters from the local district attorney's office, the latter declining to prosecute because of the complete unwillingness of inmate witnesses to testify in what would otherwise be prima facie cases. Even in those few instances where a pressure victim initially agrees to testify against his attackers, a sudden "lapse of memory" often occurs just before the case goes to court. Typical of such situations was the statement made by a young inmate who had resisted a group of jockers, only to be knifed by one of their number. He initially agreed to name the inmate who assaulted him, but soon backed down, stating to a prison official from his hospital bed, "You and I both know who 'shanked' [knifed] me, but nothing could make me testify. If I did, my life wouldn't be worth two cents."

The anxiety which prison administrators often feel because of their repeatedly unsuccessful attempts to suppress the formation of pressure cliques is evident in the irate letter of one prison warden to the director of corrections in the wake of a stabbing incident perpetrated by one such group:

> It is indeed a deplorable situation when a young man, helpless and frightened, is nearly murdered four days after his arrival at this institution because he would not submit to the will of a group of criminals. The most unfortunate part of the picture is that it is by no means the first, nor will it be the last such incident. [Author's file]

It is likely that there would be many more injuries and deaths resulting from the aggressiveness of pressure cliques were it not for the willingness of a few inmates to secretly "rat" in order to avert bloodshed.

In addition to often injuring their victims, pressure groups

---

[21] Kinsey *et al., loc. cit.*

sometimes come into violent conflict with one another, much in the manner of rival delinquent gangs who engage in periodic "rumbles." These incidents, which sometimes escalate into full-scale prison riots, usually arise from an altercation over the ownership of a particular "punk"; sometimes sexual "claim jumping" assumes a racial dimension. This may occur if a Caucasian punk is "ripped off" by a Negro pressure clique, or if a white group begins "burning coal," that is, "punking" a Negro prisoner. The latent racial tensions which characterize contemporary America permeate the walls of this miniature society where they often erupt into internecine violence between white and black prisoners. The following is an account of one such incident:

> The leader of a white pressure clique, who was killed, became involved in an argument with leaders of a Negro clique over the homosexual favors of another Caucasian inmate. This argument resulted in an unexpected attack by the Negroes on Caucasians in the A Wing dayroom on the evening of October 26. During the fight, the Caucasian leader was stabbed to death and several other Caucasion and Mexican inmates were injured by knives and struck by heavy objects . . . The incident was precipitated by the transfer of a particularly aggressive Caucasian inmate to another prison. This man was feared by all inmates because of his ability to pick out prisoners who would be most vulnerable to pressure. This inmate left behind a homosexual partner who was regarded as one of the more prized "punks" in the prison. A sale of this inmate to a Negro clique promptly followed, but was objected to by many white inmates. Arguments, and meetings with the Negroes in an attempt to nullify the sale, preceded the outbreak of violence. [Author's file]

The author's two-year period of research at a major California prison led him ineluctably to the conclusion that the "homosexual problem" derives largely from the fear and violence which are produced by the attempt of a relatively small number of men to secure substitutive sexual gratification. No attempt has been made here to evaluate the psychological damage which doubtless befalls many men who are sexually victimized by such inmates. It is certainly true, however, that ". . . the impact of incarceration on a man's sex life [is] unquestionably important and must be made the sole subject of an intensive study at some later date." [22] Also beyond the scope of this paper has been a discussion of the numerous proposals which have been advanced as solutions to the problem of prison homosexuality; for example, conjugal visitation, improvements in custody and staffing, isolation of known predatory homosexuals, and architectural changes.

"Homosexuality," as Tappan laconically observes, "is a universal concomitant of sex-segregated living." [20] To reiterate an earlier point, its existence in prison must be constantly dealt with on both a psychological and sociological level by every inmate. The typology of homosexual roles discussed here is certainly neither exhaustive nor immutable; hopefully, however, it provides a reasonably inclusive overview of a highly complex and constantly changing system of social behavior, and will also serve to encourage further research on the subject.

[22] *Ibid.*, p. 224.

Impersonal Sex and
Perceived Satisfaction

LAUD HUMPHREYS

In a previous study of sexual activity in public restrooms, I have indicated that many American males—perhaps millions of them—resort to these facilities because of the opportunity they afford for fast, economical, and impersonal sexual relationships: "What the covert deviant needs is a sexual machine—collapsible to hip-pocket size, silent in operation—plus the excitement of a risk-taking encounter. In tearoom sex he has the closest thing to such a device. This encounter functions, for the sex market, as does the automat for the culinary, providing a low-cost, impersonal, democratic means of commodity distribution" (Humphreys 1970: 154).

It is the fleeting nature of the activity they shelter that makes tearooms popular for most participants. Recently, in the course of research in an Eastern seaboard city, I discovered that the closing of park restrooms merely results in the relocation of impersonal homosexual activity. For reasons unknown, officials of that large metropolitan center closed every rest facility in its public parks. The locks are now rusty and the doors nailed shut; nevertheless, impersonal sex still flourishes. Such encounters now occur in the restrooms of subway stations and parking facilities, among reeds that line the rivers, behind the bushes along free-ways, or in the shadowy environs of truckstops. In other words, the marketing of impersonal sex appears to be highly adaptable to pressures from social control forces. "I want the quick thing," says one respondent, "and there's always someplace to get it . . . I'm just too damned busy and involved to look for anything else!"

In *Tearoom Trade: Impersonal Sex in Public Places,* I discuss the risks taken by participants in these "quickie" relationships. Not only do young toughs present physical dangers, but there is the constant threat of blackmail, assault, and arrest by the police. During a recent year, for example, the Sheriff's Department of Los Angeles County arrested seventy men in one public restroom (Gallo 1966: 688). From available arrest data, it appears that the majority of criminal charges involving homosexual activity in this country have their source in police surveillance of public restrooms.

The fear of exposure for tearoom activity has resulted in the creation of a lookout role, one well suited for sociological observation of these sexual encounters. I played this role while observing some 200 acts of fellatio between men, for fifty of which I made careful and systematic notes. In connection with such participant observation, I also collected a sample of participants (representative on the bases of both time and place) by tracing license plate numbers. Later, I interviewed the sample of fifty participants, under the pretext of a public health survey. A control sample of men, randomly selected from the population but matched with the participants on the bases of race, occupational level, area of residence, and marital status, was also interviewed (Humphreys 1970: 26–44).

Social factors, primarily occupation and marital status, influence the amount of "drive" behind the search for impersonal sex. Tearoom encounters are not only games of chance, risk-taking adventures but also sexual outlets for those who require them. The overall task of this paper is to assess the sexual needs and performances of those who seek impersonal sex and to relate those needs and activities to their social characteristics.

Researching Sexual Needs and Performance

When a mate, lover, or friend knows that a person engages in a particular type of sexual act, he or she commonly identifies the performer with that act or set of acts. One's sexual identity is formed, in no small part, around such reports or observations of one's erotic activity. Thus, among adolescents, a boy who has exhibited his prowess at masturbation on a Scout outing may find himself shackled with a nickname like "J.O." Another may build a reputation as a stud with the girls. As Kitsuse (1964: 96) has noted, such labeling may result from an isolated instance that gives rise to a process of retrospective reinterpretation of past interaction with the subject.

The problem, of course, is not only that such labels are adhesive but that they also tend to subsume other characteristics of the individual. Hughes (1958: 111) has discussed this phenomenon as "master status-determining traits." An unfortunate choice of time, place, or sexual partner frequently converts the "weak moment" of an experimenter into a permanent social identity. A girl with little (or no) coital experience may be stigmatized as a "slut," or an otherwise faithful husband may become an adulterer or a "queer."

This is the stuff of which both nightmares and short stories are made. It also contains serious pitfalls for one who does research in sexual behavior. He, too, may commit the fallacy of labeling a subject on the basis of behavior once observed or reported. In the course of studying homosexual activity in public restrooms, I observed some 200 acts of fellatio. The vast majority of participants in these encounters were seen only once by the researcher in such behavior. Although I had actually observed each respondent engaging in an act of fellatio, I had no way of knowing, in most cases, whether these men engaged in repeat performances of homosexual acts, much less of gauging the degree to which this behavior may have been habitual for them. The extent of my observations did enable me to identify a few as "habitual insertees," those who frequently occupied stalls to receive the penises of others into their mouths. Others became known to me as tearoom habitues. It is, nevertheless, possible that some men may have become data upon the occasion of their single, experimental venture into that stigmatized activity.

Apart from theoretical considerations, that is why it is unwise for a sex researcher to refer to any person as "a homosexual." Hooker's research indicates that standard psychological tests fail as indices of sexual orientation (1963: 141–161). But even a method as empirical as direct observation tells us little of such matters as the individual's overall orientation or self-image.

For this reason, I refer to research subjects only as participants in homosexual encounters. In a particular instance, one may have played the role of insertor, another the insertee part. But, even when observed once in a particular role, they cannot properly be characterized as "insertees" or "insertors" for purposes beyond the description of the interaction itself. Such categorization is prohibited by the tendency of those observed to switch parts in subsequent sexual games.

If it is our purpose to enter into a scientific analysis of sexual activity, then it is essential to acquire longitudinal data on the sexual actors. We must know not only what we saw them do (important as that may be) but what they did, by way of sex, during the days and weeks and years before they were "caught in the act." Such long-term observation is impractical, if not impossible. We are driven back, then, to methods that are only secondarily empirical. For much of his data, the sex researcher must rely on interview material.

At best, such interview data—subject as they are to both intentional and unintentional distortion—consist of accurate reports of the respondent's own perception of his sex life. He may believe (as, indeed, many who think of themselves as being homosexual do believe) that his sexual fantasies have always been homoerotic. The researcher may doubt it, cannot prove otherwise, and must record it thusly.

The man whose average rate of intercourse is 2.5 coital acts per month may think he enjoys such relations "about once a week." On an annual basis, the difference is that between 30 and 52 acts. The researcher can only report the latter rate (although, if an ethnographer, he may add a footnote to read: "Subject also goes to tearooms from time to time for a blow job.").

Any distortion of data resulting from such reports, however, need not be seen as a deterrent to knowledge. Apart from a strictly biological orientation to the question, the important information to be gained from interviews concerns the subject's *perception* of his performance, needs, and satisfaction.

The interview schedules used in my study of tearoom participants contain questions concerning the frequency of intercourse (frequency of orgasm for single men). They also cover the
respondents' perceptions of sexual needs in relation to others, of
the importance of having his sexual needs satisfied, as well as his
assessment of whether these needs are currently being met. These
questions were asked of the fifty men in my participant sample
and of fifty who were randomly selected from the general population of the metropolitan area. Additional data were gained
from numerous open-ended interviews with cooperating respondents.

Perceived Drive and
Professed Normalcy

The questions on need and relative importance were intended
to serve as checks one on the other and were effective for that
purpose. Among the married and single men of both samples,
most of those who perceived their sexual needs as being "greater
than most other men" also felt it "extremely important" that
those needs be met. Conversely, all those who judged their needs
as being less than those of others perceived their fulfillment as
being "not at all important."

A strong majority of both samples reported that it is "very
important" for their sexual needs to be met—but there the similarities end. Perceptions of the importance of sexual need-satis-
faction (which, for the sake of brevity, I shall call "drive") differ
along the lines of the social characteristics of age, marital status,
and occupation.

One variance in perceived drive between the participant and
control samples is in the tendency of participants to profess ignorance of what other men's sexual needs may be. Forty-two percent of those observed in tearooms answered with a variation of
"How should I know?" when asked to compare their sexual needs
with those of other men. Only 16 percent of those in the control
sample failed to make some estimate of comparison.

Presuming that those who engage in sex with other men
have at least as much knowledge of the sexual needs of other

males as do their nondeviant counterparts, we can only conclude
that this professed ignorance is an instance of deviance disavowal
(Davis 1964: 129–130). This manner of professing normalcy is
more pronounced among the married participants than the unmarried; however, this is clearly a function of the age differential
between married and single respondents of both samples. (Although the median age of the controls is five years above that of
the participants, that of the combined married men is fourteen
years above the median age of the single men of both samples.)
Nearly all of those in both groups who professed ignorance of
the needs of others were age thirty or older.

There is also evidence that the impact of aging differs somewhat between participants and controls. Those over age fifty-five
in the nondeviant sample consistently reported a low level of
both drive and frequency of intercourse. In spite of declining
conjugal activity, however, the older participants claimed a normal level of sexual drive. The following examples illustrate the
differences in these perceptions of drive between the participants
and controls:

> A member of the randomly selected control sample, Gus, is sixty-
> one. He has been on his job as a machinist for thirty-six years and
> professes being happily married. Never having suffered a major
> illness, Gus has missed one day of work in the last five years. "I
> had the flu," he says. He has intercourse with his wife, "once in a
> while"; but, when questioned about his sexual needs, he reports:
> "Son, when you start getting my age, you don't have too many
> needs anymore."
>
> Arthur was observed in the insertee role in a tearoom. At
> sixty-seven, he is retired. In the last five years, he has suffered a
> coronary occlusion among other ailments. He blames his lack of
> intercourse on his invalid wife, claiming that his marriage does not
> meet his "average" sexual needs.
>
> Bill is manager of a small store. At sixty-one, he has two grown
> children. He thinks it is unimportant to have sexual satisfaction.
> "I don't have sex anymore," he says. "I'm too old." This member
> of the control sample has no sex life to report. He is matched with
> Frank, a sixty-seven-year-old tearoom participant. Frank's son is
> also grown and in Vietnam. Like Bill, this salesman has had no
> serious illness in more than five years. His weekly intercourse with

his wife is, he feels, very important. We did not discuss his extra-marital sexual activity.

A similar pattern holds for older single men in the two samples:

> A fifty-nine-year-old accountant, whom I shall call Mike, is un-married and in good health. This member of the control sample reports sex needs that are less than those of other men he knows. How often does he have an orgasm? "Nowadays, almost never." His counterpart among the tearoom participants is Al, a salesman, age fifty-eight. This single man has an orgasm "four times a week." He thinks his sexual needs are "about the same as those of other men" and "very important."

The staff of the Institute for Sex Research, in their study of sexual offenders, conclude that homosexual offenders vs. adults appeared to have the strongest "sex drive" of the groups studied, if frequency of activity is taken as a measure (Gebhard 1965: 351). The tearoom research provides no evidence of greater *activity* on the part of participants that might support this finding; but it does indicate that, at least for the older men, the *perception* of sex drive is stronger among those who engage in homosexual behavior.

On the basis of social scientific evidence, it is difficult to explain these differences in sex drive and performance among the older respondents. In his original study, Kinsey (1948: 213) found that "the boys who are earliest adolescent, by age twelve at the latest, are the ones who most often have the highest rates of outlet in the later years of their lives." He also reported that "homosexual activities occur in a much higher percentage of the males who became adolescent at an early age" (1948: 630). Might this correlation between earlier puberty and higher rates of out-let in later years account for my findings? If so, my data do not support it. There is no difference between the two samples in the tearoom study, at least in so far as my respondents were able to recall the ages at which their puberty began. As regards the older men, the median age for onset of puberty among the par-ticipants was fourteen, compared with thirteen for the median age of the controls.

Certainly, as evidenced by the case histories reported above, health was not a factor in declining sexual interest and activity, that group of participants with somewhat poorer health reporting greater drive and intercourse than the healthier controls. Perhaps, then, those who engage in homosexual activity may be "oversexed." If that were true, however, the younger participants would also report greater sexual activity and drive. As we shall see, this is not true for the younger men. Those interested in the sociology of sex should beware of imposing an interpretation of abnormality (in the sense of "unhealthiness" or "unnaturalness") upon these indications of greater sexual interest and activity on the part of the aging tearoom participants. Perhaps, being less discriminating in their choices of sexual outlet, the tearoom patrons are leading more "natural" sex lives than do the "straights."

Tearoom Sex as an Alternative to Masturbation

The interviewer asked Sam, a young grocery clerk: "How often do you have an orgasm by any means?" "Almost every day," this member of the control sample answered. "But that's almost totally by masturbation." Another single man from the same sample answered: "I masturbate every day, if that's what you mean."

These examples illustrate one side of a dichotomy within the control sample of unmarried men that differentiates them from the single deviants. Half the men in the control sample were quick to mention masturbation as their primary sexual outlet, and those were the single straights who perceived their sexual needs as the same or greater than those of other men. Men of their type who did not mention masturbation generally rated their sexual needs as less than others they know.

Typical of the latter group is Jeff, a handsome university student, who says that having sex is only "somewhat important" and who reports his sexual needs as being less than most. "I have an orgasm very infrequently," he reports. "I can't remember the last time." This asexual sort of response was provided by nearly a third of the single men in the control sample, compared with only two among the unmarried participants.

Although a number of unmarried participants were quite open in admitting homosexual activity, few mentioned masturbation as a sexual outlet. If their reported assessment of sexual outlet is reliable, we must conclude that the single controls rely on masturbation to a far greater extent than do their deviant counterparts—with much the same result in terms of frequency of orgasm. The mean frequency of reported orgasms for unmarried participants is 11.5 orgasms per month, compared with 9.9 per month for single members of the control sample.

From the interviews, there is no evidence of masturbaphobia on the part of tearoom participants. The most obvious explanation of the observed differences is that the alternative to masturbation for those who enjoy homosexual activity is more readily available than is the alternative acceptable to men of the control sample. In spite of the pill, willing girls are not as easy for the single man to find in our society as are the willing seekers of impersonal sex. Moreover, it takes a great deal of time to court a young lady. In terms of time outlay, the average fifteen-minute encounter in a tearoom is almost as cheap as automanipulation. Evidently, for many men, it is a viable alternative to the latter.

Religion and Frequency of Intercourse

In terms of frequency of outlet, if not form, there is little difference between unmarried participants and controls. They are a younger population than the married men, and a rate of orgasm slightly greater than twice a week should not be surprising. For the married men, on the other hand, there are striking differences in the reported frequency of intercourse—not only between samples but between occupational classes and religious groups within each sample.

The mean frequency of conjugal outlet for the tearoom participants, 7.6 per month, is slightly more than half that reported by the controls, 12.8 per month. By eliminating those who consider themselves too old for intercourse from the calculations, the rate of the nondeviants is just double that of the men observed in tearooms. It is, of course, important to note that the range of frequency is wide within both these samples, from none to sixty acts of intercourse per month. It is also strongly correlated with the age of respondents, but median ages for the two samples of married men differ little—forty for the participants, forty-three for controls.

By projecting the mean total sexual outlet per week for men in the original Kinsey study (including all those between adolescence and eighty-five years of age) to a monthly rate, it is possible to compare the frequencies reported in this study with Kinsey's data (1948: 194). Kinsey's figure of 2.74 per week projects to 11.9 sexual acts per month, compared with the 12.8 reported by my married controls. Kinsey's mean includes all outlets—marital intercourse, extramarital activity, masturbation, nocturnal emissions, and homosexual and animal contact—about "85 to 89 percent" of which are accounted for by marital intercourse (1948: 257). Since the ages of my married respondents range only from twenty-two to seventy, including neither of the less active extremes found in the Kinsey data, it should not be surprising to find a mean of marital intercourse for my control sample (median age forty-two) somewhat higher than that indicated by *Sexual Behavior in the Human Male*.

The purpose of this comparison with data from the Kinsey study is to establish the mean monthly frequency reported by the married controls as a base rate, paralleling the "American norm" of approximately twelve outlets per month. Granted this, it is possible—lacking evidence to the contrary—to infer that the sexual needs of the average married man in the control sample are being met in his relationships with his wife. With one exception, a man who reported that his wife has "warped views on sex," all of the married controls claimed that their sexual needs were met in their marital relationships.

A very different picture emerges from discussions of the conjugal relations of tearoom participants. If we recall that their perception of sexual needs and importance roughly parallels that of the controls—and that their reported frequency of intercourse is about half that of the nondeviants—we should not be surprised that they also complain of not being satisfied in the marriage bed.

When asked if he thought his sexual needs were adequately met in his relationships with his wife, a forty-two-year-old machinist answered sharply: "No! Does any man?" He hesitated in replying when questioned on the frequency of intercourse. "My wife's been sick," he said. Later, when discussing his marriage in open-ended questions, he was careful to cover the hostility revealed in earlier answers.

I have indicated elsewhere (Humphreys 1970: 105) that, from surface appearances, tearoom participants maintain exemplary marriages. Longer interviews with cooperating respondents, on the other hand, sometimes shatter these superficial reports. An upper-class man, who makes the tearoom scene almost daily, expressed his feelings thus: "Madge is the classic bitch! Her most striking point is her limited understanding and intelligence. Financial security is her only interest. . . . We haven't had intercourse for years—and I don't want it!"

A factory foreman, age thirty-eight, says that his wife "has troubles in bearing children. Our little daughter is very important to us; but the wife had lots of trouble with a miscarriage a few months ago and we just don't want to take the risk." Devout Roman Catholics, they will not use "artificial" birth-control devices. How often does he have intercourse with his wife? "Not very often right now—once a month or so." He hesitated when asked whether his sexual needs are met in these relationships: "I guess so—no, not really." He gave no sign of remembering the interviewer-lookout who had seen him, a year earlier, taking the insertor part in an act of fellatio.

Half the married participants are either Roman Catholics or married to Catholics, compared to 26 percent of the married controls. In both groups, the Roman Catholics report a rate of marital intercourse 40 percent below that of their Protestant, Jewish, and nonaffiliated counterparts. In spite of this lower frequency of marital intercourse, Catholic respondents have more children than those of other religious affiliations. Although these data do not justify the inference that Roman Catholics are more apt to engage in tearoom encounters than those of other religious affiliations, they do strongly indicate that those who seek sex in public restrooms are twice as likely to be Roman Catholics and dissatisfied with their conjugal relations as those in the nondeviant sample.

I asked a Roman Catholic respondent, who cooperated in lengthy interviews, about the effect of his religion on his sexual activity. He reported a great deal of drive and was a daily tearoom visitor:

> "Sure," he said, "my being a Catholic has a lot to do with [my] going to the tearooms. You remember I told you that a priest was the first to put the make on me, but I'd also probably screw my wife a lot more if she'd take the pill."
>
> "But I don't understand," I said. "You won't violate the church's teaching on birth control, yet you will engage in homosexual acts. Isn't that adultery?"
>
> "The church says masturbation is a sin, too," he replied. "But I don't think of what I do in the park as adultery. I don't get involved with those people. It's just as sinful to beat your meat or—or take a pill. This way, at least, my wife isn't sinning."

A Participant Typology

From the interviews, I constructed a typology of tearoom participants, differentiated along the lines of marital and occupational autonomy (see Table 1). The question of marital autonomy was determined by the characteristics of marital status. For the purpose of this paper, however, it should be noted that the three men in each sample who were divorced or separated must be classified as "single" for the purposes of analyzing sexual behavior. In earlier analyses of the data, where the emphasis was on the respondents' life styles, these individuals were grouped with the married men (Humphreys 1970: 110).

Because the impersonal sexual activity found in restrooms is furtive and fear laden, the relative resources of participants for controlling information and avoiding exposure are of crucial importance. Along with marital status, then, occupational status must be seen as a decisive variable. Men who work for large industries or the government, who work as truck drivers, salesmen, schoolteachers, or in clerical capacities, have little autonomy. Stigmatization would almost certainly result in the loss of em-

TABLE 1. PERCEPTIONS OF SEXUAL NEED, SATISFACTION, AND OUTLET OF TEAROOM PARTICIPANTS BY TYPE, COMPARED WITH MATCHED PAIRS FROM THE CONTROL SAMPLE

	Participants	*Controls*

Type I:
 	
Dependent
occupations,
Married men
	("Trade")
	Drive: "normal"
	Opportunity: "inadequate"
	Frequency
	  of intercourse: 8.7 *
	Median age: 38
	N = 17
		("Straights")
		Drive: "normal"
		Opportunity: "adequate"
		Frequency
		  of intercourse: 16.3 *
		Median age: 42
		N = 17

Type II:
 	
Independent
occupations,
Married men
	("Ambisexuals")
	Drive: "high"
	Opportunity: "inadequate"
	Frequency
	  of intercourse: 5.7 *
	Median age: 43
	N = 10
		("Straights")
		Drive: "normal"
		Opportunity: "adequate"
		Frequency
		  of intercourse: 9.1 *
		Median age: 43
		N = 10

Totals: Married men	Mean frequency: 7.6 * Median age: 40 N = 27	Mean frequency: 12:8 * Median age: 43 N = 27

Type III:
 	
Independent
occupations,
Single men
	("Gay")
	Drive: "high"
	Opportunity: "adequate"
	
	Frequency
	  of orgasm: 15.0 *
	Median age: 28
	N = 9
		("Straights")
		Drive: "normal"
		Opportunity: "inadequate"
		  plus masturbation
		Frequency
		  of orgasm: 11.6 *
		Median age: 21
		N = 9

Type IV:
 	
Dependent
occupations,
Single men
	("Closet Queens")
	Drive: "normal"
	Opportunity: "inadequate"
	
	Frequency
	  of orgasm: 8.0 *
	Median age: 34
	N = 14
		("Straights")
		Drive: "low"
		Opportunity: "inadequate"
		  plus masturbation
		Frequency
		  of orgasm: 8.7 *
		Median age: 34
		N = 14

Totals: Single men	Mean frequency: 11.5 * Median age: 30 N = 23	Mean frequency: 9.9 * Median age: 25 N = 23

* Mean reported frequency per month.

ployment. These men are generally of lower-middle or upper-lower socioeconomic status, possessing little capital with which to pay off policemen or otherwise defend their moral histories. If married, they have been classified as Type I participants. I refer to them as "trade" because that term is applied by the homosexual community to men like these whose self-identity is heterosexual and who generally take only the insertor (penetrating) role in homosexual activity. To avoid jeopardizing their family relationships, the trade are isolated from the sexual markets provided by both homosexual and prostitute subcultures. In their furtive search for an inexpensive, expedient form of sexual activity, they turn to public restrooms (Humphreys 1970: 110–116).

Single men with little occupational independence (Type IV participants) I have labeled as "closet queens." In the homosexual vocabulary, closet queens are men who recognize their own homosexuality but are afraid to admit it to other than a few close friends (Humphreys 1970: 125–130). Neither trade nor closet queens are active in the homosexual subculture. They avoid the gay bars and public baths, those "gay" (homosexual) marketplaces providing too much danger of exposure for covert deviants. Together, these groups comprise 62 percent of my sample of tearoom participants.

Married men who are self-employed or who fill a managerial capacity were classified as Type II participants or "ambisexuals." Although most men involved in tearoom sex have had both heterosexual and homosexual experiences, and thus might be called ambisexual, this group from the upper-middle and upper classes are most apt to identify themselves as such. As might be expected, income, educational level, and other indicators of social class increase with occupational independence. The ambisexuals, like respondents of Types I and IV, avoid the meeting places of the homosexual society. In their case, however, there are strong friendship networks binding these prosperous men together and providing them with the advantages of increased communication and mutual protection.

Type III respondents, the smallest group in the participant sample, are called "gay" because of their approximation to the homosexual stereotype. (Men with dependent occupations are sometimes called "gay," as those with greater autonomy may be labeled "closet queens"; however, for the purposes of this typology, I use these terms as tags of my marital-occupational subgroups.) They are single men with relatively high occupational autonomy: students, artists, hair dressers, and merchants. Because they are likely to patronize gay bars, they resort to tearooms for sex only for an occasional "change of scene" or because a lover is out of town.

The less vulnerable participants, ambisexuals and the gay, have less to fear in the tearooms because their resources decrease the threat of exposure. They are attracted to the tearooms both because of the wide variety of sexual objects provided by the influx of non-subcultural working men to these settings and because this is adventurous activity, a source of "kicks."

Occupation and Frequency of Intercourse

Upon dividing the participant and control samples of married men into these classifications, strong differences appear between the Type I and Type II respondents within each sample. The trade report a mean monthly frequency of marital intercourse of 8.7. Ambisexuals claim a much lower average of 5.7 per month. Members of the control sample, matched on an occupational basis with participants, evidence means of 16.3 conjugal relations a month for those in Type I, contrasted with 9.1 for Type II. Although the frequencies for both types of nondeviants are higher than those reported by the matching groups of tearoom respondents, it is evident that the upper class men of both samples engage in much less intercourse with their wives than do those of the lower classes.

Of these four groups, the ambisexuals (upper-class participants) report the strongest perceptions of sexual drive, along with the lowest frequency of marital intercourse. Thus, those who engage in the least conjugal activity perceive the importance of their sexual needs as being the greatest! They suffer, then, from a *sexual bind*—the discrepancy between perceived and fulfilled sexual needs.

Nondeviants with high occupational autonomy may also be seen as victims of the sexual bind; however, such interpretation is doubtful in their case. In the first place, their conjugal relations are 40 percent more frequent than those of the participants matched with them; moreover, their perception of sexual drive is less. During the interviews, not one of the upper-class controls complained of lacking sexual fulfillment in marriage. Thirty percent of the participants in this class reported that their marital relationships were inadequate, compared with none of the controls.

Apparently, the sexual needs that most upper-class men perceive as normal, "about the same as those of other men," are not as great as the perceived needs of men in the working class. If we are to trust their claims of satisfaction—and lacking evidence of extramarital relations other than those observed on the part of participants—we must conclude that they are satisfied with a rate of intercourse that is about 60 percent of that enjoyed by men of the lower classes.

As there are no bases, including age differences, on which a biological difference can be postulated for men of the two occupational groups, it may be assumed that this contrast in perceptions of sexual drive is socially determined. Not only do men of a like occupational level communicate norms to each other, but the nature of their work and life style may result in satisfaction with less in the way of sex.

The Swedish economist, Staffan Linder, has suggested one such determining factor in his study of "the harried leisure class": in writing of the "increasing scarcity of time" in our age of affluence, he quotes Warner and Abegglen (1956: 65) who find that an executive's wife "must not demand too much of her husband's time or interest. Because of his single-minded concentration on the job, even his sexual activity is relegated to a secondary place." Linder's point is one that busy executives in my samples affirm: they are often too tired to engage in sex at the end of a day.

It is questionable whether the sexual effects of time's increasing scarcity are equally felt by all members of highly industrialized, consumption-oriented societies. Linder (1970: 84) notes that affairs are becoming "less attractive; the time spent on each occasion of lovemaking is being reduced; the total number of sexual encounters is declining." Data from this study support his latter point only as regards those with greater occupational autonomy (and then only in rough comparison with data from the Kinsey study). What is certain is that the time spent on each occasion of lovemaking is being reduced, at least for those men who choose impersonal action in the tearooms.

The trade (Type I, or working class, participants) suffer from a sexual bind without the distraction or excuse of executive pressures. Their perceived need being slightly higher, their frequency of marital sex is little more than half of the control counterparts. If it were not for one, newly married, black soldier in this group who reported "at least twice a day, when I'm home," as his frequency of intercourse, the mean frequency of this group would drop sharply. This man's wife was giving birth to their child at about the time I observed him as an insertor in a tearoom. Had I not seen him, the mean frequency for the lower-class sample of participants would drop to less than five acts of marital intercourse per month or less than a third that of the matched controls.

The reported frequency for the control group from the lower classes is about four acts per week. Again, three individuals report intercourse with their wives at least once a day. In spite of these exceptional performers, these men evidence no sexual bind and are in general agreement that their conjugal relations meet their sexual needs. They do not appear to be more masculine than the participants matched with them. Their perceived needs are somewhat lower. By every indication, these two groups differ most in terms of their frequency of sexual outlet in marriage. Only religious differences are so strong between the two samples.

The Question of Causality

These data, then, confront the student of sexual behavior with a choice: does the sexual bind serve as a causal factor of the inverse correlation between observed sexual deviance and reported satisfaction in conjugal relations, or is it merely a phantom explanation? Are some men, at least, driven from a sexless marriage bed to the impersonal sex of public restrooms; or do other factors, perhaps psychological, produce a desire for furtive homosexual activity which, in turn, decreases their performance at home?

Longitudinal data from interviews with cooperating respondents support both directions of causation. Married men of the upper classes indicate a great deal of premarital reinforcement in homosexual activity, beginning in preparatory school or at summer camp. After marrying (largely as a concession to social pressures), they tend to remain sexually faithful to their wives for as long as three or four years. Then the sexual bind appears: the Roman Catholic wife will not use birth control measures, in spite of their wish to have no more children; or the man is stationed overseas in wartime. He then returns to homoerotic experiences—activities that, although generally of a one-night-stand variety, may involve long-term relationships. This, in turn, tends to decrease the need for conjugal activity. The ensuing chain reaction, combined with the pressure on time in their professional careers, results in a portrait of the ambisexual.

With the trade, the pattern is somewhat simpler and more unidirectional: there is little evidence of early homosexual activity. From cooperating respondents, I conclude that there may have been isolated experiences of a homoerotic nature: some hustling in the milieu of a teenage gang (Reiss 1964: 181–210); instances of serving as insertor in an act of fellatio with an old man or army buddy, accompanied by financial reward in the former case or by heavy drinking in the latter. Few of these men have had extensive reinforcement in homosexual behavior, nor is there any evidence that they think of themselves as being "gay" or ambisexual.

"At lower (educational and social) levels," writes Kinsey (1948: 508), "there are definite taboos against masturbation . . . Most males of this level find it difficult to understand how a grown man could think of masturbating, particularly if he is married and living with his wife." We have seen, however, that single males of the working class control sample resort to masturbation at least often enough to bring their mean frequency of orgasm up to 8.7 per month. To many married men of the same socioeconomic level, however, masturbation is unthinkable as a sexual outlet. When caught in the sexual bind, therefore, they turn to other interpersonal outlets. Half a century ago, they would have been customers in two-bit bordellos, where madams carefully timed the encounters to maintain a profit-making volume. Like modern tearooms, these facilities provided a relatively inexpensive, expedient, noninvolving outlet for men of the working classes who want to supplement (but not supplant) their conjugal outlet. As I have stated previously, "Men with heavy emotional commitments to families and jobs . . . may not be able to afford investment in other than the most transient and impersonal types of extramarital sex" (1970: 154).

At least as regards the trade, the largest group in my sample of participants, the sexual bind appears to have a causal relationship to tearoom activity. This conclusion is further strengthened by the observation that at least one variable causing the sexual bind, religious affiliation, is prior in time to the deviant activity. The interviews provide strong evidence of a cause-effect sequence: the prohibition of artificial birth control devices are seen to produce a decline of sexual satisfaction in marriage that, in turn, drives some victims of that sexual bind to the tearooms for satisfaction.

Sexual Bind and the Single Man

It might be assumed that all single men suffer from the sexual bind between perceived needs and available outlet. For most of the unmarried men in the samples, this appears to be true. In the case of those participants active in the homosexual subculture (the "gay" men), however, this generalization does not hold. They report a perceived adequacy of outlet that compares only with the married controls. With little mention of masturbation as an outlet, they maintain a frequency of orgasms of 15.0 per month, greater than the mean reported by the controls matched with them, 11.6. With the sexual markets open to them in the gay world, it should not be surprising that they manage to exceed the base frequency for the married controls without resorting to either marital sex or masturbation.

The control sample of single men and the working class participants are less satisfied with their sexual lives. Whereas none of the controls who lack college education mention masturbation as an outlet, two-thirds of those who had completed at least one year of higher education give masturbation as their primary source of orgasm. Automanipulation, then, relieves the sexual bind of the unmarried, better educated nondeviants, providing them with a frequency of outlet second only to that achieved by the working class, married controls through marital sex.

Two-thirds of the single controls with less occupational autonomy complain of the inadequacy of their mean 8.7 orgasms per month to meet their sexual requirements. Although some of these men have premarital heterosexual partners, the majority will probably get married in order to ease the sexual bind. In their interviews, at least the younger men indicated their intentions of future matrimony.

Finally, the sexual bind is strongly felt by the closet queens. Their frequency of orgasm (8.0 per month) is lower than any other group of unmarried men reported. Although their needs are perceived as being "about average," masturbation is not thought to be a viable alternative outlet. Few of these men have any intention of marrying or of taking part in the sexual markets of subcultural homosexuality, which they fear and despise. Their tendency is to engage in what may best be described as "lone wolf" activity: furtive excursions to the tearooms, picking up teenage hustlers, even the seduction of boys with whom they work. Unlike the gay men, their acceptance of the homosexual self-image is a begrudging one. Unless they find a "permanent lover," their sexual lives are apt to continue to be inadequate and marked by guilt and self-hatred (Humphreys 1970: 139–148).

Reciprocal Trade

Tearoom activity constitutes a free market in the sexual economy. There is no exchange of money between the participants in restroom fellatio; rather, certain "goods" are traded for certain "services." In summarizing the above data, it may help for us to think of the male sex organ as the essential "goods" for this exchange. My respondents assure me that these goods must be supplied in sufficient quantity and variety for the market to be viable.

In return for the erect penis the insertee supplies a needed service, the sucking action that produces orgasm. It should be made clear that it is equally possible to view the mouths of insertees as the "goods" and the insertion of the penises as the "services." Regardless of the viewpoint taken, it should also be remembered that the man who provides the goods in one encounter may provide the service in another. From the tearoom observations, however, it is evident that there is a central tendency for certain men, generally those of the lower classes, to serve as insertors while others prefer the insertee role.

What emerges from this analysis is that the two groups most caught in the sexual bind, most dissatisfied by the discrepancies between perceived sexual needs and actual frequency of outlet, are those who provide the essential supply of goods for the tearoom market. Together, the trade and closet queens constitute 62 percent of the participant sample; but these types were observed providing 75 percent of the desired goods. Three of every four insertors in the encounters from which my sample was collected were men of lower occupational autonomy.

Ambisexuals, the gay, a minority of the closet queens, would not venture into tearooms if there were not a variety of men to be found there who are unavailable in other one-night-stand marketplaces. The most crucial group of participants in this exchange are aptly called "the trade." Masculine in appearance and heterosexual in self-concept, they enter the public restrooms in search of a service they seldom find at home and cannot afford to acquire in any other place. Without this abundant supply of goods—or lacking the services offered by those who share a more homosexual identity—the tearoom market would atrophy.

Some men choose impersonal sex over the alternative of masturbation. Others find satisfaction in their marital or premarital heterosexual relationships. All act in response to the pressure of certain social factors: their religious beliefs, occupational or educational restrictions, the increasing scarcity of time in an affluent society. Those caught in the sexual bind produced by

these characteristics will seek that form of reciprocal trade relationship that provides the lowest costs in terms of personal involvement, money, and time expended. At present, the social
control forces can only determine whether such markets will be
located in bordellos, roadside bushes, or restrooms. The lack of
perceived sexual satisfaction will, no doubt, continue to provide
ample customers in the foreseeable future.

Summary of Findings

By comparing participants in tearoom encounters with a randomly selected control sample, I found that those who seek the
impersonal sex of public restrooms are caught in a sexual bind
between their perceived sexual needs and the satisfaction of those
needs by socially prescribed means. The largest group of participants (34 percent) are married men with little occupational autonomy. Due, in part, to the Roman Catholic proscription of
artificial contraceptives, these men seek relief from a frequency
of marital intercourse that is half that reported by their counterparts in the control sample.

The more affluent married men, ambisexuals, present a more
complex portrait. In their case, a higher perception of sexual
drive combines with religious, occupational, and other marital
factors to cause inadequate opportunity for sexual outlet in their
conjugal relationships. Although married men with independent
occupations from both samples evidence less marital intercourse
than do the working class men (perhaps a result of "the increasing scarcity of time" in our consuming society), the ambisexuals
report both the lowest frequency of marital outlet and the highest perception of sexual drive.

Those who are least apt to be encountered in tearooms, the
overtly gay respondents who are unmarried and enjoy relative
occupational autonomy, report greater satisfaction in their sexual
lives than any other group of participants. The "straight" single
men, while complaining of "inadequate" sexual opportunity, employ masturbation as a major form of outlet.

Finally, the working class, unmarried tearoom participants
(largely due to a lower educational level and other factors that

make masturbation unacceptable) seek impersonal and furtive encounters to relieve the sexual bind. The chief difference between participants and controls who are single is in their acceptance of masturbation as a viable sexual outlet.

Such social characteristics as religious affiliation, occupational demands, and level of education are seen as explaining the drive behind the search for tearoom sex. If combined with the normative push for expedient, impersonal relations that our consumption-oriented, market economy provides, these social factors alone are strong enough to explain the sexual activity in public restrooms. It is unnecessary to look for interior, psychological factors behind such behavior.

REFERENCES

Davis, Fred. "Deviance Disavowal: The Management of Strained Interaction by the Visibly Handicapped." In *The Other Side,* edited by Howard S. Becker. New York: The Free Press, 1964, pp. 119–137.

Gallo, Jon J. *et al.* "The Consenting Adult Homosexual and the Law: An Empirical Study of Enforcement and Administration in Los Angeles County." *UCLA Law Review 13* (March): 643–832, 1966.

Gebhard, Paul H.; Gagnon, John H.; Pomeroy, Wardell B.; and Christenson, Cornelia V. *Sex Offenders.* New York: Harper & Row, 1965.

Hooker, Evelyn. "The Adjustment of the Male Overt Homosexual." In *The Problem of Homosexuality in Modern Society,* edited by Hendrik M. Ruitenbeek. New York: Dutton, 1963, pp. 141–161.

Hughes, Everett C. *Men and Their Work.* Glencoe, Ill.: The Free Press, 1958.

Humphreys, Laud. *Tearoom Trade: Impersonal Sex in Public Places.* Chicago: Aldine Publishing Co., 1970.

Kinsey, Alfred C.; Pomeroy, Wardell B.; and Martin, Clyde E. *Sexual Behavior in the Human Male.* Philadelphia: W. B. Saunders Co., 1948.

Kitsuse, John I. "Societal Reaction to Deviant Behavior: Problems of Theory and Method." In *The Other Side,* edited by Howard S. Becker. New York: The Free Press, 1964, pp. 87–102.

Linder, Staffan B. *The Harried Leisure Class.* New York: Columbia University Press, 1970.

Reiss, Albert J., Jr. "The Social Integration of Queers and Peers." In *The Other Side,* edited by Howard S. Becker. New York: The Free Press, 1964, pp. 181–210.

Warner, W. Lloyd, and Abegglen, James C. "Successful Wives of Successful Executives," *Harvard Business Review,* March–April, 1956, pp. 64–70, as cited in Staffan B. Linder, *op. cit.*

An overview
of sex research

Sex Research and Sociology: Retrospective and Prospective

EDWARD SAGARIN

The literature of sex is as old as the written word of mankind, and then goes back further, beyond the era when modern man can count years, to mythology and folklore not reduced to writing. But "the literature" of sex, now using the expression within quotes in the special meaning that it has for scientists, was sparse until very recent times, and it is only beginning to arise in sociology. For The Song of Ruth, the dramas of Sophocles and Aristophanes, and the poetry of Ovid are the fantasies of dreamers and the expressions of those who saw humankind as sexual beings, as lovers and frustrated people, in ecstasy and in tragedy. When man turned to *examining* his needs, passions and desires, not to speak of his behavior, rather than glorifying them in poetry or deploring them in sermons, sex research was born.

Research in the Biological Era

Early sex research was dominated by the field of biology, particularly medicine, for sex was seen as a physiological process, and the problems of sexual maladjustment, of deviation from the

I am indebted to Leo P. Chall, Paul H. Gebhard, Albert Ellis, and the editor of this book, James M. Henslin, for suggestions and criticisms that they made after reading an earlier version of this paper.

normal and normative, were seen as diseases, quite obviously a category for examination and understanding, diagnosis and treatment, by the physician. From the viewpoint of the sociology of knowledge, then, it would be expected that in the first wave of scientific investigation that was ushered in by the publication on November 24, 1859, of the book that became known by its abbreviated title, *The Origin of Species,* a work that marked the initiation of what was much later to be called "the century of Darwin," biology (including under that rubric medicine) was at least partially liberated from theological and moral prejudices, and was able to turn toward sex. At the same time, as Chall points out,[1] the study of sexuality was made possible by the Enlightenment, which permitted its separation from the discussion of morality. So that although one cannot state that there were no efforts previous to the latter third of the nineteenth century to examine this aspect of life, there were few, until Krafft-Ebing, Moll, Forel, Freud, Bloch, Hirschfeld, and Havelock Ellis, all of whose major works in this area span the years 1875–1925. Furthermore, all of these men were physicians, although there is much in their writing and thinking that went outside of and beyond the domain of the medically trained.

With these thinkers sex research began to be liberated from the shackles of puritanism, censorship, and moral (particularly but not exclusively theological) judgments. Even Krafft-Ebing,[2] whose depiction of the abnormal, deranged, demented, and dangerous brought forth images of deviants to which many still cling, and whose work is replete with judgments of a moral and ethical nature often harsh, ethnocentric, and not supported by the evidence, must in retrospect be seen as the first of the major writers to gather information, including particularly numerous case his-

[1] Leo P. Chall, "Advances in Modern Sex Research," in *The Encyclopedia of Sexual Behavior,* 2 vols. ed. Albert Ellis and Albert Abarbanel (New York: Hawthorn Books, 1961), pp. 25–34.

[2] Richard von Krafft-Ebing, *Psychopathia Sexualis,* first German edition published in Stuttgart in 1886; English-language editions in 1906 and 1922. Complete English translations, with Latin passages translated into English for the first time, were published in the United States in 1965 (New York: G. P. Putnam's Sons, 1965, and New York: Stein and Day, 1965).

tories, on those whose sex lives differed markedly from the vision of what they ought to be.[3]

Of Havelock Ellis and Hirschfeld, whose work was imbued with moralization of the reverse type, especially with sympathy for those unable to fit into the categories of the "normal," several comments seem to me significant. First, it is now clear and it can be said, or at least can be repeated (for it has been said before), that both "suffered from" (if that is the correct phrase) sexual problems and difficulties of their own.[4] Havelock Ellis, it

[3] For a harsher view of Krafft-Ebing, see Edward Brecher, *The Sex Researchers* (Boston: Little, Brown Co., 1969), pp. 50–60.

[4] To what extent the study of sexuality has been initiated or conducted by those seriously beset by doubt or guilt over their own sex lives and interests, or obsessed by fears and driven by compulsions, one does not know. Some would argue that all mankind is so guilt-ridden over sex that unresolved Oedipal difficulties, fears of rejection and of being a failure in sex, conscious or unconscious sadomasochistic predilections, are human foibles, part of the human condition, or at least the price man pays for bridling his instinctual drives and becoming a social animal. Freud has argued in this manner in *Civilization and Its Discontents* (first published, 1930; English translation by Joan Riviere, Garden City, N.Y.: Doubleday, paperback, n.d.); more recently, and starting from an entirely different (in fact, anti-Freudian) vantage point, Albert Ellis has suggested that man is basically an animal with many biological and inborn tendencies that lead him, in the sexual as well as other areas, into self-defeating pathways. See Albert Ellis, *Reason and Emotion in Psychotherapy* (New York: Lyle Stuart, 1962).

Neither of these two men, nor others who from a variety of theoretical stances might come to similar conclusions, would fail to differentiate between a deeply distressed and consciously pursuing deviant, as was Hirschfeld or Havelock Ellis, and the man with an average amount of doubts and problems about his sex life and interests, that he defines (and that he knows significant others define) as normally and socially within the boundaries of the acceptable.

On the other hand, to what extent the study of sexuality has been inhibited by the fear that a social stigma will be placed upon one who conducts the study—this, too, is an area of important investigation. Certainly, one who investigates murder or armed robbery is not suspected of being personally involved in such acts, or of having a secret life that both motivated him to conduct the research and gave him access to the materials; and while the same is not true of marijuana research, where many young teachers have become suspect by reason of their interest in pursuing such investigations, the fact is that such professors would only be slightly injured by suspicion falling on them. While jobs might be difficult to come by if one is suspected of being a marijuana user, one is not overwhelmingly stigmatized, as is the sex deviant. So that, although beginning to diminish, the inhibitory effect

is reported, was highly inhibited, a virgin until his late twenties; was married to and in love with a practicing lesbian; and was deeply involved in receiving sexual excitement from watching females urinate (an interest known as urolagnia).[5] Hirschfeld was himself a homosexual,[6] and I am told by a colleague who knew him quite well, was a masochist, not in some figurative or symbolic sense, but one who pleaded with his sex partners to whip him.[7]

Although both Ellis and Hirschfeld were physicians, their work, studies, and writings went far beyond the medical-biological, or even beyond the psychiatric, if that is to be subsumed as a branch of medicine; but like Krafft-Ebing, they leaned heavily on a clinical approach, using case histories of their own and others' patients, to substantiate their findings. Havelock Ellis was a man of letters, a literary critic and a social thinker, active in the feminist movement and other causes. His great work in the field is called *Studies in the Psychology of Sex*,[8] but it is an all-embracing study that goes far beyond its title; in fact, it contains material that is historical, medical, philosophical, juridical, literary, and not far from what would be called social philosophy bordering on sociology without methodology. His interests were in the frequency of certain types of sexual orientations (then usually called "impulses" or "instincts") and behavior, such as sexual

---

of possible gossip and ostracism is still an effective force in determining whether one will study and publish material on mate-swapping, homosexuality, and certain other aspects of sex. See James M. Henslin, "Observing Deviance in Four Settings: Research Experiences with Cabbies, Suicides, Drug Users, and Abortionees," in *Observing Deviance,* ed. Jack D. Douglas (New York: Random House, 1971).

[5] Brecher, *op. cit.,* pp. 3–49.

[6] *Ibid.,* p. 129.

[7] This statement, to my knowledge, has not hitherto been published, and inasmuch as I cannot reveal my source, and even if it could be revealed the information could not be substantiated, the reader may prefer to disregard it. But the point that I make, that Hirschfeld, like Ellis, was beset by sexual problems, seems to be both true and significant.

[8] Havelock Ellis, *Studies in the Psychology of Sex;* published at various times in several volumes between 1896 and 1928; reprinted, New York: Random House, 2 vols., 1936.

inversion,[9] the conditions under which they would arise, the origins of moral codes, and other aspects of life closer to the domain of sociology than to the discipline mentioned in his title. Hirschfeld headed a movement that fought for the repeal of the antihomosexual laws; was founder and leader of an influential institute concerned with sex research; made at least two studies to determine the extent of exclusive and partial homosexuality among German males; and was a founder and first president of the World League for Sexual Reform (in which he was associated with Bertrand Russell, among many others).[10]

Of the early medical scientists mentioned above, Bloch, Moll, and Forel are today almost forgotten, Krafft-Ebing, Ellis, and Hirschfeld seem to have had a greater influence and continue to be read, but it was indubitably Freud who made sexual behavior a proper area for investigation.[11] The influence of Freud was so all-pervasive, however, that it encouraged the channeling of sexual research into the psychological, analytic, and particularly psychoanalytic directions. This meant that sociological orientations, which would not have been anti-analytic (at least would not of necessity have been such), but would have focused in entirely different directions, were largely preempted. In sum, one did not discover what great numbers of people did, and what the relationship of their behavior might be to the social structure and

9 The phrase "sexual inversion" was at the time synonymous with what is now called homosexuality and was probably a euphemism for sexual perversion. Today sexual inversion usually refers to sex-role inversion; see Daniel G. Brown, "Transvestism and Sex-Role Inversion," in Ellis and Abarbanel, *op. cit.* (note 1), pp. 1012–22.

10 Some of this information is found in Hedwig Leser, "The Hirschfeld Institute for Sexology," in Ellis and Abarbanel, *op. cit.* (note 1), pp. 967–70; also Robert Wood, "Sex Reform Movement," *ibid.*, pp. 956–66. Leser mentions what Hirschfeld's disciples summarized as his contributions: the influence of sex hormones on personality, a statement that "all (!) sexual anomalies are caused by irregularities of physical development," and application of psychoanalytic findings to sex anomalies "of physiological origin." While it is true that Hirschfeld leaned toward the belief that there was strong correlation between physiology (even anatomy) and sex personality, I would say that this is the weakest point in Hirschfeld's contributions.

11 There is, of course, a vast literature on Freud and his influence, too long and too well-known to make it practicable or necessary to cite.

such aspects of society as class, religion, and education, because the major insights, in that period, were to be obtained from depth analysis of a single individual, or of a few. When one looks at the reception of the Kinsey studies by some psychoanalytically oriented sociologists, the significance of this statement is seen.

Sex and the Sociologist

The first stage in the history of sex research, then, was dominated by the biological sciences and reached its apex and point of highest influence in the work of Freud. Sociology, a new discipline whose areas of study were not at all clearly circumscribed, was long and hesitant about entering this hitherto forbidden domain. Sociologists at the time were seeing the world from other vantage points, largely macrosociological, with emphasis on social structure, class, institutions, power, and groups, in which sexuality seemed to play little or no role. However, the same lack of attention to sex could not be found in the sister discipline, anthropology, and many sociologists were deeply immersed in cross-cultural and hence anthropological studies. Frazer, Westermarck, and later Malinowski in Europe and Sumner in America, were among the many who were collecting and analyzing data on primitive peoples.[12] A major interest among these scholars was

[12] The four names mentioned here all seem to me to be significant, but many other illustrious names could be added. Sir James Frazer's great work was *The Golden Bough* which appeared in many editions as early as 1890 (London: Macmillan & Co., 12 vols., 1911–26; New York: Criterion Books, 1 vol. condensation, 1959); he also authored a smaller work, *Totemism and Exogamy: A Treatise on Certain Early Forms of Superstition and Society* (London: Macmillan & Co., 1910). Edward Westermarck, known for his several-volume *The History of Human Marriage* (London: Macmillan & Co., 1891), also wrote *The Origin and Development of the Moral Ideas,* 2 vols. (London: Macmillan & Co., 1906–08), and continued the theme of this last work in *Ethical Relativity* (New York: Harcourt, Brace & Co., 1932); other works relevant to his contributions to the study of sex were *Three Essays on Sex and Marriage* (London: Macmillan & Co., 1934) and *Christianity and Morals* (London: K. Paul, Trench, Trubner, 1939). Bronislaw Malinowski authored *The Sexual Life of Savages in North-Western Melanesia: An Ethnographic Account of Courtship, Marriage, and Family Life of the Trobriand Islands, British New Guinea,* with a preface by Havelock Ellis (London: G. Routledge & Sons and New York: Halcyon House, 1929); *Sex and Repression in Savage Society* (London: Routledge & K. Paul, 1953); and *Sex,*

in the nature of social organization, which for primitive societies implied family and kinship structure; this in turn brought the researchers into an investigation of incest, endogamy and exogamy, and puberty rites, all of which implied the study of sexuality.

It is one of the ironies of this period that sociologists were able to look into the sexual life of primitive peoples (i.e., the so-called uncivilized) but not of modern societies and especially not their own; and although the work of Westermarck is diffused with the concept of ethical relativism and the rejection of ethnocentrism (a term coined, in fact, by Sumner), the avoidance of sex studies in modern urban societies—and again, I note, especially the anthropologists' own—with the implication that the rites and customs of the uncivilized people were exotic, peculiar, and strange, all had an ethnocentric bias built into it.

How far removed sociology was from the study of sex can be seen from an examination of two works which in this regard promised more than they delivered. The first had the challenging title, *Sex and Society,* and was written by the renowned and influential, but at the time still young, American sociologist, W. I. Thomas.[13] The essays in Thomas' book (note the subtitle, in fact: *Studies in the Social Psychology of Sex*) are almost entirely anthropological in orientation, with more psychology than sociology, and the word *sex* is mainly used in the sense of gender. A second work that likewise belies its title, and a very interesting book at that, was Georgene H. Seward's *Sex and the Social Order.*[14] Here, again, is psychology, biology, anthropology, almost anything but what the title indicates.

Here and there an investigation, a minor paper, a little data, particularly in the literature of criminology (as, e.g., the study of prostitution) and what at the time was called social disorgani-

---

Culture, and Myth (New York: Harcourt, Brace & World, 1962), this last work published posthumously. The work of William Graham Sumner on sex is found in *The Science of Society,* in collaboration with A. G. Keller, 4 vols. (New Haven, Conn.: Yale University Press, 1929).

[13] William I. Thomas, *Sex and Society: Studies in the Social Psychology of Sex* (Chicago: University of Chicago Press, 1907).

[14] Georgene H. Seward, *Sex and the Social Order* (New York: McGraw-Hill, 1946).

zation (later this term fell into disrepute and was replaced by the term deviance), marked the totality of sex literature in sociology. Some of these studies, as related to premarital intercourse, were summarized by Ehrmann and discussed by Chall; [15] a cursory glance indicates the limitations: small samples, college students as subjects, and other obvious shortcomings. Sociology, however, did produce some major work of a nonempirical nature in this area, in the period previous to the Second World War, in the form of several contributions by Kingsley Davis.[16] This work, dealing with such aspects of sexuality as prostitution, illegitimacy, and jealousy and sexual property (much later Davis was to write on homosexuality as well) constituted the first serious effort (and to my mind the best to date) to understand the nature of sexual mores in terms of social structure, particularly in a functionalist framework.

In short the period from the Darwinian revolution to the Second World War was quite barren of any sociology of sex, Davis being the most noteworthy exception in this regard. It was not only because of the influence of Freud and because of the biological (including the psychological) orientation of this time that sociology was not yet entering this scene. It was also because a great deal of the difficulties of people with their own or others' sexuality was seen in terms of personal problems (here the exception was prostitution, believed to be caused by poverty); hence these problems could be understood in the light of idiosyncratic rather than social analysis, and they would be corrected, if correctible (and this was considered to be only a matter of awaiting better therapeutic techniques) by therapy, the domain of psychiatrist or psychologist. Sociologists were interested in crime and

[15] Chall, op. cit. (note 1), p. 29; the reference is to Winston Ehrmann, Premarital Dating Behavior (New York: Henry Holt & Co., 1959).

[16] Kingsley Davis, "The Sociology of Prostitution," American Sociological Review 2 (1937): 744–755; "Illegitimacy and the Social Structure," American Journal of Sociology 45 (September 1939): 215–233; "Jealousy and Sexual Property," Social Forces 14 (March 1936): 395–405; and "Sexual Behavior," in Contemporary Social Problems, 2nd ed., ed. Robert K. Merton and Robert A. Nisbet (New York: Harcourt, Brace & World, 1966). The last article contains Davis' analysis of homosexuality, together with further material on prostitution.

the criminal, and hence they were interested in sexual difficulties that led to a conflict between the individual and the law; but both because of the supposed origin of most sexual problems and because of the hoped-for method of saving lost souls or curing people, it was a field to be left to others.

Kinsey and After

Now we come to the second great period in this history, and to an even greater irony: namely, that the man who was to usher in the era of sociological research into sex was himself a biologist, working with a staff that did not include a single sociologist, and despite homages to his own field by the use of such conceptual frameworks as mammalian behavior, he approached his subject matter from a vantage point almost entirely sociological. The man, of course, was Alfred C. Kinsey.[17]

Kinsey founded the most long-lived, the most productive, the most heavily financed, and the most scientifically organized research group for the study of the phenomenon of sex that the world has seen. Known as the Institute for Sex Research and often, particularly since Kinsey's death in 1956, called the Kinsey Institute, it was brought to the attention of the public in 1948 when its first volume was issued, *Sexual Behavior in the Human Male*.[18] Although filled with tables and statistical data, the work became a best-seller, sold at least a quarter of a million copies in English, and was translated into several languages. In 1953 it was followed by a second volume on the female.[19] Since that time, successive volumes have dealt, among other topics, with aspects of reproduction (birth, pregnancy, and abortion) and with sex

[17] For a brief historical account of the work of Kinsey, see Wardell B. Pomeroy, "The Institute for Sex Research," in Ellis and Abarbanel, *op. cit.* (note 1), pp. 970–975.

[18] Alfred C. Kinsey, Wardell B. Pomeroy, and Clyde E. Martin, *Sexual Behavior in the Human Male* (Philadelphia: W. B. Saunders Co., 1948).

[19] Alfred G. Kinsey, Wardell B. Pomeroy, Clyde E. Martin, and Paul H. Gebhard, *Sexual Behavior in the Human Female* (Philadelphia: W. B. Saunders Co., 1953).

offenders.[20] Many papers on homosexuality, prostitution, pornography, and other subjects have resulted from work at the Institute, and at various times it has been announced, with different degrees of authority, that volumes would be planned and published on a variety of subjects, such as transvestism and transsexualism, homosexuality, prostitution, and erotic art, among others.[21]

The basic method of the Institute has been to compile interviews, or sexual life histories or biographies, by orally obtained responses to a questionnaire. In so doing, Kinsey's approach seems to have been deeply influenced by several disciplines: biology (with its emphasis on mammalian behavior; and within biology, taxonomy, or a system of measurement and orderly classification); behavioral psychology (in which the emphasis is on what one does, rather than on the meaning imputed to the act by oneself or others—which is not to imply that the latter emphasis was lacking, but that it was not primary in Kinsey's work); and sociology (with its effort to differentiate people according to social class, educational level, religious affiliation, degree of devoutness, race and other variables that were becoming popular in sociological studies—not yet of sex—but were to gain greatly in an empirical age following Kinsey, not only, or even mainly, due to his influence, but to that of computers on the one hand, and of Gallup and the pollsters, on the other).

Where previous researchers had obtained a hundred case histories and in rare instances a thousand, seldom of people reflecting heterogeneity, Kinsey's first volume was based on the case histories of approximately 5300 males, all of whom were white but who, in other respects, reflected the wide diversity of people in America.[22] Actually, the title of the book might more accu-

[20] Paul H. Gebhard, Wardell B. Pomeroy, Clyde E. Martin, and Cornelia V. Christenson, *Pregnancy, Birth and Abortion* (New York: Harper & Brothers, 1958); Paul H. Gebhard, John H. Gagnon, Wardell B. Pomeroy, and Cornelia V. Christenson, *Sex Offenders: An Analysis of Types* (New York: Harper & Row, 1965).

[21] Wardell B. Pomeroy, *op. cit.* (note 17); and Edward Brecher, *op. cit.* (note 3), pp. 119–120.

[22] The question of why the number of persons in the 1948 and 1953 samples was reduced by the elimination of nonwhites has never been satisfactorily answered. I have been informed that the difference between black

rately have indicated that the study was restricted to white American males.

In addition to the large sample that he obtained, which he contrasted with nineteen previous sex studies which could be called taxonomic,[23] Kinsey went to some lengths to insure the representativeness of that sample [24] and to determine that the respondents were telling the truth about their sex lives.[25] Many challenged the validity of the Kinsey statistics, but for the most unprejudiced account of the work (which offers some criticism but is in general tone favorable, particularly in comparison with other studies in this area), one should turn to the report of the American Statistical Association.[26]

Many criticisms of Kinsey's work appeared, and some have been coming from time to time since. Social scientists argued with Kinsey because of what he had not studied: love, for example; further, that by counting orgasms, or outlets, he was, in the words of Margaret Mead, reducing sex "to the category of a simple act of elimination." [27] Gorer expressed amazement that one could speak of "mammalian analogues to adultery." [28] Simpson, a psychoanalytically oriented sociologist, challenged the entire idea that the self-selected sample could be indicative of behavior of wide groups of people; he asked, in fact, why the volume on women had not been entitled *5,940 Selected Case Histories of*

---

and white biographies was sufficiently great so that they could not be grouped together, and that the sample of blacks was too small for it to be presented separately.

[23] Kinsey *et al., op. cit.,* 1948 (note 18), pp. 23–24.

[24] *Ibid.,* ch. 3, "Statistical Problems."

[25] *Ibid.,* ch. 2, "Interviewing."

[26] William G. Cochran, Frederick Mosteller, and John W. Tukey, *Statistical Problems of the Kinsey Report on Sexual Behavior in the Human Male* (Washington: American Statistical Association, 1954); reprinted in part in *Sexual Behavior in American Society: An Appraisal of the First Two Kinsey Reports,* ed. Jerome Himelhoch and Sylvia Fleis Fava (New York: W. W. Norton and Company, 1955).

[27] Margaret Mead, "An Anthropoligst Looks at the Report," in *Problems of Sexual Behavior* (New York: American Social Hygiene Association, 1948), cited by Chall, *op. cit.* (note 1).

[28] Geoffrey Gorer, "Nature, Science, and Dr. Kinsey," in Himelhoch and Fava, *op. cit.* (note 26), p. 55.

Human Females in the United States.[29] But what Simpson and other Freudians objected to was the lack of interview information on the *meanings* of the orgasms that were being counted; in other words, they objected to Kinsey's work because of what it did not contain. One must take more seriously the criticisms of many who have pointed out that the lower social class sample, for example, was represented by a disproportionate number of prisoners, and that one cannot assume that the sex life of prisoners, either before or during incarceration, is similar to that of people of the same social class, educational level, and other groupings outside of prison. Furthermore, almost a quarter of a century since Folsom raised certain questions inspired by reading the first Kinsey volume, little progress can be recorded toward relevant research on such matters. Folsom noted that the Kinsey study makes us "wonder if we know what the real mores are," compels us to ask what is the process of change in culture, what is the role of economic and ideological factors, and do lower class mores filter upward.[30]

In my view, however, Kinsey's work caught American sociologists with their pants down. It was a bitter experience for them to have to confront the fact that the most comprehensive study of the behavior of people in the area of sex (the mores and their violation) had been conducted by scholars of other disciplines. Sociologists felt compelled to criticize and to seek to impeach the work; otherwise, what was their professional competence that they could be outdone in their own field of specialization by outsiders?

However, simply because much of the criticism of Kinsey's work cannot be taken seriously is not to indicate that the work is beyond valid criticism. Maslow, for example, demonstrated experimentally some of the dangers of using volunteers.[31] Kinsey

[29] George Simpson, "Nonsense about Women," in Himelhoch and Fava, *op. cit.* (note 26), p. 63.

[30] Joseph K. Folsom, Review of Kinsey, Pomeroy, and Martin's *Sexual Behavior in the Human Male* in *American Sociological Review 13* (1948): 224–226.

[31] Abraham H. Maslow and James M. Sakoda, "Volunteer-Error in the Kinsey Study," *Journal of Abnormal and Social Psychology 47* (April 1952): 259–262, reprinted in Himelhoch and Fava, *op. cit.* (note 26).

then went over more and more to using 100 percent samples: that is, obtaining all of the members of a given group as respondents.[32] But even this does not answer the question of how to determine what that group is representative of. A single Catholic church, a single club in a Jewish center in a small town, a single high school class in a private school in New England—each such church, club, or class is different from all others in the same category. If scientific sampling were to be applied to the 100 percent sample technique, it would require that there be a sufficiently large number of churches, clubs, classes, and other groups, to insure that *a representative cross-section of groups* had been obtained. So that the technique that eliminated volunteer self-selection and the potential error therein was a vast step forward, but it was fraught with new sources of error that have as yet received insufficient attention.

The statisticians mentioned in general terms, and several critics have pointed out, that Kinsey's work is filled with interpretations not supported by his own data. For example:

> The opinion that homosexual activity in itself provides evidence of a psychopathic personality is materially challenged by these incidence and frequency data. Of the 40 or 50 per cent of the male population which has homosexual experience, certainly a high proportion would not be considered psychopathic personalities on the basis of anything else in their histories.[33]

Of course, while it is entirely possible that there may be some people who would want to label as psychopathic *everyone* who has had even the slightest amount of homosexual experience, no responsible scholar in the field had ever made such a judgment, but many have stated that exclusive and near-exclusive homosexuality, with strong preferences and compulsions in that direction and great fears of the other sex, do constitute psychopathy, and nothing in the Kinsey incidence and frequency data would tend to deny (or for that matter to confirm) this.

What, in retrospect, were Kinsey's great contributions, and

32 Pomeroy, *op. cit.* (note 17), p. 971.
33 Kinsey *et al., op. cit.,* 1948 (note 18), p. 600.

continue to be the contributions emanating from the Institute that he launched? I suggest:

1. The scope, methodology, and findings, as well as the discussion evoked by them, resulted in sex research obtaining an aura of scientific respectability that it had not previously had.

2. Kinsey demonstrated that it was practicable to obtain sex data, and that methods were available to determine whether respondents were telling the truth. For the latter purpose, he and his colleagues developed such techniques as comparing the histories of husbands and wives, redoing case histories after a lapse of several years in order to compare the new and old answers to the same questions, and constructing the questionnaire in such a manner that contradictions would appear without being noticed by the respondent.

3. The Kinsey group introduced the concept of the continuum, particularly in scaling the degree to which a person was homosexual or heterosexual (a concept that had been used, but not so well defined or refined, by Hirschfeld). Sexual behavior, like most other human behavior, can both be seen as falling into categories and at the same time as a continuum with constant gradations, where the lines of demarcation dividing the categories are always blurred.

4. The research emanating from the Institute for Sex Research demonstrated that there is not only diversity but widespread frequency of sex behavior of deviant, strange, and unusual natures, participated in by a considerable number and not (as hitherto believed) by a miniscule sector of the population.

5. As a result of this research, and particularly resulting from the disclosure of this widespread diversity, there arose in America a frontal attack on some popular prejudices and on the tightly held stereotypes that had hitherto been an impregnable part of the view of reality of many Americans.

Sex research was undoubtedly stimulated by the work of the Institute; yet for all of this, Kinsey may have had, in certain respects, an inhibitory or undesirable effect on such research, knowledge, and policy. First, and in line with (1) and (2) above, many sex investigators after Kinsey were to count, and were to accept, willingly and gladly, what their subjects were stating, without the safeguards that Kinsey had taken to determine whether there was concealment, exaggeration, lapse of memory, or outright prevarication. Then, in line with (3) above, some persons interpreted the continuum as a denial of the polar categories, although the majority of Kinsey's male subjects, and an even higher percentage of his female respondents, fell precisely at the polar ends. Further, in line with (4) above, many scholars (including some members of the Kinsey group), influenced by the diversity that they discovered, sought to deny the evidence for the maladjustments, sufferings, frustrations, and unhappiness of large numbers of those engaged in this diverse behavior. Finally, as part of the frontal attack on prejudice mentioned in (5) above, a widespread underdog ideology began to permeate the newer post-Kinseyan literature on sex deviance. This has taken many forms: value-free descriptions that imply that it is improper to evaluate one way of life as more fulfilling than another; a search for "normal," nonpathological respondents among deviants; a belief that because the deviant is a victim of injustice, any criticism of the deviant's way of life implies conspiracy with the victimizers. Nor does this exhaust the mechanisms of the ideologues.[34]

For none of these consequences can Kinsey be "blamed," nor

[34] It would require an entire article to elaborate on and offer evidence of the various points made in this paragraph. Some of these points I have made elsewhere (see note 69, *infra*). I am referring to much of the work on transsexualism, particularly that of Harry Benjamin, Richard Green, and John Money (see note 45, *infra*), but I would exempt from the allegations I have made here the equally sympathetic approach to the transsexuals of Robert J. Stoller, *Sex and Gender* (New York: Science House, 1968). I would place in the category of those seeking to deny evidence of maladjustments, or to place responsibility for this squarely on the shoulders of an oppressive society without examining the psychodynamics of the development of deviance but only of the development of social hostility, such persons as Martin Hoffman (see note 68, *infra*), and Lars Ullerstam, *The Erotic Minorities* (New York: Grove Press, 1966). I return to the problem of deliberately chosen samples and the search for nonpathological respondents a little later; see the references to Evelyn Hooker and to William Simon and John H. Gagnon (notes 66 and 67, *infra*). Wardell Pomeroy, a major co-worker of Kinsey, uses (and in my view misuses) his own figures to deny the concept of statistical abnormalities of homosexuality in an article, "What Is Normal?" *Playboy 12* (1965): 3. As for the statement that many have counted and few have used safeguards, I feel reluctant to single out a few investigators when the body of sociological literature is vulnerable. It would be preferable to make this the subject of another study: an evaluation of the methodology of quantitative sex research since 1948.

for the most significant of all, namely, that his figures have been interpreted as gospel, rather than as indications, and that the very size, scope, and cost of the great accumulation of life histories make it unlikely that this work will be replicated by others who can correct some of Kinsey's shortcomings and errors and at the same time bring the figures up to date. If, for example, as Bergler argues,[35] the Kinsey figures on the prevalence of homosexuality were exaggeratedly misleading, it is still possible that they might be correct for today although wrong for their own time; yet who can launch a study to determine whether it is true that 16 percent of American males (one out of six, or the sixth man, as a popularizer called him) [36] has significantly more homosexual than heterosexual experience and/or "psychic" reaction (including, of course, in this figure the exclusive homosexuals)? And if true today, was it so in the early 1940s—this is a matter even more difficult to investigate.

After Freud, one analyzed, one probed, one studied the symbolism of sex, the unconscious, the mechanisms and consequences of sublimation and repression. It was an era for the psychoanalyst and others therapeutically oriented, aided by the insights of men of letters. *After Kinsey,* one counted: who, how many times, with whom, where, why—and sometimes to these was added the participant's view of himself, his partners, and his peers. It was the era of the sociological study of sex, and during the decades since Kinsey, many important contributions have been made.

Masters, Johnson, and the Return to Biology

Freud, Kinsey—and like the skyscrapers in Kansas City that had gone about as high as they could go, so it was thought of sex research—it had gone about as far as it could go. But those who so believed (or hoped, or feared) were counting without two fac-

---

[35] Edmund Bergler, *One Thousand Homosexuals: Conspiracy of Silence, or Curing and Deglamorizing Homosexuals* (Paterson, N.J.: Pageant Books, 1959), pp. 4–7.

[36] Jess Stearn, *The Sixth Man* (New York: Doubleday & Co., 1961).

tors: the work of Masters and Johnson, and the decade of protest against the mores of American society.

The work of Masters and Johnson, deeply influenced by Kinsey (without whose pioneering Masters and Johnson could hardly have been possible), likewise attained best-seller status, although couched in medical and physiological terminology that made it almost unreadable to the layman.[37] In a sense, this marked the completion of a circle, for with Masters and Johnson sex research had again returned to biology, which it had never fully abandoned. But the generally favorable reception of this work, the high esteem in which it was held, and the ability to withstand the criticism of it on ethical grounds meant that no holds were barred in sex research. The influence of this study on sociological investigation is quite readily understandable. Without digressing to summarize the Masters and Johnson report, but only confining my remarks to a few words to illustrate and highlight the foregoing, these scientists were concerned with the physiological process and the psychological concomitants of sexual arousal leading to orgasm and post-orgasmic relaxation. For this purpose, they not only interviewed men and women, but observed them (with instruments and in other ways) during sexual foreplay, intercourse or other forms of contact, and post-intromission. It is not their findings that here concern us, important as they are; nor the very real question (which they tackled with remarkable scientific ingenuity) of whether the conditions of *observed* sexuality are indicative of what occurs in the unobserved privacy of the bedroom. It is rather that Masters and Johnson, investigating at a university, publishing in scientific journals, proved as formidable in the removal of barriers to sex research as had Freud and Kinsey before them.

It is not a coincidence that the work took place, was published, and received a generally favorable reception from professionals and laymen, in the decade of the 1960s, although the

---

[37] William H. Masters and Virginia E. Johnson, *Human Sexual Response* (Boston: Little, Brown & Co., 1966). See also Ruth and Edward Brecher, eds., *An Analysis of Human Sexual Response* (Boston: Little, Brown & Co., and New York: New American Library, 1966). Less helpful is a chapter on Masters and Johnson in Brecher, *op. cit.* (note 3).

research was started some years before, and an unpublished monograph is dated 1959.[38] The sixties were the years of the sexual revolution—a revolution at least in the open discussion of sex, and in the display of things sexual; and, concomitant with it, and not at all unrelated thereto, it was the decade of protest, particularly in the world of youth. The young, disillusioned with a far-off and unpopular war, alienated in a mass society, making common cause with the civil rights movement, were challenging all of the cherished values, mores, and shibboleths of American society. This challenge brought the youth to two simultaneous stances on sex: first, a considerable questioning of the formerly taken-for-granted morality; and second, an application of the politics of confrontation to the world of the erotic.[39] In this last and to my mind almost uninvestigated development, the youth utilized sex (as they did so many other phenomena at their disposal) to confront and harass parents, the Establishment, and all others seen as denizens of the world of squares. Just as Masters and Johnson pushed to new frontiers and brought to new respectability the area that could be available for scientific study and the methods that might be employed for that purpose, so the rebellion and the protest of the sixties, particularly of the young, likewise pushed to new frontiers the language that could be printed, and the activities that could be overtly defended (even, albeit to a limited extent, by participants). These two forces, not entirely

[38] References to these early publications are found in William H. Masters and Virginia E. Johnson, "Orgasm, Anatomy of the Female," in Ellis and Abarbanel, *op. cit.* (note 1).

On the reception of the Masters and Johnson work, *Human Sexual Response,* I am informed by the authors (through a private communication to James M. Henslin, March 16, 1970) that they examined about 780 reviews of the book which had appeared in both lay and professional journals and found approximately 90 percent were favorable. The authors met more opposition in St. Louis than elsewhere, no doubt because that was where the work was done. There was a rumor that Masters had been fired from the Medical School of Washington University, but this was false, and probably arose because of a separation that took place in order to maintain separate funds. Masters does believe, however, that there is still a great deal of opposition to sex research; my own view is rather that there is some suspicion that falls on the researcher. Perhaps this is a concealed form of opposition.

[39] I have dealt with this subject briefly in an unpublished address before the American Association for Public Opinion Research, 24th Annual Conference, Bolton Landing, New York, May 16–19, 1969.

unrelated, but interactive at least to a limited extent, served to aid one another and thus to facilitate sex research.

Social Forces Influencing Research

Thus are seen what I would cite as the three highlights, marking the three major stages, in sex research: the early biological-medical-psychiatric breakthroughs (Krafft-Ebing, Havelock Ellis, and Freud), the taxonomic and sociological studies (Kinsey), and the return to biology in the midst of the sexual revolution and the youth rebellion (Masters and Johnson). But two other influences might here be cited. The first is the demographic—the widespread realization that most parts of the world (including America) had a severe and rapidly deteriorating problem of overpopulation; the second was the growth of liberal propagandists, among both scientists and laymen, for reevaluation of sex codes and attitudes.

Overpopulation might conceivably have resulted in movements in either of two directions: a glorification of abstinence and a new effort to embrace ultrapuritanical codes, or a definition of what is right or wrong in sex behavior based on an acceptance of sexuality for fun and pleasure (which need not eliminate love or monogamous fidelity, as some people seem to think) rather than for reproduction. The former pathway would be extremely difficult for a large society, highly secular and urbanized; it would have been almost impossible in the social atmosphere of the second half of the twentieth century, at least in America and the Western world, and probably for most of the world.

The sexual freedom, liberation, or liberalization movement, not identical to but interrelated with the sexual revolution, arising from the latter and in turn encouraging its development, takes on several forms. Organizationally, it has involved such a group as the Sexual Freedom League,[40] with its amorphous program, generally bent on diminishing social (including but not limited to legal) restrictions on sexual behavior and having a pro-sexual, rather than a pro-heterosexual, orientation. This implies accept-

40 This organization is briefly discussed by Brecher, *op. cit.* (note 3).

ance of homosexuality, without emphasis thereon. Then, larger, with many more groups as well as more members, have been the homophile organizations: lobbies, social action and civil rights oriented people, and social clubs, mainly of men, but sometimes with a smattering of female members, and one devoted entirely to women.[41] Finally, there have been a few lesser known but interesting organizations of transvestites and transsexuals.[42]

The voices of these protesters have sometimes been synchronized with but on important occasions have sharply clashed with professionals propagandizing against puritanism and for less restrictive sex codes. Of these, the most prominent and most influential, in my prejudiced view (for I largely share his outlook and admit that my own was influenced by him), is Albert Ellis.[43] Others include professionals with psychotherapeutic orientations similar to those of Albert Ellis, and many, such as Socarides and Bieber,[44] who share Ellis' outlook on sex norms and values, but not his nonpsychoanalytic views; and those, like Benjamin and Money, who share the permissiveness of these men, but not their view that many sex deviants are severely disturbed.[45]

[41] Edward Sagarin, *Odd Man In: Societies of Deviants in America* (Chicago: Quadrangle Books, 1969). There is a considerable literature of and on the homophile movement, a good deal of which is cited in this book.

[42] George L. Kirkham and Edward Sagarin, "Transsexuals in a Formal Organizational Setting," *Journal of Sex Research* 5 (1969): 90–107. This was published in slightly altered and expanded form, in Sagarin, *op. cit.* (note 41).

[43] The major works of Albert Ellis in this regard are: *Sex Without Guilt* (New York: Lyle Stuart and New York: Grove Press, 1965); *The Art and Science of Love* (New York: Lyle Stuart and New York: Bantam Books, 1969); *The American Sexual Tragedy* (New York: Lyle Stuart and New York: Grove Press, 1962); *Sex and the Single Man* (New York: Lyle Stuart and New York: Dell Books, 1965); and *The Search for Sexual Fulfillment* (New York: Macfadden-Bartell, 1965).

[44] Charles W. Socarides, *The Overt Homosexual* (New York: Grune & Stratton, 1968); Irving Bieber *et al.*, *Homosexuality: A Psychoanalytic Study* (New York: Basic Books, 1962).

[45] Harry Benjamin's rejection of the theme that transvestites and transsexuals are necessarily or even in substantial numbers disturbed is expressed in his book, *The Transsexual Phenomenon* (New York: Julian Press, 1966), a view which I have criticized (see note 69, *infra*). For a view somewhat similar to that of Benjamin, expressed by John Money and many of his colleagues, see Richard Green and John Money, eds., *Transsexualism and Sex Reassignment* (Baltimore: Johns Hopkins Press, 1969).

A third branch of the sexual freedom movement is found among the popular propagandists, who have glorified the erotic in magazines and books that have likewise been influential in pushing further the frontiers of the proper, acceptable, or tolerable. Among these have been Hugh Hefner, publisher of *Playboy*, and Ralph Ginzburg, publisher of *Eros* and later of *Avant Garde*.

Sex research stimulated further sex research, not only in the sense that research by Kinsey and by Masters and Johnson encouraged investigation into sexual behavior but also such research laid the groundwork for the formation of the first professional organization, genuinely interdisciplinary, of men and women interested in this area. The Society for the Scientific Study of Sex brought together psychologists, sociologists, physicians, lawyers, social workers and others: it was both a landmark in sex research and an impetus for it.[46] The same can be said of the volume, *The Encyclopedia of Sexual Behavior*,[47] not the first encyclopedia in the field, but more comprehensive and more authoritative than any previous effort; this, too, has had a wider sale than anticipated, and its influence has probably been in the direction of encouragement of serious work in this field.

Now, when we take these several forces (the advances in the researchable and the acceptance of the respectability of research, culminating in the work of Masters and Johnson; the youthful scorn of adult mores and restrictions, in the midst of both the decade of protest and the sexual revolution; the sexual freedom movement, sponsored by and resulting in organizational formation; professionals and scientists becoming propagandists; and popular literature on the subject attaining mass distribution), it can be seen that the way was clear for sociologically oriented research into areas difficult to penetrate, many still condemned as deviant and way-out, if not illegal and criminal, many in which the researcher, were he a participant-observer, must needs be re-

[46] The Society for the Scientific Study of Sex was founded in the late 1950s; its members include leading physicians, psychotherapists, sociologists, marriage counselors, attorneys and others doing research in the field of sex; it publishes *The Journal of Sex Research*.

[47] Albert Ellis and Albert Abarbanel, *The Encyclopedia of Sexual Behavior*, 2 vols. (New York: Hawthorn Books, 1961).

luctant to so acknowledge. Yet, at the same time, while the areas
of *activity* were not yet respectable, the areas of *research into
such activity* became respectable and sufficiently so that there followed a proliferation of term papers, masters' theses and doctoral
dissertations, and government-funded as well as elsewhere-funded
(and nonfunded) investigation not only into prostitution and
homosexuality but also child molestation, forcible rape, wife-
swapping (or better, because it is not a male ethnocentric term,
mate-swapping), sex want ads, and research into who knows what
other people and conditions whose very names were not too long
ago unmentionable in the company of ladies.

Impediments to Sex Research

Sex, despite many statements to the contrary, is not as easily researchable as any other topic, but it is not alone in offering the
investigator numerous impediments, although a major one, the
lack of scientific respectability as a legitimate subject of study,
seems to have been overcome. But in sociology, it shares with
crime, race prejudices, and other aspects of social life, an aura
of secrecy that is inherent in the condition itself; and deriving
from this, dangers in attempting to penetrate into groups as participant observers (including the danger that one may be forced
to testify or may be compelled to commit illegal acts, in which
one might become a conspirator, an accessory before or after the
fact, or a participant in the forbidden act itself).[48] An even more
difficult methodological problem is the vested interest of the re-
pondent (including the volunteer) in concealing, exaggerating,
purifying, censoring, prettifying and in other ways distorting the
truth in his responses. It is apparent both to the investigator and
to the respondent that the latter is lying when he claims never
to have masturbated; and Reiss suggests that one might be able

[48] Problems of this type have been raised by Lewis Yablonsky, "On
Crime, Violence, LSD, and Legal Immunity for Social Scientists," *The American Sociologist 3* (1968): 148–149; Carolyn Symonds, "Risky and Rewarding,"
The American Sociologist 3 (1968): 254; also Ned Polsky, *Hustlers, Beats,
and Others* (Chicago: Aldine Publishing Co., 1967), particularly ch. 3, "Research Method, Morality, and Criminology," pp. 117–149; and by Jack D.
Douglas, James M. Henslin, *et al.* in Douglas, *op. cit.* (note 4).

to account for middle-class boys denying masturbation by a possible unwillingness on their part to make the admission to a middle-class investigator.[49] But it may not be equally apparent to the respondents themselves (nor in this case to the same investigator) that lower-class youths who make themselves available for fellatio may have similar reluctance to admit the pleasures and attractions of these acts.[50] They, too, may be structuring their vision of reality in order to continue to be defined by the investigator, their peers, and themselves as not being "queer" or even partly so (although they may not be sophisticated enough to understand the middle ground between the heterosexual and homosexual entities).

"How do you know that the respondent is telling the truth?" many sociologists have asked.[51] Is it all a put-on? It is a question particularly pertinent to a facet of one's biography as anxiety-provoking as sexuality; and it is one of the great achievements of the original Kinsey group that remarkable precautions were taken to solve this question.[52]

In a previous statement, I suggested that there are four major problems facing sex researchers; here I should like to elaborate on them. They were described as "the *ethical* problem of the effect of the research on the subject, the *ideological* one of researchers' biases, the *social* one of the effects of the sexual revo-

[49] Albert J. Reiss, "The Social Integration of Peers and Queers," *Social Problems 9* (Fall 1961): 102–120. This article has been widely reprinted; I have on hand five readers that contain it: Howard S. Becker, ed., *The Other Side: Perspectives on Deviance* (New York: Free Press of Glencoe, 1964); William A. Rushing, ed., *Deviant Behavior and Social Process* (Chicago: Rand McNally, 1969); Earl Rubington and Martin S. Weinberg, eds., *Deviance: The Interactionist Perspective* (New York: Macmillan Co., 1968); Hendrik M. Ruitenbeek, ed., *The Problem of Homosexuality in Modern Society* (New York: Dutton, 1963); and Gagnon and Simon, eds., note 66, *infra*. All of this may speak very highly of the paper, or perhaps less highly of the originality and energy of editors. My own view was expressed in an unpublished critique, "Was It a Snow Job—Or Was It a Blow Job: Reflections on Sociologists Who Can't See the Loopholes for the Gloryholes."

[50] Reiss, *op. cit.* (note 49).

[51] John P. Dean and William Foote White, "How Do You Know If the Informant Is Telling the Truth?" *Human Organization 17* (1958): 34–38.

[52] As cited earlier, see Kinsey *et al.*, *op. cit.*, 1948 (note 18), ch. 2, "Interviewing."

lution on behavior and on human fulfillment, and the *norma-tive* one of the establishment of guideposts for sexual activity in a world in which sex and procreation are but slightly related." [53] One can quite readily dismiss all but the ideological as a factor for the researcher, and then go a step further and declare that the good researcher has his biases but does not let them inter-fere with his investigation, handling of data, or interpretation thereof. But one cannot escape either one's ideology or the social responsibility of one's work and its dissemination.

The ethical problem is one that plagues the social sciences, and it is not much different for one who researches sex behavior than for one who researches other forms of activities or other statuses that may be troubling an individual. A brief interview or written questionnaire, responses to which may be made public only in a concealed form, may have only minimal effect on the subject, but "minimal" is not the same as "none." However, it is not the respondent alone who is here concerned; it is an entire category of people to which he belongs. Did Kinsey's work serve (as Bergler in fact contended) [54] as a self-fulfilling prophecy, caus-ing a proliferation of activity that people had come to believe, because of Kinsey, was frequent, and then had come to confuse the concepts of frequency, normality, acceptability, and desira-bility? Does a researcher confer status, legitimacy, and respectabil-ity, and hence does he reinforce deviant values and outlooks on life, by coming to an organization of deviants and asking for the right to research them; and does he confer stronger beliefs in the propriety of his (the deviant's) own way of life by an examination in which he (the interviewer) retains his ethical neutrality?

This is not to argue against neutralism, and certainly not for a return to the type of questionnaire in which boys were asked if anyone had ever tried to give them "the mistaken idea that

[53] Edward Sagarin, "Taking Stock of Studies of Sex," in Sagarin, ed., "Sex and the Contemporary American Scene," *The Annals of the American Academy of Political and Social Science 376* (March 1968): 1–5.

[54] Bergler expressed this view on many occasions; see particularly Ed-mund Bergler and W. S. Kroger, *Kinsey's Myth of Female Sexuality* (New York: Grune & Stratton, 1954).

sex intercourse is necessary for the health of the young man"! [55]
It is only to point out that a human subject cannot be the same
after having been "researched." In human behavior, there is never
a *status quo ante* anything.

Some of my colleagues have expressed amazement at this
argument; they contend that I am objecting because the researcher may *benefit* (not harm) his subject or the group of people that his subject represents. The alleged benefit derives from
ego-building and from the enhancement of a damaged feeling of
self-worth. These are noble aims, but they are not properly the
domain of a researcher *qua* researcher; rather of the psycho-
therapist in dealing with the individual, or of the sociologist,
social thinker, man of letters or anyone else, in promulgating a
view and polemicizing for it. It is entirely possible, in fact very
likely, that ego-building and enhancement of self-worth emanating from research, through the intermediary of the reinforcement of a deviant value system and a deviant view of reality,
might prove far less satisfactory than the same effects brought
about through a restructuring of personality and outlook lead
ing to or following an abandonment of the deviant pathway. But
this is to impose the normative value judgment of the society as
the better one, which it may not necessarily be for each individual.

This is not a problem for which there is an answer, no less
an easy answer. Research is dangerous, as is living itself. But
whether in research or in living, to be aware of the dangers may
assist in diminishing them.

Ideological bias in research is by no means limited to sex;
if anything, such bias is even stronger in politics. But in sex, there
had traditionally been a prejudice against research itself, and
that ideology has been overcome. In addition, there was bias
against permissiveness and for enforced conformity to a very narrow view of the normal and the normative. Sex outside of marriage, and in positions or with partners socially disapproved, was
conceptualized as sin. At times, however, these nonmarital rela-

[55] Kinsey *et al., op. cit.,* 1948 (note 18), p. 26, quoting from W. L.
Hughes, "Sex Experiences of Boyhood," *Journal of Social Hygiene 12* (1926):
262–273.

tions were known but totally ignored for social class reasons, serving to reinforce class and, in interracial relations in America, caste inequities. Later, with the rise of a secular view of the world, many types of sex behavior were labeled and treated as crimes rather than sins, and in the terminology of sociologists of the 1930s and 1940s, as social disorganization.[56] With such prejudgments, these sociologists were ill equipped to look at the objects of their study without distortion, distaste, and overt hostility.

Still later, sociologists abandoned the theme of social disorganization in favor of deviance, which to many meant (although it did not have to) not only social disapproval but sickness. Parsons defined sickness as deviant,[57] and many others defined the deviant as being sick; this was particularly true of the sex deviant, although less so for such a deviating person as the armed robber, for example, or the check forger.

Under the influence of the labeling school of sociology (ushered in no doubt by Lemert,[58] although he of course had his predecessors, as Polsky has pointed out,[59] and he has had many who followed, such as Becker, Kitsuse, Erikson, Lofland, and Matza),[60] sociologists began to focus on the persons and groups that label others as deviant, and the effect of this labeling process on the activities and self-image of those so labeled. This orientation led Becker to ask: Whose side are we on?,[61] and if not quite explicitly, then very strongly by implication, stated that the sociologist must be on the side of the victims of oppression, not the victimizers'. It is thus a new bias, the reverse of the earlier one,

[56] The history of this change is traced by John Lofland, *Deviance and Identity* (Englewood Cliffs, N.J.: Prentice-Hall, 1969).

[57] Talcott Parsons, *The Social System* (Glencoe, Ill.: Free Press, 1951), pp. 476–477.

[58] Edwin M. Lemert, *Social Pathology* (New York: McGraw-Hill, 1951).

[59] Polsky, *op. cit.* (note 48), pp. 195–196.

[60] Among the best examples of the work of this group are Howard S. Becker, *Outsiders: Studies in the Sociology of Deviance* (New York: Free Press, 1963); Lofland, *op. cit.* (note 56); David Matza, *Becoming Deviant* (Englewood Cliffs, N.J.: Prentice-Hall, 1969); and numerous articles appearing in various journals and in readers on deviance, particularly the readers edited by Becker and by Rubington and Weinberg, *op. cit.* (note 49).

[61] Howard S. Becker, "Whose Side Are We On?" *Social Problems 14* (Winter 1967): 239–247.

that enters into research, as Gouldner,[62] Bordua,[63] and others have indicated.

At the same time, those engaged in activism in the age of protest broadened to take in organized homosexuals and even transsexuals, who proclaimed themselves as fighting for minority group rights, and who denounced the label of sick as another mechanism for oppression and for continuation of the status of outcast.[64] These people found support in the work of Szasz who, protesting against incarceration and oppression committed against such victims in the name of mental illness, proclaimed that the entity of mental illness was a myth.[65]

If deviance is sickness, and the label of sickness is a continuation of the mechanism of oppression formerly used by a hostile and stigmatizing society with such abandoned notions as sin and crime, and if furthermore the sex deviant is a victim of injustice which no self-respecting opponent of injustice can support, then (it is reasoned) one must oppose the label of sickness and the concept and evaluation that accompany it. By this line of reasoning, many sex researchers began to see nonconformity without pathology or abnormality in homosexuals and even in transsexuals and others; they found the difference between heterosexual

[62] Alvin Gouldner, "The Sociologist as Partisan: Sociology and the Welfare State," *The American Sociologist 3* (May 1968): 103–116.

[63] David J. Bordua, "Recent Trends: Deviant Behavior and Social Control," *The Annals of the American Academy of Political and Social Science, 369* (January 1967): 149–163.

[64] I refer here not only to the homophile movement (Mattachine clubs, Daughters of Bilitis, and many others), but to Women's Liberation, anti-war groups, and even Black Panthers, all of whom have engaged in a general denunciation of the powers that be, the allegedly oppressive society, system, or Establishment, and the agents of that oppression, the police, alternately denounced as enemies, entrappers, or pigs. Finally, this militancy emerged in the form of an ultra-left and largely anarchistic homosexual group (as distinct from the middle class-oriented Mattachine), named, with an obvious eye on the anti-war movement, Gay Liberation Front. For all of these people, "sick" has no objective referents, except when used as an adjective before the word "society." For a discussion of the emergence of radical or revolutionary homosexual protest movements, see Edward Sagarin, "Behind the Gay Liberation Front," *The Realist,* No. 87 (May–June 1970).

[65] Thomas S. Szasz, *The Myth of Mental Illness* (New York: Hoeber, 1961).

and homosexual not unlike that between right- and left-handedness.[66] And they searched for and found relatively happy lives among the nonconformists,[67] and attributed such distress as they did encounter either to social hostility, to the normal amount of neurosis and psychosis to be found distributed in any population, or to the fact that previous investigators had used an atypical sample (subjects who had come to them for therapy and hence are by self-definition sick, or were in prison or similar settings).[68] What seems to be missing from this entire research is a study of whether the "sick" label, or any other label that is misused to justify oppression and maltreatment, can still have logical referents and be properly applicable by scientists who disdain the improper use of their findings.

This is not the occasion to digress into an argument responding to the entire question of ideological bias; I have done so elsewhere.[69] My only point is that such bias is an impediment to research, whether it is on one side or another, on both sides or on many. To answer the question posed by Becker: "Whose side are we on?" I suggest that there are many sides, that as social thinkers we can be on the side of the oppressed and the pariahs, as social activists the side chosen depends upon the forces and

[66] An example of this type of reasoning is seen in this quotation by William Simon and John H. Gagnon: "We are arguing that it (female homosexuality) is unnatural, but unnatural in the way that all human behavior is unnatural; that is, it is without an absolutely predetermined and fixed shape and content, and it is a complex condition which derives from man's unique abilities to think, act, and remember and his need to live with other humans." ("The Lesbians: A Preliminary Overview," in *Sexual Deviance*, ed. John H. Gagnon and William Simon [New York: Harper & Row, 1967], p. 282).

[67] An example of one who deliberately searched for and succeeded in finding well-organized lives among homosexuals is Evelyn Hooker, as expressed in several papers, such as "The Adjustment of the Male Overt Homosexual," *Journal of Projective Techniques 21* (1957): 18–31; and "Male Homosexuality in the Rorschach," *Journal of Projective Techniques 22* (1958): 33–54.

[68] This theme runs through many works, such as Martin Hoffman, *The Gay World: Male Homosexuality and the Social Creation of Evil* (New York: Basic Books, 1968). The subtitle of the book clearly expresses the viewpoint of its author.

[69] Edward Sagarin, "Ideology as a Factor in the Consideration of Deviance," *Journal of Sex Research 4* (1968): 84–94.

the program, while as sociologists we can only be on the side of investigation, research, and validatable findings. Furthermore, it is highly questionable whether human suffering is alleviated in the long run by research bias, even when it seems to lead to befriending the innocent and the friendless.

Bias in the social area: the effect of the sexual revolution on behavior and on fulfillment—this is an altogether separate problem for research, but research is part of the problem. For while the liberalization of sexual mores makes research possible by preparing a social climate for it, at the same time the research contributes toward the liberalization. It is a cumulative and circular process, but one to which insufficient thought has as yet been given. If one could assume, as many would like to do, that the more permissive codes (ultimately, a few say, the lack of codes, but this is never reached, nor is it imaginable in terms of social living) are beneficial, increasing the potential for happiness, releasing all human beings from the bondage of senseless repression, then research that contributes toward permissive guidelines could be initiated with the same value-free attitudes as investigation aimed at finding a preventive or cure for a debilitating disease. But sex research may be more in line with research on insecticides or on atomic energy, with effects on society highly problematic.

Searching for guideposts for sexuality is the fourth great problem, but it is more properly a problem for research than a problem of research. What are the desirable normative codes in the world of the pill (or its substitutes if it is abandoned), of controllable venereal disease, of overpopulation that is engulfing us faster than had been predicted by the direst of neo-Malthusians? Some will argue that to prescribe (and proscribe, for proscription is prescription) is not the task of research; it is only to describe, and then of course to draw the *theoretical,* not the *normative,* implications therefrom. The argument is enticing, but it has two drawbacks. First, those who have investigated are presumably more knowledgeable than others, and they cannot escape the obligations of delineating the implications for social policy of the findings that they have unearthed. And, further, research must lead to policy formation, unless it be sterile and useless; and if this policy is not formulated by the researcher, then it will be by others, who may misinterpret the findings or misuse them for a variety of reasons and purposes.

Theory, Investigation, and the Future of Research

Where do we go from here? From the viewpoint of the researcher, it is clear: to more and better research. But where will that lead, how should it be undertaken, what paths are to be pursued, and with what instruments?

It would seem to me to be highly desirable for scientists working in the field of sex to enter into the same type of debate that has punctuated the literature of deviance, and particularly the literature of juvenile delinquency (see the sharp criticism leveled at Cohen, Ohlin and Cloward, Miller, the Gluecks, Matza, and their colleagues, not only by each other but by large numbers of sociologists).[70] While Kinsey was subjected to tremendous criticism, studies of sexuality have usually tended to ignore (rather than build upon or refute) the mass of pertinent literature.

Further, it would seem desirable to integrate empirical and theoretical research: that is, to integrate information gained about the small group and the individual participants with theories of the social structure, institutions, value consensus, and conflict. There are little data in the work of Kingsley Davis, for example, to support his theories, and there is little that is theoretical in the body of empirical studies that have poured forth since Kinsey. Here and there the two are interwoven: an outstanding example, to my mind, would be Goode's study of the effect of urbanization and industrialization on family structure, including sex behavior.[71] But by and large there is a gap separating theory from investigation, and it is a gap reminiscent of the broader

[70] It would be a digression to give references to substantiate this point; for one brief summary of these controversies, see Leonard Savitz, *Dilemmas in Criminology* (New York: McGraw-Hill, 1967).

[71] William J. Goode, *World Revolution and Family Patterns* (New York: Free Press of Glencoe, 1963).

question in sociology: How do you go from the analysis and findings of the individual actor, the dyad or small group (the work
of Goffman, for example), to findings on the nature of society,
its class structure, institutions, and ideologies?

The recent literature on sex, furthermore, is filled with speculative material, intuitive, sometimes extraordinarily brilliant
and insightful, at other times almost self-evident, yet unsup-
ported by convincing data (at least data cited, presented, or published). As an example, there is a simple statement by Simon and
Gagnon: "To most people, the lower class, certain minority
groups, a number of occupational roles, and the female who is
not linked to a conventional family role are seen as differentially
available sexually and, consequently, as more sexually active.
Such persons are seen as having greater sexual appetites and less
self-control over these capacities." [72] Here, Simon and Gagnon
are assuming the existence of stereotypes and publicly held prejudices; it remains to be determined whether "most people" do
see these groups in this manner, how many such people, what
groups of people, and how firmly held their images are. Statements of this sort can be extremely valuable as assumptions, as
educated hunches, but the task ahead is to examine the facts and
amass the data with such insights as guides. And if sociology is
to be a "debunking" discipline, it must not only debunk the
masses of their illusions, but it must debunk itself of its images
of the illusions held by the masses.

Finally, the sociology of sex is largely bereft of any association with the great founders and theoreticians of sociology. There
is a need for a theoretical framework, or many such frameworks,
within which to study this field. Role theory has been utilized to
some advantage, as well as the Weberian concept of *verstehen,*
while occasionally one encounters the approaches of Mead and
Cooley. One might start with the simple assertion, to use a phrase
that Simon and Gagnon are fond of, that sexual behavior is socially scripted. It would remain for the researcher to determine
whether a given behavior is a departure from the script or a following of it, and how those who deviate from the script become

---

[72] Simon and Gagnon, *op. cit.* (note 66), pp. 247–248.

followers not only of a deviant script, but of the major social script itself as adapted to the deviant role.

Theory will enrich the study of sexuality, just as the lowering of taboos will encourage it. In the intertwining of these two strands a tremendous field of study begins to emerge. If the impediments can be overcome and the problems handled, this research will yield results for the individual investigator, the discipline of sociology, and humanity.

NOTES ON CONTRIBUTORS

MAE A. BIGGS is a Teaching Assistant in the Department of Sociology at Washington University and an Instructor of Sociology at Southern Illinois University.

DUNCAN CHAPPELL, on the faculty of the Department of Sociology of the State University of New York at Albany, has co-authored (with P. R. Wilson) *The Police and the Public in Australia and New Zealand,* St. Lucia: University of Queensland Press, 1969.

MARVIN CUMMINS is an Assistant Professor of Sociology and Associate Director of the Social Science Institute at Washington University. He has written *Coppers: A Sociological Study of Suburban Police,* Chicago: Aldine Publishing Company, forthcoming.

NANETTE J. DAVIS is a doctoral candidate in the Department of Sociology at Michigan State University. She has contributed both to journals and to anthologized volumes.

GILBERT GEIS is Professor of Sociology at California State College at Los Angeles. He has authored *White-Collar Criminal,* New York: Atherton Press, 1968 and co-authored (with Herbert A. Bloch) *Man, Crime, and Society,* New York: Random House, 2nd ed., 1970. He has also contributed numerous articles to journals.

GEORGE W. GOETHALS is the Chairman of the Department of Social Relations of Harvard University. He has contributed to numerous journals in addition to authoring (with Wesley Allinsmith) *The Role of the Schools in Mental Health,* New York: Basic Books, Inc., 1962, editing (with Leon Bramson) *War: Studies from Psychology, Sociology, Anthropology,* New York: Basic Books, Inc., 1963, and writing (with Dennis Klos) *Experiencing Youth: First-Person Accounts,* Boston: Little, Brown & Co., 1970.

MICHAEL GORDON is an Associate Professor in the Department of Sociology at the University of Connecticut. He has published in journals, has edited *The Nuclear Family: The Search for an Alternative,* New York: Harper & Row, forthcoming, and he has authored *Juvenile Delinquency in the American Novel, 1905–1965. A Study in the Sociology of Literature,* Bowling Green, Ohio: Bowling Green University Press, 1971.

JAMES M. HENSLIN is an Assistant Professor in the Department of Sociology at Southern Illinois University. In addition to this collection of papers and numerous articles in journals and chapters in anthologized volumes, he has edited *Down to Earth Sociology: Introductory Readings,* New York: The Free Press, 1972, and co-edited (with Larry T. Reynolds) *The Structure of American Society: Social Institutions as Appendages to Market,* and *Social Problems in American Society: Divergent Perspectives,* both forthcoming from Holbrook Press of Boston.

LAUD HUMPHREYS is an Associate Professor at the School of Criminal Justice of the State University of New York at Albany. He has authored *Tearoom Trade: Impersonal Sex in Public Places,* Chicago: Aldine Publishing

Company, 1970, for which he won The Society for the Study of Social Problems' 1969 C. Wright Mills Award for the best book written on critical social issues. He has also contributed articles to journals.

GEORGE L. KIRKHAM is a research criminologist at the Stanford Research Institute and Assistant Professor of Sociology at San Jose State College.

PETER K. MANNING is an Associate Professor of Sociology and Psychiatry at Michigan State University. In addition to articles in sociological journals and chapters in anthologized books, he has edited *Deviance and Change,* Englewood Cliffs, N.J.: Prentice-Hall, forthcoming and (with Marcello Truzzi) *Sociology and Youth,* Englewood Cliffs, N.J.: Prentice-Hall, 1971. He has also authored *Explaining Deviance,* New York: Random House, forthcoming.

CHARLES H. MCCAGHY is an Associate Professor in the Department of Sociology at Bowling Green State University. In addition to contributions to journals and books, he has edited (with Mark Lefton and James K. Skipper, Jr.) *Approaches to Deviance: Theories, Concepts and Research Findings,* New York: Appleton-Century-Crofts, 1968, and *In Their Own Behalf: Voices from the Margin,* New York: Appleton-Century-Crofts, 1968.

EDWARD SAGARIN is an Associate Professor of Sociology at the City College of City University of New York. He has authored *The Anatomy of Dirty Words, Odd Man In: Societies of Deviants in America,* and, (with Albert Ellis) *Nymphomania.* He has edited *The Other Minorities* and (with D. E. J. McNamara) *Problems of Sex Behavior* and *Perspectives on Correction.* He was also the special editor of the "Sex and the Contemporary American Scene" edition of *The Annals of the American Academy of Political and Social Science.* In addition to being the vice-president of the American Society of Criminology, he has contributed to numerous journals.

STEPHEN SCHAFER is Professor of Sociology at Northeastern University. He has authored *The Victim and His Criminal,* New York: Random House, 1968, *Theories in Criminology,* New York: Random House, 1969, *Compensation and Restitution to Victims of Crime,* Montclair, N.J.: Patterson Smith, 2nd ed., 1970, and (with Richard D. Knudten) *Juvenile Delinquency: An Introduction,* New York: Random House, 1970. He has also contributed many articles to journals.

DAVID F. SHOPE is a Psychologist who is currently engaged in private practice as a marriage counselor. He has previously contributed to journals and books.

LARRY SIEGEL is a member of the Department of Sociology at The State University of New York at Albany.

JAMES K. SKIPPER, JR. is a Visiting Professor of Sociology at the University of Western Ontario. In addition to his journal contributions, he has authored (with Emily Mumford) *Sociology and Hospital Care,* New York: Harper & Row, 1967, and (with Powhatan J. Wooldridge) *Behavioral Science, Social Practice and the Nursing Profession,* Cleveland, Ohio: Press of Case Western Reserve University, 1968. He has also edited (with Robert C. Leonard) *Social Interaction and Patient Care,* Philadelphia: J. B. Lippincott Company, 1965, and (with Mark Lefton and Charles H. McCaghy) *Approaches to Deviance: Theories, Concepts and Research Findings,* New York: Appleton-Century-Crofts, 1968, and *In Their Own Behalf: Voices from the Margin,* New York: Appleton-Century-Crofts, 1968.

CAROLYN SYMONDS is a graduate student in the Department of Sociology of the University of California at Riverside. Her paper in this volume is a revision of her Master's thesis.